A POLITICS OF MELANCHOLIA

A Politics of Melancholia

FROM PLATO TO ARENDT

*George Edmondson
and Klaus Mladek*

PRINCETON UNIVERSITY PRESS

PRINCETON & OXFORD

Published by Princeton University Press
41 William Street, Princeton, New Jersey 08540
99 Banbury Road, Oxford OX2 6JX

press.princeton.edu

All Rights Reserved

Library of Congress Cataloging-in-Publication Data

Names: Edmondson, George, 1964– author. | Mladek, Klaus, author.
Title: A politics of melancholia : from Plato to Arendt / George Edmondson
    and Klaus Mladek.
Description: Princeton : Princeton University Press, [2024] |
    Includes bibliographical references and index.
Identifiers: LCCN 2023018166 (print) | LCCN 2023018167 (ebook) |
    ISBN 9780691251295 (hardback) | ISBN 9780691251301 (paperback) |
    ISBN 9780691251448 (ebook)
Subjects: LCSH: Melancholy (Philosophy) | Melancholy in literature. |
    Political science—Philosophy. | BISAC: LITERARY CRITICISM / General |
    PSYCHOLOGY / Emotions
Classification: LCC BF575.M44 E34 2024 (print) | LCC BF575.M44 (ebook) |
    DDC 152.4—dc23/eng/20230911
LC record available at https://lccn.loc.gov/2023018166
LC ebook record available at https://lccn.loc.gov/2023018167

British Library Cataloging-in-Publication Data is available

Editorial: Anne Savarese and James Collier
Production Editorial: Natalie Baan
Cover Design: Chris Ferrante
Production: Lauren Reese
Publicity: William Pagdatoon
Copyeditor: Leah Caldwell

Jacket image: Caspar D. Friedrich, *Two Men Contemplating the Moon*. ca. 1825–30.
Oil on canvas. Wrightsman Fund / Metropolitan Museum of Art

This book has been composed in Miller

10 9 8 7 6 5 4 3 2 1

CONTENTS

ACKNOWLEDGMENTS

A BOOK SO long in the making as this one teaches protracted lessons in gratitude and humility. We are particularly grateful to Dartmouth's John Sloan Dickey Center for International Understanding for hosting a seminar devoted to our manuscript and to Timothy Campbell and Dominiek Hoens for generously agreeing to read our work in progress. Alongside our Dartmouth colleagues who took part in the same seminar—Andrew McCann, Margaret Williamson, Azeen Khan, and Donald Pease—they helped us transform a folie à deux into a book-to-be. An added note of thanks is due to Azeen Khan, whose timely intervention put the whole project back on track. For their support and friendship over the years, we thank our Dartmouth colleagues Aden Evens, Patricia Stuelke, Colleen Boggs, Michael Chaney, Nirvana Tanoukhi, Alexandra Halasz, Veronika Füchtner, Rebecca Biron, Michelle Clarke, Klaus Milich, Yi Wu, James Godley, Marc Dixon, and Jason Houle. Eric Santner, Gerhard Richter, Adam Sitze, Carsten Strathausen, Kristina Mendicino, Martin Puchner, Amanda Claybaugh, Heather Lukes, Molly McGarry, Jack and Shelley Dumpert, and Reagan Arthur have each done something to sustain the project and its authors, and we thank them. A fellowship from the American Council of Learned Societies funded a year of uninterrupted writing and research near the beginning of the project, while the efforts of our indefatigable research assistant, Leah E. Casey, helped ease our workload toward the end. We are forever grateful to our anonymous reviewers at Princeton University Press for returning two deeply engaged, detailed, and generous readings of a long manuscript, and to our editor, Anne Savarese, for showing us that good things do indeed come to those who wait. Finally, we thank Hazel-Dawn Dumpert and Kristin O'Rourke, without whom we wouldn't be melancholic, just miserable.

Some paragraphs from the prologue made their way into "Chaucerian Humor," *Studies in the Age of Chaucer* 41 (2019): 73–105. Material from chapter 4 appears in "The Noise of Neighbors: An Essay on 'The Blacksmiths' and Unrelated Matters," *Modern Philology* 117, no. 1 (2019): 1–23. Language from chapters 1 and 6 shows up in the entry on "Gerechtigkeit," in *Enzyklopädie der Genauigkeit*, eds. Markus Krajewski, Antonia von Schöning, and Mario Wimmer (Konstanz University Press, 2021),

161–174. A section of the prologue was first published as part of "A Politics of Melancholia," in *A Leftist Ontology*, ed. Carsten Strathausen (University of Minnesota Press, 2009). Parts of chapter 5 were first published in the chapter "Natural History" in our edited volume, *Sovereignty in Ruins: A Politics of Crisis* (Duke University Press, 2017).

A POLITICS OF MELANCHOLIA

Prologue

"WHAT THEN IS Melancholia?" So inquired Socrates of the courtesan Aspasia, the lover of Pericles. "Is he mortal?" "No," replied Aspasia. "What then?" pursued Socrates, reputedly the wisest man of his age. "As in the former instance," explained Aspasia, "he is neither mortal nor immortal, but in a mean between the two." Socrates, intrigued now, grew impatient. "What is he, Aspasia?" Her answer: "He is a formidable ghost (*deinos daimon*). . . . But God mingles not with man; . . . [T]he wisdom which understands this is spiritual; all other wisdom, such as that of arts and handicrafts, is mean and vulgar. Now these ghosts or intermediate powers are many and diverse, and one of them is Melancholia." "And who," pressed Socrates, "was his father, and who his mother?" "The tale," responded Aspasia, "will take time;

nevertheless I will tell you. On the birthday of Hades there was a feast of the gods in the underworld, at which the god Zagreus or Overabundance, who is the son of Persephone and Zeus, was one of the guests. When the feast was over, Penia or Poverty, as the manner is on such occasions, came about the doors to beg. Now Zagreus, who was the worse for nectar (there was no wine in those days), went into the cellars of Hades and fell into a heavy sleep, and Poverty, considering her own straitened circumstances, plotted to have a child by him, and accordingly she lay down at his side and conceived Melancholia. . . . And as his parentage is, so also are his fortunes. In the first place he is always poor, and anything but tender and fair; . . . and he is rough and squalid, and has no shoes, nor a house to dwell in; on the bare earth exposed he lies under the open heaven, in the streets, or at the doors of houses, taking his rest; and like his mother he is always in distress.

Like his father too, whom he also partly resembles, he is always plotting against the fair and good; he is bold, enterprising, belligerent, a mighty hunter, always weaving some intrigue or other, keen in the pursuit of wisdom, sorrowful, but not bereft of resources; a philosopher at all times, terrible as an enchanter, sorcerer, sophist. He is by nature neither mortal nor immortal. But now he springs to life when he gets his way, now he dies—all in the very same day. Because he is his father's son, however, he keeps coming back to life, but then anything he finds his way to always slips away, and for this reason, Melancholia is never completely without resources, nor is he ever rich.

The curious reader may be wondering where they should look for this fragment of dialogue. Let us spare them the effort: it is nowhere to be found. If it sounds familiar, that is because we have constructed it out of some language from Plato's *Symposium*, where it masquerades as Socrates's myth of the birth of Eros, which he credits not to the historical Aspasia but to the fictional Diotima. We make this construction, drawing on the Freudian technique of fabricating a narrative audacious enough to force a confrontation with a forgotten part of the analysand's history, not to try the reader's patience, but to unsettle the history of philosophy just enough to help recover the place of melancholia within it: a place unjustly usurped by love. Having forgotten Freud's insight that the melancholic temperament is an expression of love, that indeed love can take the ambivalent form of perpetual conflict, undying fury, and discontent in the face of injustice, we have instead grown accustomed to thinking of melancholia as, at best, an ethical disposition or, at worst, a merely personal affliction. What has been lost is the understanding, possessed by both Freud and Aspasia, that the true lover is always melancholic, the authentic melancholic always a lover.

That will come as no great revelation to anyone familiar with the Galenic tradition, or the history of medieval and early-modern medicine, or heartache. Our point, however, is not simply the obvious one that there exists an intimate, affective connection between love and melancholy. Our point is that melancholia, being one of the proper names for love, is an interpersonal condition rather than a personal one; and being an interpersonal condition, it exists within the realm of politics. According to Hannah Arendt, one of the "reasons why philosophy has never found a place where politics can take shape" is "the assumption that there is something political in *man* that belongs to his essence." Such an assumption, rooted in philosophy's myopic fixation on *man*, is fatefully misguided. "*Man*," insists Arendt, "is apolitical." Politics, by contrast, "arises between *men*, and so quite *outside* of *man*. There is therefore no real political substance. Politics arises in what lies between men and is established as relationships."[1] Politics is immaterial, a spirit—a *daimon*, to borrow some language from Aspasia. Or perhaps we should say: politics is a ghost, an intermediary spirit shuttling between human actants ("for God mingles not with man," as the wise Aspasia tells us). But for that very reason, Arendt is wrong to conclude that philosophy has never found a place where politics can take shape. It did once find a place; but then it just as quickly repressed its knowledge of that place. It silenced the historical Aspasia's tale of Melancholia, progeny of Poverty and Abandon, in favor of the fictional Diotima's myth of Eros. It replaced the deinos daimon of melancholia, the daimon of conflict, contestation, and righteous fury, with the doctrine of ideas. Politics was sealed up within a fable of philosophical love.

With that in mind, let us return to our construction. Like all constructions, ours is staged in order to release the spirit of encrypted loss; it thus already takes part in a politics of melancholia. Philosophy became melancholic the moment it turned its back on politics following the death of Socrates—the one death it could neither forget nor forgive.[2] But in melancholically turning its back on the daemonic realm of politics, philosophy also, in the paradoxical way of these things, ended up banishing Melancholia. Socrates was made to speak, long after his own death, of the transcendent love that would drive philosophy to seek the truth that would reform the polis. Meanwhile, the deinos daimon Melancholia continued to haunt the outskirts of the city, the lone inhabitant of the lost place of politics, incapable of forgetting the death encrypted in the name of Eros. This was the great injustice, the unforgettable outrage: everything that Socrates was made to say about love in the *Symposium*—that it was bold, enterprising, belligerent; terrible as an enchanter, sorcerer, sophist; prone to plotting and intrigue; keen in the pursuit of wisdom, sorrowful but not bereft of resources; dying and springing to life again, continually; a philosopher at all times—could also be said, should also be said, about Melancholia. Melancholia's place had been usurped; Aspasia had been supplanted; their words and characters had been attributed to others. The thing about a spirit, though, is that it can never die; it will always haunt. And so it is with the daimon Melancholia, who, despite being displaced by Eros, has nonetheless managed to maintain a furtive, immaterial existence in certain literary and philosophical texts. Returning to those (mostly canonical) texts, this book seeks to redress the injustice done to the demigod Melancholia by restoring his acolytes to their rightful position as the poets, by turns inventive and destructive, outraged and inspired, of political thought.

We realize, of course, that a critical work on melancholia must seem, at this point, like an exercise in melancholia itself. After all, wasn't the great age of academic melancholia over and done with by the early aughts? Isn't melancholia a bit passé? Isn't W. G. Sebald dead and gone? The ancient disposition of melancholia did indeed enjoy, after long years of confinement, a burst of scholarly interest in the last decade of the twentieth century and the early years of the twenty-first. But as if aware of melancholia's infernal origins, the representative works from this period— *Postcolonial Melancholia, The Melancholy of Race, The Psychic Life of Power*—all tend to politicize melancholia only insofar as they cast it in a negative light: an obstacle to authentic political engagement, an affliction in need of a remedy.[3] Adding a Foucauldian twist to an uncritical (if also widespread) reading of Freud's essay "Mourning and Melancholia," these works bequeath to us a vision of melancholia as doubly sinister: not just morbid and pathological, a species of failed mourning that hinders us from working through the traumatic legacies of the past, but a mechanism of governmentality to boot.

Paul Gilroy's *Postcolonial Melancholia* offers a simple case in point. Gilroy's central claim is that white Britons suffer from—and, more to the point, inflict—a melancholia that amounts to an unethical form of collective forgetting, an almost willful refusal to reckon with the shameful burden of the past. At the most basic level, carriers of postcolonial melancholia find themselves unable to work through, and, in working through, accept, the painful reality of the loss of empire. Exhibiting only the most morbid and pathological characteristics of melancholia, they test the reality of multiculturalism—test it in the way that Freud says the melancholic tests the painful reality of the loss of the loved object—and reject it, managing thereby to forget the shame of the past while at the same time refusing to acknowledge the loss of empire or confront its lasting costs. Not only, then, do white Britons refuse to accept what they view as an impoverished present; their refusal prevents everyone from advancing into a more egalitarian future, one freed from the burden of empire's supposedly glorious past.

The drawback of this thesis, as we see it, is that it is too quick to cede the power of melancholia, which comes across as little more than an insidious instrument of reactionary oppression, to the wrong parties. Misconstrued as *ressentiment*, melancholia is left drained of its capacity to challenge, even arrest, existing power formations. Like Anne Cheng, for whom the raced American subject assumes an identity formation indistinguishable from the denigrated object of melancholia—an object disciplined and rejected by turns, an object not fully incorporated into the very body (politic) that paradoxically cannot do without it for its own identity formation—and Judith Butler, who argues that the lacerating and immobilizing grief of the melancholic interiorizes the violent tactics of social regulation, Gilroy takes what was the conflictual disposition of melancholia and turns it into a form of affective panopticism. No longer recognizable as the spirit of politics, melancholia is hereby transformed into the opposite of itself: a disciplinary instrument through which the subject of power, forced to adopt the thwarted position of the abjected lost object, is denied political participation and full citizenship.

A corrective to this disciplinary version of melancholia was offered by a second tradition—let's call it the sorrowful-recollective—inspired by Derrida's revision of melancholia as the ethically retentive counterpart to forgetful mourning.[4] The wellspring of this tradition, David Eng's and David Kazanjian's preface to their edited collection, *Loss*, deserves special comment, which we will reserve for later. A more recent example, and one that shows just how fluid and heterogeneous these traditions can be, is Joseph R. Winters's *Hope Draped in Black*. There is much we admire in Winters's approach, in particular his fruitful campaign to make "strange bedfellows" of the Black literary tradition and the critical theory of the Frankfurt School.[5] We likewise share Winters's desire to liberate melancholia from the orthodox Freudianism that arguably ends up constraining the work of Butler and Cheng. And we are fully on board with his critique of the American model of amnestic progress. Where we part company is over the *potenza*—the power and potential—of melancholia itself. In keeping with what we regard as the self-imposed limitations of a merely ethical, as opposed to fully political, melancholia, Winters is too quick to reduce melancholia to a program of remembrance and the recollection of loss, as if Walter Benjamin's angel of history, whom Winters invokes, were not being irresistibly propelled (albeit backward) into the future. Such an approach, we feel, downplays the poietic dimension of melancholia, its capacity for making as well as for remembering, "registering," and "unsettling." If there is hope, it is not only because "expressions of 'death and disappointment'" can "simultaneously voice longings for a better, more just existence"; it is because our situation is utterly hopeless, and hopelessness is the mother of political poesis.[6] That is why, though we have no wish to deny anyone their historical claim to incomparable sorrow or question the "heightened receptivity to loss" acquired through the intergenerational trauma of "race-inflected violence and suffering," we resist the idea that the cause of melancholia is temporal rather than lost, or that the melancholic's contemplative gaze must be directed backward rather than downward—that its perspective must be historical and not, as we will go on to argue in these pages, drawing on the language of Marxian critique, natural historical.[7] As we understand it, the power of melancholia, like that of thought and judgment, belongs to everyone (the pallor of our canonical representatives notwithstanding). The political melancholic affirms, sorrowfully but also jubilantly, our common condition of living in the midst of the worst.

That common condition has been brilliantly diagnosed, and at times brilliantly countered, by the works of what we will call the affective tradition, works such as Jonathan Flatley's *Affective Mapping*, Rebecca Comay's *Mourning Sickness*, and Jonathan Lear's *Radical Hope*.[8] Indebted as much to Heidegger and Benjamin as to psychoanalysis or poststructuralist ethics, these works make a powerful case for understanding melancholy as both persistent and ubiquitous: nothing less than the *Stimmung* of a modernity ushered in by the French Revolution. But melancholy, however ubiquitous as a mood, is not in and of itself political; or, rather, its affirmative political dimension remains latent if it is treated only as an affective atmosphere or as the basis for a "counter-mood."[9] Where the governmental and recollective traditions leave us with a mostly negatively politicized melancholia recuperable only as the work of mourning, these later works bequeath us a melancholia that manifests as a mood to be managed rather than as a form of thought capable of transforming the outside world. Correspondingly, they figure a melancholic who has attunement but lacks praxis.

Our melancholic is different. A figure standing both for what needs to be done and for what remains unrealizable in the world's political aspirations, our politicized melancholic, far from being indifferent, marginalized, or affectively disciplined, embodies the universal condition of communal life: a discontent that so vexes and irritates a community's members that it becomes the common symptom binding them together. In that respect, the affective dimension of the melancholic disposition remains most faithful to the common cause of a polity. Faithfully, then, this book returns, in true melancholic fashion, to some of the unforgettable offenses on which communities, whether imagined or historical, have been founded: the death of Socrates; the fratricide in *Hamlet*; Woyzeck's killing of Marie in Georg Büchner's *Woyzeck*; the murder of Moses in Freud's last text; the violent appropriation of nature by the invisible hand of the market; the intergenerational betrayal of the revolutionary idea that Hannah Arendt detects in the aftermath of the revolutions of the eighteenth century. Such returns are neither nostalgic nor recuperative. Rather, they repeat the melancholic gesture of holding on to the worst—of affirming the common sense that there is indeed something rotten, not only in the state of Denmark, but universally. Yet even as our melancholic practice remains attuned to histories of wreckage and grief, it follows Hamlet in turning the tactical ruses and surprises of the nocturnal temperament to a different end than self-laceration or, just as important, self-recovery. Political melancholia, as we have come to understand it through our readings of literary and philosophical texts, is mournful but also jubilant, catastrophic but also poietic. It is the name we give to the restive dimension of an ageless affect, an immemorial mood of unbending disconsolation. And while its presence can be detected in the recorded histories of successive political orders, it cannot be said to belong to or arise from any of them. More closely aligned with what Roberto Esposito, reflecting on the commencement of a continuously emergent revolutionary beginning, terms "the origin of the political" than with any conventional concept of politics, melancholia is political in that it organizes the other volatile sentiments, particularly shame, anxiety, and wrath, that human culture carries over from its prehistory.[10] Following in the footsteps of a tradition of melancholic thinkers descended from Aristotle, we argue that those affective registers of melancholia, in affirming the worst, are what enable us to open a space for "the existence of the unreal" that not only makes us courageous and just but that also enjoins us to think something new.[11]

Among modernist proponents of that tradition, Benjamin is surely the most well-known, and with good reason, as we will see in a moment. Yet Benjamin was not alone in recognizing what he called the "motorial" force of melancholia; he had precursors.[12] When Kierkegaard, for example, raised the restlessness of anxiety to the dignity of a philosophical object, he declared melancholia to be the "ailment of our age"—but an "ailment" so dear to him, of such "utmost importance," that he could never do without it. "The strange ideas of my melancholy," he wrote, "I do not give up."[13] It is not the destruction of traditional beliefs that causes this epochal ailment. Rather, what occasions this crisis is the melancholic way of thinking itself: the revelation of another history and another politics brought about by what Theodor Adorno, in his study on Kierkegaard, calls the melancholic's "specific engagement with historical *realien*."[14] In making a ruin appear out of the flotsam washed ashore from the tradition of the forgotten, melancholia makes a crisis. The melancholic, as Kierkegaard emphasizes, has "uncommon powers" in dealing with reality, even when he is inwardly shattered by it and his immense capacities are concealed from him under the guise of providence.[15] The melancholic recalls something essential from history—remnants of long forgotten figures and past struggles—and discovers in them the necessity of another path, a deeper passion. That passion is attuned to an affirmative mode of mourning, of "standing face to face with nothingness," of wishing that the echo of your mourning and your emptiness would reverberate back to you.[16] As Adorno demonstrates, Kierkegaard's philosophy originates in melancholia, which becomes something akin to a transcendental affect. From out of a specific struggle with historical realities, melancholia makes possible not just the emergence of new truths, but the different aesthetic and attitude toward life those truths require.[17]

Benjamin's *Origin of German Tragic Drama* takes this philosophy a step further. For Kierkegaard, melancholy was the "ailment of our age" precisely because it named an interior state, albeit one pensively engaged with historical realities. Benjamin transforms the melancholic disposition into something impersonal, a generalized mood of the world that sur- passes any compensatory schemes pursued by the interiorizing "work of mourning" (*Trauerarbeit*). Mourning plays, observes Benjamin, "are not so much plays that cause mourning, as plays through which mournful- ness finds satisfaction"; they are "plays for the mournful" (119). This is a historical claim about the experience of the profaned world after the death of tragedy. But it is also a way of acknowledging that mournfulness, now freed from the cell of subjective dejection, has become persistent and pervasive, detectable in all objects and spheres of life. When Benjamin ties "the theory of mourning" to a feeling "which is released from any empirical subject and is intimately bound to the fullness of an object," when he cel- ebrates the "astounding tenacity of intention" "at the heart of mourning," "capable of a special intensification" "matched perhaps only by love," he thus does more than diagnose melancholia as a reaction to a world sud- denly emptied of meaning. He describes a world "which is revealed under the gaze of the melancholy man": a world in which the subject is appre- hended by the "solemn" intention "within the object itself." "Mourning is the state of mind" that is "bound to an a priori object." Persevering like love, "and that not playfully," as Benjamin is quick to clarify, the melan- cholic state of mind is more persistent, more pervasive, and more general- ized than it first appears. "Only called a feeling because it does not occupy the highest place," melancholia is shown by Benjamin to be categorical, an ontology, the a priori condition of life in modernity (139).

What finally makes that melancholic ontology affirmative, and not merely a new version of acedia, is the place of repetition within it. "The never-ending repetition" characteristic of the *Trauerspiel*—its reliance on grave processions and ostentatious displays, on empty ceremony and pomp—"secures the bleak rule of a melancholic distaste for life," according to Benjamin (140). That way of describing the staginess of *Trauerspiel* may make it sound as though the genre trafficked in a clichéd version of the melancholic temperament, which is often accused of being fixated, ruminative, spiraling, tedious: repetitive in the worst sense. But what Benjamin in fact describes is how the melancholic passion for stilted ostentation and halting procession reveals an enigmatic dynamism stored up in historical phenomena, precisely by bringing those phenomena to a standstill, objectifying them, and draining them of their vitality. In the deadening "depersonalization" performed by *Trauerspiel*, Benjamin locates the mechanism of a peculiarly melancholic poesis. Offstage, "the deadening of the emotions, and the ebbing away of the waves of life which are the source of these emotions in the body, can increase the distance between the self and the surrounding world to the point of alienation from the body." When staged as *Trauerspiel*, "the concept of the pathological state, in which the most simple object appears to be a symbol of some enigmatic wisdom because it lacks any natural, creative relationship to us, was set in an incomparably productive context" (140). Yet productive how, one might ask, and of what? One answer to that question comes by way of Howard Caygill's gloss on Benjamin's claim that there will eventually come a point "where the universe has been taken over by that despair which is actually its secret *hope*." "When there is only repetition," explains Caygill, "then the affirmation of it creates a novelty and thus breaks the immanence of repetition."[18] Analogously, the melancholic affirmation of repetition, dramatized in "the never-ending repetition" of *Trauerspiel*'s paradoxically frozen processions, breaks the immanence of mere repetition by performing a transmutation of mourning that is truly novel.[19] Repeatedly replaying the alienation of the self in relation "to the surrounding world," increasing the "symptom of depersonalization . . . to an intense degree of mournfulness," *Trauerspiel* gives rise to a new, and newly redeemed, form of mourning. The "contemplative paralysis" formalized in the genre's incessant repetition reveals that mourning is double: that the self-absorbed object of mourning does not coincide with itself; that it is outside of itself, different from itself, a surprise to itself (140).

As Benjamin demonstrates, nowhere is this turn of melancholia toward affirmation clearer than in Shakespeare's *Hamlet*: "[Hamlet's] life, the exemplary object of his mourning, points, before its extinction, to the Christian providence in whose bosom his mournful images are transformed into a blessed existence. Only in a princely life such as this is melancholy redeemed, by being confronted with itself" (158). Melancholia grasped in this fashion, at the point where it encounters and interrupts itself, where it is repeated and affirmed and where it is no longer contained in a form but effects a transformation, "inspires itself to new life" and awakens "within itself the clear light of self-awareness" (158). Even the most despairing and destitute melancholia, once fully affirmed, would become something other than mere despair and destitution. In fact, it may pass over from being affirmative to being, like divine violence or the proletarian general strike, "afformative": the insertion into history of a caesura, a pause or paralysis that is also a fundamental interruption.[20] This paralysis, wherein "no work is done, nothing is produced, and nothing is planned," not even the work of mourning, is the political event of affirmative melancholia.[21] It manifests a new sociality, a melancholic collective attuned to the bleak rule of an empty world, like the mourners in the frozen processions of *Trauerspiel*.

The reader can be forgiven for thinking that this affirmative version of melancholia bears only a passing resemblance to melancholia as it is commonly understood. How did it come to that? How did it happen, to pose the question a different way, that the figure who inspired an awestruck Aristotle to wonder, "Why is it that all men who have become outstanding in philosophy, statesmanship, poetry or the arts are melancholic?" got driven underground, forced to endure a furtive and disreputable existence on the outskirts of the polis? Should we blame Cassian, who warned his fellow cenobites that "our sixth combat is with what the Greeks call ἀκηδία [acedia], which we may term weariness or distress of heart"? Or should we blame Pinel, who, after describing melancholia in the usual fashion ("The symptoms generally comprehended by the term melancholia are taciturnity, a thoughtful pensive air, gloomy suspicions, and a love of solitude"), declared that "nothing . . . can be more hideous than the figure of a melancholic, brooding over his imaginary misfortunes"?[22] Many commentators would be inclined to point the finger at Freud and at his 1917 essay "Mourning and Melancholia," in particular. We, however, wish to point a different finger in a slightly different direction, toward an overly deferential reading of Freud's essay and of its revision, six years later, as part of *The Ego and the Id*.

Freud begins "Mourning and Melancholia" by drawing a contrast—too sharp, in the opinion of later commentators—between the work carried out by "normal" mourning, on the one hand, and "pathological" melancholia, on the other. The former process, avers Freud, holds little mystery. Having first "shown that the loved object no longer exists," "reality-testing" then "proceeds to demand that all libido shall be withdrawn from its attachments to that object."[23] Understandably, this process, which gets "carried out bit by bit, at great expense of time and cathetic energy," can drag on, and it often arouses an opposition on the part of the ego "so intense that a turning away from reality takes place and a clinging to the object through the medium of a hallucinatory wishful psychosis" (14:244). In the end, though, concludes Freud, experience shows "that when the work of mourning is completed the ego becomes free and uninhibited again," ready to transfer its libido to another object (14:245). In melancholia, by contrast, no transference of libidinal energy to a new object occurs; instead, that free libido is withdrawn into the ego, where, Freud tells us, "it [is] not employed in any unspecified way, but [serves] to establish an *identification* of the ego with the abandoned object" (14:249). The result, according to Freud, is an entrenched ambivalence, on the part of the ego, toward the object—that is to say, toward that portion of itself that identifies with the object. On the one hand, the ego's "narcissistic identification with the object . . . becomes a substitute for the erotic cathexis, the result of which is that in spite of the conflict with the loved person the love-relation need not be given up" (14:249). Or, as Freud puts it a few pages later, "by taking flight into the ego, love escapes extinction" (14:257). At the same time, however, the melancholic continues to harbor feelings of aggression and hostility toward the object that abandoned, injured, or otherwise disappointed the ego. "If the love for the object—a love which cannot be given up though the object itself is given up—takes refuge in narcissistic identification," writes Freud, "then the hate comes into operation on this substitutive object, abusing it, debasing it, making it suffer and deriving sadistic satisfaction from its suffering" (14:251). Inwardly directed, played out again and again ("In melancholia . . . countless separate struggles are carried on over the object, in which hate and love contend with one another" [14:256]), ambivalence ensures that it is not only love for the object that the melancholic preserves but conflict, too. As Freud puts it in a famous passage:

> [T]he shadow of the object fell upon the ego, and the latter could henceforth be judged by a special agency, as though it were an object, the forsaken object. In this way an object-loss was transformed into an ego-loss and the conflict between the ego and the loved person into a cleavage between the critical activity of the ego and the ego as altered by identification (14:249).

Having declined the reality principle's injunction to transfer their libidinal energies to another object, the melancholic gets ambivalence and internalized aggression instead.

That, at least, is one way of reading the situation. We believe, however, that there is more implied by, even embedded in, Freud's diagram of the psyche than ambivalence or a conflict turned inward. What the diagram gives us instead is a model for neutralizing sovereign power, which in turn frees us to pursue a politics bereft of the consolations of mastery. Consider the intersection of identification and the ego ideal. The superego, Freud tells us in *The Ego and the Id*, arises out of the nascent ego's identification with the ego ideal.[24] The gestures of melancholia, meanwhile, repeatedly stage a history in which the feelings associated with what Freud calls "the loss of an ideal kind"—outrage, disappointment, disillusionment, "dissatisfaction with the ego on moral grounds"—get transferred onto the object, which is then criticized, in turn, by the "institution" or "agency" that Freud will eventually label the superego (14:246). In "Mourning and Melancholia," Freud presents this as a quasi-political parable in which a "mental constellation of revolt" has "passed over into the crushed state of melancholia" (14:248). But here Freud misapprehends as capitulation what is in fact a peculiar tactic of the melancholic. The superego, we know, needs the ego in the same way a sovereign needs cowering subjects. Like the sovereign, the superego thrives on the cultivation of particular affects: dread, certainly, but also the pleasures associated with failure and resignation. Yet Freud says something else about the melancholic ego. He says that "the complex of melancholia behaves like an open wound, drawing to itself cathectic energies . . . from all directions, and emptying the ego until it is totally impoverished" (14:253). This is one key to understanding melancholia as a political disposition: the fact that it drains the psychical complex of the affects, the dread and suffering and perverse pleasure, on which the superego ordinarily feeds. With the ego thus depleted—a situation too easily mischaracterized as impotence or a lack of agency—the superego becomes bonded to the object, becomes, as it were, completely absorbed in the object, like a monarch who, deprived of cowering subjects, spends all day staring at his moldering coronation robes and dented crown. Far, then, from laying out a straightforward political parable— cruel and oppressive superego on one side of the barricade, crushed ego on the other—Freud's diagram in fact schematizes a self-enclosed system collapsing in upon itself, with the superego berating and denigrating an object that is really only a part of the self-same complex: the derivative of an ego ideal lacerating itself for its own loss.

Freud himself provides us with a compelling image of this dynamic. Describing the unconscious nature of melancholia—oftentimes, the melancholic "knows *whom* he has lost but not *what* he has lost in him," suggesting "that melancholia is in some way related to an object-loss which is withdrawn from consciousness"—Freud notes the following:

> In mourning we found that the inhibition and loss of interest [in the outside world] are fully accounted for by the work of mourning in which the ego is absorbed. In melancholia the unknown loss will result in a similar internal work and will therefore be responsible for the melancholic inhibition. The difference is that the inhibition of the melancholic seems puzzling to us because we cannot see what it is that is absorbing him so entirely (14:245–246).

That Freud himself should fail to see what it is that absorbs the melancholic so entirely is instructive, if not altogether surprising. For it never seems to occur to Freud, as it never seems to occur to certain critics of melancholia, that there could be a form of melancholia that has nothing to do with, and cannot be understood by, any would-be sovereign figure: a melancholia that, far from being beholden to the superego, circumvents it altogether. For such a melancholia, the superego represents, at best, an obstacle to be overcome—a pretender seeking to claim credit for a disposition that precedes it—on the way to accomplishing a larger goal. The melancholic has no choice, then, but to develop tactics; and here we encounter one of them. Freud confesses that he cannot see what absorbs the melancholic so completely. And yet Freud himself remains completely absorbed in the melancholic's absorption in the unconscious object. Absorbed by absorption, with no ego to distract him, Freud becomes lost to the realm of the lost object.

Meanwhile, the melancholic is free to direct her pent-up energies elsewhere. "The most remarkable characteristic of melancholia, and the one in most need of explanation," observes Freud, "is its tendency to change round"—the language already evokes revolution—"into mania" (14:253). "What has happened here," Freud goes on to conjecture, "is that, as a result of some influence, a large expenditure of psychical energy, long maintained or habitually occurring, has at last become unnecessary, so that it is available for numerous applications and possibilities of discharge"—among which we would like to include, not just political action alone, but that paradoxical combination of discontent and sublime fury which allows us to contemplate the unreal (14:254). Freud then arrives at the following conclusion:

> In mania, the ego must have got over the loss of the object (or its mourning over the loss, or perhaps the object itself), and thereupon the whole quota of anticathexis which the painful suffering of melancholia

had drawn to itself from the ego and "bound" will have become available. Moreover, the manic subject plainly demonstrates his liberation from the object which was the cause of his suffering, by seeking like a ravenously hungry man for new object-cathexes (14:255).

As Freud interprets it, mania amounts to something like an extreme resolution of mourning: evidence that the subject has at last "got over" the object. But if mania seems triumphant, it is not because the melancholic has abandoned the object (although he may have transcended loss, which is something else entirely); it is because he has devised a strategy to neutralize the superego. What mania signals is not the final convergence of melancholia with mourning. That would be to misunderstand how melancholia perpetuates and even intensifies the conflict that mourning seeks to resolve. What mania signals is the next, furious phase in the melancholic's project, made possible by abandoning the superego to the object.

But not, let us reiterate, by abandoning the object. Freud contends that the manic subject, newly liberated from the crushed state of melancholia that inevitably follows the psyche's failed revolt against reality, seeks like a ravenously hungry man for a new object in which to invest their libidinal energies. That, however, is to assume that melancholia and mania are mutually exclusive states. It is also to ignore the possibility that they exist on a continuum, with mania functioning as a more heightened, and indeed more radicalized, version of melancholia: a melancholia that has overcome being crushed and, newly emboldened, returned to a "mental constellation of revolt." Recall that Freud characterizes melancholia as a state of sustained ambivalence, an admixture of love and hate for the incorporated (and unrelinquished) object, a confusion of fidelity and conflict. Eager to identify any evidence that "healthy" mourning always wins the day, Freud imagines an uplifting scenario in which the emancipated maniac, having freed himself from the object whose incorporation has caused him so much suffering, seeks after new object-cathexes. But what if the melancholic turns manic not because they have relinquished the object but because they have figured out the true power of cathexis? What if melancholics were demonstrating their liberation not by seeking new object-cathexes in the outside world but by cathecting to the object in just the way that Freud says they do: by investing their free libidinal energies not in the object as such but in the "vehement passions," the conflict of love and love of conflict, associated with it?[25] When Freud observes that the most remarkable thing about melancholia is its tendency to turn round—to make a revolution—into mania, he bears witness to the liberated melancholic's recovery of the mental constellation of revolt, now under the furious, inspired guise of mania.

So: the political melancholic has the power to arrest the would-be, superegoic master by absorbing the latter's attentions in the realm of the object. They also have the capacity to liberate themselves from the suffering caused by their incorporation of the object, not by ravenously seeking after new, compensatory object-cathexes (the melancholic is nothing if not faithful), but by cathecting their libidinal energies to the mental constellation of revolt, the undying love and endless conflict, associated with the object. With that reframing of the melancholic temperament in mind, we would now like to raise a more fundamental question: What exactly *is* the "lost" object of melancholia? Freud himself is somewhat vague on the topic, associating it both with the loved object and with an unspecified "what"—an ideal, say, or an aspiration, or some grand plan—that is lost when the object as such is lost. In the specific case of political melancholia, however, the "what" that is lost is politics itself. Here we diverge from Giorgio Agamben, who in his own reading of the lost object of melancholia argues that melancholy "would be not so much the regressive reaction to the loss of the love object as the imaginative capacity to make an unobtainable object appear as if lost."[26] Melancholia is reassuringly deceptive, according to Agamben. If the object in question has never in fact been possessed, melancholia will delude us into believing that it is merely lost; if the object in question could never be possessed only because it never existed, melancholia will delude us into believing that it may be appropriated, imaginatively, as something lost. This, we wish to argue, both is and is not the case with politics, and has been from its origin. We have never known, nor ever had, politics. But neither is politics "lost" in the way that Foucault implies when he argues that the death of Socrates ushered in "a form of veridiction peculiar precisely to philosophical discourse, and the courage of which must be exercised until death as a test of the soul that cannot take place on the political platform."[27] Politics is lost, like the object in melancholia is lost, only insofar as it has never been possessed. And therein lies the true cause of melancholic grief, as well as its power of affirmation. We have had any number of spurious, compensatory objects in the place of politics—governmentality, war, the sovereign exception, postpolitical competition, and political economy all come to mind—but we have only ever known politics as something lost. The political melancholic has been dissatisfied with every one of those substitutes, every one of those compensatory objects soliciting their, and our, libidinal cathexis. The political melancholic is not so naïve, however, as to believe that politics is merely lost, that it once existed in reality and might thus be recovered. Even the melancholic sense that politics was lost with the death of Socrates is lost to the melancholic, for whom no such consoling fiction will satisfy. Rather, the melancholic counters philosophical veridiction with affirmation: affirmation that politics is lost, and that its loss is the origin of politics. Affirming that all ideals, including the ideal of loss, are lost, the melancholic is then free to open a space for the unreal—which is as much to say that the melancholic enters into open conflict with a reality that continues to demand that they give up their devotion to the lost object of politics and instead seek another, more wholesome and profitable object-cathexis. To this repeated injunction the melancholic says No, just as they have done for millennia. And thus does their love for the object escape extinction.

In fact, this is how the melancholic both affirms that love and, by the same gesture, shows that love to be a power of affirmation. In his preface to *The Description of Misfortune*, Sebald programmatically writes that melancholy "at the level of art . . . is anything but reactive or reactionary. . . . Melancholy, the contemplation of the movement of misfortune, has nothing in common with the wish to die. It is a form of resistance."[28] Melancholia is to be understood in precisely this fashion, as resistance; but in just that way it is also the affirmation of another politics, one keyed to division, grief, and misfortune. The melancholic, writes Sebald, "goes over again just how things could have happened"; he cannot help but recount, repeatedly, the "description of misfortune."[29] How can the incessant recounting of misfortune be a political act and create a shift in the meaning of the political? According to the classicist Nicole Loraux, every politics begins "with a call to oblivion." Amnesty—and amnesia—are deployed to renew the bond of life in the city, but always at the terrible cost of replacing the memory of misfortune (*kakon*). Granted, as Loraux notes, there is a good reason for the members of a polis to put an end to the alliance of "terrible wrath" and "unforgetting grief" (*penthos alaston*), for it "wanders" (*alaomai*) in the community like an accursed ghost that, in Plutarch's reckoning, "must absolutely be avoided (*aleuasthai*)."[30] And yet, Loraux observes, the exhortations made to the Athenian citizens to remember to forget their *menis*, their wrathful grief, render visible another strength, a much more formidable remembering (*mneme*) and the politics it makes possible:

> Wrath in mourning, the principle of which is eternal repetition, will- ingly expresses itself with an *aei*, and the fascination of this tireless "always" threatens to set it up as a powerful rival to the political *aei*

that establishes the memory of institutions. . . . I renounce my *menis*—
is never pronounced. . . . *Menis*: a word to hide the memory whose
name is concealed by it. Another memory, much more formidable than
mneme. A memory that reduces itself completely to nonoblivion. [. . .]
And just as it was necessary to forget the strength behind the "ills,"
a recurrent utterance shows the renunciation of memory-anger: it is
necessary to deny—assuming that it is possible—the denial that has
stiffened upon itself.[31]

Here Loraux brings the forbidden-but-not-forgotten memory of *menis*
in closest proximity to Nietzsche's eternal return, and thus to the edge
of affirmation. In the never-renounced *menis*, "the eternal repetition"
of mourning-wrath, modeled by the Athenian citizen, we encounter a
"powerful rival" to the "memory," rooted in amnesty and amnesia, of
political institutions.

The unforgetting melancholic is thus not a transformative figure
because she struggles with her melancholic condition. Rather, melancholia is itself the engine of transformation because in it struggle, now recognized as fidelity to a loss or a sorrow that does not forget and thus is
not to be overcome, becomes political. Melancholia, liberated from being
merely an individual affliction, passes over to a mode of courage, a virtue,
as Badiou might call it, that takes time and involves "holding on, in a different duration from that imposed by the law of the world."[32] This fidelity
to a different time and duration can express itself, according to Benjamin's
"Theses on the Philosophy of History," as "courage, humor, cunning, and
fortitude"—each of which can be found in the arsenal shared, for example,
by Socrates and Hamlet. But it can also manifest itself as hatred, love,
unforgetting anger, and grief: in short, as all those vehement passions that
have been unwelcome in the city basically since Pericles gave his funeral
oration, but which are seized, externalized, and deployed by the melancholic to create another "concept of the political."

For who could ever engage in a discourse on melancholia without taking a stand, or without a transcendental commitment to the persistence
of what Loraux calls "nonoblivion"?[33] The sorrow that cannot forget itself
demands an affirmative gesture, an unconditional engagement with the
cause of loss, with the promise of a memory that is more originary than
any institutionalized politics or philosophy.[34] As Loraux argues, politics
and philosophy *presuppose* the fidelity of the melancholic to this inscrutable thing, the "unforgetful."[35] The melancholic finds, in the sphere of
sorrow, an insistence of nonoblivion that demands what Foucault calls the

"courage of truth": that way of accounting for unforgettable loss which has not yet become Socratic or philosophical questioning. Keyed to pervasive, universal sorrow and the inevitability of conflict, the melancholic in this way reorients "the concept of the political" as one that is at once antagonistic, mournful, and communal. Contrary to Derrida's double affirmation, the "arche-originary pledge" anterior to any determinate content, his "yes, yes" that situates a "vigil" and opens up the space for politics, albeit without giving a specific position, a politics of melancholia as it is understood here entails an intensely determined attitude toward an intensely determined thing.[36] A politics of melancholia determines—and in determining, affirms—why one is always already subject to a vigil, why one takes a stand, remains vigilant, in relation to the "movement of misfortune" alluded to by Sebald. Hamlet and Woyzeck are mad in a double sense: they are furies, yes, but they are also lovers, given over to Plato's *mania*. It is this madness that makes their mourning affirmative, and thus melancholic. They are not going to let politics fall into oblivion just because it is lost.

Arguably this amounts to a different understanding of loss and the object—and so, too, of the melancholic disposition—than the one encountered in the restorative version of melancholia exemplified by the preface to the collection *Loss*. For the editors of that collection, David Eng and David Kazanjian, the question "What is lost?" gives way, "invariably," to another question—"What remains?"—that in turn gives way to a statement: "What is lost is known only by what remains of it."[37] Understood in those terms, the object becomes whatever can be recovered from what Eng and Kazanjian call "the domain of remains"—a definition that effectively drains melancholia of its radical potential by reducing it to a form of defiant curation (4). Setting aside the obvious Lacanian rejoinder that the lost object may not wish to be recollected any more than the beggar wanted half of Saint Martin's cloak, we raise a more basic objection: namely that the object of melancholia is "known," if it can be said to be "known" at all, not by what remains of it but by its absence, galling and overwhelming, from the impoverished domain of world history.[38] The melancholic looks about her and declares, "This is not it; this has never been it." The question raised by the melancholic is thus not "What is lost?" or (perish the thought) "What remains?" It is, "Should a world that has never been 'it' be reassembled at all?"

For that reason, we wish to revise Eng's and Kazanjian's otherwise crucial insight that "the work of mourning remains becomes possible through melancholia's continued engagement with the various and ongoing forms of loss—as Freud writes, 'of a loved person' or 'some abstraction which has taken the place of one. Such as one's country, liberty, an ideal, and so on'"

(5). There is indeed something continuous about the work of melancholia, and it does transpire at the level of Freud's "and so on." But where Eng and Kazanjian take the "melancholic excess" implicit in that "and so on" as necessitating the work of "mourning remains," we understand it as Freud's tacit admission that melancholia concerns the ongoing accumulation—the piling up, as Walter Benjamin might put it—of ruins (5). The one mode is merely recuperative. The other is a process of infinite unmaking, carried out in the name of what can never be forgotten precisely because it has not yet been. The one is a version of renunciation, now reiterated as "the adamant refusal of closure" (3). The other is an expression, manic and furious at times, of a mode so transitive and impersonal that it could never be reduced to anything like a conscious recollection of what remains.

This is not to suggest, however, that the melancholic has nothing to do, no purpose in life. Just because a politics of melancholia entails something other than constructively mourning what remains of a broken world does not then mean that it is not affirmative. It is simply affirmative of the ruination that a program of "mourning remains" takes it upon itself to remedy. Once again, this way of understanding melancholia requires a correspondingly new understanding of the object. Earlier we argued that the melancholic cathects to the loving conflict (and conflictual love) associated with the object more than to the object as such. In fact, it may be—and the actions of a figure like Hamlet bear this out—that the only reason the melancholic retains the lost object at all is so they will have a pretext for continuing the conflict and love which they would otherwise have to relinquish. Freud himself intuited as much. The self-reproaches and complaints of melancholics, he observes, "are really 'plaints' in the old sense of the word": "reproaches against a loved object which have been shifted away from it on to the patient's own ego" (14:248). Strictly speaking, then, the reproaches voiced by the melancholic are not *self*-reproaches (although they might be misinterpreted as such) so much as objective complaints: the externalization, in plaintive speech, of an internalized sense of injustice. The melancholic is the lead plaintiff in what turns out to be a collective action taken against the outside world.

Perhaps, then, when speaking of the melancholic object, we should not speak of an object at all, or at least not in the strict, Freudian sense of a loved object retained through incorporation or a "what" whose remains we mourn. Perhaps we should speak instead of a particular disposition toward the object that the melancholic externalizes, literally objectifies, in the world around them. Perhaps, borrowing some language from Adorno, we should speak, not of the object, which implies something determined by the subject (including the mourning subject), but of "objectivity." In Freud's theory of melancholia, where narcissistically internalized libidinal energy forms an identification between the ego and the abandoned object, one can still hear echoes of the bourgeois belief that there exists an identity of subject and object. It was that identity which Adorno, following the example set by Benjamin, made it his business to disintegrate, precisely by demonstrating that not only the identity between subject and object, but the categories of subject and object themselves, are never immune from the natural forces of decomposition, decay, and dissolution.[39] As the fact that Adorno's thinking was influenced by Benjamin's work on the *Trauerspiel* suggests, however, this was an understanding of the relation of subject to object already arrived at by the melancholic. Long before Adorno, the melancholic grasped that the object, when properly understood as objective—that is, as both a source of truth and as something that, existing in the material world, was prone to decay— announced the dissolution of the reality whose dictates, Freud tells us, the melancholic strenuously rejects. Benjamin was of course invariably sympathetic to what we have taken to calling the politically melancholic disposition. But when Adorno, building upon Benjamin's work in the *Origin of German Tragic Drama*, proclaims that "the objectivity of history . . . is natural history"—that historical reality, like the secure identity of the subject, remains open to the same natural decay that befalls any material object; that the eternal decay of all objects is the objective truth disclosed in history—he, too, is speaking in the language, or at least the tonality, of the political melancholic.[40] What Freud could not see, and what generations of commentators have repeatedly dismissed as sullenness, alienation, despondency, or worse, was simply the melancholic's absorption in natural history. Meanwhile, what Adorno clearly perceived was that such absorption repeated, in objectified form, the melancholic's own disconsolate and conflictual disposition toward the lost object.

At its most basic, the term *natural history* refers to Adorno's insight that the second nature created by society's "natural law of motion" leads to "the negation of any nature that might be conceived as the first."[41] Nature and history, observes Adorno, writing under the influence of Benjamin's own, earlier ruminations on the concept of natural history, are present in one another: nature is "present as transience" in any historical formation, while history is present in nature "as something that has evolved and is transient."[42] Just as the presence of transient nature means that no historical formation can ever resolve itself into a given, inevitable, "natural" state, so too does nature remain subject to historicization, to transformation by

humans—to its own form of transience. And just as all historical formations succumb, in time, to the natural forces of evolution and decay, so
too are humans never simply fated to be engulfed by natural forces that
exist entirely outside of or apart from their own nature, their own capacity
for historicizing action. Insofar as nature is worked on, it is implicated in
history; and insofar as nature is implicated in history, it is never merely
anomic and abysmal. "The attitude of melancholic contemplation," as
Adorno calls it, doesn't just remain absorbed in such natural history; it
is an outgrowth and an engine of it. This comes across most clearly in a
lecture that Adorno delivered on January 12, 1965. There Adorno seeks to
clarify why, in his view, "the relationship of nature and history provides us
with the primal image of interpretive behavior."[43] Evoking Benjamin's *Origin of German Tragic Drama*, Adorno reminds us that this primal image
of natural historical interpretation has been with us for a very long time,
"handed down," as he puts it, "through intellectual history in the form of
allegory." He then continues:

> Beneath this gaze, the profound gaze of allegory, which is perhaps
> the model for the philosophical gaze as such—because the attitude of
> melancholic contemplation may well be the attitude on which philo-
> sophical inquiry has been founded—nature stands revealed. Nature, I
> say, reveals itself beneath this gaze as history, just as in all allegory the
> death's head owes its central importance to the fact that as a natural
> object its own expression reveals its historical nature. Conversely . . .
> beneath this gaze history stands revealed as nature in so far as it turns
> out to be permanent transience.[44]

Such a melancholy attitude, because it "perceives transience in everything
historical," is not just recollective of the past, according to Adorno; it is
also "critical," given over to the dialectical negation of both nature and history. Thus "we might even say," picking up on Adorno's argument,

> that the transition from philosophy to criticism represents something
> like a secularization of melancholy. This is a melancholy that has
> become active, not a melancholy that makes do, that remains stuck fast
> in an unhappy consciousness, not at home with itself, but a conscious-
> ness that exteriorizes itself as a critique of existing phenomena. Such a
> melancholy is probably the pre-eminent critical, philosophical stance.
> In other words, if you read the phenomena of history as the cyphers of
> their own transience or their own natural deterioration, they will also
> always be defined by their own negativity.[45]

If melancholia has been misconstrued as dejection rather than absorption—if we have squandered, as it were, our philosophical inheritance—it is largely due to having forgotten this understanding of melancholy and, with it, our capacity to recognize natural historical dissolution as the objectification of our critical consciousness. The shadow of the lost object has fallen, not only across the ego, but across the objectivity of history, which is natural history.

This collective forgetting of a melancholia inseparable from natural history has had effects both immediate and far-reaching. Immediately, it is has led politics to submit to the logic of our own historical formation, where capitalism thrives on the assumption of groundlessness and flux—the assumption, that is, of a wild, anarchic nature anterior to law and order and in need of a strong, guiding hand, preferably of the invisible sort. Worse still it has meant that we continue to submit to a much older, and indeed persistent, logic, a logic that might be said to constitute the primal sin of political philosophy. From the moment that Pindar's sovereign law (*nomos basileus*), conjured to justify violence "with the strongest hand," joined forces with the Sophists' fantasy of a natural "right of the strongest," political philosophy has stumbled over the egregious conflation of might with right, violence (*Bia*) with justice (*dike*), that constitutes the inner workings of both sovereignty and government. (Agamben would go so far as to claim, in fact, that "the hidden paradigm guiding every successive definition of sovereignty" is precisely Pindar's sovereign *nomos*, which works by melding the principle of superior force with a force of law said to have originated from a natural source.[46]) Precisely because of that initial misstep, however, political philosophy has never stopped dreaming of a noncoercive nomos and an immemorial *physis* capable of eluding the grasp of sovereignty and governmentality even while remaining essential to their self-conception. Consider, for example, the idea of *chora* (space) in the *Timaeus*, Plato's dramatized theorization of cosmogony and natural history.[47] Plato's reflections, "as in a dream," on the unsettled and yet indestructible chora seem to be driven by a single-minded pursuit of a third, bastard nature capable of breaking open the dichotomy between a changeless sphere of commanding, lawful being (a "source" and a "father," 50d) and an anomic nature of becoming and semblance apprehended by changeable opinion (*doxa*). Here and elsewhere in his political philosophy, Plato tends to multiply the terms nature (physis) and law (nomos) to avoid the false alternative between a sovereign nomos that becomes one with nature, as in Pindar's poem, and the Sophistic notion of an anomic, brute nature anterior to nomos. For such a notion of lawless nature serves either to justify the violence of the strongest or, in

Hobbes, the intervention of the sovereign into the state of nature. Meanwhile, Plato's chora, this nearly incomprehensible space, formless and yet
capable of receiving and giving form, compels us to think a nomic nature, a
nature suspended between the hypernomic order of unchanging forms and
the anomic sphere of visible nature: a *physionomos*.[48] It is as the Athenian
remarks in Plato's *Laws*: such a physionomos would replace and displace
Pindar's "decree of nature . . . that the stronger should rule and the weaker
should obey" (690c). The Platonic pursuit of physionomos effectively derails
the operative fantasy of the Sophists that a physis can be severed from its
nomos—that underneath law and logos roam the unfettered forces of a wild
state of nature in need of despotic rule. Taking up Plato's unfinished project,
then, the political melancholic remains absorbed not just in natural history
but, more specifically, in the pursuit of physionomos.

It is with this idea of a physionomic natural history in mind that we
come around, in good melancholic fashion, to Albrecht Dürer's much scrutinized engraving *Melancholia I*. This engraving, which Dürer dedicated
to the Emperor Maximilian I, makes a strange gift for a prince. As Erwin
Panofsky points out, the engraving's saturnine figure wears keys, signifying power, and a purse, signifying wealth: meet emblems for the power of
the emperor over the Earth.[49] Yet the image sends mixed signals; for it
also depicts the power of melancholia to dismantle the emperor's Earthly
realm. The saw, nails, and plane, scattered seemingly without sense, suggest that Melancholia is aligned more with the undoing than the building
of a world, more with derailing current orders than with restoring old ones
(let alone mourning them). Nor is Melancholia unaware of what it can do.
As if cognizant of their own transformative powers, the engraving's saturnine figure and child exhibit a strange sort of resolve, at once frozen and
purposeful. Together with the dog and the bat, they form a community
of melancholic creatures bound together only by an affect that possesses
them, citizens of neither of the orders, worldly or divine, that they take it
upon themselves to undo. The night vision of the bat, the ghostly light of
the rainbow, and the lurid gleam of the comet seen in the background of
Dürer's work catalog the nocturnal weapons of melancholia: nimble in
twilight and obscurity, attuned to spectral forces and to the transformative
events of natural history, winged and prophetic.

Meanwhile, the saturnine figure's baleful stare and clenched fist (a new
motif introduced by Dürer into the iconography of melancholia) hint at the
resolve and power latent in the melancholic temperament. There is a fury
at the root of that temperament, yet it would be a mistake to reduce that
fury to anger or, worse, ressentiment. The peculiar fury of melancholia,

and the clenched fist used to signify it, associate melancholia with stasis, the ancient term naming a standstill in the workings of the polis, the stalemate that obtains once the norms and rules that ordinarily govern civic life have been dismantled.[50] Even today, the melancholic stands accused of bringing political life to a grinding halt. To this accusation we say, Yes, exactly. Stasis, a standing still in order to stand up (or a standing up that is also a standing still: the term derives from the pregnant moment when someone stands up to challenge someone else), is an insurrectionary gesture: a baleful stare, a clenched fist. Frozen and yet momentous, almost imperceptible and yet striking enough to captivate those who witness it, the stasis inaugurated—inaugurated at every moment, one might say—by the melancholic gesture introduces a genuinely revolutionary time into the regulated time, the dependable tick-tock-ticking, of the polis. This revolutionary, melancholic time is a plodding time, a patient time. Set to the speed of natural historical phenomena, it is revolutionary in the way that Saturn revolves around the Sun.

And in its plodding, revolutionary way, that time carries us back, returns us, both temporally and spatially: temporally, to the early days of the polis; spatially, to the scene of the polis's first encounter with itself. In 458 BC, shortly before the performance of Aeschylus's *Oresteia* trilogy, a section behind the orchestra was cut off from the theater located on the Acropolis in Athens: the *skene*. It was in this separate structure, hidden behind the playing area, withdrawn from the view of both the audience and the chorus, that all the inadmissible acts and unimaginable horrors that might haunt the city could now be staged—staged, but not witnessed.[51] In the case of the *Oresteia*, those acts and horrors include not only Agamemnon's murder but also, in the *Libation-Bearers* (the most ghostly of the three tragedies), the taciturn powers of Apollo and Agamemnon's ghost, whose presence can be felt "from the other side of the mound where his dismembered limbs lie entombed."[52] Just as important, the skene conceals from view Electra's and Orestes's plan to kill Clytemnestra, a plan that also involves the secret schemes and machinations of Pylades, the courtier and secret counselor *avant la lettre*. Along with acts of murder, brooding gods, and restless spirits, the skene thus harbors, while also hiding from view, the presence of strife: in the house, in the family, in the souls of the actors, and in the city. The fallout of stasis, its humus, so to speak—its fertile breeding ground and residue—lies dormant in the skene. As a gathering place for a forgotten history, the skene becomes the backstage haunt of strife, the site where its catastrophic past and future is stored as though its melancholic contents retained a glimmer of redemptive power.

The question of stasis—or rather, of what to do with stasis—thus becomes the abiding, if unstated, question at the heart of the *Oresteia*. In *Agamemnon*, for example, Cassandra furiously affirms stasis: "Let the insatiable spirit of strife [stasis] raise a cry of triumph over the family" (1116–7). Meanwhile, the chorus can only lament its ruinous powers, followed by a death wish: "Io, Earth, Earth, if only you had swallowed me up / before I saw this man lying / in the lowly deathbed" (1538–40). It is the presence of stasis, sitting like a crypt not only between the opposing factions but in their midst, in *oikos*, that prompts the silencing discourse at work in the trilogy. Words are chosen carefully or else become a means of deception. Secrets are kept and plots hidden from sight. Either muteness, the blockage of information itself, is on dramatic display in the *Oresteia*, or else the cacophonous sounds of the vengeful furies.

But while emerging from oikos, the institution of stasis—its status as a permanent, if muted, feature of civic life—combats *oikonomical* stasis by partitioning it further, making finer critical cuts within its seemingly self-contained economy. As J. Peter Euben notes, Orestes's political focus is striking, particularly compared to how his mother triumphantly justifies the killing of her husband. Unlike Clytemnestra, who harps on private wrongs, Orestes begins his speech after the murder of his mother with a vow to break the rule of "the twin tyrants of this land" (973). In *Agamemnon*, the aftermath of the Trojan War gets redirected into the oikos, with the fall of Troy repeated in the downfall of the House of Atreus. In the more melancholic *Libation-Bearers*, a wrathful Orestes returns home and, having avenged his father, brings the force of downfall out of the oikos and into the city. The fall of Troy, which had become the downfall of the House of Atreus, now becomes the downfall of tyrants. Perhaps, then, Agamben is on the right track when he claims that, ultimately, "stasis does not originate in the oikos; it is not a 'war within the family,' but forms part of a device that functions in a manner similar to the state of exception. . . . Oikos is politicized and included in the *polis* through stasis."[53] In that case stasis, traditionally considered the greatest calamity that could befall a city, is to be welcome, for it makes politics, which is coterminous with the overcoming of tyranny ("the twin tyrants of this land"), possible in the first place.

Now if there exists anything like a determinate politics of melancholia, a tactics or program, it will be found here, in the melancholic's ability to effect stasis. Stasis is, in the first place, temporal, a time of standstill. It is also gestural. Yet in both these ways, stasis—and the frozen gestures of fury in Dürer's engraving only emphasize the point—is structural, even diagrammatic. Look again at the dismantled tableau of *Melancholia I*. The melancholic, having picked up on the underlying mood of the polis, then reintroduces that mood in the frozen gestures of stasis. That which he extracts from his historical formation, he then reinserts, this time as an inert diagram, a frozen constellation. Surrounded by the ruins of both the material and cosmic orders, the static figure of Melancholia—seated, perhaps, or forever on the verge of standing up—succeeds in rearranging her historical formation so thoroughly as to redirect the onlooker's attentions into the workings of natural history. This is a genuinely revolutionary gesture not only in the usual sense of reversing an intolerable situation but in the sense that, by introducing the furious, frozen gesture of stasis, the melancholic allows for the possibility of a new and, strictly speaking, unthinkable discourse. Unlike the other discourses available to us—those of the master, the university, the analyst, and the hysteric—this new discourse, the discourse of the melancholic, cannot be established by a quarter turn but only by a revolutionary reordering: an impossible inversion of object over subject, knowledge over master.[54] A thorough overturning—truly, a re-volution—of the power latent in the discourse of the hysteric, the discourse of the melancholic introduces the possibility of the impossible and thus provides the political subject with a cause so immemorial, it can only seem new.

In that respect, our understanding of melancholia differs from that found, for example, in Esposito's work on melancholia and community. Esposito compares melancholia, which he describes as being "made of nothing and impossible to appropriate," to the putative lack of *das Ding*, the Thing.[55] But here it would do to recall the genealogy of the Thing as psychoanalysis understands it. The Thing first appears in the *Project for a Scientific Psychology*, where Freud imagines the process by which "a human-being learns to cognize" in relation to "a fellow human-being." "The perceptual complexes proceeding from this fellow human-being," conjectures Freud, "will in part be new and non-comparable" to the subject's own, whereas

> other visual perceptions . . . will coincide in the subject with memories of quite similar visual impressions of his own, of his own body. . . . Thus the complex of the fellow human-being falls apart into two components, of which one makes an impression by its constant structure and stays together as a *thing*, while the other can be *understood* by the activity of memory—that is, can be traced back to information from [the subject's] own body.[56]

Picking up on this idea of a bifurcated fellow human being, split between a visual register we recognize and a "new and non-comparable" component that we judge to be "strange and even hostile on occasion," Lacan then draws a connection between the constant, structurally inert Thing detectable (but not understandable) in the fellow human being, and the implacable death drive.[57] What Lacan draws out is thus the Thing's association with destruction: with externalized sadism and a disruption of the pleasure principle. And that association becomes even stronger when we consider that, from the perspective of the subject, the Thing is "new and non-comparable," a description that calls to mind Adorno's observation that "'the new,' the dialectically produced, actually presents itself in history as the archaic."[58] The appearance of the new, an appearance precipitated, according to psychoanalysis, by a judgment leveled against the Thing in the neighbor, signals transience and so occupies the same register as the archaic—the register, that is, of something so "strange and even hostile" that it announces the passing away of what is given and familiar.

We thus agree with Esposito—what melancholic wouldn't?—that community is not a substantive *res*, and certainly not our *res*.[59] We agree, in other words, that community is impossible, precluded from cohering by the Thing.[60] But if the Thing makes community impossible, that is not because it is nothing, not because it is lacking in a groundless, insubstantial way—not because it fails to assemble, as the Heideggerian overtones in Esposito's use of the term *Thing* would imply—but because it is all too real, in the properly Lacanian sense of being constant and inert, lacking from the place of lack. Esposito assumes that the melancholic is fixated, Hamlet-like—or, rather, pseudo-Hamlet-like—on the *delinquere*, the failure or crime, that cuts across community.[61] But what absorbs the melancholic is not a lacerating fault, exactly, but rather, as Benjamin perceived, a realm of infinite perishing or eternal passing away. The "crime" in this case—the crime that is actually the source of our secret hope—is not that the ghost is dead but that the ghost remains unburied. The Thing, missing from its grave, missing from the place of foundational lack beneath the polis, is always (and therefore never fully) perishing, eternally (and therefore never fully) passing away. The Thing is simply one of the names we give to indestructible transience.

Melancholia, then, as commentators have long perceived, comes down to an absorption in the Thing. But it is not the Thing as a gathering or assembly at the site of groundlessness; nor is it the Thing as a simple fault or lack. It is the Thing made unforgettable and indestructible: unforgettable by having never been "known" in the first place, indestructible by virtue of its having been encrypted, lodged in a state where it is always perishing, never past. It is the Thing as the lack even of lack, even of the groundlessness that allows for assemblages. It is the Thing as the objectivity of history. In this respect, the melancholic has a particular (non)-relationship with the law. It is not the nomos that concerns her, since the nomos, to follow Esposito's logic, is predicated on a lack or fault that draws each subject into a guilt history registered by the *delinquere* aspect of community. For the melancholic, there is no foundational crime anterior to or under the law. There is not even what Esposito refers to as the primal murder of community as such. What the melancholic perceives instead is the delinquent nature of law itself, the scandal that brought nomos into existence and that continues to inhere within it. That scandal is simply this: the violent separation of nomos from physis, either under the guise of a nomos justified by a spurious conception of natural strength (that the strong should rule the weak) or a nomos called upon to subdue, while also claiming for itself, a wild, brutish nature anterior to the law. That violent separation, as the melancholic unconsciously recognizes, is neither right nor just. It therefore must be reversed.

Earlier we imagined the melancholic looking about her at an impoverished world and declaring, "This is not it; this has never been it." Now we need to amend that declaration somewhat, if for no other reason than to distinguish the stance of the melancholic from that of the hysteric. For in fact the melancholic looks about her and declares, "There is nothing but this; the eternally perishing, indestructible Thing is what we have. It is the new cause of a new community, the basis for a thinking of the unreal." The seduction (or perhaps the danger) of mourning has always been that it will endorse the ancient, decisionist logic of *krísis* by putting an end to crisis: by declaring, in essence, that the diseased body is dead, the great wrong righted, the rituals dutifully enacted, the crisis masterfully resolved. Melancholia, by contrast, perpetuates and intensifies crisis. Where mourning installs lack at the center of community, melancholia reorients community around those permanent causes that confound krísis: disease, discontent, dissolution. A preponderance of the black bile, as the ancients well knew, keeps any body, including the body politic, in a state of permanent disequilibrium.

The melancholic is typically regarded as unhappy or despairing; but he only despairs of the nomos, which, existing on the order of a spurious second nature, cannot be redeemed. The melancholic's hope lies elsewhere, in the physionomos. Pitched somewhere between the hypernomic realm of unchanging forms and the anomic realm of visible nature, physionomos names a nomic form of nature—in short, a natural historical nature, a critical nature. Freud was surely correct to note how the melancholic exhibits little interest in maintaining life. But what Freud could not have known, although he clearly intuited as much, is that the life eschewed by the melancholic is the "life" we now identify as the product of the sovereign exception: life as something qualified by sovereign power, animated by sovereign power—in short, biopolitical life.[62] That is a life which the melancholic has no interest in perpetuating. Rather, the "life" that interests the melancholic is the natural historical life realized in the death drive. This is a physionomical life, a life neither qualified by nomos, to which it remains indifferent, nor natural in the sense of being available as the grounding of law. This life, this life that concerns the melancholic, is more akin to the chora theorized in Plato's *Timaeus*: formless and yet capable of taking form; indestructible because subject to constant destruction; unforgettable because encrypted in the unconscious; revolutionary because caught up in incessant transformation; a realm of creaturely delight not subject to the intervention of nomos into physis. Head bent, the melancholic gazes into this realm, his eyes set, not on despair, but on future happiness.

CHAPTER ONE

The *Eros* of *Stasis*

PLATO'S MELANCHOLIC REPUBLIC

"I fail to understand the stasis of the winds: one wave rolls in from this side, another from that, and we in the middle are carried along in company with our black ship, much distressed in the great storm" (Alcaeus, fr 208).[1]

"Plato's Socrates laughed only once, in the face of the death that his companions feared" (Phaedo 84d, 115c).[2]

ACROSS HIS VAST body of writing, Plato employs the word *melancholy* only once, in the *Timaeus*, and then only as a cognate with "bad temper," "forgetfulness," and "stupidity" (87a). To be fair, we can hardly blame Plato for wanting to purge his philosophical vocabulary of a word burdened by its association with disease and disorder. But just because Plato eschews the term melancholy does not mean that his work is therefore free of the melancholic temperament and the dark political vision that attends it. When it comes to melancholia, which by its very nature is furtive, secretive, and interstitial, the trick is knowing where to look; and the place to look in this case is where Plato himself locates what is best: in philosophical *eros* and the philosophical form of life it inspires, a life embodied by Socrates, the wisest man of his age, as the oracle says in the *Apology* (21a). For eros, it turns out, is a concept in conflict with itself—a concept already given over to stasis. Understood as the philosophical desire for that which lacks—for truth and justice—eros is the best. When, on the other hand, eros is understood as shameless, insatiable lust—in the *Republic*, the tyrant steps forth as eros incarnate (573b-c)—the concept is also found to carry the signature of the worst. Paradoxically, then, as Leo Strauss points out, Plato's great work, which otherwise celebrates love as the driving force behind the philosophical life, "almost opens with a curse on eros."[3]

Cursing eros: Is that not precisely what the melancholic does best, at least in the way that Freud understands the distinction between mourning and melancholia? Inattentive readers of Freud's "Mourning and Melancholia" might be too preoccupied with the question of mourning over the loss of an object to notice that melancholia originates from the bond between love and conflict. One of the most important passages in Freud's text can be found in his discussion of the continued conflictual cathexis poured into the object of love. Loss is marked by the permanence of discord, by a life-long quarrelling and sparring with the love object, be it an ideal, a thing, or a person. Unresolved conflict and unceasing ambivalence are the hallmarks of melancholia. In fact, all destructive energies of melancholia, whether they are directed inward or outward—Freud mentions hate, anger, abuse, masochistic self-laceration, and sadistic satisfaction with torment, among others—stem from the conflict of love and the love of conflict. Right before Freud describes how "an object-loss [is] transformed into an ego loss" so that "the conflict between the ego and the loved person" might be perpetu-ated as "a cleavage between the critical activity of the ego and the ego as altered by identification with the ego" and how "the shadow of the object fell upon the ego" so that "the latter could henceforth be judged by a special agency"—descriptions, that is, of the critical partitioning that characterizes melancholia—he confronts us with disturbing scenes of unrest and insur-rection. Deploying powerful images, Freud stages a tumultuous drama of melancholic eros, love, intermingled with *eris*, strife: of "self-reproaches" that are really "reproaches": of "complaints" that "are really 'plaints,' in the old sense of the word"; of "the *pros* and *cons* of the conflict of love [*Liebe-sstreit*] that has led to the loss of love"; of the feeling of having been slighted or "treated with great injustice." As Freud sees it, the rebelliousness of the melancholic is not surprising, for her thinking and attitude "still proceed from a mental constellation of revolt."

More, then, than a simple victim—grief-stricken, crushed, and disappointed—the melancholic remains ensnarled in the perseverance of Liebesstreit, the conflict of love. She is an irreconcilable aggressor, an unrelenting and unforgiving agent of conflict who plagues her object without remorse. Freud's seductive image invoking the shadow of loss that falls upon the ego is too often misconstrued as an instance of smother-ing defeat when in fact it stages a scene of conflict: the subject devours the love-object of strife and thereafter speaks, feels, and acts through this incorporated object as if he (or perhaps it) were a ventriloquist. Freud himself designates the melancholic act as a beastly act of aggression. "The ego wants to incorporate this object into itself," he observes, "and . . . it wants to do so by devouring it [*auf dem Wege des Fressens*]."[4] The Fressen of Liebesstreit, the devouring of the conflict of love. Is there a better motto for the discordant visions of the melancholic?

Certainly there is no better motto for the melancholic procedures—some call it the erotic philosophy—developed by Plato through his mouth-piece, Socrates. Plato may have sought to purge his writings of even the word melancholy. But by repeatedly staging the conflict of love, putting philosophical eros into dialectical conflict with tyrannical eros so as to effect a kind of stasis, he established the template for a politics of melancholia, as we shall now see.

The Tyrant and His Melancholic Eros
(Socrates, Alcibiades, Lacan)

"Penia (Poverty) is a grievous thing, an ungovernable evil, who with her sister Amakhania (Helplessness) lays low a great people" (Alcaeus, fr. 364).[5]

What did the Pre-Socratics do without love? Or, to ask the question another way, how did ancient philosophers go about instilling melancholia in tyrants, kings, and men of power without the example of Socrates's cruel play with the love of Alcibiades in Plato's *Symposium* to guide them? One might of course point to the long tradition, going back to Diogenes's scornful attitude toward Alexander the Great, of scenes that stage the encounter between the sage and the king. In Plutarch's rendition, when Alexander, ruler of Greece and Asia, visits the philosopher in the market square at Corinth, Diogenes, after noticing Alexander and his entourage, only raises himself up far enough to say, contemptuously, "Stand a little out of my sun." To this slight of his sovereign splendor, Alexander admiringly replies, "If I were not Alexander, I would be Diogenes."[6] Alexander, visibly moved, has an inkling of the melancholic wisdom underneath Diogenes's saying—a wisdom neatly summarized in Diogenes Laertius's version of the same episode. This time the exchange begins with the mutual intro-duction of the beggar and the king: "'I am Alexander the great king.' 'I am Diogenes the dog.'" When asked whether death is a bad thing, Diogenes replies with another laconic apothegm: "How can death be evil when in its presence we are not aware of it?"[7] As in similar episodes employing the same motif—Silenus speaking to King Midas, for example, or Solon to Croesus—here the melancholic philosopher confronts the sovereign with the same Thing, the same pure expression of the death drive: "Not to be born is best."

This expression of the death drive knows multiple variations, but the idea itself is always the same, as if the encounter between the philosopher and the king can give birth to only one scene: that of the ruler's humbling confrontation with the death drive. In *Oedipus at Colonus*, the chorus woefully sings: "The Helper comes at last to all alike, when the fate of Hades is suddenly revealed, without marriage-song, or lyre, or dance: Death at the end. Not to be born [*me phunei*] is, beyond all estimation, best; but when a man has seen the light of day, this is next best by far, that with utmost speed he should go back from where he came" (1220–25). The *stasimon* is directed at Theseus, and indeed at all human beings; but the old, destitute Oedipus, the king of shreds and patches, could just as soon impart the same message to his former self, Oedipus, the King of Thebes. Similarly, in the *Histories*, Herodotus famously recounts how Croesus asked Solon which man can be considered the happiest and most prosperous of all. Croesus is of course hoping that Solon will declare Croesus himself to be that man. And so when Solon instead replies with the wisdom of the gods, "that it is better for a human being to be dead than to be alive," Croesus becomes visibly annoyed.[8] Surely, though, the matrix scene that influences all subsequent ones of this type is that of the capture of Silenus, the wise tutor of the god Dionysius, by King Midas after a hunt. Plutarch in *Consolation to Apollonius* quotes a passage from Aristotle's lost dialogue *Eudemus*, or *On the Soul*:

> When Midas had used every possible means and at last forced Silenus to speak, he said, when thus constrained, "Ephemeral seed of laborious genius and harsh fortune, why do you force me to say what it would be better for you not to know? Ignorance of the woes one is heir to is what makes life least painful. . . . [T]he best thing for all men and all women is not to come into being, but the next after this and the first that men can attain is to die as soon as possible after coming into being."[9]

The admixture of empathy and contempt found in Silenus's dark wisdom expresses itself with even greater ferocity in Nietzsche's rendering of the tale in *The Birth of Tragedy*, where Silenus "at last . . . gave a shrill laugh."[10] For Nietzsche, this encounter between the sagacious satyr and King Midas manifests the deepest insight into Greek tragic knowledge, a knowledge that, in Nietzsche's telling, the incorrigibly optimistic Socrates simply could not avow. Socrates remains for Nietzsche the slayer of tragedy, despite the fact that Alcibiades himself, in the *Symposium*, compares

Socrates with those statuettes of Silenus which, on being opened, revealed the overwhelming *agalma*, the much beloved, much treasured images of the gods (215f). According to Aristotle, this comparison shows that Silenus's melancholic revelation holds not merely shock value but also, when encountered in the person of Socrates, a profound philosophical point.

Nevertheless, Nietzsche is right: Socrates does not induce melancholia into rich, beautiful, and powerful young Athenians like Alcibiades in the same manner as does Silenus, Solon, or the chorus of *Oedipus at Colonus*. Nor does Socrates confront the king in the manner of Diogenes, the cynic. The role of the philosopher in relation to the king is, for Socrates, not that of the contemptuous "anti-king king," as Foucault calls the cynic: "the true king and other king" who will outlast, as a beggar king of destitution, the fragile royalty of Alexander.[11] Unlike Diogenes, Socrates shows little interest in reversing and scandalizing the sovereign position or in transforming the master signifier so as to posit a real and hidden sovereign of derision, dirt, and combat. That would still be the kind of sovereignty that Foucault describes, after Bataille, as a powerless sovereignty, a "nonpositive affirmation."[12] Socrates in the *Symposium* proceeds differently, more obliquely, one could say, and never by way of direct confrontation. Although Plato knows Silenus's wisdom well (Lachesis in the "Myth of Er" expresses it clearly as a warning to the living [617d]), philosophical eros, the unconditional love of lack, is not an unrecognized countersovereign. Instead, the truly melancholic philosopher embraces the tyrant tightly, smotheringly, hugging him until death would feel like a relief. The melancholic immerses the tyrant in too much loss and engages him in desirous lack. True eros attaches itself at the most vulnerable spot of tyrannical eros—at the point of bottomless greed (*pleonaxia*), the insatiable desire for more—and then redirects its boisterous energies toward melancholic means and ends: toward examination, dissolution, and the loving embrace of lack. Within despotic eros, there suddenly arises another eros—a melancholic eros—able to reconfigure the entire symbolic universe of the sovereign and master. The tyrant exits the stage to enter the world of melancholic eros, there to encounter, in agalma, the death drive. Diogenes was right: we are not aware of the presence of death. But we are particularly oblivious when we deem ourselves most alive—that is, when we are in love.

And that's not the worst of it (or the best of it, depending on one's philosophical position). For to be "struck and bitten by philosophy," as by a snakebite, in "the most sensitive part," is a communizing event, as

Alcibiades says in the *Symposium* (218b). The snakebite of philosophical eros is what initiates us into an alternative community of inhumans,
of beasts or satyrs who are capable, like Silenus, of feeling shame and
embracing death. Affirmative melancholia, the erotic embrace of lack, is
in this sense the most effective antidote against tyrannical injustice not
because it is powerless but because it creates a tyrannical counterdesire, a
more enduring and unconditional form of madness. Contrary to the mysterious "tyrant-makers" mentioned in Book 9 of Plato's *Republic*—those
"clever enchanters" who plant a destructive and "powerful erotic love,
like a great winged drone" in young men—philosophical eros deflates
this "enormous drone" and transforms its sweet treasures into worthless
matter (572e–573a). Such is the profaning power of love.

But what does Socrates actually say about love that the act of saying
alone can bring a tyrant like Alcibiades to his knees? He calls it a kind of
wisdom; for Plato, eros is raised to the dignity of the best philosophical
Thing. This peculiar mode of human wisdom points to one of Socrates's
most important statements about knowledge, the one expressed in *Symposium* 177e: "The only thing I say I know are erotic things [*ta erotica*, translation altered]." Socrates claims to have a knowledge about erotic things
that at once adheres to and exceeds human wisdom. Eros, as we hear from
Diotima in the *Symposium*, is a third thing, "something in between" con-
traries, "in between mortal and immortal" like "everything spiritual, you
see, is in between god and mortal" (202b-e). In this sense, wisdom about
erotic things would be a kind of human-inhuman protoknowledge that
draws on, and breaks with, both mortal and divine wisdom. Erotic wisdom
shuttles "back and forth between the two," like the unyielding, shoeless
vagabond and schemer Eros in Diotima's birth myth of the *daimon*,
recounted in *Symposium* (203c-d, 202a). Eros inhabits an unsettled space
from which human and divine wisdom can be examined and rendered
lacking; his mother, *Penia*, who had nothing to offer but her own lack
of resources, is first and foremost a capacity for encountering things that
are lacking and for producing such encounters with lack (203c). As David
Roochnik writes with respect to Diotima's teaching of eros in the *Symposium*: "Eros is a capacity to enter into relationships with objects. To love is
to love something (199d). Furthermore, what is loved is something lacked
(200b)." The erotic philosopher himself embodies this lack and therefore
has a peculiar relation to things that are lacking. He dwells in an area
imbued with *daimonic* truths that, positioned midway between wisdom
and ignorance, have the capacity, precisely by being incomplete, to extract
the true erotic nature of human beings and things. Knowledge of erotic

things means to be cognizant of being possessed by ignorance and lack; it is to be seized by "an awareness of the incompleteness of all activities."[13] Knowledge of eros can thus never become a teachable *techne*. It can only ever take the form of an unconditional, practical commitment to voiding the mastery of knowledge and to derailing all attempts at covering up the constitutive hiatus between knowledge and truth.

This commitment to voiding and derailing is what Lacan seeks to capture when he declares, in his own reading of love in the *Symposium*, that the erotic philosopher "gives what he does not have" and "loves with this lack."[14] The philosopher of erotic things confronts his interlocutors with judgments and declarative opinions without then providing a discourse to explain them. The erotic discourse consists of speaking truths without knowing or of not knowing what one thought one knew, as Agathon confesses to Socrates: "'It turns out, Socrates, I didn't know what I was talking about in that speech'" (201c). Hence, the erotic philosopher, akin to Socrates in the *Apology*, wishes to continue infinitely with his just discourse despite the discordant truths of love that effectively render his discourse inconsistent and the truth of his logos unknowable.

For the philosophical discourse in the *Symposium* does not simply speak about love; rather, as Lacan repeatedly insists, that discourse lets love speak and, in speaking, perform the cacophonies of love. The daimon eros threatens to disown its speakers in the same way the commands of the *daimonion* or the dreams and oracles disown Socrates's voice in the *Apology*. Like the speech of the poet who hides behind his muses, the discourse of the erotic philosopher gets irredeemably split into conscious and unconscious truths. When Socrates's Eros enters the dramatic *Darstellung* carried out in the stages of the dialogue, it does so as a dissolving dual power: the power of conscious speech, coupled with the power of transfiguration. During the course of the six speeches that make up the *Symposium*, figures undergo transformation, switch positions, and constantly fall victim to interruptions (as in Aristophanes's hiccup) before the whole banquet ends in turmoil with the intrusion of the drunken Alcibiades. For Lacan, it is the latter's rambling, passionate seventh speech—a speech that no longer talks about love but is the speech of love itself—that most fully reveals the degree to which the real of love prompts an affective, scenographic, combinatory play among the figures of the dialogue. The real of love is a dialogic bonding agent. Little wonder, then, that when Socrates finally breaks with the transference love performed by the philosopher and his pupil, the other characters are left feeling empty (*kenosis*), their only sure knowledge being the discovery of a booming hollow in the center of knowledge.[15] To be sure, Lacan took an

abiding interest in Plato, finding in the latter's thought a powerful affirmation of his own, particularly concerning the expropriating power of speech.
Thus, for Lacan, the discourse of the analyst (and the hysteric) speaks
through Socrates, qua erotic philosopher, while the discourse of the master
(and the university) speaks through Plato's episteme. Unlike the stranger
in the *Statesman*, who hopes that we might be able to transform the truths
of dreaming opinion into waking knowledge—the traditional Platonic procedure of converting truths into knowledge—Lacan adheres to the philosophical aspiration of the *Symposium*: to transform knowledge into truths
of love (as a knowledge about erotic things) (278e).[16] When that aspiration
is realized, the figure of Socrates, the analyst, rebels against his author, disowning Plato and his writing as the site of mastery and knowable truths.[17]
Plato himself, by means of his philosophical dramas and their staging of
Socrates as the quintessential erotic philosopher, provides the organon for
a systematic self-expropriation of his thought.

So much for the effects of love upon the philosopher (and his author).
What are the effects of melancholic eros on the lover (*erastes*), on the one
who falls madly in love? What does Alcibiades speak, in his drunken state,
about Socrates? Is the tyrant becoming melancholic? Here it would help
to backtrack a bit, if only to clarify the scandal that Plato stages for his
readers. Alcibiades, the tyrant and hot young thing (*eromenos*) of Athens,
charming, gorgeous, and seductive, has had the unfortunate good luck to
fall in love with Socrates (eromenos), considered by many the most unat-
tractive man alive.[18] As the quintessential tyrannical man of antiquity,
Alcibiades confesses that Socrates, the satyr and monster, is an expert at
dissolving one's most treasured bonds. Socrates, he laments, "makes it
seem that my life isn't worth living" and "that my political career is a waste
of time" (216a). The philosopher injects a counteracting poison—a kind of
philosophical *pharmakon*—into the life of "young and eager souls [whose
grip] is much more vicious than a viper's and makes them do the most
amazing things" (218a). Such "young and eager souls" "have all shared in
the madness, the Bacchic frenzy of philosophy" and are therefore imbued
with the power to envision other, more intensive and far-reaching communities, ones full of strange creatures—demons, satyrs, animals, gods—and
bizarre ideas (218b). The community of inhumans is immunized with a
poison that instills more zeal, more fidelity to the cause of eros, than any
human will or tyrannical desire could ever realize.

According to Alcibiades, a whole bestiary, amounting to an extensive disfiguration of Plato's conceptual persona, surrounds the figure of
Socrates, who gets compared to a viper, a monster, even the deadly Typhon

from Hesiod's *Theogony*. By drawing out the most bizarre, inhuman features of Socrates, Alcibiades moves him closer to the inanimate sphere, to the realm of things (221d). Indeed, according to Alcibiades, Socrates is himself a misshapen thing, albeit one capable of completely unhinging the minds of his followers and distorting their habitual vision of life. Yet in charging Socrates with such monstrous powers, even with the power of the "thing itself," Alcibiades is merely echoing the object of his love (218e). For Socrates himself continually drains the image of the sage who possesses the gift (agalma) "truly worthy of a god" (222a). Try as his young followers might to place him in the role of the precious, omniscient thing to which they might then transfer all their (tyrannical) love, Socrates rebuffs their efforts. "You could be wrong and I may be of no use to you," Socrates warns Alcibiades (219a). If Socrates is the "thing itself," it is a thing that is good for nothing, a thing in its most depleted form, "always making the same tired old points in the same tired old words," like a broken record (221e). Alcibiades knows full well that Socrates's whole persona, his ideas and speeches, are at some level completely ridiculous, egregious, even devoid of any substance, "just like those hollow statues of Silenus" (221d).

Even according to the one who is most in love with him, then, Socrates, the philosophical hero who is supposed to replace the great Trojan hero Achilles and the political idol Pericles, is in some sense a thoroughly profaned void, a melancholic. In Hamlet's words, he is "a thing of nothing." But by interrupting transference love and presenting itself as excessively desirous, this thing is nonetheless able to extract philosophical eros from tyrannical greed. Socrates leaves the members of the philosophical community deeply dissatisfied, out of place and hollow, but, paradoxically, more in love. Being in love, philosophically, makes one "more miserable" and "deeply ashamed," as Alcibiades adds (216c). But it also makes one more resourceful in inhuman affairs and more immune to the sting of another form of love that "has long been called a tyrant" (*Republic* 573b).

Melancholic Stasis and Eros in Plato's Republic

When Socrates introduces the question of stasis at the end of Book I of the *Republic*, the line of argument seems to be straightforward: civil war (stasis) is the greatest calamity that can befall a city because it dissolves the common and divides the people into factions, rendering them incapable of collective action (351c–352c). As the Athenian stranger says in the *Laws*, civil war is "the harshest of all wars," the war that most captures the disastrous essence of war as such (629d). There is simply no "greater evil" than a city torn by division, and for this reason alone stasis must be understood as the cause and epitome of injustice (462a). Stasis generates an atmosphere of enmity and strife that "in every way" is the opposite of justice (352a); vice versa, injustice "causes civil war, hatred, and fighting among themselves, while justice brings friendship and a sense of common purpose" (351d). Moreover, since stasis is a civil war, that is, a fighting of a unit against itself, Socrates can then draw an analogy with the individual as an enemy of himself. This shifting from politics to the individual and back again is the origin of the *Republic*'s city-soul analogy, which, not surprisingly, begins with a reflection on stasis as the self-destruction of city and man alike. Stasis is the juncture between man and the city, the knot that braids together political practice and Plato's novel concern with the care for the soul. When stasis and injustice arise within a single individual, Socrates continues, man cannot accomplish anything, like the city that is torn by faction, "because he is in a state of civil war and not of one mind" (352a). Stasis makes him not only his own enemy, but also the enemy of just people in general and even of the gods (352b).

This catastrophic diagnosis of enmity and strife has been the mantra of political philosophy ever since. Volker Gerhardt, for example, has summarized Plato's legacy for politics as follows:

> Man, as we know from the *Laws*, is determined by internal opposites. But whoever does not become master of the war in his inside, is not capable of politics. Hence, the Athenian stranger demonstrates to the Cretan Kleinias . . . that war cannot be the goal of politics. Politics needs external unity to accomplish its goals. And this unity becomes the measure for the internal unity of every single man.[19]

Is a corresponding internal and external unity truly the precondition for political action? How do we determine this "becoming master" of the war inside man, this unity that must be projected both inward and outward? Does it mean, for example, that conflict is acknowledged, but somehow overcome or at least reduced to a minimum, as in postpolitical forms of conflict resolution? Being infinitely fearful of the convulsions of a worldwide civil war, contemporary politics has perfected the art of managerial supervision, of the organization and privatization of conflict.[20] Most political theorists would subscribe to the idea that the well-governed polity today must be achieved through democratic procedures of power-sharing, parliamentarian debate, and processes of mutual recognition; through community building, the fair distribution of resources, and the development of capabilities. If conflicts cannot be resolved preemptively in this fashion, they are relegated to the adversarial process of adjudication and arbitration and the mechanisms of market competition.

Nicole Loraux sees a more violent dynamic at work, one resting on the persistent latency of stasis. According to her, politics *is* division, and the primordial discord that underlies the city has been repressed, forgotten, and violently turned into a benevolent power, both in the poetic tradition and in political philosophy.[21] But while Loraux's contention, shared by most political theorists, that the origin of political philosophy, Plato's dialogues, takes a leading role in the pacification and suppression of unforgettable discord might be true for Platonism, it is emphatically not true for Plato's philosophical dramas. It is certainly accurate to say that Plato's *Laws* begins, more boldly than the *Republic*, with a damning assessment of stasis within man, household, and city as the greatest calamity of politics: to wit, that "being defeated by oneself is the most shameful and at the same time the worst of all defeats" (626e). At the same time, however, both *Laws* and the *Republic* thrive on the worst, at times inconspicuously, at times openly, and articulate welcome forms of stasis in all its expressive, theatrical, and political declensions. In that way, Plato pays ambivalent homage to his predecessors, whose wary views on conflict he at once heeds and aims to surmount. The Athenian stranger, for instance, makes the following comment in passing: "Let's set aside whether the worse can ever somehow be superior to the better (that would require a longer discussion)" (627b). To have opened that longer, and long deferred, discussion is the merit of Loraux's *The Divided City*; but the discussion itself must now be extended to involve Plato and the tradition of philosophy and political theory his work initiates.

Where to begin? Plato's melancholic assault on the goodness and happiness of ordinary political existence in the *Republic* opens on a scene of daily Athenian life. Socrates and Glaucon go down from Athens to the Piraeus to watch the celebrations of Bendis, featuring horseback races and torch relays, and enjoy the "all-night festival that will be well worth seeing" (328a). The year is probably 421, during the Peace of Nicias. By the time of the *Republic*'s composition, about fifty years later, most of the principal characters will be dead, and few of them peacefully. J. Peter Euben notes that three (Polemarchus, Niceratus, and Socrates) will have been executed on political charges, with the first two murdered for their fortunes by an oligarchic faction led by members of Plato's own family. We watch these peaceful interactions, then, with apprehension and a sense of impending violence—a violence nourished by the desires of the spirited (*thumos*) and appetitive (*epithumia*) parts of the soul. Socrates's dialogic construction of a just polis is immediately imperiled by the very passions and forces that are necessary for the city's vitality and strength. *Pleonaxia* ("greed," "covetousness," "insatiable desire"), the root cause of stasis in the *Republic*, haunts the inaugural book of political theory from the beginning. As Euben remarks, "The men who are friends in the *Republic* will soon be killing one another for power and property outside it. Under such circumstances the community of philosophical dialogue constituted and led by Socrates is hardly a promising paradigm for political life."[22] This ominous sour note will hereafter accompany Plato's great political design and also signal its collapse. The wisdom gained from the *Republic* is melancholic; it instills a trepidation and sense of regret in its readers that not only plagues them but that also recounts the constellation of desire and impasse that led to the catastrophe in the first place.

But we were enjoying a festival. Between the spectacle and the torch race, these Athenian democrats would seem to have little time for philosophical dialogue. And yet their nocturnal conversation about justice and politics will last all night, at least for those few who have the desire to sustain it. Most of the other characters, however, are already described in the *Republic*'s opening scene as quintessential democratic men, men who give themselves over to the whims of appetite. This type of man, the *homo democraticus*, is for Socrates the incorrigible adolescent, enslaved to circulation and enthralled by ever-changing anarchic urges bellicose, given to the pursuit of petty pleasures, fully engrossed in the idolatry of youth as well as in the fear of death. For fear of seeming old, tiresome, and overbearing, the democratic man abases himself before everything youthful. Socrates proceeds with his analysis: "He often engages in politics, leaping up from his seat and saying and doing whatever comes to his mind. . . . There's neither order nor necessity in his life, but he calls it pleasant, free, and blessedly happy, and he follows it as long as he lives" (561d). The community of democrats, avers Socrates, is on the road to perdition and civil war—to stasis. This form of democracy, as Badiou argues in his dramatized translation of Plato's *Republic*, is formless, rife with impending doom and "the despotism of the death wish." The democratic life is acephalic and lacks the divisions of *eide*; it is deprived of ideas and therefore of the world.[23] As Socrates will later put it, in Book 8 of the *Republic*, the delights of democracy will unerringly end with the "nightmare of tyranny."[24]

First, though, the *Republic* will make room for the advent of a salutary stasis (one tied, we argue, to melancholia) in the struggle between Socrates and his adversary in Book 1 of the *Republic*, the would-be tyrant Thrasymachus. After alluding, in 350b, to what Thucydides in chapter 3 of *The*

Peloponnesian War (particularly 3.82) had already ascertained to be the symptoms of civil war—that men strive to outdo each other simply for the sake of winning; that everyone engages in acts of senseless audacity regardless of justice—Socrates tightens the screws on Thrasymachus.[25] Socrates concludes his argument that only the unjust person knows no limits and will scheme to get the better of the just and the unjust person alike with an indirect accusation against Thrasymachus: advocating for injustice also means fostering ignorance and badness. Socrates's act of shaming works wonders. "Thrasymachus agreed to all this, not easily as I'm telling it, but reluctantly, with toil, trouble . . . that was a wonder to behold. Then I saw something I'd never seen before—Thrasymachus blushing" (350d).

Socrates, it seems, has awakened Thrasymachus's sense of shame. Thrasymachus's bold-spiritedness and passion (thumos), by which Glaucon is so impressed, comes in touch with the honorable form of shame (*aidos*), thereby disclosing a divided self that has lost its bearings in the new world of justice that will now be created. Thrasymachus's unequivocal own, now thrown into disarray, is given over to an impersonal own—proof that just words prompt real justice effects, that *logos*, word, can be turned into an *ergon*, a practice. Socrates's speech has become a deed that can split subjects into two and estrange them from themselves. An internal struggle ensues within Thrasymachus's old self that gradually liquefies his dearly held beliefs: that justice is the advantage of the stronger, that it promotes one's self-interest and is about the satisfaction of greed (*pleonexia*), which Socrates singles out as a chief cause of stasis. Speech has rendered such ideas shameful; they are now felt as shame. All that remains is for Socrates to ensure that Thrasymachus's blushing is only the beginning of his resistance against Socratic justice and that a just form of struggle, once initiated, will persist.

In this way the philosophical drama, by performing an interruption of tyrannical reason that brings out the fissures in Thrasymachus's entire symbolic universe, stages what drives Socrates the most: namely, to show that justice and wisdom are stronger than injustice and ignorance (351a). Once again, Socrates alludes to Thucydides's diagnosis of stasis in post-Periclean Athens, this time by bringing up the example of the unjust enslavement of other cities, as described in the Melian Dialogue (351b). Suddenly, Thrasymachus becomes capable of engaging in a form of doublespeak—holding up both claims to justice and rubbing Socrates's argument ("If what you said") against his "own" ("but if things are as I stated")—which is already involved in a process of self-dissolution (351b-c). But while Socrates praises the internalization of his argumentation as an act of genuine thinking,

Thrasymachus interprets it as an act of transference, as nothing but an attempt to please his interlocutor. Thrasymachus's transferential inclination does not bother Socrates. On the contrary, he fosters it, knowing well that wanting to please him "some more" only facilitates the excavation of long buried sentiments (351c). For it seems clear that, like Polus in the dialogue *Gorgias*, who "himself unwittingly confirms that, deep down, he has harbored these beliefs all along," Thrasymachus has wished to express different, more provocative ideas about justice all along, ideas that destroy the idiotic justice of the stronger.[26]

How do we know this? Because the fact that Thrasymachus is willing to subject his ideas about justice to the destructive work of the Socratic elenchus betrays a desire for a just struggle within the soul (336b–338b). From the earliest days of Hippocrates, the question of stasis had been part of a nosological discourse. Thus Polus in the *Gorgias* can admit, once his sense of shame has been aroused in the course of the dialogue, that committing acts of injustice generates sickness of soul (477b-c). Ever mindful of that tradition, Platonic drama counteracts the general malady of stasis in soul and city with its development of struggle and transference love in the process of adversarial speaking. In the case of Thrasymachus, this process works beautifully: where once he had believed that wisdom and justice impede action and only make one suffer from the exercise of unjust power, Thrasymachus now begins to embrace the kind of suffering that derives its transformative power from the restlessness of justice. Homing in on *dikaiosune*, "justice," a word that emphasizes, more than dike or *dikaios* (terms that are bound to established ethical norms and political power), virtuous behavior both in the individual and in collective life, Socrates is able to dislodge the advocate of self-interest from the ideology of the self and thereby from existing practices of justice.[27] Against his will but in keeping with his desire, Thrasymachus has become engaged in a new form of struggle, one where it becomes clear that, the more he pursues customary dike and his own, the more he is restored to his original estrangement, while the more he fulfills his desires, the more he is drained of his idea that justice is the justice of the stronger. Socrates's dramatic form of justice thus constitutively denaturalizes Thrasymachus's sense of justice. He once held that dikaiosune is nothing but an unnatural restraint on desire; now it dawns on him that an impersonalizing form of justice has opened up a completely novel type of infinite desire, a desire for restless dike. During the exchange, a kind of civil war within Thrasymachus's self has broken out, a stasis that combats the other, pernicious civil war that arises from what Socrates in Book 4 calls *polypragmosyne* (the meddlesomeness of the curious busybody who dabbles in multifarious activities), *allotriopragmosyne* (interference, the meddling in another's affairs), and *metabole* (the change of one's occupation) (434b-c; 444b). Justice (dikaiosune), understood as "doing one's own," is a defense arrayed against this meddlesomeness, this propensity for change and inequality that Socrates designates as the root causes of stasis. In the end, Thrasymachus abandons the struggles of tyrannical meddlesomeness and enmity to assume a new form of struggle, that of philosophical eros.

If it seems that we have tarried awhile in the first book of the *Republic*, it is only to emphasize how much the problem of strife animates the play of questions and answers that together add up to the origin of political philosophy. If stasis is indeed, as Roberto Esposito has emphasized, *the* great problem in response to which political philosophy comes into being, then the *Republic* offers us a lesson about the way political philosophy originally attempts to resolve the puzzle of civil war.[28] The *Republic* appears to reveal that political philosophy cannot think through the problem of stasis in a purely philosophical manner—in a manner where the order of the intelligible will have given shape and form to the order of the sensible—rather than the other way around. Instead, the disaster of stasis can only be disclosed in a melancholic manner, as both an indication and failure of the ambitions of the political.

Crucially, though, that failure fails and, in doing so, yields a kind of success in the course of working through stasis. For stasis is not only the dangerous contagion in response to which political history and political philosophy come into being; it is also, as John R. Wallach has stressed, the unbearable condition that necessitates the discourse on justice pursued in the *Republic*.[29] It is important to remember that another form of enmity, the opposition between friend and enemy, structures the first attempts at defining political justice in the *Republic*, an idea that Socrates tries to deflect, but whose aggressive, bellicose content continues to reverberate throughout the dialogue (332d). After all, this enmity has far-reaching consequences. Not only does it lead to an initial act of injustice that makes the guardian class and the practice of warfare necessary; it also acts as the reason for abandoning the prepolitical system of needs in the healthy city (which Glaucon terms the "city for pigs" [372d]) in order to constitute the first self-governing city, the city of luxury (373d-e).[30] Only with the arrival of the inflamed, luxurious city—the polis of insatiable desires and strife—has justice even become an issue. Moreover, the discussion of enmity and civil war marks the beginning of Plato's city-soul analogy, the theory of the tripartite soul, and the degeneration of the just city, all of which stand as crucial passages in the *Republic's* staging of the antithetical meaning and transformative content of the term stasis (352a; 440b; 545d-e).

As Loraux has shown, stasis lies at the origin of politics and is constitutive of its destiny. The intimate relation between stasis and politics can be expressed with full ambiguity in the following way: the end of stasis is the end of politics. As if Plato were aware of this perplexing conundrum, the *Republic* interweaves the origin, purpose, and performance of politics together with the process of thinking through stasis as an idea—a disturbing and potentially disastrous one, but an idea nevertheless. Rather than being a catastrophic occurrence that at any time can befall a city, and rather than designating a kind of political "institution" that means "revolution in the city," Socrates raises stasis to the level of pure thought, to the dignity of an eidos that breaks with the confinements of history and reality.[31] It is true, as Loraux holds, that Plato "continually returns to the problem of stasis"; but rather than provide a showcase for all "the modalities in which conflict is repressed," Plato continually invites stasis into the midst of his dialectical performances. He plays, stages, and often even escalates the unrest of strife in the soul and the city to such a degree that his philosophical drama becomes the very form of rebellious discontent and restlessness for which stasis has always been loathed.

To be sure, Plato's intellectual dramas treat political stasis with great apprehension, working overtime to transfer its calamitous power into a distinctly philosophical terminology and dynamic. They do so, however, not, as Loraux suspects, to fantasize a free play of stasis in the soul in order to escape from the political reality of division in the city.[32] Rather, when Plato submits the political phenomena of his time (civil war, faction, the enslavement of people and cities) to an eidetic analysis, he does so to extract the immanent laws of transition among political regimes and to distill the constellations of strife from which such phenomena emerge.[33] Once again elevating the idea of stasis to the level of pure thought, Plato has Socrates identify "civil war (stasis) breaking out within the ruling group itself" as the "simple principle" and "cause of change in any constitution" (545c). The stasis in the constitutive class of the best regime (aristocracy) is the primal sin behind the disintegration of the beautiful city (*Callipolis*) and the origin of the emergence of timocracy. All successive stages of transformation in the soul and the city, often precipitously and pejoratively called a "decline," stem from this internal discord among the rulers.[34] Stasis dissolves the "one mind" of the city, the seemingly unchanging "own" which has been its governing principle and its source of stability and happiness (545d). Socrates discerns a natural tendency toward self-destruction in Callipolis and in the four other regimes—or, to express the matter more properly, a propensity of the city's soul, embodied by the ruling class, to destroy itself. Not having a word for melancholia, however, Socrates can only express this suicidal drive underpinning all forms of decline and dissolution in "tragic tones" (545e).

Yet Socrates's philosophy, too, must be expressed in tragic tones; for Socrates is no less melancholic, no less prone to destruction, than the ruling class. If, for example, the just city has already been accomplished, at least officially—both in word and in deed—in Books 4 and 5 of the *Republic*, why does Socrates continue his detours, footnotes, and suggestions for the "one change" "that would enable our city to reach our sort of constitution" (444e–445b; 471c–473a)? Is this proposal for "one change" not the very obstacle to the creation of the just city? Does not the philosopher, by constantly inserting more complexity into the master signifier, permanently sabotage himself, his happiness, and his performance of justice in the manner of a melancholic? Socrates is aware of this problem and therefore tries to limit change to the "fewest in number and the least extensive" (473b). Yet there is no getting around the fact that both the shocking proposal to make philosophers rule as kings, which is drowned in a "wave of laughter," derision, and contempt—a curious symptom of anxiety—and the analysis of discord within the ruling class found in Book 8 are equally willful constructions of stasis within the kingly thing (473c).

It could be, of course, that Socrates undertakes a kind of philosophical experiment, one that tethers the governing principle to the source of perdition, a move that seems altogether unnecessary, even dangerously frivolous, so as to track every aftershock of discord and every permutation of unrest. More likely, though, is that Socrates pursues the tremors of stasis in order to turn the one thing that most bedevils politics and philosophy into their constituent force. We may call this force, after Agamben, "destituent," for it grinds down the "own" (*okeion*) of soul and city and prompts the creation of a continuously self-dissolving "stasis-own" which is the kernel for the communizing "bond of division" among citizens.[35] What Plato in *Letter VII* calls the "Thing itself" is the medium and effect of this bond and the engine for the constitution of a destituent *koinois nomos* (common law). In this way, Plato's philosophical drama incorporates the destructive energies unleashed in strife to make his quest for concord fail. But the demonstration and performance of such failure fails, that is, it accomplishes something else, albeit only indirectly, by way of gesture and indication. The power of the enemy that plagues both philosophy and politics, namely enmity, can now be used to combat stasis. The traces of the death drive, detectable everywhere in strife, are deployed to tease out the internal unrest and fragility within the master signifier. The proliferation of faction prompts a movement of self-reversal in a ruling element that, unbeknownst to itself, has seized philosophy's aspirations for mastery and wisdom.

A movement of self-reversal headed where, we might ask. Where does the road to perdition end? The answer is that it ends in a place of nonending, of a movement that never comes to rest. "Change" (*metaballei*, 545d), "movement" (*kinethetai*, 545d, 546a), "decay" (*phthora*), "dissolution" (*luthesetai, lusis*, 546a), "civil war" (stasis, 545d, 547a, 547b): with the proliferation of these terms, Socrates draws his interlocutors back and, as it were, down, immersing them, incrementally and at the level of speech, in the experience of an originary, melancholic stasis: an *Ur-stasis*. It is to this primordial form of stasis, Socrates suggests somewhat reluctantly, that Homer's prayer to the Muses at the beginning of the *Iliad* bears witness: "Do you want us to be like Homer and pray to the Muses to tell us 'how civil war first (*proton stasis*) broke out'?" But where Homer speaks of a "fire" that first erupts among the Greeks, Socrates seeks to identify the precise moment, the exact site, of a first outbreak of stasis, which always occurs from the inside against the inside, like an autoimmune disease.[36] To that end, he extracts from the vast field of discord the "proton stasis," a first space and time (proton means "first" both temporally and spatially) from which all subsequent modes of conflict derive and by which they can be explained. Socrates strives to isolate the primordial idea, the spatiotemporal stasis-ness, of stasis. In other words, Socrates distills the *first principles* that make movement and change in politics thinkable and possible. And yet to purify such a universal form, the movement of stasis must be momentarily arrested so that the philosopher can proclaim, again with Homer's *Iliad*: "[c]ivil war, we declare, is always and everywhere 'of this lineage'" (547a).

Socrates, then, wishes to lay claim to stasis. But to do so, he must first perform stasis, the complex, syncopated rhythm of his diction indiscriminately mixing repetitions, natural historical laws of perdition, and increasingly complex arithmetic-geometric calculations with forms of melancholic presentation. There is no other way: Plato's philosophical drama must, at this juncture, draw on those "tragic tones" of the poetic Muses to provide the cause and master genealogy of all strife and self-destruction. Philosophical discourse must submit itself temporarily to the contagious dynamic of stasis, whose laws Homer, the political expert and poetic lawgiver, has revealed.[37] Assuming the voice of Homer's poetry, philosophical speech presents the bewildering Janus-face of philosophical poetry ("Do you want us to be like Homer?") (546a). When the question of Ur-stasis emerges, philosophy morphs into philosophical poetry to mimic the formless "form" of stasis. Homer's mixed, meddlesome, and stasis-inducing mimesis—the same Homer whom Socrates later declares to be the "leader" and principal teacher of "all these fine tragedians"—turns here into the paradigm, both in content and in form, for the philosophical drama of stasis (378b–380a, 392a, 392d–393c; 595b, also 607a). When it comes to explaining and performing proton stasis, there is simply no better source than the master of poetic mimesis. More to the point, only when the mixed mimesis of Homeric poetry, the shifting back and forth between the speeches of the author and his characters, has fully confused the reader can the latter be released from the pressures of discerning who is the mouthpiece for whom. Polyphony and the cacophony of speeches abound; we no longer know whether Socrates, Plato, Homer, his Muses, or the tragedians narrate the reasons for the downfall of the rigid, arithmetic order of Callipolis. As soon as we follow the melancholic maxim that "everything that comes into being must decay," all forms and ideas (eide) that sustain the narrative order also fall into ruin (546a). Book 8 enacts, in tones pitched somewhere between grief (chalepon in 546a means "hard to bear," "painful," "grievous") and delight, the collapse of the whole symbolic universe that the Republic has worked so hard to create. In the end, philosophical play combats political stasis with the melancholic-philosophical performance of stasis, which now takes the form of a devotion to the figure of the worst. Stasis-politics, the politics of what Glaucon in Book 8 of the Republic calls a "still finer city and man," surmounts Callipolis by playfully performing change and conflict (543c, also 592a-b).

Accordingly, it is Homer's divine Muses who enact and observe the spectacle of stasis in Book 8 of the Republic to "indicate" the laws of the best and truest play (Laws 804b). Contrary to the theatocracy of the day, which supposed that serious things (the Athenian stranger uses the example of "war") were for the sake of playful things (peace), this true play instead turns to and thinks through playful things—singing, dancing, enchanting, educating (Laws 803e)—for the sake of "the most serious thing" (803d). Plato's serious play in Laws and the "playing and jesting with us as if we were children" in Book 8 of the Republic both have a redemptive power (545e). For the degeneration of cities and souls is recounted, one could almost say "replayed," as a "truest tragedy" that indicates, obliquely, the best of life through the presentation of the worst. Serious play functions as a dialectical process of purification in the course of dialogical exchange; this play is coterminous with the dialectical process of division (which is also a complication) whereby every important term is temporarily isolated in order to encounter its philosophical counterpart, its truer kin. As the poverty (*penia*), madness, and dispossessing strategies of philosophical eros reorient the possessiveness and manias of tyrannical eros, and the self-dissolving tendencies of philosophical logos combat the self-satisfied binary logic of sophistic discourse, so serious play exploits the fact that terms and practices are cleaved internally (like the antithetical meaning of stasis, but also so the terms and practices "play," "philosophy," and "theater").

When the genealogy and principles of Ur-stasis must be performed, then, the Muses of the philosophical theater and the Muses of poetry must be brought into agreement with each other. "And we'll declare that what the Muses say is right. It must be, since they're the Muses": Socrates's and Glaucon's slight tone of irony insists that philosophy and poetry must maintain at least a minimal distance, but both discussants cannot mask that only the shift to the tragic-comic perspective of the divine Muses can adequately perform the effects of time, motion, and stasis (547a-c). Only poetic mimesis can express in content and form "the way this transformation begins" and the origin of "striving and struggling with one another" (547b-c). The "true Muse, that of discussion and philosophy," shakes hands with the Homeric Muses, a handshake that endures, with many reservations, until Book 10 of the *Republic* (540b), for the people must ultimately be persuaded by serious play, the charms of poetry and philosophy, and not by "force" (548c). Ur-stasis, by putting the whole world at play, allows us to comprehend the entire process of decline as at once a political, a tragic-comic, and a cosmic event.

Beyond its mixed tonality, however, what makes the *Republic*'s philosophical drama of stasis so deeply melancholic is its not-altogether-human cast of characters: the ideas, types (cobblers, weavers, sophists, guardians, philosophers, tyrants, etc.), props (the cave, the sun), affects, and characters (the soul and the city) that Socrates, Glaucon, and Adeimantus conjure up in the course of their conversation; the personified concepts, affects, and types that make up the dialogues' inner drama of ideas; the outlandish crossbreeds (like the guardian-philosopher-dog), inhuman characters, and figures (somewhere between thought and person) that engage each other on the invisible stage of Plato's philosophical theater. Arguably, this cacophony of inhuman voices reaches its crescendo in Books 8 and 9. For there, the ideas that jolt the drama of downfall into action are, like civil war, divisive ideas about division, internally conflicted ideas about conflict. And Socrates proposes rather strange ideas indeed.

"If there are five forms of city," he proposes, then "there must be five forms of the individual soul" (544e). In the place of political regimes (aristocracy, timocracy, oligarchy, democracy, and tyranny), which he wrests from their historical moorings, and of their corresponding types (the king, the democratic man, the tyrant, etc.), which he wrests from lived personal experience, the Socrates of Books 8 and 9 creates ideas (eide) that make distinctions in confusing situations possible and render the contours of the underlying conflict clear. After the arousal of primordial stasis, discord appears everywhere: in families, between generations (father and son), among changing values, between affects, within the soul. Plato is not interested in political institutions. Instead, he tries to capture change by concentrating his attention on the collision of the dominant ideas that govern the specific character—the peculiar soul—of the cities in question. For Plato, as for Solon and Thucydides, regime analysis is essentially a psychodrama. What it explores is not the legal framework of a regime but the subjective type and figural structuration of its soul. In a nutshell, Socrates approaches the constitution of a city as he would the constitution of the soul, excavating the governing principles of its master signifier so as to reveal the desires, fears, and aspirations of the aristocrat, the oligarch, the democrat, and the tyrant.

Plato thus responds to the crisis of Athenian politics by developing a new practice, a kind of "soul-practice," that entails the complete reconstitution of the individual as well as the collective psyche, both in speech and in deed. This transformation requires the conversion of both the individual soul and the soul of the city into ideas with the capacity to uproot traditional belief and to estrange established educational, rhetorical, and political practices from themselves. As ideas, concrete political phenomena turn at once into typological determinations of thought, possessed of a quasi-personal status. It is characteristic of Plato's political philosophy that ideas and concepts are dramatized in this fashion, that they become impersonal impersonations of thought with the power to conjoin the concrete physical existence, specific attitudes, and affective moods of political actors with the pure divisions of dialectical speech. In the *Republic*, one could say souls and cities attain what Deleuze and Guattari call "features of conceptual personae, or *thought-events*." Such conceptual personae can never be abstractions; they are dramatic actors who provide access to the historical context in which they appear precisely when they transcend those contexts and turn them into figures of thought. The dramatic performances of conceptual personae, by dislodging concrete political actors from their habitual environment, allow us to apprehend the former's "pathological symptoms, their relational attitudes, their existential modes, and their legal status" as part of a larger "thought-event."[38]

For example: although the typological analysis of the twisted use of language by the democratic man in Book 8 is, as Adam Parry notes, reminiscent of Thucydides's account of the Corcyrean stasis, Socrates refrains from naming the protagonists and from describing the socio-historical milieu in which these events occurred.[39] Rather than recounting the concrete instances of suffering, murder, and disease, he instead focuses on the psychogram of the democratic man, the psycho-political economy of affects and desires within the democratic soul. As Arlene Saxonhouse shows, the democratic regime betrays an inherent form- and lawlessness that dissolves the boundaries between gods, humans, and animals. The democratic soul is characterized by an unrestrained flux of words and thoughts, "unbounded by history, tradition, or past usage," that stems from a fundamental lack of structuring ideas. While this incapacity for imposing ideas on the world "creates an underlying unease" and is full of melancholic impasses, Socrates is far from condemning the democratic soul altogether.[40] What has been traditionally read as a linear story of degeneration and decline (from Callipolis to the unbearable stasis of tyranny) might have to yield to a more complex genealogy of political ideas (which includes the very lack of ideas) that also necessitates a reevaluation of stasis.

Breaking the tyranny of ideas and destroying the compulsive order of the just and beautiful city, Saxonhouse rightly observes, has, after all, a liberating, perhaps even a redemptive, effect. Hence, "at first there is something very appealing about the multihued regime that transcends categories to include all women, slaves and horses," something beautiful even: "Socrates uses the word *kalos*, beautiful (three times in 557c), to describe this regime," a use that cannot be easily dismissed as ironic.[41] The Platonic drama navigates, sometimes carefully, at other times boldly, between an unabashed love of ideas, a bewildering delight in exposing ideas to ruination, and a willingness to employ ideas as the principle of destruction. The philosophical drama performs this navigation as if it were a ship of state that must traverse Alchaeus's stasis of contrarian winds, tacking in order to aim at divisive units—things—that dwell in a field of division without any preexisting unity or harmony.[42]

This is worth bearing in mind as we return to the city-soul analogy; for there is nothing comforting or "imaginary" in the incessant inversions, from inside-out to outside-in, between the commonwealth and the individual. On the contrary, should the city assimilate, in letters of "larger size and surface," all the mental attributes of the individual, including the excesses of anger and aggression, of madness (*mania*) and melancholia, of anxiety, love, and shame, then political strife will be in danger of becoming further deepened and amplified, not soothed (368d). Plato's dramatic strategy is less about imbuing every citizen with the intensity of such affects than it is about bestowing upon the idea of the city itself the capacity to speak, think, act, and feel. The city is not only turned into an idea, it is turned into a *prosopopeia* with soul, eros, and character (435d-e; 544d–545c). Conversely, if the soul becomes a city and imports the dynamics of political domination and violence into its economy, including the city's factions, plots, imperial ambitions, and enemies, then the play of unrest in the soul swiftly turns into a serious political matter. Political stasis, now carried into every single person as their innermost condition, renders the drama within the soul a politicized affair even when there is no mention of politics. Plato's philosophical drama constantly shifts back and forth between the political and psychological contexts, rubbing them against one another, like "fire sticks," to bring to light the singular-universal thing of stasis (435a).

Socrates is well aware of both the benefits and dangers of blending the small letters of the psyche with the large letters of the city. On one hand, the justice that is found in a single man can be extrapolated to the city as a whole (individual characters might "tip the scales . . . and drag the rest along with them" [544d-e]) and vice versa. The construction of a just city can serve as a model for the education of just characters and is itself the performance of a just practice (ergon, 472a–473a) (369a). On the other hand, when the energies of soul-stasis and city-stasis converge, as they do in tyranny, a mutually reinforcing feedback loop is set in motion, seizing every part of the soul and the city to produce what Loraux might call a "*stasis kinete*," which "would indicate a movement twice over."[43] This accelerated form of stasis culminates in the nightmare visions of the tyrannical man, when the tyrant, by feasting on the city's dormant desires, realizes them in practice. Hence, in the tyrant, as Richard Parry notes, "the ills of such a public life" (fear of survival, flattery, becoming the object of disgust) are "added" to the internal psychopathological miseries of the tyrannical soul.[44] Although Socrates never uses the expression stasis kinete, such progressive strife lies at the heart of the monstrous, tyrannical eros that never shrinks "from trying to have sex with a mother, as it supposes, or with anyone else at all, whether man, god, or beast" (571d). The extreme hubris of the tyrant, his satiety (in Greek, as Charles Kahn notes, *satiety* "suggests *hubris* and carries connotation of disaster"), combined with the inflammations of tyrannical eros, leads to a conflagration in just the way that Heraclitus envisioned in his Fragment 65.[45]

This inflammatory vision of the worst as eros run amok happens to be found in Book 9; but Plato's images of the worst haunt the entire *Republic*, and he never misses a chance to evoke the kind of stasis that the acts of tragic heroes incite in the city ("Oedipus of course, but also Elektra or Medea," as Bernard Baas has observed), as if tyranny and tragedy shared a common root.[46] Socrates holds up the worst—wretchedness and injustice—and the best—happiness and justice—side by side, rubbing them against each other to tear down the tyrants' "theatrical façade" and illuminate the underworld of the tyrannical city until "every corner" of its lawless edifice comes to light (576d–577a). However, as with the democratic soul, this intercourse between the worst and the best reveals disturbing proximities and overlaps between the tyrant and the philosopher, between injustice and justice, unhappiness and happiness, madness and melancholia. Thus, even if the "finest sketch" of human beings were realized both in man and the city, the justice carried out by dike would continue to contain strife, perhaps precisely because the divine sphere is its model. Socrates cites here what "Homer called 'the divine form and image'" as the paradigm for the "finest sketch," apparently forgetting what he had argued in Book 2: that the Homeric gods are always "warring, fighting, or plotting against one another," and therefore stories about them ought not be "told nor even woven in embroideries" (501b; 378c). In short, there is nothing in "Homer's divine form and image" to suggest concord in the world of gods. On the contrary, as Socrates states in *Euthyphro*, "the gods are in a state of discord (*stasiazousin hoi theoi*) . . . they are at odds with each other . . . at enmity with each other" (7b).

What happens, then, when that conflictual model takes root in human thought? As Socrates had explained in the *Philebus*, the soul is neither immune from pains and pleasures nor from "irritation" and "infection," which often are "inside and cannot be reached by rubbing (*tribe*) and scratching." All the scratching and rubbing that goes on in the soul bears witness to a constitutive disquiet in psychic life, to wounds of the soul that are only further aggravated by the promise of "relief from itching by rubbing" (46e–47a; 46a). In *Phaedo*, one is tempted to say that Socrates develops the whole dialogue about the fate of the soul from a reflection on the pleasures of a rubbing that does not soothe but rather intensifies the pain of the shackles around his legs (60b-c). When Socrates speaks of his body, he always points to the true spectacle, to the rubbing of scars, infections, and bonds of the soul. Likewise, in *Philebus*, the irritations caused by itching and scratching can procure "enormous pleasures," but more often are outweighed by pains: they go "from one extreme to the other in their distress," sometimes creating "wild

palpitations" where one "is almost dying of these pleasures," and sometimes causing the most painful deprivations (46d–47b).

Now that we know all about the stasis of the soul, should we be surprised to find that, once Socrates steers the conversation away from
scratching and back to poetic mimesis in Book 10, the question of pleasure
and pain and of "civil war with himself" returns (603c-d)? Poetic mimesis
and the idea of mixed pleasures is the model for stasis, for the fact that
"our soul is full of a myriad of such oppositions at the same time" (603d).
Eros likewise is not about harmony, but about the expression and pursuit
of this myriad of opposites; the "nature of the real lover of learning,"
Socrates argues in Book 6 of the *Republic*, is "to struggle toward what is,
not to remain with any of the many things that are believed to be" (490a).
"What is," is eros as the struggle and unrest of the soul, which involves the
complete revaluation of the "many things that are believed to be." Eros is
at once manic and melancholic, devoted to the excess of strife.

Anxious Stasis: How to Make the City Melancholic (Plato's Apology)

Now that we have come to appreciate the effect of melancholic eros on the
city-soul, it is time to ask the obvious follow-up: How does a melancholic
operation grounded in eros work concretely with regard to the life of the
city itself? This question can only be asked—indeed, it can only be understood—by fully assuming the peculiar mode expressed in Socrates's terrific (*deinon*) form of speaking, as his accusers call it in the *Apology* (17b).
Socrates, as we saw in his ambivalent deployment of the Homeric Muses,
routinely turns philosophical speech into a kind of mimetic conjuration,
a practical exercise in mythic self-enchantment with the power to transform words into deeds and dialectics into the lived experience of immortal
existence. Such dramatized speech frees itself from too much dependence
on logos, which, as we know from Plato's discussion in *Letter VII*, remains
weak and vulnerable. Or, to state the matter more accurately: the stirring
Socratic *logoi*, as we find them in the *Apology*, reverberate through dialectical *logos* as its fiery, mad undercurrent, as if to demonstrate that logos—word, speech, reason, discourse—cannot become fully truthful, erotic,
and melancholic until it is also sufficiently delirious. This is an idea that
Plato will return to elsewhere in his writings. When in the *Phaedrus*, for
example, "reason and madness, at a certain level, converge" and a "double-
voiced discourse . . . occurs at the heart of Socrates' second speech," erotic
mania acquires a melancholic truth-content that precludes its playing the

role of unphilosophical, irrational excess to philosophy's calm reason.[47] Instead, mania actualizes the unrest of stasis, which once more asserts itself both as the principal philosophical condition of the soul and as the theater-idea of the Platonic dialogue—an idea that the form of the dialogue will then smuggle back into the city.

It is an inhuman, beastly idea, as Plato well knows. As soon as Socrates and his companion Phaedrus venture outside the city walls and stray from the familiar walking path, the dialogue inadvertently turns to outlandish myths and their preoccupation with monsters whose "absurd forms" incorporate body parts from a number of different creatures (229a–230d). Although Socrates refuses to be sidetracked by the overwhelming task of giving a rational account of such multiform monsters (to follow the Delphic order "know thyself!" is infinitely more important), he does not altogether dismiss such mythic speech. He even flirts with the idea of himself being such a monster, a monster more frightening than the most frightening of all monsters: "I accept what is generally believed, and . . . I look not into them but my own self: Am I a beast more complicated and savage than Typhon?" (230a). Nietzsche always claimed that Socrates, and indeed the Platonic drama as a whole, were tyrannical, multifarious monstrosities far more charged with extreme affects than the equanimity Socrates displayed at his death might lead one to assume. Here in *Phaedrus*, Socrates affirms this observation by comparing himself, his own soul and speech, to the angry and most fearsome of all monsters, Hesiod's Typhon (830–44).

What happens, then, when Socrates, this Typhonic monster with a gift for therianthropic speech, returns to the center of the city from his mad ventures along its walls? Socrates's procedure of shaming his fellow citizens in the *Apology* aims at the very origin of the desire for values even as it performs their radical revaluation. In fact, both the indictment of Socrates and his defense put the city's passionate attachment to certain concepts of truth, wisdom, and piety on display for further examination. In the process, every term under scrutiny is reveled to be, like the words in Freud's essay "On the Antithetical Meaning of Primal Words," a duplicitous combination of contradictory values. A kind of stasis thus appears within the terms themselves, as if the faith in opposite values has been shattered, replaced by a logic besides the *logic* of binary logos, a logic so charged with internal unrest that it can restore words to their primal duplicity. In Socrates's accusation against the city, the most cherished goods of Athens (its wisdom and power, its piety, its system of truth and justice—its whole ethos) suddenly appear worthless, while new philosophical practices and beginnings emerge to revolutionize the very definition of political life.

For the erotic philosopher who sustains the practice of refutation is not content merely with devising mad speeches. His task instead is an eminently political one: to insert more and more lack into people and things, bonding them to each other through their mutually shared incompletion and estrangement, their common melancholia. In other words, the erotic philosopher gives to the people with whom he communes the capacity, first, to void themselves of their illusory completion and, second, to transform themselves into plagued monsters. The philosopher in this way continuously hollows out the spaces in which he dwells, for his persistent love of lack pursues intimate relations with those forms of knowledge and human activities that share in the incompleteness of erotic things. The voiding capacity of erotic truths has a communizing power. This is the reason why, as Socrates says in the *Apology*, all those "young men" follow him around "of their own free will" and "take pleasure in hearing people questioned; they themselves often imitate me" (23c). The confrontation of received opinion (*doxa*) with erotic truths in the process of examination creates heretofore unknown philosophical communities, communities that instill as much enjoyment and mimetic desire in their members as they produce anger and distress (23d).

There is no fuller expression of this procedure than the one found in the *Apology*, a dialogue organized around Socrates's unconditional willingness "to face death many times" over the charge of having corrupted the youth (30c). He would not always be so courageous. In the *Republic*, Socrates warns that the spirited philosopher-guardian, if unguarded, can swiftly turn from a gentle dog to a wolf, from a kindly ally to a savage master (416a-b). Likewise, in Book 9 of *Laws*, Socrates views the spiritedness (thumos) of the guardian as both cause and response to corruption. Hence, the guardian must, above all, guard against the dangers coming from guardianship itself. The Stranger in the *Statesman*, meanwhile, is, like Socrates in the *Republic*, afraid of spiritedness (thumos) and courage. After all, he notes, it is the very obsession with devising a best regime, one that would enduringly quell stasis, that leads to the permanence of stasis. And yet: Who is it that maintains that obsession? It is the philosopher. The philosopher is himself the dangerous supplement that induces unrest in the city; the inauguration of political philosophy has given rise to a new form of stasis, one between the philosopher and the polis. And as in the civil war between moderation (*sophrosyne*) and courage (*andreia*), the adversaries in this case are often "extremely hostile to each other [*allelas echthran kai stasin*] and occupy opposed positions in many things" (306b). It is this version of the courageous, erotic philosopher, the one engaged in stasis with the city, that we encounter in the *Apology*. Contrary to Protagoras's warning, in the dialogue bearing his name, that visiting a city as a self-professed sophist intent on persuading the youths is a dangerous business, and that lots of protective measures must be taken because "jealousy, hostility and intrigue on a large scale are aroused by such activity," Socrates in the *Apology* is determined to aggravate division and unrest in the city (316d). And so the stories he narrates in that dialogue, about the oracle and Achilles's shame, about his refusal to try the ten generals and hand over Leon from Salamis to the Thirty Tyrants, are designed as divisive interventions, as subtractions of the philosopher from the city (32 b-c). For courageous philosophical teaching cannot, in the end, foster consensus. It can only foster, as Clifford Orwin puts it, "a new kind of discord—between itself and the city."[48]

Once again, this comes down to a particular practice of speech. When Socrates embarks on his investigative journey through the different strata of Athenian society (the politician, the poet, the craftsman) to examine those who are "reputed wise" (*tina ton dokounton*), he genuinely wishes to learn about the truths of their doxa, "which reveals itself to him in distinction from all others," as Hannah Arendt writes (21b).[49] There is good reason to believe, however, that Socrates already suspected that his examination of the reputable sages of Athens would end in disillusionment. But if that is the case, then what kind of truth does he really seek with his investigation? The answer—that Socrates pursues an erotic truth outside knowledge that can serve as an orientation for the labor of justice—becomes clear when Socrates examines the first self-professed wise man (the politician), and an intense, very acrimonious scene develops:

> Then, when I examined this man . . . I was affected (*epathon*) something like this: he seemed (*edoxe*) to me that he seemed (*dokein*) to be wise to many people and especially to himself, but he was not. I then tried to show (*deiknunai*) him that he thought himself wise, but that he was not. As a result he came to dislike me, and so did many of the bystanders. So I withdrew and thought to myself: "I am wiser that this man . . . I am likely wiser than he to this small extent, that I do not think I know what I do not know" (21c-d, translation altered).[50]

What immediately strikes one here is that Socrates is also affected by his demonstration (deikunai) of the discrepancy between reputation and wisdom. He does not triumphantly delight in his ability to expose this semblance (dokein) of knowledge; instead, he suffers from (epathon) the disintegration of reputation into a "matter of seeming."[51] But while

Socrates is deeply affected by this theater of semblance and revelation, this masked performance organized around the terms dokein, doxa, and deiknunai, the visual evidence presented in the demonstration that "he was not" wise is simply too compelling to ignore. "[T]hat he thought himself wise," in particular, sadly expresses a genuine self-deception that goes beyond the mere imitation or pretense of wisdom. At first sight it seems as though the illusion of wisdom simply comes from believing that the truths of one's doxa could ever be merged with knowledge. This is the case, for example, with the wisdom of poets and tragedians who, like seers and prophets, "say many fine things without any understanding of what they say" (22c). Then wisdom would have to be a constant awareness of the incongruity between truth and knowledge, between genuine reputation and a teachable techne. And the task of the philosopher would consist of shaming self-professed sages who plug up this difference, of showing them all the ways they fail to live up to the truth of their reputation. But Socrates, the angry politician, and the bystanders all seem to be affected by something more radical: namely, the revelation that no truth can be distilled from their doxa other than the truth that comes from the complete ruination of doxa itself. Arendt writes:

> The search for truth in doxa can lead to the catastrophic result that the doxa is altogether destroyed, or that what had appeared is revealed as an illusion. . . . Truth therefore can destroy doxa; it can destroy the specific political reality of the citizens. . . . The inconclusiveness of many Platonic dialogues . . . can also been seen in this light: all opinions are destroyed, but no truth is given in their stead.[52]

This destruction of all opinions without giving a truth is the quintessential melancholic operation, producing as it does a stasis, a permanent state of arrested unrest, in thought and expression. The Athenian citizens notice that Socrates's examination of the sages does infinitely more than disprove their individual wisdom or reveal the vanities of their profession. Their anger about Socrates has a political content, for his intrusive investigations of doxa effectively threaten the Athenian citizens with the destruction of their "specific political reality," that is, with the collapse of their entire symbolic universe. Polite Athenian society held that someone's doxa should not be treated simply as a subjective construct but acknowledged as the appearance of a political truth. By destroying the truths that adhere to someone's doxa, Socrates shatters not just the very foundation of Athenian collective wisdom; he shatters trust in the power of words and opinions to speak the truth.[53]

Socrates's destruction of doxa thus amounts to nothing less than an attack on the basic grammar of beliefs by which his fellow citizens sustain the order of political life. Dismantling the opinion and wisdom of the Athenian sages constitutes a wholesale political assault on the allocation, determined by separate spheres of professional expertise and technical knowledge, of roles and places in the structured life of the city. Whereas Socrates in the *Republic* praises mutually exclusive domains of knowledge, Socrates in the *Apology* acts as a transgressor of all forms of knowledge who completely disregards the virtue of minding one's own business. Instead, the melancholic thinker searches for destructive truths and a universalizing form of wisdom by which distinct epistemic territories can be transcended. Socrates's truths cannot help but turn the hierarchies of Athenian political life upside down: "I must tell you the truth—I was affected (epathon) by something like this: . . . the highest reputations were nearly the most deficient while those who were thought to be inferior were more knowledgeable" (22a).

Again, Socrates does not revel in his discovery that the current hierarchies of knowledge and reputation are so misguided as to beg for a complete reversal. Socrates is aware of the anxiety his repeated call for a "revaluation of all values" where "somebody" can quickly turn into a "nobody" causes among his fellow citizens (35a, 41e). He only reluctantly dismantles the most precious opinions of the city and replaces them with completely desiccated truths: the wisdom about the worthlessness of wisdom; the ruins of doxa; the injustice of legal justice; the superiority of death over life; the insignificance of the most cherished things (30a). It is thus not quite accurate to say, as Arendt does, that in Plato's early aporetic dialogues "all opinions are destroyed, but no truth is given in their stead." Socrates gives us infinite amounts of truths, but none for us to have. Instead, his obstinate truths are the effect of a practical demonstration, like the stages in a philosophical drama: the distressing enjoyment of examination; the constitutive discord between the philosopher and the city; the shame of doing wrong; the disturbing force of just speech; the communizing power of destructive truths or the blessings of the death drive. What we should say, then, is that Socrates's dramas of destruction are an *affirmative* act and must be counted as part of truth and justice procedures. The destruction of the truths of doxa is the prerequisite for truths to appear; the destruction of opinion is a prerequisite for the emergence of true opinion and genuine reputation (34e); the exposure of shamelessness is the revelation of shame (aidos); the examination of the gods and of conventional piety is the precondition for "*examined piety*"; and, finally, the destruction of legal and state justice is the precondition for the event of justice.[54] Taken altogether, such destructive acts manifest a primordial strife that itself attains a positive political content. The labor of Socrates's melancholic examination results in the inclusion of dissolution within the political.

Yet the labor of melancholic examination accomplishes something else of equal importance: it allows Socrates to redefine the very idea of the examined life as the ability, not merely to bear, but to practice, the (erotic) presence of worthless wisdom. The "small extent" to which Socrates can designate himself as "wiser" (Socrates hesitates to use the word *wisdom* in relation to himself) than everyone else is a residue that can be embraced only after the procedure of examination has ruined all forms of traditional wisdom and fully traversed the thing of ignorance (21d). The minimal difference that separates Socratic wisdom from that of the Athenian sages is not a question of more knowledge about certain substantial topics. It requires a particular habit of thought, an attitude that affirms the distress of being at a loss (*aporia*) in the following terms: "that I do not think I know what I do not know" (21d). Whereas his accusers try to gloss over the moments when they are at a loss, Socrates fully exhibits such aporia, thriving on its groundlessness and declaring it to be the distinctive mark of his true doxa (23d). As far as he is concerned, it makes him both "superior to the majority of men" and *courageous* (35a). Socratic courage with regard to knowledge means to not recognize any limits to the depths of ignorance. Bottomless ignorance intrudes into all those carefully separated epistemic territories, all those jealously guarded fiefdoms designed to establish the boundaries between wisdom and ignorance.[55] Like Lacan in his reading of the *Meno*, many have proceeded from the assumption that Plato, and indeed the philosophical project as a whole (particularly Hegel), is mainly concerned with distilling the episteme of the master from the knowledge of the slave. Invariably, though, they encounter a strong countervailing current: time and again, Plato's Socrates declares the methodical production of a bottomless ignorance his principal philosophical task.[56]

Socrates's devotion to this paradoxical form of wisdom has the most devastating political effects, for what is at stake is the intimate bond between wisdom and political power, between the professional of political knowledge—personified in the sophist—and the discourse of the master, embodied by the tyrant. In "Truth and Juridical Forms," Foucault argues that before the sixth century, "the tyrant was the man of power and knowledge, the one who ruled both by the power he exercised and by the knowledge he possessed."[57] To judge from the myths surrounding legendary kings in the past, European societies for millennia believed that holding political power necessarily implied possessing secret, special knowledge about the gods, the future, and the memory of man. According to Foucault, Sophocles's *Oedipus Rex*, which would be followed by Plato's philosophy a few decades later, stages the complete breakdown of this mystique of privileged political knowledge and solitary power and can therefore be seen as the starting date for the long decomposition of the union of political power and occult wisdom. Thereafter, Foucault contends, the positions were split: men of power were considered blind and men of knowledge powerless. Whereas "the man of power would be the man of ignorance," the seer, the prophet, and the philosopher were now the ones who communicated with the gods and the realm of eternal truths. "With Plato," Foucault argues, "there began a great Western myth: that there is an antinomy between knowledge and power. If there is knowledge, it must renounce power."[58] However, Socrates, not only in the *Apology* but in many other dialogues, discredits both positions, that of an exclusive political knowledge *and* that of a deeper philosophical wisdom capable of communing with the forces of the earth and the heavens. Even what Foucault calls the deeper knowledge postulated in Platonic philosophy, "the essential memory that is the recollection of what was seen in intelligible heaven," amounts to a rather tenuous form of "knowledge," more problematic than authoritative, a wisdom often cited from unverifiable sources and part of an ambiguous mythical narrative (30).

Pace Foucault, then, Socrates does not simply sever political power from the wisdom of the sages. Instead, he dismantles the wisdom both of the powerful (Athens, the politician, the sophist) and of the seers, prophets, and philosophers (for example Anaxagoras in the *Apology* and in the *Phaedo*). Even gods fall under scrutiny or get absorbed into the philosophical project of voided wisdom. God and the philosopher become in the end so indistinguishable that it remains unclear who takes the lead and who follows in the itinerary of examination. As soon as the discourse of the master appears, whether it manifests itself as power or as knowledge, Socrates sees only blindness and wrongs. Whereas Oedipus was doomed because he knew and did too much, Socrates is condemned because he insists on sapping, in consummate melancholic fashion, all significance from wisdom and political action. In this way, as Benjamin notes, Socrates is justifiably the foundational figure of the Trauerspiel.

There are those, such as Sean Kirkland and Bruce Johnstone, who have argued that Socrates is doomed from the beginning of the *Apology* to play the monstrous thing of the city, the beast-man with which contact is dangerous, even contagious, because of the "awe-*inspiring,* wonder-*provoking*, or terror-*inducing*" nature of his speech.[59] Their conclusion is understandable. After all, the main charge against Socrates is that he has corrupted (*diaphteirei*) the youths and spread the disease of discord everywhere (*Apology* 23d, 24c).[60] Socrates is the pied piper of Athens whose words are so forceful and seductive that they can spoil, maim, or even destroy the polis. The adjective deinos, used by Socrates's accusers when they caution their fellow citizens that he is a "terrific speaker" (*deinos legein*), means not only "clever" or "accomplished"; it also means "wondrous" or "terrible," as in the first stasimon of the Chorus, the famous ode to man, in Sophocles' *Antigone*.[61] "*Ungeheuer ist viel*," "much is monstrous," is how Hölderlin translates the famous "*polla ta deina*," and Socrates, no less than the nature of man in the eyes of the Sophoclean Chorus, radiates this affective power across the city. Yet Socrates enters the stage precisely to drain his speech and his truth of such a wondrous, monstrous charge and return them to the simplicity (*atechnos*), austerity, and sobriety of the common, unembroidered language spoken in the marketplace. His speech and his truth are certainly "disruptive," but less because they are "*overwhelming*" and "*excessive*," like the terrible speeches and truths of tragic heroes, but because they are the opposite. Eschewing tragic truths, Socrates consistently portrays himself as a man firmly placed within the confines of sober, human wisdom, a man who is neither "high in the city," like a god, nor "without city," like a beast. Socrates, in fact, cannot wait to deflate the attempts of his accusers (going back to Aristophanes) to confer upon him all of the secret magico-religious wisdom that was once believed to be the exclusive possession of the magic king (18b-c).

That is because Socrates knows that his devotion to the nothing of wisdom confronts the imperial ambitions of Athens with a crisis far more potent than that brought about by the destruction of traditional truths and divinities. The Athenians might be able to cope with the lack of their truths; but Socrates, this "pestilential fellow who corrupts the young," embodies something far more confusing: a strangely contagious and seductive form of life that has descended upon the city like a plague sent by the god (23d). This philosopher-daimon is a healer like Apollo, the source of the Phrygian oracle, but one who cures the city by bringing the Socratic plague. Like Freud, who on his first visit to America is said to have remarked that he was bringing the plague of psychoanalysis to the new continent, this melancholic god-philosopher purges the plague of mad Athenian politics through the dialogic plague of erotic elenchus.[62] Socrates is simply too much in their face with his unbending demonstration of the obtrusive presence of lacks: the flaunting of his ignorance and of his poverty, his overly dramatic subtraction from political and private life, his constant "shaming-reproach," as Robert Metcalf calls it, that calls on every citizen to give "an account of your life (*elenchos tou biou*)" (39c).[63]

Socrates is all too aware that the city longs to be released from the shame and anxiety that his roaming presence there elicits, even if they have to resort to ignoble means to secure it. The corrupting power of philosophy is so unbearable and contagious that Athens cannot let Socrates live. But Socrates also knows that he will not be gotten rid of so easily, for one simple reason: the philosophical form of life "cannot be harmed" or laid to rest (41d). Indestructible and infinite, its destructive spirit haunts perpetually from a future to come so long as shamelessness and injustice persist in the city. In a sarcastic tone and full of foresight, Socrates confronts his accusers with their conundrum: "You cannot avoid executing me, for if I should be acquitted, your sons would practice the teachings of Socrates and all be thoroughly corrupted" (29c). Socrates never assuages their anxiety. On the contrary, Socrates intensifies their shame and anxiety, as if only the maximal immersion in crisis and destruction could serve as redemption "for not living in the right way" (37d; 39d).

Socrates's destructive melancholia, which emerges in response to a fundamental wrong in the city, thus has a foundational character. it gives birth to new philosophical communities, new philosophical spirits. After hearing his death sentence, Socrates, the future Hades-examiner, parts from his countrymen with a menacing prophecy about a future people who will be more youthful and even "more difficult to deal with" in their manner of testing and reproach than he has been (39d). Socrates now fully unleashes the anxiety-inducing spirit of philosophy, lending its disturbing power a vast spatial and temporal expanse. The philosophical form of life is now firmly lodged inside Athenian democracy and Panhellenic myths, in the idea of death and in the view of the underworld, stretching forward into distant futures and back into immemorial pasts. Socrates never misses a chance to connect the present, his speech before the jurymen of Athens, to ghostly domains, the migration of the soul to "another place" and "for all eternity" or, above all, to the "true jurymen," Minos and Rhadamanthus, who will sit in judgment "there" (40d-e; 41a). His prophecies conjure an entirely different city, populated with philosophized spirits (the daimonion, the soul, the demigods, the shadows of the mythic heroes) but open to the living. Continuing the work of examination, these prophecies, philosophical in kind and irreducible to either tragedy or epic poetry, confront the glories of immortal heroic life with something far more allur-ing: the "extraordinary happiness" of infinite philosophical life (41c).[64]

However, while Socrates's discussion of the dead in the *Apology* is ordi-narily full of such assurances, there comes a brief moment when he con-templates the possibility that "the dead are nothing," an idea that, when expressed in the *Phaedo*, unleashes an anxiety great enough to result in the temporary breakdown of the dialogue (40c; 89b).[65] Lacan is no doubt right when he argues that Plato in the *Phaedo*, despite all appearances, not only demonstrates that the immortality of the soul cannot be proven but even aims at the opposite: to show the imminent possibility of the soul's death.[66] In *Phaedo*, the "care of self" (*epimeleia heautou*) is cotermi-nous with the "practice of death" (*melete thanatou*) (81a). Learning how to die primarily means learning how to maintain the philosophical discourse on the immortality of the soul: namely, that the dialogue itself must never die. If life were truly finite and the dead were "nothing," as Socrates allows himself to imagine—if "all eternity" were "no more than a single night"—then the dark wisdom of Silenus would return and the whole Socratic dis-course would forfeit its strongest support (40e). The mutually reinforcing relay between the infinity of philosophical discourse and the practice of immortality would break apart and render Socrates's ignorance more per-vasive and his mode of stasis more irreconcilable. Melancholic eros would overwhelm Socratic discourse. Plato has ensured that it will.

CHAPTER TWO

Hamlet, the Melancholic Prince

IN 1527, ROUGHLY three-quarters of a century before the first recorded performance of Shakespeare's *Hamlet*, Albrecht Dürer published a pamphlet outlining his theory of fortification.[1] The pamphlet is dedicated to Ferdinand I, and one can only wonder what the emperor made of it, assuming he bothered to read it at all. Did he notice the aggression of his most loyal servant, hidden in plain sight? Did he suspect that Dürer had devised the perfect prison for him: a citadel curiously removed from the territory over which he, the prince, claimed jurisdiction; a fortress permanently beleaguered, forever anticipating a siege that would never come? Did he understand how cunning Dürer had been, consigning his own sovereign to a dead zone, a no-place, a site that would end up being bypassed by the very armies it was built to withstand? Could Ferdinand ever have predicted that the fortress to which his most humble and obedient servant planned to consign him would find its ideal use, centuries later, as a prisoner-of-war compound or concentration camp—a haunt of bare life? Did he realize how utterly Dürer had drained the sovereign of his charisma and personality, how thoroughly he had transformed the sovereign into a new, entirely lifeless and placeless technology: a diagram and a function?[2]

Dürer's theory of fortification has a strangely antiseptic elegance. Immunitarian to the core, the fortress, as Dürer conceives of it, combines all three of what Foucault calls the *dispositifs*, or apparatuses, of power: the care of the sovereign; the disciplinary apportionment of professions and functions; the biopolitical partitioning of the secular from the sacred, the living from the dead, fresh air from vapors.[3] Though intended to protect and even foster life, the fortress is notably devoid of liveliness. Within its walls one will find both prisons and workshops, but one seeks in vain for a courthouse. On its light and airy streets, one will encounter inhabitants who have not just sacrificed their lives to the promise of security, but who have exchanged the philosophical demand for a just and good life for the lifeless servicing of goods. And at the center of it all stands a tower, a pyramid, as Dürer calls it, wherein the sovereign dwells in the utmost security, having withdrawn himself into the innermost recesses of the fortress. Sequestered in his tower, the sovereign leads his subjects in anxiously anticipating the arrival of a crisis that will surely come. The fortress designed for him by his faithful servant is nothing more than the imposition of anxiety rendered in architectural form.

Dürer's ideal fortress might accurately be described as a place that meets all the needs of its inhabitants, a place without lack; but accuracy in this case only misses the point. The fortress does indeed schematize a fantasy of completion, perfection, wholeness, usefulness, industriousness: a utopic space where all professions live and work together and where everyone's needs are fulfilled in a fantastically closed economy. Yet it does so in a way that, underscoring and indeed conjuring the manic side of sovereignty, goes well beyond any normal expectations of use. The fortress dissembles autonomy and self-containment. True, it lacks for nothing, but it does so only at the level of imagination, as realized in a garrulous and hyperabundant commentary on use that knows its own uselessness. This peculiar capacity—this capacity to return the sovereign's enjoyment to him as utter uselessness, dead on arrival—speaks to Dürer's own position as an affirmative melancholic. Exhibiting the melancholic's capacity for being completely engulfed by the insane logic of the fortress while also living outside of it (the melancholic always living in internal exile within the polis), Dürer maps out the craziness of the sovereign position for all to see, daring his patron to construct and then inhabit the claustrophobic lack of lack realized in his plan.[4] The plan itself could never be accomplished, exceeding as it does all reasonable functionality. And yet this is the only way that the real of the (perceived) sovereign demand can be felt in all its insanity: by overfulfilling it. There is an aspect of cryptography to Dürer's cartography—the labels and definitions, the naïve inertia of the battle scenes—that verges on embarrassing. But that is only because its presentation, at once serious and adolescent, draws us into the ambit of an enjoyment now drained of all its liveliness. That is how Dürer preserves his own enjoyment: by dissipating the sovereign's enjoyment in the very act of overfulfilling it.

While it might seem, then, as though Dürer props up an actual, living master, building the invulnerability of the position into the very

landscape (now carefully indexed as a flat topography of river, moun-
tains, forest, shelter, fruited plain), what his theory of fortification in fact
does is imaginatively preserve a place for the master that is dead at the
moment of its presentation: petrified, schematized, monumentalized in
a tomb disguised as an industrious fantasy of communal, interconnected
life. Yet that is not the only way in which Dürer's odd text encrypts his
own enjoyment at the expense of the prince's. The satisfaction the pamphlet takes in staging battle scenes and in demolishing the fortress, the
delight it takes in imagining the new weapons to be tested against the
structure's walls: these gestures betray a desire for the destruction of
the very security state the pamphlet lays out so carefully. In this way,
the pamphlet realizes, in diagrammatic form, a particular version of the
sovereign: one inherently destabilized, undermined at its foundation,
filled with anxiety about its own position, a position now given shape not
by pomp and majesty but by a hyperorganization of space and vocation
placed under the constant threat of violence and bombardment. Not only
is Dürer's plan too expensive and fantastical to be realized, the sacrifice
too great to be carried out; it maps, with mathematical precision, with
right angles and careful arrangements, the fantasy that the sovereign
position might not be defensible at all—that the fortress is erected in
the expectation that it will be demolished, its defenses surmounted, its
solitary tower taken.

What are we to make of this ambivalence? We might note that Dürer's
imaginary fortress seems to solicit its destruction in the same way that
psychical defenses allow for passage toward the Good, as understood in
psychoanalytical terms—that is, toward the object.[5] Or we might pursue
the analogy further and say that the fortress is merely the blueprint, the
imaginative realization, of Dürer's own psychical topography as an affirmative melancholic: a psyche occupied by a master whose simultaneous
destruction and preservation it alone has carefully planned. Consider the
design of the fortress. The shapes of the buildings, the space inhabited by
no one: these are rigidly laid out, but they devolve into a central space,
occupied by a tower or pyramid (already, a hint of entombment), to which
no living person could gain access and from which no escape is possible.
At the very heart of Dürer's imaginary fortress, then, we find not only a
tower but a crypt: the mapping of an inaccessible, but also inescapable,
core, a place where the sovereign might remain hidden away, protected
from the outside—but where he might also be forgotten.[6] As Agamben
describes it in *Stanzas*, the enigma of melancholia is that it "offers the

paradox of an intention to mourn that precedes and anticipates the loss of the object." "From this point of view," concludes Agamben,

> melancholy would be not so much the regressive reaction to the loss of the love object as the imaginative capacity to make an unobtainable object appear as if lost. If the libido behaves as if a loss had occurred although nothing has in fact been lost, this is because the libido stages a simulation where what cannot be lost because it has never been possessed appears as lost, and what could never be possessed because it had never perhaps existed may be appropriated insofar as it is lost.[7]

Melancholia emerges here as the necessary precondition for imagining an escape from, or perhaps an alternative to, the impoverished world, the world of lack. There is always a crypt to be revisited, a lonely tower to be viewed from a distance. In Dürer's genuinely melancholic fortress, by contrast, there is no escape route, no elsewhere to be imagined outside of this imaginary place. This sequestered, claustrophobic, constipated space has no outlet; only by destroying it can one hope to discharge the tensions internal to the psychical foundation on which it sits.

Now if Agamben's model of melancholia is predicated on a paradoxical form of immunization—the immunization against loss, guaranteed by a lack that ensures the imaginative capacity to believe otherwise, to escape the reality tested and found wanting—then the model outlined in Dürer's theory is predicated on a lack of lack, undergirded by a structure with no outlet. For Agamben, the melancholic can revisit a loss possessed in its very loss, a crypt that can always be found. Dürer's affirmative melancholia is more radical, more anti-immunitarian. Not only is there no protection from loss; there is no exit that one might take to avoid a confrontation with the lack of lack that ensures ruination. Instead of resting on a crypt that one might revisit in its absence, Dürer's fortress is itself a re-visitation, in language, of the becoming-stone of enjoyment, the deadening of liveliness, the objectification of quickness. Immoveable and at the same time easily bypassed, the fortress already looks ahead to its ruination.

And who, or what, will haunt this ruin? Recall the sovereign in his lonely tower, his isolated pyramid. His enjoyment, as perceived by Dürer, was to have at his disposal the perfect fortress. Dürer dutifully returns that enjoyment, only in inverted form—drained of its liveliness, realized so fully and so earnestly that it not only verges on parody but goes beyond parody and turns into anxiety: the anticipation of a siege and a bombardment that never happens. And even if that siege were to happen, there would still be no way out. The sovereign is alone in his tower, bereft of his own enjoyment and yet possessed of that offered up, with dedication, by his servant. And there he will wait and wait, prince of a ruin. The inert character of the fortress, its inky stoniness, removes its inhabitants from historical time as only a work of imagination can. But in doing so, it subjects those inhabitants to the time of natural historical decay.[8] The space of the sovereign is reimagined here as a space turned in on itself, already contemplating its eventual ruination at the hands of natural history. The fortress, understood as the schematization of the sovereign position, is nothing but a ruin haunted by the enjoyment of the one who planned it, who plotted out its walls.

Fortress Elsinore

Hamlet, too, takes place in a fortress. The play starts off sparsely, almost desolately: at midnight, on a platform.[9] We are introduced to a couple of sentinels, Bernardo and Francisco, who are guarding—what, exactly? Are they guarding, as appears to be obvious, Elsinore castle from its enemies? Are they policing the perimeter of the castle, as if to contain some internal threat? Perhaps they are guarding the play itself, defending it against the reader in search of some hidden truth. Or might they be there to put the spectator on her guard, whether against the shattering effects of the play or her own transferential desires? Whatever the answer, *Hamlet* opens in an atmosphere of profound insecurity and distrust, and with good reason: a king is dead, a new king has taken the throne, and hostile neighbors threaten the border. Act I confronts us with a state in the state of emergency, a time of crisis in which one is required to come most "carefully upon [his] hour" (1.1.6). But can that state of emergency alone account for the profound distress manifested by the presence of armed guards? The first line of the play, "Who's there?" might be read as announcing, however tentatively, the emergence of the modern liberal subject: a subject defined by agency, doubt, lively emotions, depth of feeling, and the ability to experience an existence no longer constrained by the bounds of tradition.[10] But the lines that follow—"Nay, answer me. Stand and unfold yourself"; "Long live the King!"; "You come most carefully upon your hour"—already counter that fantasy of the subject by presenting a couple of sentinels who know how to interrogate (and to be interrogated), to answer when called, to know and even bless the name of the master, and to know the time of their Other (1.1.1–6). This would be a subject that is acknowledged only at the moment when it discloses its secret, its interior life. But what does the subject actually reveal at the moment of questioning? "Long live the

King": a pledge of the servant to the master at whose behest he willingly sacrifices his own being. Instead of a subject, we get a police exchange: the asking and giving of a proper name, the reassurance that nothing has happened, the order to move along, to go to bed, and the expression of thanks for at last being "relieved" of one's duty. Finally, Francisco will be allowed to enjoy the few hours of private time allotted the public servant. But what joy can he expect, being "sick at heart"? Guarded and guarding, the subject emerges here only to disappear, replaced by an expression of discontent, an admission of melancholia that, never answered, lingers long after Francisco has left the stage. This is the clearest sign that the law of the home—paternal succession, the order of peace, contractual obligations—can no longer claim to be the home of the law, that Elsinore has lost jurisdiction over itself. The moment when the ghost appears is the moment when Marcellus proclaims, "Peace, break thee off," thereby articulating, in words that evoke secrecy and rupture, what had previously been hinted at: Elsinore is in a state of emergency (1.1.40). There will be no rest for anyone—no comfort, no sleep, no peace of any kind—from now until the end of act 5.

This broken peace returns us to the question of what it is the sentinels are guarding against. The answer appears to be easy: Fortinbras, the hostile neighbor, having "sharked up a list of lawless resolutes," imports martial law into the state (1.1.98). There must be a state of emergency, because the state is under siege. But as even a cursory reading of act 1, scene 1 reveals, the logic of martial law has already so thoroughly penetrated the characters' speech that storytelling itself becomes a fortress designed to guard against the realization that the threat externalized onto the neighbor really comes from within. Each phrase, though intended to displace aggression onto an outside enemy, inadvertently draws our attention to the fact that the usurper is already housed in the home of the law. It is only fitting, then, that at the very moment the guards "sit down awhile" with Marcellus and Horatio to tell the story about "this thing" that they "have two nights seen," the events of the story should unfold before them (1.1.21, 33). The ghost suddenly appears, almost as if it had been conjured by the story of its previous appearance. Indeed, the four companions not only never get to finish the stories by which they would orient themselves in the master narrative of which they are a part, they barely get to begin them. They don't even get to repeat them.

The occupant of this fortress that chiefly concerns us is, of course, Hamlet—Hamlet, because, as the only character in the play possessed of "a heart unfortified" (1.2.96), he is both the heir to this fortress and also the one who will destroy it. We have described how the appearance of the ghost of Hamlet's father prevents the creation of a coherent communal narrative—a narrative, we might add, that would serve in part to lay that ghost to rest. Another way of putting this would be to say that the appearance of the ghost prevents the establishment of a particular type of plot; and in that, it also gives us occasion to consider the various meanings of *plot*, one of which is the site of a fortress.[11] Hamlet, the son of the ghost, follows his father in retarding the development of the plot, in both senses of the word. But Hamlet goes further than the ghost ever could, or would ever want to, by introducing a counterplot that both parallels and undermines the edifice of Elsinore, understood as a stand-in for the fortified state as such. Hamlet ensures that the plot of the fortress gets unmade—that the very ground on which it stands is abolished—through the destruction of all plots, including the revenge plot promoted by his father's ghost. Walter Benjamin's claim that "a major work will either establish [its] genre or abolish it; and the perfect work will do both," however gnomic it may sound, is to the point; for *Hamlet* itself depicts that very gesture: the founding of a fortress that abolishes its own foundation, a fortress whose foundational gesture is its own abolition.[12] Hamlet's counterplot is a plot that unplots itself and, in so doing, precludes the writing of any plot in its place.

Let us say it again: *Hamlet* is not a tragedy.[13] It is not even a tragedy about the tragedy of *Trauerspiel*—namely, that the genre is haunted by the memory of the tragic function it can no longer perform. That function, simply put, was to found the idea of the polis, as often as not through the burial of a melancholic figure.[14] (Oedipus, seeking out an unmarked grave in order to clear a space on which the polis might regenerate itself, is the prime example.) Trauerspiel, as *Hamlet* already demonstrates, is different. *Hamlet*, rather than allowing the state to claim for itself the power of the theater, instead forces the state to confront (or, better, be seized and struck by) the gestural theater-idea of Trauerspiel.[15] In *Hamlet*, play, *spiel*, is something that takes place on a side stage adjacent to, or rather aside from, the state. The state, rather than being able to lay claim to the power of theater, is instead forced to become absorbed in the plot of a play dedicated to the unplotting of the foundations of the state. *Hamlet*, to round it off to a formula, forces the would-be immunitarian state to recognize that it is already haunted: haunted neither from within nor from without, but from the wings.

Haunted by what, though? Jacques Lacan's argument is that the play revolves around the absence of mourning; but that is not to say that it is simply about the aberrations or insufficiencies of mourning.[16] It is about the impossibility of locating the place of lack—call it the proper tomb, the well-tended crypt—at the foundation of the state. There are no places in *Hamlet* where mourning might take place; its crypts are present not as sites but as citations: rumors (the father's crypt); travesties (Ophelia's); nonburials (those of Polonius and of Rosencrantz and Guildenstern); or grotesque unburials, like that of Yorick. Rather than performing the work of tragedy by providing the polis with a place of lack in the form of a foundational crypt, *Hamlet* realizes—and, in realizing, abolishes—the ends of Trauerspiel by disrupting the logic of lack. The logic of lack, after all, is nothing but the logic of prohibitory law. The lack of lack, by contrast, is the source—or, better, the absent cause—of anxiety. Hamlet fills Elsinore, the fortress, with anxiety. In that respect, Hamlet presents us with a veritable ground zero, the not-all, of the politics of melancholia. Too often, the melancholic stands accused of reactively turning anger inward. *Hamlet* shows us that, on the contrary, the melancholic forces the polis to assume the structure of melancholia, albeit without being able to appropriate it for its own ends. Like the Trauerspiel, which prevents the state from laying claim to the workings of tragedy, instead demanding that the state be struck by the frozen gestures of impossible mourning, the political melancholic forces the fortified state to be struck by the melancholic's own absorption in the object that does not lack, that indeed does not stop not existing. Lacan did not go far enough, even for a Lacanian. There is no desire in *Hamlet*, for desire proceeds from lack. In other words, there is something more than a phallus, even if that phallus is a ghost. In *Hamlet*, even the ghost is haunted, haunted by the insistence of an object that precludes the possibility of the ghost's lack at the site of a new foundation for a new polis. All that truly remains at the end of *Hamlet* is the melancholic's still-living enjoyment, housed in a ruined fortress, secured by what we will go on to describe here as the objectivity of natural historical decay.[17]

Enter the Ghost

What plot does the ghost of Hamlet's father want? Or, to put it another way, to what plot does the ghost already belong? Toward the end of act 1, scene 5, Hamlet describes the ghost as a "perturbed spirit," a spirit who is himself haunted by something (1.5.182). One might be forgiven for wanting to attribute that hauntedness either to the father's unavenged murder or to his guilt over his own, unexpiated crimes. For this is what the ghost desires above all, that the play should assume the plot of a revenge drama, a drama of crime and guilt, of recrimination and expiation. But of course that plot never comes off in *Hamlet*. There is no restoration of justice in the play, no fulfillment of the father's demand. Until the very end, Hamlet resists the impulse to make good on the father's desire to become a specter, a spirit of fear and dread. The ghost remains a ghost and nothing more. The ghost wants to be relieved of whatever it is that haunts him, that turns him into that most paradoxical of figures, the melancholic ghost. But Hamlet, dutiful son that he is, refuses to let that happen.

What transpires instead is a grotesque mix of gothic horror and wheeling slapstick. In a manner at once deft and madcap, Hamlet deploys comedy, so often treated as a strategy for evading a direct confrontation with enjoyment and anxiety, to prevent the ghost from using another form of evasion—the plot of crime, sin, deprivation, and expiation—to disavow the overwhelming proximity of the object and the anxiety it evokes.[18] There is much at stake in act 1, scene 5; the risk of betraying its evental character runs high. In its monstrously mixed structure, however, the scene somehow teaches us to be faithful to the event—a faithfulness that always, as the scene reminds us, carries the risk of making us appear foolish and ridiculous—albeit without succumbing to the self-aggrandizing drama of the Master, as performed in this case by the ghost of the father (or at least as the ghost would *like* to perform it). If there is a comedic aspect to the play, it emerges here, in the fact that the ghost is merely the ghost of a ghost—a pathetic, castrated failure; an imposter playing the role of haunting figure—rather than a truly threatening specter able to take revenge against his enemies. The ghost is an "honest ghost," as Hamlet puts it: genuine, and not a demon, but also painfully earnest, a little worried, touchingly conscientious, almost domesticated—but hardly threatening (1.5.138).

Yet the self-aggrandizement and self-pity of the ghost, his way of presenting himself as the nobly suffering victim, his efforts to seduce Hamlet with the romance of his story of murder and purgatory: these are deployed not only to mask the comically insufficient position of the father but to conceal the very thing that registers the pathetic nature of the ghost in the first place: the overproximity of the second death, the utter obliteration of the father's name and the order it grounds.[19] This, in fact, may be the most profound effect of the comedy at work here. Rather than neutralizing the anxiety generated by the overproximity of the object, which comedy sometimes does, the comedic elements in Hamlet's initial interactions with the ghost symptomatize the father's pathetic ignorance of his absence from the place of lack he longs to occupy. Put otherwise, Hamlet's comedic treatment of the ghost only underscores the becoming-object of the ghost. One can hear as much in Hamlet's language—his "poor ghost," his labored pun on the Globe Theater, his vow to "wipe away all trivial fond records" so as to remember nothing but the ghost—which tends to reduce the father to the level of comic or even base matter: to something impoverished, inert, an isolated prop on the stage of Hamlet's "distracted globe" (1.5.97). If Hamlet seems vaguely unmoved by the ghost's histrionic attempts at tragic heroism—if he tends to turn the ghost's inability to stop mourning lack into slapstick—that is because he detects how the ghost is already haunted by the specter of anxiety, the specter of becoming object, of being subjected to the second death. The ghost mouths the belief that the time can be put right, that his crimes can be redeemed, that propitiation is all that the state requires to restore an economy of lack in which Hamlet, too, might take his proper place as king.[20] But Hamlet hears something else. Hamlet hears the ghost's unstated anxiety that he is the lack that lacks—that he inhabits an Other time in which no act, and no desire, is possible.

Consider that the ghost of the father, rather than acting as the agent of prohibition, issues Hamlet a command. This is no fearsome, castrating Father of the Law; this is a vaguely desperate father, urging his son to enjoy the jouissance denied to the father himself. In this way, the ghost seems to tempt Hamlet to exceed, even to destroy, the boundaries of the very law he ought to secure. Yet that would be to assume that the ghost in fact embodied the myth of the primal father, that he stood at the head of a story rooted in crime, castration, exceptionality, and the law of lack. But the ghost, as we have argued here, does not haunt. He is haunted, possessed even, by a secret prehistory quite different from that of the primal father, a history of suffering and torment without redress, unrelieved by ritual or mourning—a history of the unhistorical Other time of the second death. The ghost wants Hamlet to set the time aright, to restore an economy of lack by returning the father to his proper grave, to make the basis of the law a crime acknowledged and avenged. But the time is not out of joint because a crime has been committed; the situation in Elsinore cannot be reduced to an unavenged regicide or the normalization of martial law.[21] The time is out of joint because an Other time, a time of utter eradication, insists within its midst. The ghost may be unaware that he is an emissary from that Other time; thus he continues to agitate for the unfolding of a particular plot, that of the revenge drama. And perhaps even Hamlet persists, for a short while at least, in the belief that he is fulfilling the ghost's stated demand to fix the time through a definitive act of vengeance. Yet in his actual behavior, Hamlet remains true, not to the ghost, but to the Other time that haunts the ghost. Hamlet, to put it crudely, is twice the ghost his father is.

One sees this most clearly in act 1's oath scene. At its most basic, an oath should bind together a community through something like a verbal contract. Yet even the verbal register gets undermined here, unmade through its very use. In Lacan's reading of *Hamlet*, the phallus gets transformed into a ghost.[22] We should not take this to mean, however, that the phallus is therefore comparable to the primal father: a figure capable of haunting by its very absence. The phallus works to ground signification; it is the signifier that makes signification possible. But in this scene, the phallus, in the figure of the ghost, is "*hic et ubique*": here and everywhere (1.5.156). There exists no solid ground to signification, no phallus to secure it, to guarantee its comprehensibility. Instead, the phallus, which ordinarily would ground the order of signification, takes the form of a ghost under the stage, and more (at least as Hamlet sees it); the ghost-phallus is a pioneer, an old mole, an agent of slow destruction. To the extent that Hamlet identifies with the ghost or agrees to pursue the ghost's mission, he too becomes an agent of destruction.

That is not to say, however, that Hamlet serves merely as an advocate of groundlessness or a follower of the ghost. He swears allegiance to something of which not even the ghost is aware: the ghost behind the ghost, as we have already put it. Consider Hamlet's revision of the ghost's plaintive command, "Adieu, adieu, adieu, remember me," which Hamlet, in his repetition of it, later reduces by one adieu. What might seem at first like a rewriting of the ghost's command, or even a violation of its injunction to remember, turns out, upon reflection, to be a fulfillment of it.[23] Hamlet hears far more than what the ghost says; for he knows that only by destroying the ghost's command, only by violating it, can he realize its thrust. That is true fidelity—fidelity to the destructive imperative voiced in the ghost's command. Hamlet pledges fidelity, not to the ghost's stated desire for revenge, but to the drive toward destruction that the demand can be made to carry. To fulfill the command, in essence an injunction to remember the ghost by laying him to rest—by saying goodbye—Hamlet must break it, destroying even the language of the command itself, forgetting something (an adieu) as an act of destructive preservation: the observation of the command in its breach.[24]

Which, as it turns out, is a breach that also serves to intensify the command's spirit. Like melancholia itself, the ghost's command—remember, goodbye—is impossible and paradoxical. Yet the impossibility at work here, an impossibility that undermines the functionality of language, gets intensified by Hamlet's concluding words to his companions—"Nay, come, let's go together"—where negation serves to affirm the destructive drive encrypted in the ghost's call for revenge (1.5.190). In essence, Hamlet redirects that drive, or rather the enjoyment of that drive (take revenge!), into the wider workings of life in Elsinore. The phallus should ground language; but here there is no ground, nor even any groundlessness. There is only repetition. Repetition wears away at the language of the ghost, dissolving three adieus into two.

Eventually, Hamlet prevails upon the other witnesses of the ghost to swear, in the ghost's name and yet to Hamlet in person, never to reveal what they have seen, or heard, or know. The language of the oath shifts repeatedly—and that is significant. First Hamlet asks his companions to swear never to make known what they have seen; then, getting more specific and objective, never to speak of *this* they have seen; then never of this that they have heard; and finally, never to let on that they "know aught" of Hamlet, even if—especially if—he appears to be feigning madness (1.5.79). With each repetition of the oath—an oath that never seems to hold, to find its guarantee in the real—language moves closer both to the objective realm, the realm not of *what* but of *this*, and to the *aught* of Hamlet. Each iteration revolves, moreover, around an oath to silence and nonknowledge. The others are not to speak—meaning, in essence and in practice, that they verbally swear an oath to the unmaking of language: to the introduction of something ghostly, something shifting and disruptive, into language itself. And while they begin by swearing (albeit without knowing as much) to the ghost, they end by swearing to Hamlet himself; and that, too, is significant. The phallus is a ghost, according to Lacan, a ghost into whose symbolic place, into whose vacated place, the subject gets to slot himself. But the phallus is also the signifier that authorizes signification, and here that function is undermined in the operations of language, which work through repetitive dissolution, the movements of the object, and, finally, the silence that gathers around the *aught* of nonknowledge. Hamlet does indeed assume the place of the ghost; but in so doing, he forces the other characters to swear, in a speech act that turns upon itself, to something other than the phallus in its guise as master signifier. Hamlet not only displaces the ghost of his father; he contracts the ghost behind the ghost, taking over the place of repetition and anxiety, taking over the place of the object—a fact attested to by Ophelia, who, in the next scene, describes a ghostly, ghastly Hamlet

> with his doublet all unbraced,
> No hat upon his head, his stockings fouled
> Ungartered, and down-gyved to his ankle,
> Pale as his shirt, his knees knocking each other,
> And with a look so piteous in purport,
> As if he had been loosed out of hell
> To speak of horrors

(2.1.78–84).

So Hamlet supplants the pathetic ghost while at the same time contracting the anxiety-generating ghost behind the ghost. What then? As a purely dramatic matter, this helps to explain why Hamlet hesitates to kill Claudius when he has the chance. In the first place, to kill the king would only end up concealing the Other temporal space that Hamlet inhabits, the time out of joint. To kill Claudius would be to risk perpetuating the fantasy that the time can be redeemed, that things can be set right. To kill Claudius would be to play into the one plot, the revenge plot, that Hamlet the melancholic has no interest in pursuing. To not take revenge: that is to make visible a mission irreducible to rivalry or succession or restoration or any of the other trappings of phallic jouissance. A revenge drama can only backslide into a fantasy narrative of crime and punishment, a narrative realized through rituals of sacrifice and mourning. Hamlet's apparent inaction, by contrast, makes it known that something more than crime is at stake: namely, that the far greater betrayal is to seek an escape from betrayal in the ritual reestablishment of law and order, in the righting of things. The "crime" in question here is not the murder of one king by his usurper—a crime on the order of phallic jouissance.[25] The crime here is the ongoing effort to deny the fundamental rottenness of Elsinore: not the rottenness of corpses or a time out of joint, but the rottenness of burying those corpses before they begin to stink and of hastening the return of a time that is not out of joint.

Another way of putting this would be to say that Claudius doesn't know that his position, based on the illusory enjoyment of transgression, the enjoyment of phallic jouissance, is pathetic. Claudius does not know; and in not knowing, he is guiltier of a far greater crime than murder. He is guilty, if that is the right word, of believing in the phallus as the signifier of power. Hamlet, by contrast, does know, knows that the position of sovereign that Claudius occupies is itself pathetic. Hamlet's inaction concerning Claudius has thus been misread.[26] Claudius is simply too pathetic to be killed, just as the sovereign phallus is too pathetic to resist the workings of the lost cause to which Hamlet, as a political melancholic, has declared fidelity. Claudius, the king of shreds and patches—the king who truly exemplifies the pathetic nature of the king—is not worth killing, whereas his continued existence seems to realize Hamlet's melancholic project. Claudius, the king, is a thing—of nothing (4.3.28–30). Which is to say: He is a thing drained of the enjoyment supposedly provided by phallic jouissance. His very position, which would only be validated by a revenge killing, is instead drained of its significance.

This frank indifference to the position of the sovereign, aligned with the phallus, has a surprising effect. It frightens even the ghost of Hamlet's father. We argued earlier that the repetitive time scheme inhabited by Hamlet wears away with each return. One sees the same phenomenon at work here as well. By not killing Claudius when he has the chance—an act that would set the time aright by accurately repeating the killing of his own father—Hamlet achieves what a straightforward act of revenge could not: it allows him to display, repeatedly and gratuitously, an emptied sovereign, a sovereign so pathetic that he does not even realize he has been drained of enjoyment and had his interior replaced by a fixation on the anxiety object actualized by Hamlet. Claudius is weak, incapable of castration or of containing enjoyment. And Hamlet's decision to leave *that* king intact and in tatters initiates a repetitive pattern in which the would-be master, hereafter embodied in a series of figures that includes (at the very least) Polonius and Fortinbras, gets displayed as hollowed-out, agitated, anxious and scheming, deprived of both interiority and agency.

The figure that exemplifies this new version of the sovereign, the figure of the skeletal master drained of stature and enjoyment, is of course the ghost of Hamlet's father, who reappears briefly in act 3, scene 4. Superficially, the ghost returns to goad Hamlet into action. Yet note the ghost's appearance: not purposeful or robust but caught off guard, a little sleepy, dressed in his nightshirt, slightly deranged (3.4.102). Hamlet's inaction conjures the ghost; but it does so only because the ghost has been made anxious by Hamlet's indifferent dismantling of the position of the king. The ghost returns, in other words, not because Hamlet hesitates or shows compassion toward the hapless Claudius—that is, not because Hamlet refuses to follow the plot of the revenge tragedy devoutly wished for by the ghost—but because Hamlet shows no respect for the position of king that the ghost most wants to preserve.[27] Ironically, the allies here are not Hamlet and the ghost but the ghost and Claudius, who together seek to militate against Hamlet's utter evacuation of the phallus, against his conjuring of the ghost that terrifies even the phallic ghost.

And then—the ghost disappears, never to be heard from again within the play. Where does he go? Why does he leave? Psychoanalytic criticism would argue, has argued, that the answer rests on Hamlet's dissolution of the Oedipus complex.[28] Hamlet, according to this reading of the play, comes to *know*, know that the father is pathetic, that the phallus is a ghost. But at the same time Hamlet, as a melancholic, does not know; the cause is lost to him. These stances are not irreconcilable, however. Hamlet's knowledge does not set out to redeem what it undoes. In that respect, he is not a cynic. Rather, he maintains fidelity to what he does not know: to the lost cause that absorbs him, and to which he rallies others. This is what makes Hamlet such a threat to the state—such a threat, in fact, that Claudius issues a warrant for his death; he wants to preserve the political structure of the Oedipus complex in its very dissolution (4.3). Hamlet really does go so far as to assume the place of the father, to lay claim to the phallus. Only now it is an objectified phallus, a phallus that provides no ground even to the groundlessness of an order guaranteed by the phallus—here and every-where—as ghost. From this point on, Hamlet betrays no feelings of guilt, no signs at all that he is in league, even half-heartedly, with the transgressive-restorative fantasies of the revenge drama promoted by the ghost. For by now he is well on his way to advancing his counterplot, his mounting of another, melancholic polis on the side stage apposed to Elsinore. And for this, he has his mother to thank.

Gertrude as Flesh

When Hamlet arrives in Gertrude's closet—Gertrude's private chamber, where he has been summoned, where his presence has been demanded—he arrives burdened by the fantasies, lurid and lustful and shameful, of imaginary flesh (3.4.41ff).[29] It may be a critical cliché, but it remains true nevertheless: Hamlet is disgusted by the very idea of his mother having sex with Claudius. The shame that Hamlet feels most keenly is shame for others—shame, very specifically, for the others around him who have given themselves over to the shamelessness of institutional life. So when Hamlet, coming close to overplaying the Oedipal scene, bursts into his mother's closet, it is to catch Gertrude out, to discover whether she is part of the plot against him (an essentially Oedipal, rivalrous plot in which he risks being cut out and off), to test her and shame her in order to confirm that she is, in fact, guilty of the sins of imaginary flesh that he has projected upon her. Is she penetrable? Does she feel?

Yet Gertrude turns out not to be the embodiment of imaginary flesh at all. On the contrary, she turns out not to be shameless but oblivious, lost in a haze of forgetfulness.[30] Suddenly, as if a spell of shame had been broken, Hamlet himself begins to exhibit a strange sort of shamed resolve: the shame of knowing that he had become fixated on lust; the shame of having lost himself, even for a while, to imaginary flesh. Imaginary flesh had been a lure, a distraction. But now, at the moment when he simultaneously enacts and dissolves the Oedipal scene, Hamlet comes into contact with real flesh: the flesh of the world that has no partner, that is beholden to no master signifier.[31] And at that moment, he enters into a bond with Gertrude—a genuinely melancholic bond—infinitely more powerful than that promised by the Oedipal fantasy.

That bond is sealed at the point of forgetfulness. Strangely, almost inconceivably, Gertrude has forgotten that Hamlet is "for England" (3.4.202). How could she forget such a thing, his own mother? Yet that oblivion, that forgetfulness, is crucial, because it is a forgetfulness of the law. Gertrude has forgotten, as if it were utterly inconsequential, Claudius's injunction. This is in striking contrast to Hamlet, who, so far as we can tell, never sleeps, never dreams, never forgets. He remains, instead, utterly absorbed by the shamelessness of the law; and in that respect, he is not quite melancholic enough to be genuinely *politically* melancholic. Gertrude, on the other hand, is *truly* melancholic in that she *does not know*. She has forgotten everything, including the law. That only means, however, that she remains unaware of the power of her own melancholia. In a sense, then, Hamlet, with his repeated "good nights" to Gertrude, needs his mother: needs her both to give him her flesh, and so retire, and also to remain in the somnambulant state of melancholia, the "witching time" that Hamlet, too, must learn to haunt (3.4.160ff; 3.3.396). This is the pivotal moment in the play, then, where melancholia is made to confront itself and, in the process, become political. Hamlet and Gertrude need one another.

What does it mean, after all, to dissolve the Oedipus complex? It means accepting that you will neither kill the father nor gain access to the mother's body. It means accepting the belief that you have been castrated, or might be castrated. It means buying into a quasi-legal order predicated on the dread of castration and the force of repression. Yet this is not quite what Hamlet accomplishes. He contracts the objectified phallus, thereby moving into the place of the dead father; but he does so without perpetuating an economy of substitution—that is, without endorsing an Oedipalized economy—while at the same time gaining access to the power embodied by Gertrude: the power of real flesh. Real flesh, the flesh of the world, exceeds representation.[32] In that respect, it remains out of debt to the phallus as S_1, the signifier invested with the power to represent the subject for all other signifiers. Exceeding and eluding the economy of lack and succession, flesh thwarts the felicitous marriage of the body and the state. Note, for example, that Gertrude shows little interest in the mourning rituals that would guarantee a future rooted in an economy of lack perpetuated by a particular use of the body and of life: procreation, reproduction, productivity. She flaunts her desire in such a way as to emphasize how little that desire is or can be overcoded with the biopolitical interests of the state. She has abundant desire, and yet, somehow, it seems to have no basis in castration.

Paradoxically, this lack of castration only ends up deepening—and, in deepening, undercutting—Hamlet's relationship to the institution or situation (to borrow a term from Alain Badiou) of which he is a part.[33] On the one hand, women in the play only seem to deepen, or at the very least solicit, identification with the institution and its needs. They serve as the physical conduit of population and succession. They speak to Hamlet normally, lovingly, and in perfectly rational terms. They care about Hamlet in a way that holds out the promise of earthly fulfillment. On the other hand, the same women serve as bearers of an Other jouissance not tied to the phallus or to a phallic economy of castration and lack. What their overbearing proximity bodies forth, then, is not lack but the lack of lack. Thus Hamlet's dilemma: How is he to disentangle that knotting together of two conceptions of fullness, the fantasy of earthly fulfillment versus the anxiety-provoking lack of lack? The first merely guarantees Hamlet's complete immersion in the institutional frame. The other constitutes a traversing of the same frame in order to touch upon "that within which passes show": the flesh that cannot be represented (1.2.85). This is how Hamlet at once realizes and dissolves the Oedipus complex: by gaining access to the flesh already at work in the institution of the body politic and its discourses. The point at which Gertrude and Ophelia are embedded in the life of the institution is the point at which Hamlet can reveal to the institution and its inhabitants something more about themselves than they can know, namely that they are immunized against their own internal workings.

The tension between body politic and flesh, played out mostly at the level of language, is evident from the very opening of the play: "Who's there?" That wary question, we noted earlier, can be read as announcing the arrival of the modern liberal subject. And yet to frame Hamlet, the character or the play, as a harbinger of the emergence of that subject is to neglect how much the flesh of the world precedes the modes of withdrawal and self-assertion that characterize modern immunitarianism.[34] That immunitarianism, always directed against flesh, is present to an almost stifling degree throughout Elsinore. It is there in the obsessively correctional speeches that both Laertes and Polonius deliver to Ophelia concerning her relationship with Hamlet, there in the spying that Rosencrantz and Guildenstern are sent to do against Hamlet (1.3, 2.1.74–120, 2.2.1–39, 225–327). Yet in the speeches given by Laertes and Polonius, especially, flesh rebels against the rhetorical invocations of the metaphor of the body politic, which is prevented from cohering precisely by the insistence of ungovernable flesh. What is the nature of that insistence? Hamlet's first soliloquy offers us a hint: "O! that this too, too sullied/solid flesh would melt" (1.2.129). Hamlet may claim that canon law prevents him from taking his own life, but really it is the solidity of flesh, which will not melt—which, even when sullied, remains still-living. There is a lot of shame, a lot of disgust coursing through Hamlet's language, but that is the point. Flesh marks the shame that arises in the face of the shamelessness of power. What appalls Hamlet, what he cannot get beyond, is that there resides, in the very midst of the state, a looseness, a wantonness, a shameful performance of power. Flesh rebels against that abuse of itself, that unapologetic abuse of power, that disgusting display of inherently illegitimate authority. But there is an alternative to be found in the immersion in real flesh, in the investigation of its workings within a body politic that seeks to banish it even as it flaunts its imaginary counterpart. Hamlet's wish to die from shame is his first insight, his first step toward recusing himself from the master-plot of procreation, perpetuation, revenge, succession: a master-plot organized around the seriality of exchangeable bodies. Hamlet's voluntary immersion in the realm of real flesh is his new reason for living.

Yet in an odd pairing, Hamlet turns out not to be the only character in the play to understand the stakes of flesh. Polonius does as well. The difference, however, is that whereas Hamlet declares his fidelity to the cause of flesh, enlisting himself in its service, Polonius's only loyalty is to immunitarian goals: to the smooth workings of the institution and the state, both of which can function apart from the sovereign that sits at their head (2.1.101–120; 2.2.40–167; 3.1-179–189). His investments are fundamentally disembodied: in the office and not its occupant, in the state and not the regime (2.2.44–45). Polonius, to put the matter otherwise, cares mostly about fortifying Elsinore against the threat of real flesh, and to such an extent as to suggest that he remains hypervigilant in the face of flesh, aware of its insistent presence to a degree that Claudius and Gertrude are not.

That vigilance manifests itself in Polonius's obsessive tutelage of his children, a regime of instruction that amounts to protecting flesh against flesh. A case in point is his first interaction with Ophelia, following immediately upon his first appearance on the stage, where an all too corporeal Hamlet has intruded into Ophelia's private room without a legible purpose, disheveled, his knees knocking, white as his shirt: an attitude that Polonius, as has surely been noted many times before, immediately reads as passion and affliction (2.1.84ff). Here Polonius insists on interpreting Hamlet's actions as the overexcitements of the body, and not surprisingly so; for one of the few ways that flesh can be allowed to express itself is as private, and therefore easily domesticated, passion (the mad passions of the lover, say, or the angry thirst for revenge) and not as the overbearingness of something so rotten in the state that it manifests itself in the symptomatic gestures of its prince. That Hamlet is neither mad lover nor raging avenger makes his appearance as flesh all the more upsetting to a figure like Polonius, whose duty, both as father and court-ier, is to police the borders of the body against the disruptions of the flesh. After all, if Hamlet is understood as a passionate lover, then it only requires a small turn to channel that passion into procreation and thus, in time, the production of new bodies to which the sovereign can lay claim. And if he is understood as a raging avenger, then it only requires a small turn to transform him into a custodian of the sovereign, working to replace bodies with bodies.

How ironic, then, that Polonius should be undone by flesh and transformed into flesh. At one point, when performing how Reynaldo should query strangers who might be able to report on Laertes's behav-ior abroad, Polonius forgets his lines, the lines of the role he can fall into so effortlessly: the role of spy (2.1.49–51). One can easily read this as a moment when an exhausted and mechanical political vocabulary suddenly runs into a dead end of self-erasure, of oblivion and forgetful-ness. In a flash, a whole tradition of improvisational courtiership seizes up, like a malfunctioning machine. Suddenly, Polonius loses his capac-ity to play the role at all, or at least not without some prompting, not without something supplementing for the loss of a genuine connection to his role. The performative language of immunitarianism—the lan-guage, that is, of the role that courtiers are expected to play—grinds to a halt. And that moment, that moment of immunitarian failure, that is the moment when shame flares up, the moment when Polonius, exposed and agitated, registers real flesh. Flesh shames the situation that cannot contain it, the situation that tries to control flesh but fails in the effort. And we, as spectators, are also left exposed, ashamed, unable to feed Polonius the lines that might salvage the moment and save this charac-ter from utter embarrassment, that might rescue him from flesh. To do so, however, would be to violate the fidelity to flesh that Polonius, for all intents and purposes, has declared already. Flesh has filled Polonius's mouth. Yet that flesh is more alive than the mechanical language of the court whose workings it disrupts. In the experience of shame, shame powerful enough to bring the court machine to a standstill, Polonius is granted a rare and fleeting moment of dignity.

From that point on, Polonius may continue to talk (and talk and talk), but he is little more than a vehicle for flesh. His smooth language has been compromised, rendered inoperative in its very use. It seems entirely fit-ting, then, that he should be killed by Hamlet during the closet scene and rendered flesh proper: that which is extracted—literally dragged—from the Oedipal plot (3.4.218). What Hamlet hopes to achieve by crystallizing the dissolution of the Oedipus complex—the mortification of the positions of father and mother—comes when Hamlet transforms the garrulous arch-plotter and busybody Polonius into the truly grave and silent material body. "[T]his counselor / Is now most still, most silent, most grave": Hamlet can only register Polonius's final tribute as a joke, a pun (3.4.214–215). Yet Hamlet has bestowed upon Polonius the status he always craved, that of the trusted courtier, precisely by taking him out of that very economy: the substitutional economy of the court, the economy in which one gives oneself over, shamefully, to the life of the institution, the economy in which life is allowed to betray life. This is the way of the melancholic; for the melancholic cannot give respect without registering, in ironic fashion, the ridicule that inheres in the acquisition of respectability—in the humiliations, degradations, and submissions that the institution extracts from its most devoted adherents. Hamlet, in reducing Polonius to flesh—most silent, most grave, soon to stink up Elsinore like a dead rat rotting in the wall, infusing the castle with an enjoyment not tied to the workings of the state—confers upon him a type of dignity even stranger and more rarefied (because more material) than that which Polonius achieved for himself when he forgot his lines. Polonius is silent and grave only in that his body, having been dragged out of circulation and made unavailable for the rituals of mourning, can no longer be made to speak on behalf of the state. Instead, his body generates the enjoyment of real flesh, gross and rank and putrid, offensive to the nostrils because no longer managed by the tongue: an enjoyment already circulating through the workings of the state whose representative Polonius has truly become, now that Hamlet has dragged him onto the side stage.

Yet Polonius, in adding a comic dimension to Hamlet's perverse restaging of the Oedipal drama, plays another crucial role in the development of the latter's counterplot. The Oedipal fantasy is at once realized and rendered inoperative in its overperformance. Hamlet enters boldly (and by invitation) into his mother's closet, where he proceeds to dispatch the old and impotent Polonius (a compromised father figure if there ever where one) before supplanting the ghost of his father with a specter of anxiety. In this one moment, then, Hamlet manages to actualize the ghost behind the father's ghost and the flesh behind the mother's flesh. No one in the play will go on to take Polonius's place; his flesh insists at the site where substitution might emerge or where we might expect to encounter the properly Oedipalized subject in its afterlife, following the dissolution of the Oedipus complex.

But there is no such afterlife in the play. Hamlet's flat admonitions to Gertrude, his treatment of the ghost as a distraction from the task at hand—a regression into "piteous action"—his elevation of the pathetic Polonius, whom he kills without remorse, to the place of the father in the Oedipal scene: all this points to how completely Hamlet has evacuated the Oedipal scenario through the act of realizing it (3.4.129). Gone are the guilt and the care, gone the search for a substitute, gone the fate of perpetuating the scenario as such, with its mandate of crime and punishment and submission. Hamlet has replaced these with the ghost, whose place he assumes and intensifies, and with flesh, which he accesses and embraces. His dissolution of the Oedipus complex formalizes, like Dürer's plan for a fortress, the mortification of that dissolution. The plot has been so thoroughly realized that no one may occupy it.

Hamlet's parodic restaging of the Oedipal drama may thus be read as a different sort of primal scene, one that emplots an alternative economy organized around something other than guilt or lack or conscience or any of the other payments extracted by an Oedipalized symbolic order. Following the closet scene, Hamlet no longer exhibits any guilt. Instead, he directs his energies toward the workings of a counterplot that will culminate in his establishment of a counterpolis, a city of the dead. The (re)appearance and subsequent disappearance of the ghost only serves to underscore this transformation. In the place of the afterlife of the Oedipal subject, Hamlet has substituted another afterlife altogether, one that consists of nothing but a perpetuation of the pathetic state of the ghost.

The Courtier-as-Event

So far, we have been charting Hamlet's larger melancholic-political mission, that of inscribing a counterplot. Now we turn to his primary tactic in that mission: seizing upon the courtier-as-event.[35] As we saw even with Dürer, the courtier is the event insofar as he functions, by his very activities as courtier, as a harbinger of the destruction of the situation, which in this case is defined by sovereign order or the institution. The courtiers who populate the darkened corridors, the "confines, wards, and dungeons," of Elsinore do not realize that they are the event, of course (2.2.250). They do not know that their over-identification with the sovereign or their commitment to preserving an immunitarian regime spells the end of the very sovereign order they serve. But Hamlet, in his fidelity to the lost cause, at least intuits as much. If nothing else, he knows to put direct, destructive pressure on the pathetic devotion that the courtier shows to the sovereign, knows that he need only intensify—and in intensifying, make more visible—the clandestine workings of power that the courtier naïvely repeats and repeats without thinking. The courtiers (and here we should recall that Hamlet numbers among them) draw out, by their intrigues and actions, the dead core of the situation—the shadow of the demise that their workings will bring about. The clamor of the courtier's state actions lends prosthetic support to a melancholic apparatus animated by a life that only masquerades as vitality. Let's call it a resuscitated life, a life sustained and suspended when the courtier expends his own germinating energies on servicing the sovereign's impotence. For that is what the courtier does: feeds off the sovereign's impotence, compensating for the latter's failures and shortcomings while remaining incapable even of contemplating how his very presence serves as an index of those same failures and shortcomings, that very impotence.

The evental nature of the courtier emerges at the intersection of immunitarianism and the death drive. Insisting on his civilized status, manifested in his service to the state: that is what the courtier arrays against the pressures of life—against all that we have associated with the too-much-ness of flesh. Yet that is not the courtier's only strategy. In ordinary melancholia, the death drive is directed inward; but the courtier turns the death drive outward, directing the cruelest energies of the superego against the external object—that is, against the most threatening eruptions of flesh. This much is all too evident in the workings of courtly life: in the intrigues, the conspiracies, the betrayals, the policing. Order has an enjoyment all its own. Yet we should understand how that particular enjoyment can be turned against itself. We have already noted how appeals to the metaphor of the body politic found in the play invariably succumb to the workings of flesh—flesh, which cannot be represented—within language. In a similar manner, the courtier occupies the darkened corners and out-of-the-way places in the prison that, according to Hamlet, simply is Denmark (2.2.247). That, then, is where one should look for the courtier: in the phantom limbs of the body politic. Courtiers body forth the flesh that augurs the demise of the body politic.

Consider how Rosencrantz and Guildenstern interact with Claudius and Gertrude in act 2. *Rosencrantz*: "Both your Majesties / Might, by the sovereign power you have of us, / Put your dread pleasures more into command / Than to entreaty." *Guildenstern*: "But we both obey, / And here give up ourselves in the full bent / To lay our service freely at your feet, / To be commanded" (2.2.27–32). It is not just that they essentially insist that the king and queen command them; it is that they conjure, through a particular use of language, a more powerful sovereign image than the one they see before them. Hamlet does something similar but intensifies it, conjuring a master shot through with flesh and anxiety, a sovereign conjured in all of his pathetic impotence. But back to Rosencrantz and Guildenstern. The point here is that they *over*-identify not only with the sovereign but with the institutional apparatus, at once conjuring and undermining the order they serve. They possess no genuine interior, no personal secrets. They are little more than ciphers, receptacles for state secrets. "Thanks, Rosencrantz and gentle Guildenstern," says Claudius. "Thanks, Guildenstern and gentle Rosencrantz," echoes Gertrude (2.2.33–34). And yet, paradoxically, the two courtiers do more than they need to do, more even than the state requires for its effective functioning. Going that extra mile, they perpetuate our knowledge of the pathetic reality of the state—its utter reliance on the functionaries who conjure it—even as they perpetuate the outward-directedness of the superegoic death drive. Thanks, indeed.

But here we should pause to reevaluate the death drive itself, even as it appears to be on the side of disciplinarity. At first glance, it might seem as though the courtier could not be an event precisely because the figure cannot be aligned with the traditional definition of the event as something spontaneous and eruptive. But in that respect the courtier is even more of an event insofar as he transforms the event into something plodding, incremental, machinelike in its repetition and lack of singularity. The courtier-as-event is fully in the situation that he systematically destroys. That reflects the death drive as entropic: a buildup of heat and tension that corresponds both to loss and to a too-much-ness that slowly overwhelms the circulation and distribution of energy within a closed system. There can be no promise of eschatology in such a system, no cathartic discharge of energy. There is only a repetition, a slow rotation, a withering away.

Repetition thus emerges as one of the techniques that Hamlet must wrest away from the courtier. The plotters who surround Hamlet have devoted themselves to a version of repetition that advances the plot by employing the logic of infinite substitutability found at the heart of the symbolic order. Move along, let go of the dead, nothing has happened: these are the orders that the courtier not only issues to the melancholic but that he uses to structure his own life in the hopes of keeping desire safely in check. And since those orders typically take the form of advice or counsel, it follows that Hamlet's struggle with the courtier over repetition should unfold around the language of advice, and around one form of that language in particular: the proverb. "The proverb," as Benjamin puts it in "The Storyteller," might be thought of "as an ideogram of a story. A proverb . . ." he continues, "is a ruin which stands on the site of an old story and in which a moral twines about a happening like ivy around a wall."[36] Repeating a moral dislodged from a story that, in its original form, had continued to develop over time, the proverb drops out of time only to return, as citation and fragment, to stifle further thought and arrest narrative progress. Where the mythical old story had been living, organic and robust—the narrative that a polity could tell itself about itself—the proverb is lifeless, dumb, inert, divorced from evolving forms of cultural production. This deadened quality makes the proverb useful, as a piece of counsel, only "for a few situations," according to Benjamin— as opposed to the story, which in the right hands can provide counsel in many different situations and elevate its teller to the ranks of the teacher and the sage.

It also means that the proverb can be used in one of two, apparently contradictory ways.[37] Polonius, for example, treats the proverb as a frozen index of hard-earned, communal wisdom, the sediment of a people's shared life. For Polonius, the proverb, affirming common knowledge and eliciting immediate recognition and assent, stands as the final measure of the health of the polity, the essence of all that should be passed on under the sign of tradition. One can no more argue with a given proverb than one could deconstruct the institution of the proverb as such. Yet it is precisely this fact that lends Hamlet's nonproverbial proverbs their authority; he invokes the commonsensical thrust of the proverb (itself a proverbial force on the order of "it is what it is" or "this is the way things are") only in order to show the proverb's tautological self-legitimation, the way its authority has no foundation other than its own claims to authority. Hamlet's proverbs display the naked self-authorization of a dead moral so as to strip it of its ability to reinvigorate the life and values of a culture. Proverbs, to paraphrase Nietzsche, are coins whose faces have been worn away. Passed from mouth to mouth, their origins unknown, proverbs are not spoken; they speak those who, like Polonius, traffic in them. To use a proverb in the way that Polonius does is to presume to conjure the spirit of a people. To use a proverb in the way that Hamlet does is to introduce a ghost into the *gestus* of a people. If the reader feels confused and befuddled by Hamlet's proverbs, it is because they ask us to have a knowledge we can't possibly have, to be familiar with a past that has yet to be. The force of Hamlet's nonproverbial proverbs lies in their ability to "ghostify" the reader, to ask us to conjure a "folk wisdom" that has never lived and that lacks a past wherein it might have originated. Hamlet's performance of his proverbs—proverbs, let us repeat, that have never before been heard—is convincing precisely because they seem to draw on the authority of a parallel gestus or counterhistory to the one assumed by those who say, for example, that all roads lead to Rome. Hamlet knows that Rome is a ruin.

For Hamlet, then, the proverb captures how the theater-idea of the Trauerspiel expresses the logic of the eventual act. He adheres to a repetition without model, a nonmimetic intervention without cause or purpose that deadens the paradigms of a given form of life. Building upon the pure repetition of the proverb, Hamlet calls up the eternal recurrence of the Same, making us aware of the disorienting, self-estranging knowledge that, unbeknownst to us, speaks through us in our voicing of the proverb. Introducing proverbs whose origins we can't possibly know, forcing us to contemplate the ruinous nature of the proverb—as if it were a fragment from another history—Hamlet gives us the language of the eventual act. Again, though, as with the courtier-as-event, that act is genuinely eventual in the sense of looking nothing like an event. The proverb affirms what is deemed worthy of returning and thus of affirming. Adding another turn, Hamlet's continued use of the proverb continually affirms, and so deems worthy of returning, what has never ceased to haunt us in the proverb, which is the disorienting proximity of a ghost that whispers, *You ought to know this! This ought to be common knowledge!* While Polonius implies that whoever knows the proverb shares in power and whoever doesn't is excluded, Hamlet implies that his proverbs cannot be shared and yet exclude no one. Since no one can own them, everyone is addressed by them. As in a social situation where no one wants to admit to not knowing something so familiar as a well-known proverb, Hamlet seduces us into rashly consenting to the revolutionary gestus we didn't know we know.

None of this—repetition, mortification, the externalization of the death drive, the courtier-as-event—can be separated, finally, from the role of play within the play. On the subject of play in *Hamlet*, we must quote—and, in quoting, contest—a long passage from Carl Schmitt. "[T]his drama," writes Schmitt,

> which never ceases to fascinate as a play, does not completely exhaust itself as play. It contains components that do not belong to the play and, in this sense, it is imperfect as play. There is no closed unity of time, place, and action, no pure internal process sufficient unto itself. It has two major openings through which historical time breaks into the time of the play, and through which this unpredictable current of ever-new interpretive possibilities, of ever-new, yet ultimately unsolvable, riddles flows into the otherwise so genuine play. Both intrusions—the taboo surrounding the guilt of the queen and the distortion of the

avenger that leads to the Hamletization of the hero—are shadows, two dark areas. They are in no sense mere historical-political connections, neither simple allusions nor true mirrorings, but rather two given circumstances that are received and respected by the play and around which the play timidly maneuvers. They disturb the unintentional character of pure play and, in this respect, are a *minus*. Nevertheless, they made it possible for the figure of Hamlet to become a true myth. In this respect they are a plus, because they succeeded in elevating *Trauerspiel* to tragedy.[38]

We would amend this argument in several ways. Schmitt contends, as part of his larger project of revitalizing—of making present—the sovereign figure he detects lurking behind the composite figure of Hamlet-James I, that the absence of mediating play in *Hamlet* allows for the play itself to rise to the level of authentic tragedy. Yet such a contention rests on the assumption that the real that intrudes into the time of the play would be understood, even by Hamlet himself, as necessarily scandalous or tragic and not as what it is: Hamlet's object and his cause. Hamlet's form of play—his manipulation of language, his feigning of madness, his self-alignment with the courtier-as-event—does not inhibit tragedy; it is what brings the source of the tragic, namely, "originary conflict," to light. The twist, however, is that while such shadowy conflict may be tragic for Schmitt, it is decidedly not tragic for Hamlet. Tragedy, in fact, is what Hamlet drains from the position of sovereign precisely by forcing the would-be occupants of that position to become absorbed—and in becoming absorbed, be rendered pathetic—in his own melancholic object, which Schmitt mistakenly identifies as the historical real. Truly, Hamlet allows for a fissure to open up in the time of the play; but that fissure, that eruption of the real, is less an intrusion of the historical real than it is an intrusion of the real (cause) brought about by Hamlet's cunning deployment of one aspect of the historical real: the fabrication, improvisation, and "self-fashioning"—in a word, the play—associated with the courtier.

Commenting on the passage from Schmitt quoted above, Jennifer Rust and Julia Lupton write that

the *minus* or negative space of these intrusions [of historical time] becomes a *plus* insofar as they interrupt the pure "*Spiel*" of the Trauerspiel with the "tragic" weight of genuine historicity, a weight that becomes a void with the passage of time, a cryptic cipher continually refilled by philosophical or psychoanalytical speculation. The *Einbruch*, in short, functions as the exception to the normative order of representation that, far from damaging the play, intensifies its dramatic effect.

Like the sovereign's decision, the intrusion of real time into the play of representation functions as a creation *ex nihilo*, inserting a negative space into the drama around which new forms of imaginative encounter can take place.[39]

The "new forms of imaginative encounter" Rust and Lupton allude to here are those accorded the philosophical or psychoanalytic reader of *Hamlet* the play, who gets to fill the void in legibility left behind by the passage of time with critical speculation. But let us not forget that there is another form of imaginative encounter modeled in the play itself, and that is the melancholic reality-testing practiced by Hamlet. Looking about him, Hamlet sees nothing but shamelessness and oblivion; meanwhile, he is accosted on all sides, even through the ghost, by the injunctions of the symbolic order: mourn and forget, accept an appropriate substitute for what is lost, assume the tragic necessity of your mandate and your investiture. Faced with such an impoverished reality, Hamlet reacts as any melancholic would, with a discontent that borders on disgust. But he does not stop there. Instead, he takes up the arms of fury and resolve and, using the imaginative engagement peculiar to the melancholic—the capacity to hold on to the lost object, to imagine an alternative to a corrupt history rooted in lack—mounts a counterplot, feigning madness to draw out the genuine madness, the anarchic unsaid, at the heart of Elsinore's *nomos*.[40] The negative space that Schmitt registers as the remainder left behind once historical time has been subjected to the decay of historical knowledge, we then register as the decay of historical time under the pressure of the lost object, of which "aught" can be known. This could not happen without the use of play. And yet courtly improvisation, understood as the continuous making and unmaking of self-assemblages, is clearly not what Hamlet has in mind when he begins to play; it is to do whatever it takes to stage an encounter with the object. He is the player who, knowing not "seems," uses play to introduce the real into the time of Elsinore.[41]

This is what makes Hamlet's strange encounter with the plotter Osric so intriguing (5.2.81ff). One has to wonder, in the first place, why Hamlet even bothers with Osric; he hardly seems worth the effort. But more pointedly, one has to marvel at Hamlet's audacity in criticizing Osric's speech. Here is the same Hamlet who deploys feigned madness—a kind of playing—in the process of objectifying the phallus, of dissolving the phallus as the groundless ground, the here and everywhere, of signification. It was Hamlet, after all, who made it possible for flesh to overwhelm language. So why would he and Horatio mock Osric when the latter's language runs dry or when he traffics in the language of the time, which is a performative language, a fashioned (and fashionable) language hollowed out by Hamlet himself? Partly this has to do with a certain severity on Hamlet's part. Hamlet has already taken all of the license of play for himself, insofar as he has feigned the anxiety object into revealing itself. His dissolution of play as anything other than the revelation of the real has brought to light the "it is" that "passes show," the real that exceeds representation. Hamlet has left himself, at least, no escape routes. Yet that does not mean that no escape routes exist for the other inhabitants of Elsinore. It only means that to take advantage of those routes is monstrous; for to play any other role than that of Hamlet in the wake of Hamlet is disingenuous. Yet that monstrousness only intensifies, in turn, the upsetting nature of Osric's continued presence, his insistence within the scene. Just prior to Osric's appearance, Hamlet had been waxing sentimental: "But I am very sorry, good Horatio, / That to Laertes I forgot myself, / For by the image of my cause I see / The portraiture of his. I'll court his favors" (5.2.75–78). Osric's repeated returns make it impossible for Hamlet to maintain this fleeting fantasy of brotherhood with Laertes. Such an imaginary community, based on the mere "image" of cause, could never be. Osric, then, fulfills his duty as courtier in fittingly ironic fashion, recalling Hamlet to his true cause, which only reveals itself in repetition, in the grinding, insistent event of the courtier. This is what Hamlet must lay claim to: the event of the courtier, an event that undoes the prior meaning of event as necessarily improvisational and spur of the moment, a temporary forgetting of one's self that leads to a recollection of one's self.

But the grotesque image of Osric as a "lapwing [running] away with the shell on his head" also draws our attention to the infrahuman dimension of the evental nature of the courtier (5.2.187). Even when playing, even when working and plotting—simply by doing those things—the courtier perpetuates a natural historical crisis within the very walls of Elsinore. This is what Hamlet must also conjure, since it fundamentally conjures a skeletal master; and so it is to natural history—and to the event as natural historical and not spontaneous, the event as truly revolutionary—that we now turn.

Natural History

Schmitt, in one of the great near-misses of twentieth-century criticism, contends that the many enigmas of *Hamlet* can be traced to the intrusion of historical time into the time of the play. Those intrusions of historical time register, according to Schmitt, as ciphered traces of real-life scandal:

the taboo of the queen, the composite figure of Hamlet-James I. The tragic dimension of the play then arises from how the conflict behind those intrusions, barbaric in their lack of mediation, their vital force, disrupts the order of the play and, beyond that, of early modern Europe in the wake of religious schism. So much has been lost, in Schmitt's view. Our own view, taken from the wings, is different. As we see it, the reference to the turmoil of roguish barbarism, and to the dynamic of exile and return that accompanies it, indicates that what intrudes into the play is not historical time but rather the tumultuous workings of another time, the time of natural history. If Schmitt is right that the play is no longer fully legible, it is not simply because we have lost our knowledge of the historical scandal encoded by its language. It is because natural history eats away even at the sense, the order, of the play, while introducing another sense that can only be extracted, as Schmitt clearly perceived, through a form of immanent criticism. But where Schmitt sought to use history to revitalize the lost order of the play, we want to understand how the intrusion of natural history into the time of the play calls that very order to account. We want to understand how the physionomos of natural history, to which Hamlet becomes more and more attuned as the play wears on, reveals to nomos its own shamelessness.

The natural historical strain in the play, a strain intimately tied to what we have been calling the courtier-as-event, finds its fullest expression in the "Mousetrap," the play-within-the-play of act 3, and in the graveyard scene at the beginning of act 5; but it is present from the first. And indeed, that is the point: it falls to Hamlet to intensify the workings of natural history already encrypted in the mundane life and everyday language of Elsinore. One of the first things Hamlet says to Polonius, for example, is "you are a fishmonger," an insult with multiple associations: trafficking in dead flesh; smelling up the Agora (as Polonius will do when he becomes a dead rat); the reduction of language to a vehicle, repetitious and hyperbolic, of commerce (2.2174). There is an enjoyment to Polonius's "courtierese," a near-zero degree of rote senselessness, of which he himself seems unaware, despite—or perhaps because of—the fact that it keeps the wheels of the immunitarian state greased and turning, endlessly converting a truly ungovernable jouissance into the property of the state. But Hamlet, the mad allegorician, with his freewheeling speech, goes one step further by deanimating Polonius's already undead, state-sanctioned enjoyment.[42] "For the sun breeds maggots in a dead dog," he says, "being good kissing carrion" (2.2.181–183). Hamlet, the sun/son who is himself too much in both, uses language to enliven dead matter only to speed up the natural historical process of decomposition. And the image works, stopping Polonius dead in his rhetorical tracks, forcing him to contemplate the melancholic core—the repetition of "words, words, words"—of his own courtierese. Hamlet's is a peculiarly senseless-efficacious language, the perfect inverse of the pragmatic, instrumental language of the state: a speech composed in order to decompose, to deanimate what is already degraded.

So Polonius, who traffics in that degraded language of the state, is a fishmonger, a merchant peddling the enjoyment that Hamlet then uses to undermine the foundations of Elsinore precisely by intensifying the natural historical repetition already at work in the garrulous busyness of the courtier. Yet Polonius is not the only courtier who, in his discrete language, in his intrigues and solicitous concern for the well-being of the prince, serves as a vehicle for natural history. Hamlet, when speaking to Guildenstern in 2.2, just before Polonius returns, avers that he knows "a hawk from a handsaw" (2.2.388)—a pun on birds and implements (a pickax and a carpenter's tool/heron) that already suggests how thoroughly the animal world of natural historical transformation has converged with language and how completely Hamlet has seized upon that conflation as a tool of political melancholia. And this is but one example of how an animal seems to show up, in language at least, every time a courtier appears or is mentioned: woodcock, camel, weasel, whale, fanged adders, crab, rat, and, of course, worms. Over time, the play becomes crowded with courtiers and their animal familiars. This is Hamlet's great insight, his attentiveness to the animal within the courtier (and here we should recall that Hamlet, when removing Polonius's body, drags it into a small chamber, like an animal dragging its kill back to its den). This is not to say that courtiers are simply animal-like. It is that they act as harbingers, emissaries, of the natural historical realm that will eventually undermine the world of the court. This is what Hamlet sees: that the added capacity for politics that, according to Aristotle, distinguishes the human animal is what degrades the courtier; and that the hope of the courtier, his chance at redemption from the world of the court, lies in his unwitting alliance with natural history. In this way, natural history collapses into the courtier-as-event—as natural historical event.

That natural historical event culminates, appropriately enough, in the Mousetrap, the play-within-the-play that is really the heart of *Hamlet*, its metatruth, "unkennel[ed]" by Hamlet (3.2.83). The Mousetrap is meant to surveil Claudius, to catch his conscience; and in that respect, the play merely capitalizes on the atmosphere already present in Elsinore, an atmosphere of wary gazes and "lawful espials," a theater in which "madness in great ones" never goes unwatched: a theater of luring, of stalking and catching, of fishing and hunting, of chasing prey (3.1.32, 191). "Hide fox, and all after," as Hamlet puts it, already noting the relation between policing and noble pastime. Hamlet's challenge is thus to turn the already cruel theater of Elsinore against itself (4.2.30–31).

Yet Hamlet must also be transformed, and the Mousetrap accomplishes that as well. When initially contemplating the ruse of the play, Hamlet relies on the most mainstream aesthetic conventions of early modern humanism. Language is natural, the language of animals is gestural and dumb, there exists a rational hierarchy, and so on. Such conventions rest on the assumption that all which can be expressed already exists in nature and that human language must simply imitate it—not, as will prove to be the case, that expressions and gestures can take on a life of their own and actively transform the natural model itself. Analogously, Hamlet begins by assuming that his play will induce regression in Claudius—that Claudius's conscience, having been made evident, will be revealed to all. It is such humanistic assumptions about theater that the Mousetrap will itself debunk.

The fantasy has it that Claudius's occulted guilt will be "unkennel[ed]": uncovered or brought to light, released from its confinement. Yet such a humanistic assumption fails to reckon with what it denies: that there can be a perverse nature, a horrifying action, a poisonous word, a distorted mirror. To "unkennel," as it turns out, is not to "uncover" or "expose to the light of day"; nor does it mean to unleash or set free so that the guilty man's conscience will run down the guilty man himself. There follows no revelation, no admission of guilt, no overt punishment. For who can predict what game the unkenneled dog will pursue or, more to the point, what forces the dog, once unleashed, will unleash in turn? Thus it is with the dumb show, the enigmatic power of which ends up transforming both Claudius and Hamlet. Evidently the play upsets all those who are made to watch it. But aside from Hamlet and Horatio, only Claudius has a clear idea of the subject matter of the play and what it portends: that the enjoyment he had thought was secret has now been unkenneled, that it is both too much his and no longer his own. Crucially, though, this is something other than the perverse sovereign-transgressive enjoyment that Claudius had imagined himself to wield. To reveal the king as what Lacan called the Great Fucker is no particular feat; that, after all, would only confirm the sovereign's status as primal, exceptional, enthralled by the transgressive jouissance to which he alone may lay claim.[43] The stiff and gestural theater of the Mousetrap does something much more radical: it confronts Claudius with his own transgressive fantasy, but drained of all its liveliness and enjoyment. Truly, the king is revealed to himself as a thing of nothing—a deadened, mute, and mortified thing denied further access to the transgressive enjoyment of his crime, a spectator of a dumb show whose frozen gestures intersect with his own drained interior.

Rather, then, than inducing regression in the king—reducing him to his animalistic state by turning him into a "mouse," a "deer," a "jade," or even a "peacock"—the play-within-the-play entraps Claudius, enthralling him not in "his" transgressive enjoyment but in the petrified enjoyment being staged before him. It is not the conscience of the king that gets caught by the play. The king himself is revealed to himself as the captivated creature he fundamentally is: frozen, trapped, isolated, and exposed to his shame, his enjoyment returned to him as something mortified, drained of all its liveliness.

As we say, though, Claudius is not the only character to be transformed by the natural historical pull of the Mousetrap. Hamlet is also changed. Before, Hamlet had sided with a philosophy of language that depreciated the dumb, gestural language of nature. But there is something in the very dumbness of the dumb show that opens his eyes to the transformational force that draws the king down and out, away from his humanistic essence. From that point on, Hamlet allows himself to be seized by the gestural theater and its capacity not only to drain the liveliness from the sovereign's enjoyment but to return that enjoyment to the king in mortified form, useless to power. Before this point, Hamlet was half actor and half onlooker. Now his share in the action induced by the play is, as he says to Horatio, "whole" (3.2.286). The "whole" Hamlet now gives himself over to the "company" of players that, dead or alive, make up a theater of transformation and destruction. "I'll take the ghost's word for a thousand pound," declares Hamlet after a visibly stricken Claudius has fled the scene (3.2.292–293). Yet this is more than a declaration of belief in the ghost's story or a confirmation of Claudius's guilt. The ghost's word, confirmed and grounded by a mute, gestural dumb show, is more than a mere word. It is sound enough, and disturbing enough—altogether substantive enough—to warrant investment in a destructive theater "company" (3.2.284) The word in question properly belongs neither to the ghost nor to Hamlet, to no one, really, but also to both of them and to everyone. Assuming the same role as the ghost, Hamlet too begins to act as the mole-pioneer, burrowing away in the understage of Elsinore, mining deeper than those who plot against him. Where before Hamlet had begun by paying lip service to the conventions of an early modern humanistic theater, convinced as he was that the play would extract a confession of guilt from Claudius, the taste he gets of some "talk of poisoning" hastens his transformation into the destructive character at large in the play (3.2.295). But he becomes that character not by default but through his fidelity to a word that does not accord with the words around it—that in fact gums up the metered speech of the court by inviting, in the form of a "payjock" that gratuitously fails to rhyme, the eruption of natural history into the linguistic makeup of the play (3.2.290). It is that force that ends up capturing the king, albeit at a point other than conscience.

This conflation of natural history and language only intensifies as the play wears on. The language of act 4, for example, becomes overwhelmed by natural historical substances beyond the reach of sovereign control: whispers, mobs, worms that feed indifferently on the corpses of lean beggars and fat kings. One can hear as much in the speech of Claudius and Gertrude: Gertrude, who paradoxically commands Rosencrantz and Guildenstern to "bestow" the royal palace upon its own occupants; Claudius, who detects his impending usurpation in the superfluous deaths inflicted upon him by the murmurs and whisperings of the mob (4.14; 4.5.77–96). The courtier-as-event converges with the general intellect in the service of natural historical transformation, and the rigid language of the court proves to be no match for it.

Hamlet's soliloquy in act 4 offers a case in point. Strictly speaking, this particular soliloquy betrays many of the hallmarks of clinical melancholia, self-laceration and self-denigration chief among them. What is wrong with me? Hamlet wonders. Why can I not sustain a cause (4.4.32–66)? Yet the same soliloquy also presents us with something like a limit case of melancholia. Melancholia turns all earthly causes to dirt. What then does it have left to defile, other than itself and its own lost cause? Hamlet wastes no time in debunking, even at the level of affect, the easy exit strategies of conquest and revenge. The ghost is pathetic, Claudius is a king of shreds and patches, Gertrude is oblivious: Hamlet revisits the stations of the revenge drama one last time, but without any enthusiasm. It is the first plot to be drained of all of its grandeur and enjoyment. But then Hamlet's strategy is to drain all plots of their putative greatness. Revenge, conquest: these plots are simply too small and inconsequential in comparison to Hamlet's counterplot—too small even to accommodate the graves they generate. Hamlet's counterplot at least assumes its own insufficiency, its own inability to contain the dead. Graves do not need plots; embedded in the realm of natural historical decay, the realm of worms, they actively, inexorably participate in the work of melancholic unplotting. All causes, along with all of the plots that might be used to pursue them, are inadequate, inherently lost in relation to the grave. The only worthy cause left is thus to wear down all lost causes, even and especially—or rather, finally—the lost cause of melancholic thought itself. Hamlet berates himself for not acting when he has cause, strength, and worth to do so. Yet he continues to think, and that raises the question: Can thought itself be transformed into those same three qualities? Can thought itself function as cause, strength, and worth? Hamlet ends his soliloquy by declaring that henceforth his thoughts—but only his thoughts—will be "bloody." Even the organic matter of blood will be disembodied, transfigured, melted into air. And then, in the consummate turn of his melancholic unplotting, Hamlet even curses ("bloody") thought. Simultaneously fulfilling and destroying his own melancholic counterplot, Hamlet defiles thought and turns its transformative power back upon itself.

By this point, it is clear that there are two planes, two forms of speech, in the play: one spectral, metaphorical, and uneconomical—in a word, natural historical—and the other concrete, instrumental, duplicitous, and economical, the language of the intriguer. Laertes, for example, in his own naïve way, is particularly adept at the latter. He speaks in equations; his talk revolves around balances, quotients, and compensations (4.5.115–163). Even nature gets enlisted in his economic logic of equity. Laertes wants redress, and Claudius is only too happy to promise it to him in exchange— always in exchange—for helping the king carry out his own murderous, managerial plot.

In response, Ophelia sings the words of an uneconomical physiono-mos, another law (4.5.164–198). Laertes speaks of rights, of recompense, of what is owed. Ophelia sing-speaks a language of pure loss, loss that cannot be recouped by the language, ritualized and evasive, of the court: the language of revenge and legal redress, of official mourning. Ophelia casts away everything, even "moan." Her language ("stole") disrupts the very language of rights and indebtedness and orderly repayments invoked by her brother. Yet in that, she confers some dignity upon her father by turning him into what he had not been before: an object worthy of being lamented. Institutional language would only degrade Polonius, degrade him even further than it had when he was alive to speak it. Ophelia does her father the honor of continuing Hamlet's work of embedding Polonius in natural history, something her brother, still in thrall to the language that humiliated Polonius while alive, cannot do.

And when Ophelia herself dies, she passes along that power, the power of natural historical speech, to Gertrude, who honors Ophelia by making her an object of lamentation in her turn (4.7.163–183). Such transference is entirely fitting. Gertrude, the source of the play's mother tongue—the melancholic object incorporated by Hamlet and then disseminated by him into the discourses of the court—now functions as the mouthpiece for a hypermetaphorical speech that even Laertes recognizes as being "more than matter" (4.5.173). The mad Ophelia enters reciting a taxonomy of flowers, and Gertrude's lament for the drowned Ophelia continues the theme. Unlike just about everything else in Elsinore, flowers cannot be instrumentalized. They bloom, they get picked, they wither and die, they delight or offend the senses. Perhaps we can say the same thing about the use of metaphor; Gertrude's floral-heavy lament for Ophelia is fecund in its very deathlike imagery (and vice versa). It breeds like maggots in a dead dog lying in the sun. We are shamed at this moment into realizing that the purely metaphorical and figurative cannot be dismissed as something irrational and presymbolic. We are made to feel instead that it possesses a language and a logic all its own, that it simply *is* language at its most glorious and uncourtly, its most blissfully uneconomical. The insistence of metaphoricity crowds out all other uses of language. By comparison, all other forms of speech seem corrupt, evasive, serviceable, choked with stale enjoyment. Courtly speech can only perform "obscure funeral[s]"; metaphoricity conjures specters (4.6.211). Again, though, that is not to say that such language misses logic and sense. On the contrary, the laments of both Ophelia and Gertrude have a decorum of their own: a musicality, and a tempo, and a sensory order. Lamentation shades into delight. But their logic is physionomical, indifferent to sovereign authorization. Thus Gertrude's depiction of Ophelia's death manages to capture, in a grand metaphor, the underlying logic of Hamlet's own melancholic unplotting. What kept Ophelia afloat in time—the thing that sustained her, the thing she worked for, the "element" in which she moved—is what eventually drags her down and out of time, and thence into natural history. At the moment of her passing, Ophelia comes to occupy the same critical register as the courtier-as-event.

The two clowns in act 5 perceive as much. They understand Ophelia's death for what it is: the expression of a death drive. Moreover, they understand that an expression of death drive among the nobility must be denied, covered over, hastily buried in consecrated ground (5.1.1–30). But then, the clowns would be apt to understand as much, already being allies, by virtue of their occupation, in the larger project of melancholic unplotting. The clowns here, and the gravedigger in particular, betray no commitment to an ethics of remembrance. Neither do they seem traumatized by their proximity to death or awestruck by the solemnity of the gravedigger's office. The gravedigger's job absorbs him in the administration, the continual filing and refiling, of bones. He throws up bones for contemplation—that is, as objects facilitating absorption in the workings of natural history—not for nostalgic recollection (5.1.66–120). The scene is not to be understood as an extended indulgence in memento mori; for nothing is remembered here, least of all the finality of death. Stories of past lives emerge with every unearthed bone; but that is only because those stories find their everlasting persistence in the material of the bones themselves. Lives, archived in the bones, are reanimated only by the contemplation of those bones. The absence of sentimentality surrounding lives once lived, of nostalgia surrounding past greatness, is striking. Yet the gravedigger's peculiar humor, coupled with his fidelity to the bones he administers as bones—his single-minded dedication to an ongoing task unrelieved by any overarching redemptive scheme— forbids such gestures. At this point, in fact, the gravedigger might be said to out-Hamlet Hamlet. Heretofore, Hamlet had been the agent of melancholia, the consummate student of bones. But here he meets his match in a figure whose "Hamletization" is already complete in its wittiness, its fidelity, and in its mastery of the repetitive techniques needed to organize the remains of the dead. "How absolute the knave is!" exclaims Hamlet to Horatio. "We must speak by the card, or equivocation will undo us" (5.1.139–140). The gravedigger is a strict literalist, attuned even to the density, the material baseness, of language. His absolute, uncompromising devotion is not, however, to the maintenance of hallowed ground but to the real "ground . . . in Denmark," a ground teeming with jawbones, skulls, sheepskins, parchments, worms, spades, dead letters, puns, dates, proverbs, and the long-lasting "houses" of the dead (5.1.60–164). If there is any redemption to be found in his work, it must wait until doomsday; but even the prospect of a doomsday is unwelcome, since it will only damage the gravedigger's "houses." Confronted with such refreshing frankness, Hamlet seems uncertain whether he should be disgusted or impressed. Yet it soon becomes apparent that the gravedigger is the only figure Hamlet truly admires, recognizing him as his only real peer when it comes to the endless grind of an unplotting carried out at the level of language.

And so they begin to play, to pun. Back and forth: the courtier becomes a worm, the lawyer fine dirt, their papers and dossiers dust (5.1.76–114). Their bones long outlast their terrestrial existence, leaving the lives they led to feed speculation and contemplation—and, beyond that, mockery and derision. The courtiers, lawyers, great politicians, and heroic warriors who once lived lives of institutional grandeur and world-historical signifi- cance now assume their most enduring role: that of having their bones sifted and sorted under the administration of the gravedigger. As Ham- let quickly perceives, that administration is fundamentally allegorical, in the Benjaminian sense of the term: a contemplation of the material that enables linguistic rearrangement; a sorting and a sifting and an infinite piling up.[44] At the end of a long metabolic-metaphorical process, Alexander has been transformed into loam used to stop up a bunghole, Caesar into clay used to fill a gap where the wind gets in (5.1.204–219). A life of greatness gets transformed at last into the material, inert and yet endlessly proliferating, of allegorisis.

Yet this transformation happens not only with bones and the memories attached to them. The gravedigger also imposes it upon language. For just as his bones provide the material for his puns, so his puns are like bones: inert and yet demanding of attention, the afterlife of a thought and yet bereft of a "world" (to invoke Heidegger) in which they would make sense or find a purpose. Such a world, in fact, no longer exists for the gravedigger in any practical sense. Every word he takes up, every bone he unearths, immediately loses its worldliness and gets archived—sorted, as it were—into something other than chronological time. The gravedigger measures time differently, simultaneously accumulating and exhausting it: in long intervals (thirty years); in converging events (such as the fact that the gravedigger began his job on the day that Hamlet *père* defeated Fortinbras, which also happens to be the day that young Hamlet was born); in the duration of his "houses" (5.1.146–175). While the clamor of monumental history goes on around him, the gravedigger persists in a form of unsentimental labor—a continual grinding away, an endless round of burying and unearthing—that absorbs him in another realm, another time, more authentic than the scheming world of Elsinore.

Hamlet, inspired by this encounter with a kindred spirit (the work of the gravedigger being much like that of the courtier-as-event), then begins to contemplate Yorick's skull, which he has just picked up (5.1.185–197). All at once, time collapses, and we realize that Yorick had been the "loam," so to speak, in Hamlet's earlier life: both the product and the embodiment of the melancholic disposition; a model, archived in the earth and administered by the gravedigger, for what Hamlet would later become. In life, Yorick's words had been transient and ephemeral, his actions mocking and self-defeating. But now, the rictus of the skull persists as the afterlife, inert and efficacious, of that mockery, outlasting even Alexander's worldly exploits—until finally, in death, the "infinite jest" of Yorick's life becomes the object of Hamlet's melancholic contemplation (5.1.186–187). Outlasting its day, confusing time, the persistent "grinning" of Yorick's skull casts a mocking, retroactive light on the schemes of the courtier, the subtleties of the lawyer, and the battle plans of the warrior. More powerful in death than any ruler is in life,

Yorick continues to play out his infinite jest long into the future, his skull having been transformed into the echo chamber of a "roar" that, mocking the past that once included it, splits the present from its self-absorption. We see, then, that even in life, the jester had already been what his skull will allow others to become long after he is dead: an allegorician with the power to dissipate the eschatological force of the sovereign word by subjecting it to citation, cannibalization, and ironic mortification.[45] And we see as well that the gravedigger is but another jester, an allegorician of bones, unearthing matter earlier, and in another place, than that called for in any eschatological plan, setting time itself on a roar. And we see, too, that Hamlet is an apt apprentice of Yorick's jest, for his contemplation of the jester's skull transports him to the time of his childhood, a time filled with singular and unique moments, a time so different from that of his present, rife as it is with murder, plots, and mayhem. Pah!

And does it not make perfect sense that this scene with the gravedigger should follow Hamlet's return from a trip meant to bring about his death (4.7.43–48)? It is as if Hamlet were living on borrowed time, as if whatever had sustained his investment in the present of the play had been given up for a more genuine interaction with a more authentic world, a world where Hamlet truly belongs. In stark contrast to how he acts in the crisis-ridden world of Elsinore, Hamlet is here serenely quiet, as close to being at peace with himself as we have seen. But that is to be expected. Where so much of the rest of the play remains caught up in the clamor of the present, its crimes and its chaos, this scene unfolds in a time after the worst has already happened. And now that the catastrophe has come and gone, and now that Hamlet has accepted as much, we at last enter upon the outskirts of a functioning polis, a workaday world of transformative, repetitive labor. Elsewhere, the state is in turmoil, consumed with the task of forestalling the worst. The gravedigger operates in a realm at once adjacent to that one and yet strangely untouched by its machinations. No one here is concerned with hatching schemes to prevent the catastrophe from happening. They work in the midst of the worst. And it seems entirely fitting that Hamlet should find his place among them and that they should aid him in the task of unplotting the community that exiled him.

Hamlet's *Ends*

Act 5, scene 2: We find Hamlet speaking to Horatio, recounting the tale, which he refers to as a "play," of how he outplotted Rosencrantz and Guildenstern and escaped the death sentence contrived for him by Claudius.

"Our indiscretion sometimes serves us well," he says, "when our deep plots do pall" (5.2.8–9). Plots have been central to Hamlet's fortunes from the beginning, but he, too, has been plotting, preparing the ground for another type of edifice, erected on another type of foundation. What is left to us when our deep plots, our sustaining fictions, "do pall": When they become worn out and exhausted, drained of vitality, revealed as little more than a cover used to conceal the dead? Our best option at that point is a certain indiscretion, a certain disrespect for secret machinations, a certain refusal of shame and guilt, a certain willingness to turn discretion, the courtier's greatest virtue, against the institution that virtue serves or to employ a half-forgotten ability to "write fair" against the "statists" who equate clarity with "baseness" (5.2.33–35). Such, then, is the deep plot, the self-palling plot, set in motion by a Hamlet "benetted round with villains": an auto-dissolving foundation authorized by a certain indiscretion, a certain boldness (5.2.29). That is the new "fortress," the new polis, that Hamlet will simultaneously establish and abolish, much as Benjamin claims the play *Hamlet* does its genre.

Accordingly, we want to try to understand Hamlet's treatment of his erstwhile companions—his outplotting of Rosencrantz and Guildenstern and his use of Horatio as a sometime confidant—as part of a larger pattern of betrayal; for in its patient work of mining, as in its sustained absorption in natural history, Hamlet's melancholic unplotting betrays a status quo that knows nothing other than betrayal. But that is true only up to a point, given that Hamlet never stops being a prince, never renounces his social position, even in spite of the fact that he resists Claudius's early overture "to remain / Here in the cheer and comfort of our eye, / Our chiefest courtier, cousin, and our son" (1.2.115–117). This failure of Hamlet's to abdicate leads to an odd interaction between him and Horatio during the graveyard scene, when Horatio, responding to Hamlet's fanciful mockery, skull in hand, "of a courtier, which could say 'Good morrow, sweet lord! How dost thou, sweet lord?'" answers with an "Ay, my lord" of his own (5.1.83–88). Horatio is no doubt indulging in some irony. Even so, what other choice does he have? The system hasn't suddenly collapsed. The asymmetrical nature of Hamlet's and Horatio's positions—one a prince, the other a student of no discernable pedigree—still obtains. But that is merely consistent with Hamlet's melancholic unplotting, from which he has never exempted himself. For while it may be true that Hamlet retains the title of prince, it is equally true that he has made a point of hollowing out that same position, draining it of all its sovereign splendor. That, in a sense, is Hamlet's greatest betrayal: the simultaneous evacuation and perpetuation of his own royal position. To the list of those things that are rotten in Denmark, Hamlet adds the title of prince.

But does Hamlet then betray his own betrayal? "The rest is silence": so run Hamlet's famous last words (5.2.359). Yet shouldn't Hamlet remain entirely silent—silent and grave, in the manner of courtier-as-event or the inexorable grinding and mining of natural history—if he wants to maintain fidelity to his lost cause right until the very end? Perhaps. But why should he betray his cause by remaining utterly silent, and so risk letting his cause die with him, when he could betray his betrayal by speaking up and so complete his betrayal by giving his cause an afterlife? Here we see the cunning of political melancholia at work. Hamlet's first strategic betrayal is to give the duly elected Fortinbras his "dying voice" (5.2.357). This is an act of haunting, not a political endorsement. Now Fortinbras cannot speak without allowing Hamlet's dying voice (a natural historical voice if ever there were one) to be heard through the dead cant of officialdom. To the ears of anyone who has attended carefully to the play, Fortinbras can only sound shamefully disingenuous. So let him speak; all that can be heard is Hamlet's encrypted voice, the paradoxical dying voice of silence, hollowing out the sovereign word.[46]

Hamlet's other strategic betrayal of his own betrayal, by far the more significant of the two, involves rallying Horatio to his cause (a word, we should note, that comes up repeatedly as the play winds down [5.2.340, 384, 392]). Hamlet, in what amounts to his last act as prince, commands Horatio, who is in no position to refuse, to perpetuate his cause. He could not have chosen better; for almost immediately Horatio, the assiduous and well-meaning scholar, begins to betray Hamlet's melancholic betrayal of an inherently treacherous status quo. It may not sound that way at first. On the contrary, one can detect something like an intensification of Hamlet's betrayal of betrayal in the way that Horatio speaks to Fortinbras, telling him that his tale will serve as a vehicle for a "cause" authorized by a "mouth" whose "voice" will continue, like the rictus of Yorick's skull, to wield its influence long after the life that animated it has passed away. Yet this is the same Horatio who, in rapid succession, comes close to negating five acts' worth of profanation by offering a benediction in which "flights of angels" might sing Hamlet to his rest; offers to provide Fortinbras with a dispassionate summary of events, as if his detachment had spared him from what he had witnessed; and, in practically the same breath used to advance Hamlet's cause, volunteers himself as the counselor able to draw out the moral of the story (361, 373–387). What are we to make of this apparent contradiction? One might assume, mistakenly, that a desperate, dying Hamlet had resorted to browbeating Horatio into doing his, the prince's, bidding. But Horatio clearly loves his friend; and love, as Lacan contends, "is the sign that one is changing discourses," the sign that one is taking up, in the wake of analysis, a different position in relation to the master signifier.[47] That is true in two ways here. On the one hand, Hamlet has succeeded in changing discourses for everyone, from the master's discourse (whose hollowed-out structure Fortinbras, much to our embarrassment, continues to occupy) to something else: a shadowy intimation of the patient and laborious discourse of the melancholic. Horatio, meanwhile, is also in the process of changing discourses; or, rather, he represents a larger transition into a university discourse that will continue to intersect with the discourse of the melancholic only in order to betray it: taking its cue from the latter insofar as it drains the situation of its enjoyment (the object a), but doing so only in the interests of a more attenuated, fully institutionalized master, an S_1 dressed up in the scholarly attire of S_2.[48]

That is not to say, however, that this newly ascendant university discourse is any less free from the afterlife of Hamlet's dying voice than is the master's discourse inhabited by Fortinbras. The theater-idea of *Hamlet* says otherwise. From the very beginning, Hamlet has worked to unmake the tragic plot played out, in everyday life, at the level of the Oedipus complex. And at least from the completion of the Mousetrap, he has worked to establish a counterplot to be acted out upon a side stage apposed to the main stage of Elsinore. Now we see how that counterplot, that new ground for a new edifice, will unfold. Fortinbras's master plot will go forward, with all the authoritative pomp and majesty that one might expect; but it will do so having had its shamelessness laid bare for all to see. Meanwhile, Horatio's plot, the affably treacherous plot of the university discourse, will also go forward, earnestly obscuring the shamelessness of the master with a scrim of disinterested inquiry. Yet here there will be an important twist; for in spite of everything, Horatio's love for Hamlet suggests that he has been affected by analysis enough to at least serve as the repository, however unwitting, of the memory of a prince who has mortified the position of prince, a skeletal S_1 that will hereafter share the throne with the duly elected Fortinbras. Like the university discourse, which will continue to be shadowed by the structurally impossible fifth discourse of melancholia—a discourse that cannot emerge from a quarter turn, but only from a revolutionary construction—the close association between the discourses of the master and the university means that both plots will be shadowed by a counterplot carried out on a side stage, a spectral area reminiscent of the darkened corridors and hidden alcoves haunted by the courtier but now set apart, just beyond the reach of any institution that might try to claim it as its own property. Fortinbras will order that the bodies be put out of sight and that Hamlet be given a soldier's funeral utterly out of keeping with his actions in life (5.2.396–401). Horatio, meanwhile, will seek to immunize the community from further harm (5.2.394–396). And it will be hard to say which action represents the greater betrayal of Hamlet's betrayal. But perhaps the distinction doesn't matter; both men will seek, paradoxically, to vitalize their actions with Hamlet's dying voice, a voice that speaks in terms echoed by the punning gravedigger and the courtier-as-event. At the end of *Hamlet*, as in Hamlet's end, we encounter the point at which the draining away of enjoyment cannot help but become the drawing on of natural history.

CHAPTER THREE

Woyzeck Is the Worst

IF ONE WERE ASKED to single out a life tormented enough to represent the early, tumultuous decades of the nineteenth century, one could do no worse than the historical figure behind Georg Büchner's play *Woyzeck*: the itinerant soldier, prisoner of war, deserter, and murderer Johann Christian Woyzeck. Executed in 1824 after three years of examination by Leipzig's chief medical officer, Dr. J. A. Clarus, the historical Woyzeck embodies— appropriately enough, in the form of a headless trunk—the confusions of an era that couldn't decide whether to ignore him, confine him, study him, or destroy him. Either because of or in spite of its myriad crises, the first half of the nineteenth century sees the emergence of several new disciplines, among them forensics, psychiatry, and criminology, alongside a massive buildup of bureaucracies, medical institutions, and police forces assembled to facilitate the development of a newly "normative" society.[1] Those disciplines and bureaucracies, designed to produce the docile bodies necessary for furthering the ends of population control, public hygiene, crime prevention, and security, shared one overarching goal: to foster the strength of the state. And in that they were wildly successful. Nevertheless, one can still detect, in the years after 1815 and the end of the Napoleonic Wars, a silent struggle being played out between the forces then conspiring to forge what Foucault calls a "really demonic" alliance between "those two games—the city-citizen game and the shepherd-flock game—in what we call the modern states" and another, counter arrangement, another configuration of forces, discourses, and bodies.[2] For the time being, we will call this other configuration, in a nod to Deleuze's reading of Foucault, the Woyzeck-diagram.[3]

This Woyzeck-diagram, operating at the crossroads of several discourses, is everywhere noticeable in the first half of the nineteenth century.

Opposed to any pastoral-polis game grounded in disciplinary and biopolitical stratagems of power/knowledge, it arranges itself in the gestures, attitudes, and enunciations of bodies neither docile nor overtly rebellious. Its home is those disreputable places, populated by people of questionable character, where not even the translucent sky (which isn't visible anyhow) can offer clarity and orientation. Its form is that of the immutable human suffering—in a word, the worst—detectable as the underside of the lofty aspirations of politics and political philosophy. Eschewing a tragic politics erected upon the ideas of sacrifice, destiny, revenge, purpose, and immortality, the Woyzeck-diagram instead arranges a confrontation with what Benjamin and, following him, Adorno call "the *facies hippocrita* of history," that "primordial landscape" which reappears at every stage of decay and decline, not just in human history but in human life.[4] As Benjamin puts it, "everything about history that, from the very beginning, has been untimely, sorrowful, unsuccessful, is expressed in a face—or rather in a death's head."[5]

Büchner, the student, medical doctor, and revolutionary, was intimately familiar with the Hippocratic face, the physiognomy of the worst. Sometimes it seems as though he saw it everywhere: in the French Revolution (*Danton's Death*), in the figure of the melancholic poet (*Lenz*), barely veiled in our princes and kings (*Leonce and Lena*), and, above all, in the destitution of the modern have-nots and no-counts (*Woyzeck*). In a letter to his fiancée from 1834, Büchner writes that "[t]he feeling of having died was always around me. Everyone had a Hippocratic face." Büchner then goes on to describe his fellow men, and indeed the whole world around him, in such a way that the entire cosmos ends up reverberating with the physiognomy of the worst: "glazed eyes and waxen cheeks . . . , limbs twitched, the voice grated. . . . [W]e poor wailing musicians, is our groaning on the rack only meant to pierce through the clouds, resounding higher and higher, and finally to die away as a melodic breath in heavenly ears?"[6] In *Woyzeck*, Büchner asks us to do nothing less than envision the landscape of history and nature, including the very features and disposition of Woyzeck himself, grafted onto the physiognomic traits of the facies Hippocrita. And like the facies Hippocrita, which stares out at us from every warzone, every blighted landscape, every newspaper and every screen, Woyzeck is not going anywhere. He may be traversed by discourses that are about to eliminate him, he may collide repeatedly with superior forces that can send him hurling back into the mediocrity and oblivion whence he came; yet Woyzeck remains a potent, dense particle, possessed of a relentless intensity and poetic energy that flashes up whenever he confronts the overwhelming powers called into being by his own, trouble-some existence. Taking seriously the biopolitical prerogative of life as a political object, *Woyzeck* mobilizes such life against the powers deter-mined to manage it. Like the hero of Büchner's *Lenz*, Woyzeck emblematizes the obscure individual that, not knowing enough to stop gesticulating, act-ing, speaking, and thinking, manages to unleash the forces of a richer, more expansive form of life. His interior, once exteriorized, transforms the outside. "[Lenz]," we are told, "acted like everyone else, yet there was a ter-rible void within him, he no longer felt any fear, any desire; his existence was a necessary burden.—So, he lived on."[7] We would say much the same about Woyzeck.

Set nowhere in particular—neither in the capital nor in the remote villages of Germany—and in the unclear interim between a regime of sov-ereignty (with the Captain as its placeholder) and the governance of biopo-litical apparatuses (amply represented by the Doctor and by the emerging sciences of psychiatry, psychology, and criminology), *Woyzeck* thematizes a certain stuck-ness, a certain sense of nonbelonging in a nonplace at a nontime. In *Woyzeck*, dispersed and anonymous discourses, caught here in their first stage of development, have yet to supplant the old regime of juridical power. But neither have they worked out how to absorb the guilt and agitation disseminated by the fragmentation of the sovereign agent.[8] Inherited terms are inoperative, new terms remain to be coined. The play is marked, in fact, by the flagrant, puppet-like dumbness and ineptitude of its power holders, registered most powerfully in the vulgar language they use to try to capture Woyzeck or to comprehend the unsettled time in which they toil. This is true of the Captain, who continues to traffic in the most shopworn terminology of honor, morality, and virtue. But it is truer still of the Doctor, who couches a received vocabulary of free will, self-control, determinism, and so on in a scientific language that, at the moment of its development, already sounds exhausted. "I'm revolution-izing science," declares the Doctor, "I'll blow it sky-high. Urea ten percent, ammonium chloride, hyperoxidic. Woyzeck, don't you have to piss again? Go in there and try."[9] A revolution in science predicated on the demand that a wretched creature will himself to perform a bodily function: one might call this a classic case of old wine in new skins. But this is something more, something worse. This is spoiled wine in cadaverous skins. The con-ceptions at work here are so crude and traditional that the new sciences, on the brink of ushering in a revolution, utter their first-last words—"Urea ten percent, ammonium chloride, hyperoxidic"—and are pronounced dead on arrival. In the end—that is, at the very beginning—Woyzeck proves too much for them. Like an experiment conducted in a dirty lab, the haphazard transition from sovereign rule to new forms of disciplinary and biopolitical power creates the very environment that allows for Woyzeck to emerge as a figure of the worst: a figure that, in confounding both sovereignty and governmentality, drains each one of vitality.

The play declines, moreover, to present, by way of comic relief, corrupt or incompetent caricatures of the dominant powers for which there exist, somewhere else—in some other outpost or some other play—more fully realized representatives. Instead, *Woyzeck* extracts the dumb truth about such power holders, which is that they possess neither the terms nor the means necessary to constitute, let alone organize, a more convincing form of life. The characters in the play are half-born, failing, only provisionally inhabiting their allotted roles. Who are they? A soldier who is not a soldier, a friend who is not a friend, a mistress who is not a mistress, a drum major whose rank is ceremonial, a melancholic captain, a sadistic doctor. Strangely driven, with no apparent mandate or motivation, they grope in the dark. The ramshackle dysfunction of the new disciplinary and biopolitical orders allows for no alternative to sovereign ruination, no other, more efficient configuration of power, no scene where politics is found to bring about the *euemeria* of the good life. We hear of no aspiration—no enemy to combat, no capital to conquer, no plot to be quelled, no prince to be resisted—beyond necessity. Instead, the play's characters service the feeble logic, the "it is what it is," of the unimproved life. And yet, they are never cynics. Although every one of them is a thoroughly disciplined subject operating within a biopolitical force field, the apparatuses of power are rendered so vacuous and inoperative that the situation proves to be less dreadful than we feared.

In fact, it is much worse. *Woyzeck* runs counter to the belief, held in some quarters, that the three regimes of power (sovereign-disciplinary-biopolitical) succeed one another in orderly fashion, like relay runners passing the baton cleanly from hand to hand. This belief betrays more than just disappointment in the many failings, even the impotency, of the master discourses. It actively works to prop up those discourses of power so that they can then be resisted, combatted, shamed, captured, constructed, and finally exposed in the form of counter-conducts or counter-empires. Good inheritors of Foucault that we are, we dread disciplinary regimes and biopower in just the way that cowering subjects once dreaded the sovereign. What gives many of us fear, in fact—and, in that fear, a strange sort of solace—is that the new powers work far more rationally and efficiently than the mercurial sovereign of absolutism. *Woyzeck* does not share that comforting fear. Instead, the play understands that the hardest thing to abide is the knowledge that we live in a time defined neither by sovereign power, with its right to let live and make die, nor by biopower, with its capacity to make live and let die, to adopt Foucault's elegant formulation. And so that is where it situates us: in an interregnum where neither the sovereign nor anonymous networks of power rule.

In *The Meridian*, his 1960 acceptance speech for the Büchner Prize, Paul Celan insists that we cannot choose between, on the one hand, the good figures of the nonhuman that exceed the humanist boundaries of our art and politics and, on the other, the undead, inhuman automata that pull, in sinister and mechanical fashion, the strings of our history. Büchner's plays, as Celan observes so astutely, bend the homogenous space of power according to the "angle of inclination of [the poet's] creatureliness."[10] In that way, they lead power down a particular route, a "stepping beyond what is human, a stepping into the uncanny realm turned toward the human—the realm where the monkey, the automatons and with them . . . art too" are actualized and attain an "acute accent" (5). What initiates such "stepping" is an encounter with citations, whether they come from Woyzeck or from others who incessantly summon inhuman voices—what Celan calls the "old and even ancient forms of uncanniness" (5). Celan intimates that any text, whether it be political or poetic, whether coming from the "Revolution Square" or from the terrifying poetic "breathturn," must "travel the route"—the route of art and politics—"for the sake of such a breathturn," through "the abyss and the automatons," to where "the automatons break down—for this single short moment" (3, 7). The poetry of political thought, on the path of this route, compels political thinking to catch up to the real of politics. Or, better: political thinking needs to catch up to the thinking already underway in Celan's speech or in Büchner's own writings.

Thus we turn, melancholically hopeful in the midst of the worst, to *Woyzeck*.

The Captain

Of all the symptomatic power holders who stumble their way through *Woyzeck*, none exemplifies what it means to encounter the worst more than the Captain.[11] The play's other power holder, the Doctor (to whom we will turn in a moment), may get confused by Woyzeck's enigmatic citations, but he has the advantage, so to speak, of being a harbinger of a new master in the discourse of the university.[12] The Captain, meanwhile, voices the melancholic truth of an order so weary of life that we have to worry about its suicidal tendencies, particularly when we hear the Captain's anxious and befuddled words to an uncomprehending Woyzeck:

> CAPTAIN: Take it easy, Woyzeck, take it easy. One thing at a time;
> you're making me quite dizzy. . . . [W]hat am I supposed to do
> with the extra ten minutes? . . . What are you going to with that
> ungodly amount of time? . . .
>
> I fear for the world when I think about eternity. Activity,
> Woyzeck, activity! Eternal, that's eternal, that's eternal—you
> realize that, of course. But then again it's not eternal, it's only a
> moment, yes, a moment—Woyzeck, it frightens me to think that
> the earth rotates in one day—what a waste of time, what will come
> of that? Woyzeck, I can't look at a mill wheel anymore or I get
> melancholy. . . . This discussion has really worn me out (142–143).

Typically, this might be regarded as the empty, sentimental babble of a ridiculous, exhausted soldier; yet every word, every turn, is significant. Simply put, the Captain cannot stop talking to Woyzeck not only about revolution but about the revolutionary time that threatens to depose him and his ilk from their positions of power. Holding forth, under the guise of concern, on the subject of time-management ("Woyzeck, just think, you've still got a good thirty years to live, thirty years! That's 360 months, and days, hours, minutes! What are you going to do with that ungodly amount of time? Get organized, Woyzeck"), the Captain merely plays for time, wasting and extending it, as if to stave off the inevitable. The Captain, so used to giving orders, thinks that he can order time. "Take it easy, Woyzeck," he admonishes, "take it easy. One thing at a time. . . . You can go now—and don't run like that! Slow, nice and slow down the street" (141, 144). In other words, the revolution can wait.

Woyzeck, in response, seems to abide, for he invokes Gottlieb Konrad Pfeffel's disillusioned comment on the failure of the revolution: "The likes of us are wretched in this world and in the next; I guess if we ever got to Heaven, we'd have to help with the thunder" (142). Yet who can say, to recast Woyzeck's words in a less fatalistic, more properly melancholic form, what might happen when the wretched get to "thunder" alongside the angels in Heaven? Everyone, including Woyzeck, seems to assume that they will be put to work on the making of ordinary storms. But what if they were tasked instead with helping God announce another, greater storm: that of Judgment Day?[13] The resigned image of eternal drudgery, of toiling away for the Captain's military order even in the kingdom of Heaven, assumes a new tonality once we hear the thunder as the rumbling, distant but getting closer, of apocalyptic time. The Captain seems to hear it that way. "Woyzeck," he intones, "you have no virtue, you're not a virtuous person." Echoing his earlier advice to "take it easy," the Captain advocates, when faced with a figure who might truly revolutionize the empty time that fills him with such anxiety, an embryonic version of panopticism and governmentality: "Woyzeck, you always look so upset. A good man doesn't act like that, a good man with a conscience" (142). More insidiously still, this pathetic holdover from the Napoleonic era "*cunningly*" (to borrow one of the scene's stage directions) turns a pair of explicitly revolutionary images, that of the Earth's rotation and, more romantically, the millwheel, into eternal figures for acedia and nostalgic stupefaction (142). Woyzeck, though, persists in filling empty, historical time, the time of "one thing at a time," with an evental charge. "The good Lord," he says, "isn't going to look at a poor little kid only because amen was said over it before it was created" (142). Rather than submit to the Captain's orderly regime of virtue and conscience, Woyzeck instead refers to redemptive time: to Creation and Judgment Day, to the persistence of origin realized "when we act like nature tells us." Traditional morality, Woyzeck seems to intimate, will end, and Judgment Day will usher in a sinless, transparent world, a world freed from the illusion that salvation can be had, or can only be had, through the mouthing of an *amen*.

The Captain is merely bewildered. "What's that you're saying?" he asks. "What kind of a crazy answer is that? You're getting me all confused with your answer. When I say *you*, I mean you—you!" (142). Woyzeck's "crazy answer" to the Captain's admonitions, countering, as it does, the Captain's attempts at passing judgment, is truly a cause for wonder and perplexity. The Captain's confusion of pronouns shows the effect: Woyzeck, whose physical proximity to the Captain (*you*) is momentarily obliterated by the disembodied, impersonal voice of the prophet or the oracle ("What's that you're saying?"), for a fleeting instant assumes the divine standpoint of annunciation. Suddenly, we find ourselves in the end of time, where new communities are formed: "The Lord said: 'Suffer little children to come unto me'"; "Us poor people"; "Us common people"; "We're only flesh and blood." Moments earlier, the Captain had tried to trick Woyzeck into betraying his, Woyzeck's, stupidity:

CAPTAIN: Say something, Woyzeck. What's the weather like today?
WOYZECK: It's bad, Cap'n, bad—wind.
CAPTAIN: I can feel it, there's something rapid out there. A wind like that reminds me of a mouse. (*Cunningly.*) I believe it's coming from the south-north.

WOYZECK: Yes, Cap'n.

CAPTAIN: Ha! Ha! Ha! South-north! Ha! Ha! Ha! Oh, are you stupid,
terribly stupid (142).

It may be, though, that the impossible south-north wind whipped up by the
Captain's cruel fancy—blown, as it were, out of the Captain's own mouth—
will indeed harness whatever it is that, blustering away out there, affects
the Captain like a mouse. For what else but a whirlwind, blowing in from
opposite ends of the Earth, would be strong enough to reorient the car-
dinal directions that guide our movements—to sweep away the despair
of the frightened creatures, like the mousy Captain, who no longer know
which way to turn? The Captain's cunning words were supposed to capture
Woyzeck, to expose how "stupid, terribly stupid" he is. Instead, stupidity has
spoken the truth about time.

What is that truth? Superficially, the Captain speaks of an empty,
sequential time, a time eternalized and drained of its exigency. But folded
into this voided time there is another time, a time that fills the Captain
with unbounded anxiety, and with good reason. The Captain himself refers
to it as "extra" time, and it is, ironically, his own speech that brings that
time to light. This other time, dis-synchronic and noncontemporaneous,
capable of accelerating or slowing down the measured beat of chronomet-
ric time, proceeds with different speeds and effects, for it is both expansive and self-contradicting, both "eternity" and "activity." "But then again,"
admits the Captain, "it's not eternal, it's only a moment" (141–142). The
"extra" time of the Captain's speech is terrifying and anxiety-provoking:
a time of fear, of waiting, of boredom, but also of hope, anticipation, and
expectation. An "ungodly amount of time," the Captain calls it. What is he
supposed to do with it? Now whether that ungodly extra time changes
everything while leaving it outwardly intact or whether that time draws
everything into its rotational pull while it itself stays exactly the same
remains impossible to say. But unlike the drunken spectacle of the bourgeois revolutions that, according to Marx, use the very form of revolutionary novelty only to better perpetuate the status quo, this scene presents a
repetitious time of natural history that, while seeming to confirm reality,
in fact grinds down every element of that reality until it is no longer recognizable as such—until historical time becomes uncanny and ungodly: the
very opposite of "one thing at a time."[14] Or, as one of the Apprentices puts
it in another scene from another draft, "It's all out of order!" (165).

This "extra" time, spliced together out of "eternity," "activity," and
"moment," perfectly encapsulates the temporal mode in which the

sovereign finds himself stranded after the revolutions of the eighteenth century. At one point, amid his self-pitying ruminations on empty time, the Captain also acknowledges that he is a body of sorts and that that body is in a kind of crisis. Once upon a time, the sovereign's politico-theological body was immortal, a state of affairs that demanded the immunization, and thus the potential immortalization and perfection, of his living body. Now, though, well into the nineteenth century, the combined forces of the outside and finitude have conspired to turn the sovereign's two bodies, politico-theological and mortal, inside out. The immune system that once shielded both the individual body of the sovereign and, through that body, the members of the body politic, not only from its outside but from its own, internally generated surplus, has broken down.[15] In its former place we encounter something else, something that always threatened to exceed the body's confines: layers and tissues of an expansive, de-territorialized "thing" that, traversing taxonomical, temporal, and spatial boundaries, conjoins mouse and Captain, Captain and millwheel, millwheel and Earth, Earth and wind, sequential time and repetitive time. In the vulnerable, transitory mass of flesh that flees the confines of the sovereign body after its disintegration, revolutionary time meets transformative spatiality.

If the Captain, as the play's diminished figure for what remains, circa 1840, of sovereign power, seems particularly wistful, perhaps it is because he realizes that, had it not been for the enormous pressure placed upon him by the antidotal function of the sovereign body, he too could have fled—that his flesh, too, could have disappeared into new spatial-temporal configurations and revolutionary movements. Now, though, it is too late for all that, and instead he must encounter, for the first time, the real that (he?) always truly was. *Look*, the play seems to say to the Captain, *here is all the surplus that had to be reined in by corporeal immune responses and so could never be counted as part of your sovereign* ipseity. *Natural history never belonged to you.* Worse still, surely, at least as far as the Captain is concerned, is the fact that the messenger in this case is none other than Woyzeck himself. For in scene 4.5, what Roberto Esposito calls "the idea and the practice of incarnation," a practice that systematically turns bodies and immune systems into flesh via acts of splitting, partitioning, and disfiguring, finds its devastating complement in the flesh-practices of Woyzeck.

But perhaps the Captain is despondent for another reason as well. As we learn from Foucault's staging of an exemplary scene roughly contemporaneous with *Woyzeck*—the confrontation, circa 1810, between the mad king George III and a certain Doctor Willis—flesh tends to appear particularly in those moments of oscillation when sovereign power and the medical profession face off against one another.[16] If we are justified in reading the Captain as a vestigial stand-in for the sovereign, then the comedic rivalry between the play's two power-holders, the Captain and the Doctor ("DOCTOR I take my leave, most honorable Mr. Drillprick. CAPTAIN Likewise, dearest Mr. Coffin Nail"), stages a historical encounter between the disintegrating body of the old master and the overbearing presence of the new, who wants nothing more than to experiment with the remnants of the former's flesh. In scene 4.9, we thus discover the winded Captain as he overtakes the fast-moving Doctor, hoping to persuade the latter to resuscitate a life that has grown weary of its own exhaustion:

> CAPTAIN: Doctor, I'm afraid for the horses when I think that the poor
> beasts have to go everywhere on foot. Don't run like that! Don't
> wave your cane around in the air like that! You'll run yourself to
> death that way. A good man with a good conscience doesn't go so
> fast. A good man. (*He catches the* DOCTOR *by the coat.*) Doctor,
> allow me to save a human life. You're racing . . . Doctor, I'm so
> melancholy, I get so emotional, I always start crying when I see my
> coat hanging on the wall—there it is.

Yet it is no longer to be expected that nostalgic, placeless masters will receive the help they solicit, breathlessly, from the doctors confidently embodying the emerging order. Circumstances have changed so much, in fact, that the Captain finds himself appealing to the Hippocratic oath to elicit the Doctor's sympathy. It doesn't work. Not only does the Doctor mock the Captain's wish; he makes it clear that his only interest lies, not in the physical or emotional state of the decrepit old master, but in his pathology, now that the symptoms of decay have manifested themselves and the Doctor can begin to probe the Captain's mortifying flesh. The Doctor's death wish toward the Captain, thinly veiled as a professional diagnosis but legible, finally, as a symptom of the historical confrontation between competing discourses, is palpable:

> DOCTOR: Hm! Bloated, fat, thick neck, apoplectic constitution. Yes,
> Captain, you might be stricken by an *apoplexia cerebralis*. But
> you might get it just on one side and be half paralyzed, or—best of
> all—you might become mentally affected and just vegetate from
> then on: those are approximately your prospects for the next four
> weeks. Moreover, I can assure you that you will be a most inter-
> esting case, and if, God willing, your tongue is partially paralyzed,
> we'll make immortal experiments.

Immortality under this new regime is reserved, not for the sovereign's majestic body, but for the notable experiment, the scientific breakthrough, the interesting case study.

In this one scene, then, we can observe, through Büchner's novel anatomization of power, a moment in world history when the careful administration of pathological bodies and abnormal minds supplants the obsessive attentions paid to maintaining the health of the sovereign's body—when the loosened flesh of the master, rather than being allowed to join forces with other forms of creaturely life, is instead absorbed into a new discursive practice. The curiosity and concern orchestrated by the emerging university discourse replace not only the care once taken by the sovereign for his subjects but also the care for the sovereign that had once preoccupied the learned members of the royal entourage. Perhaps, then, we ought to get better acquainted with this new discourse and its representative, the Doctor. For "dearest Mr. Coffin Nail," as it turns out, despite his self-assured arrogance, is no less hapless than "most honorable Mr. Drillprick" when confronted with Woyzeck's melancholic absorption in natural history.

The Doctor

Clearly it mattered to Büchner that Woyzeck not be reduced to the pitiful linchpin of a socially conscious play: a wretch whose thoughts are an effect of his paranoia, who must eat peas for a living, who spends his time on stage getting pushed around, beaten, betrayed, cuckolded.[17] Reversing the existing power structure altogether, Woyzeck acts as the aggressor while the power holders can only react, with curiosity and bemusement, to his provocative thoughts and bewildering citations. Far from being an object of pity and horror, Woyzeck steps forward as a kind of ragged philosopher-king, a modern Diogenes who continually deposes both himself and his interlocutors (who are just as likely to be his interrogators) with doubles and duplications. We have already seen the effect this has on the Captain. Now, in 4.8, we see what it does to the Doctor, whom Woyzeck frustrates by refusing to master "the call of nature"—by refusing, that is, to heed the Doctor rather than nature.

For Woyzeck, nature has nothing to do with free will or self-control. It has to do, rather, with "a certain character, a certain structure" being attuned, not simply to nature, but to what Woyzeck calls "double nature": a radical outside indifferent to human order. "Doctor," he asks (*Confidingly*, according to the stage directions), "have you ever seen anything of double nature? When the sun's standing high at noon and the world seems to be going up in flames, I've heard a terrible voice talking to me!" (144). This double nature encompasses, at once, in doubling fashion, the planetary order with its potential for apocalyptic, catastrophic events—flames and voices—and the underlying principles of natural history written, albeit illegibly, in "the toadstools . . . how they grow in patterns." "If only someone could read that," says Woyzeck, apparently invoking the medieval trope of the book of nature, the script of which we must all learn how to decipher (144). Now, though, Woyzeck doubles that script with another, more striated and sedimentary script inscribed in the Earth's history: a record of catastrophe that disrupts any smooth narrative of rational order and patient growth. Read this way, against the grain, the growth pattern of the toadstools no longer reveals the grandly beautiful characters of an impassive nature entirely removed from the exigency of the living. Instead, the "long lines, crooked circles, figures" that appear "when nature runs out" mark the eruption, like a fire in the sky, of an intensely historicized natural history into the temporal frame of world history: a natural history that demolishes orders even as it divulges structures (166). Falling well outside the bounds of classical geometry, the "long lines, crooked circles, figures" form hyperbolic, elliptic natural historical patterns that suddenly mushroom up one day in unforeseeable, transitory constellations. Legible both as the advent of an impenetrable disaster writing and as the promise of a prophetic insight, this eruptive form of writing conjoins, in the figure of catastrophe, one's own "character" or "structure" with the force of natural history. For Woyzeck, concrete historical crisis is made both legible and audible as a natural constellation of crisis, and vice versa: catastrophic, volcanic nature is transfigured into an idea of history as transience and downfall.[18] In *Woyzeck*, "crooked" constellations of nature and history overlap and return to us a script of a disaster, written out in unheard-of shapes.

The Captain surely would have been left speechless by Woyzeck's vision of inhuman double nature. The Doctor, by contrast, reacts by asserting a kind of mad, zealous mastery of knowledge, delivered in a manner best described as one of hyperimmunitarian scientific aestheticization. "You've got a marvelous *aberration mentalis partialis*," he intones, "second species, beautifully developed" (145). Against the natural historical real heard in Woyzeck's speech, the Doctor erects a nearly impenetrable wall of pseudoscientific wonder, almost as if he hoped to outdo the perplexing beauty and intricacy of Woyzeck's images. Taking Woyzeck's genuine engagement with the outside and translating it into a matter of curiosity, like a horse that can count, the Doctor turns Woyzeck into a fascinating case study. Worse, he turns Woyzeck into a curio, to be placed under his, the Doctor's, care: "You're an interesting case. Subject Woyzeck, you're getting a raise. Now behave yourself" (145). To his credit, the Doctor at least dimly recognizes that science must traverse Woyzeck's peculiar subjectivity in order to arrive at the revolution—or at least "a revolution." Alas, though, the only revolutionary knowledge the Doctor hopes to extract from Woyzeck is the kind that can be put toward "revolutionizing science," which in this case is a science only too eager to hand over Woyzeck, now transformed into a domesticated "subject" that knows how to "behave," to the new master. We can already detect, then, in the Doctor's reaction to (and treatment of) Woyzeck, the emergence of the university discourse as the new master. Diligently recording Woyzeck's words, thoughts, and behaviors even before any murder has been committed, the Doctor follows the modus operandi of a juridico-forensic discourse to which we have since grown accustomed, but which must have seemed strange indeed in the 1830s: namely, that it will always find an alibi, be it the risk assessment of dangerous individuals, the prevention or repression of crimes, or the need to intrude into, explore, and discipline whatever intrigues or vexes it. And whatever revolutionizing science, with its "sky-high" aspirations, cannot incorporate into an intelligible framework will be, without further ado, hounded, harried, denounced, and found guilty (144). Thus the Doctor: "You pissed on the street . . . that's bad. The world is getting bad, very bad. . . . Nature! Woyzeck, man is free; in man alone is individuality exalted to freedom. Couldn't hold it in! . . . I have it in writing, here's the contract. I saw it all, saw it with my own eyes" (144). The new discourses have evidence, eyewitness accounts, reports, and case studies, all of which conspire, under the guise of scientific certainty, to declare people such as Woyzeck guilty long before any crime has been committed.

None of that means, however, that the discourse of the university is any less impotent than the master's discourse when confronted with Woyzeck and "the important question of the relationship of subject to object" opened up by his form of life. This becomes apparent in scene 3.1 (designated, in our edition of the play, as an "optional scene"), when three creatures—a cat that barely escapes defenestration, a "rabbit louse" living in the cat's fur, and Woyzeck, a soldier who "for a quarter of the year . . . hasn't eaten anything but peas" (155)—begin to commune with one another, frustrating the Doctor's attempts at staging an experiment for the gentlemen students gathered in the courtyard below his window. It doesn't take long for the Doctor to perceive that communion—and, having perceived it, to document it, explain it, disrupt it by doing his best to translate it into the terms of the university discourse:

> DOCTOR: Courage, Woyzeck—just a few more days, and it'll be all over. Feel him, gentlemen, feel him. (*STUDENTS feel his temples, pulse, and chest.*) Apropos, Woyzeck, wiggle your ears for the gentlemen; I meant to show it to you before. He uses two muscles. Come on, hop to it!
>
> WOYZECK: Oh, doctor!
>
> DOCTOR: You dog, shall I wiggle them for you, are you going to act like the cat? So, gentlemen, this represents a transition to the donkey, frequently resulting from being brought up by women and from the use of the mother tongue. How much hair has your mother pulled out for a tender memory? It's gotten very thin in the last few days. Yes, the peas, gentlemen (155).

With one grand, sweeping pronouncement, the Doctor enacts the various exclusions—of speech, the good manners of childhood education, language, animals, women, idiots (the layman, the unscientific man), and the poor—through which scientific knowledge establishes itself. Having been made dog, Woyzeck becomes cat, becomes louse, becomes donkey. And yet in just that way, Woyzeck manages, like the cat (who simply runs off), to make an exodus from the cruelty and humiliation of the scientific scene. Against the ad hoc arrangements of science, Büchner stages another, even more experimental scene, one in which the three objects of scientific inquiry, the three curios—insect, animal, and deviant—begin to dwell with one another, like an adoptive family that truly cares. "The fellow holds the beast so tenderly," remarks the Doctor, "like it was his grandmother!" (155).

The second Clarus report points to the historical Woyzeck's "confusion of the objective with the subjective" as a symptom of his madness.[19] By contrast, Büchner's play redeems Woyzeck's "fault"—that is, his tendency to mistake his own suffering and anxiety for that of the object, and vice versa—by depicting it as the capacity for genuine empathy and care. As Büchner presents it, Woyzeck's "confusion of the objective with the subjective" is exactly what allows for the formation of new networks of cohabitation and new circuits of affect among entities. And not just living or embodied entities; for the answer that Woyzeck and his new relations pose to "the important question of the relationship of subject to object" resounds well beyond the confines of the Doctor's courtyard—all the way "to space, to the earth, to the planetary system" (155). No anatomical theater can contain it.

Much attention has been given recently to the way that Büchner's drama deploys the Clarus report. Rüdiger Campe argues compellingly that *Woyzeck* problematizes all the discursive strategies, forms of representation, and framing devices of the forensic case study, including its axioms of guilt and accountability. Contrary to the grand spectacle of punishment, atonement, and execution, the Clarus report stages a different, much more sober scene, that of scientific observation and writing. In the psychiatric report, Woyzeck's life turns into a file meant to capture his living individuality. According to Campe's reading of the case, the psychiatric gaze is no longer concerned with actions and their injurious effects, but with causes that manifest themselves in the meticulous exploration of the speech, composure, and reactions of the accused.[20] Nicolas Pethes, meanwhile, shows how Büchner's "dramatic case study," instead of reconstructing the causes of the crime, competes with its psychiatric counterpart to shed a completely different light on Woyzeck's deeds.[21] And Arne Höcker suggests going a step further, reading Büchner's *Woyzeck* "as the dramatic framing of a case history that in its mode of representation comments on the case and engages with the conditions of its formation. The drama . . . is the staging of the case, its *making*."[22]

We harbor no doubts regarding Büchner's deep engagement with all the formative gestures of the Clarus report. But *Woyzeck* is not about making the case; it is about the case's undoing, the diseasing of its axioms, narratives, and reasoning. For science does not have a case. Büchner's drama unframes Woyzeck and his "interesting case," as the Doctor eagerly describes it, by confronting the spectacle of the inquisitive gaze with another scene of reasoning and perception, that of "double nature" and what the Carnival Announcer in scene 4.3 will call "double *raison*." A procedure of mortification is at work in Büchner's citational strategy that drains all the living individuality from the case. He extracts the unaccountable residues, the deformed skeletal matter, from the scientific study and offers them to the reader as bewildering objects of immersion. The delirious speech of the drunken Barber in scene 1.10 might serve as a case in point:

> Sir, leave me alone! I am science. Every week I get half a florin for my scientific self—don't break me apart or I'll go hungry. I am a *spinoza pericyclyda*; I have a Latin backbone. I am a living skeleton, all mankind studies me.—What is man? Bones! Dust, sand, dirt. What is nature? Dust, sand, dirt (160).

Infelicitous, self-aggrandizing speech acts; pretentious discourse mixed with boasting and malapropisms: the Barber has good reasons to proclaim that he is science. His "scientific self" perfectly mimics the narcissistic, nonsensical bluster, economic calculations, and involuntary comedy—in a word, the *bêtise*—of the Doctor's rhetoric. Except the Barber is, like Woyzeck, also the exploited object of scientific studies. And this object begins to speak, as "living skeleton" or "spinoza pericyclyda": a grotesque word monster of Greco-Latin descent that exists nowhere outside of the Barber's delirious speech, not in Linné's zoological taxonomy or in the curiosity cabinets of the local prince. The Barber is in possession of this precious spinal deformity, probably a rare type of hump, and juxtaposes it with Spinoza's pantheistic spirit, which he reduces to a disfigured bone structure. This is Büchner's version of Hegel's proposition that the "spirit is a bone." Yet this funny backbone remains intensely intriguing; it wishes to be scientifically scrutinized by "all mankind." The Barber is all too aware that he is nothing but a living corpse, one whose sole purpose is to be dissected in front of hundreds of observant students in the anatomical theater of the university.

Let us not forget, after all, as we pore over the Clarus report, that the doctor from Leipzig was not a psychiatrist, but an anatomist and surgeon by training. Likewise, Büchner's professor at the University of Gießen, Johann Bernhard Wilbrand, the model for the Doctor in *Woyzeck*, was a comparatist anatomist who wrote an influential handbook on natural history.[23] When the Barber reiterates the deeply sobering insight of the Announcer that man is "dust, sand, dirt," he certainly debunks the run-of-the mill version of German idealism that ruled early nineteenth-century university discourse (140). But he also clarifies that science zealously awaits the corpse. The case study is not interested in the subject as thriving individual, but in its demise; it wants the dead body, curiously deformed bones, monstrosities to be studied and exhibited in a university lab or natural history museum. The Doctor seeks a *pericyclydic* skeleton. The Barber's speech, meanwhile, by linking the weighty question "what is man?," which according to Kant encompasses the whole of philosophy, and the Spinozist question "what is nature?" to the mundane apparatus of the scientific case, engages in an act of profanation.[24] Philosophy and anatomy, idealism and forensics, metaphysical treatise and scientific case study: these, the Barber tells us, have grown together like a peculiar constellation of mushrooms in the silence of a German forest. When the Barber confronts modern science with the Baroque vanitas motif, he reminds the audience that comparative anatomy in the vein of Clarus and Wilbrand is about the nomenclature of bones, the power of naming, and the vanity of becoming citable—about breaking down the living into its natural historical elements. Possessed of the drunkard's gift for giddy profanation, he addresses himself not as a living

individual that purportedly animates the forensic case study, but as pure
genericity, inanimate anatomical matter, to a generic audience, mankind
itself. He rants at us with the insight of a melancholic killjoy, and with a
hint of rebelliousness, not altogether different from Büchner, who argues
that "philosophy a priori still sits in a desolate desert" and whose last words
reportedly were "we are death, dust, ash, how may we lament?"[25]

What we encounter, then, in scene 3.1 is really two scenes: a crude scientific demonstration, addressed to "gentlemen"; and, dwelling within that
scene, a natural historical scene, addressed to all creatures. The Doctor had
intended to take up, for the benefit of his students, the question of the relationship between subject and object. In the event, though, the implications
of that question prove too much for him, and he instead ends up display-
ing a miniature bestiary: a living diorama where the recalcitrant animal, the
insect under the magnifying glass, and the deviant human can be exhibited
for the edification of young medical students ("Come, gentlemen, feel him!");
where demonstration and interrogation, training and experimentation meet
and reinforce one another. Confronted with Woyzeck, whose absorption in
natural history it can neither comprehend nor appropriate, the discourse of
the university quickly devolves into the crudest possible demonstration of
power/knowledge. And what is the lasting legacy of that display of power,
that implantation and extraction of knowledge? Like the medical theater,
the bestiary that the Doctor tries to throw together in his courtyard is characteristic of the disciplinary and biopolitical apparatuses of the nineteenth
century. Making a mockery of the very thing they purport to capture and
classify, those apparatuses lay out, as in a scientific cabinet of wonders,
forms of life now deemed inferior, unstable, deviant, abnormal, and, for that
reason, needful of our curious gaze. And yet such apparatuses, if they exist
today, do so only as the occasions for our own melancholic contemplation:
curious artifacts gathering dust in museums of natural history. Displays of
mummified life that have become, over time, their own forms of mummified
life, they offer up vague premonitions not only about the natural historical
truth content revealed by dejected forms of life—that not much separates
historical nature from naturalized history—but also about our own precarious position in the zoosphere, where we must now venture.

The Barker and the Announcer

In *The Meridian*, Celan identifies two figures from *Woyzeck*, the carnival
barker and his monkey, as the representatives of art (which, Celan insists,
"is the same art," again and again) "in this totally different era" after the

revolution.[26] The Barker, whose job it is to entice us, to beckon us, to draw us in, presents to us a monkey that precludes any possibility of choosing: between the good animal and the bad one, between competing versions of the human and the animal, between what we would keep and what we would reject. We must learn, the Barker tells us, to see double. On the one hand, he insists, pointing to the monkey, we are to "look at this creature, as God made it: he's nothing, nothing at all." On the other hand, we are enjoined to "see the effects of art: he walks upright, wears coat and pants, carries a sword! Ho!" (139). The monkey's performance of bipedalism, his coat and pants, his little sword: these are the effects of art, of transformation and making, that cover up the shame of living, the shame of being an animal, of being naked, of being created, of being nothing at all. Art's efforts to hide shame only call our attention to that shame.

What Celan takes to be a figure for art can also be taken as a figure for a particular kind of politics: revolutionary, political but also poetic, carried out in the name of the "majesty of the absurd" and in the place "where all tropes and metaphors want to be carried ad absurdum."[27] "Each poem," argues Celan, "has its own '20th of January' inscribed in it": its own, irrefutable datum; its element that can neither be avoided nor disavowed.[28] In *Woyzeck*, that 20th of January, that datum, is the shame of living: the prehistorical shame so intimately tied to melancholia, the shame that gives way so easily to fury, the shame that no amount of world-historical development will ever eradicate and to which it must in fact return. Act 4.3 (or 1.1, if comparing Büchner's drafts) records that datum in an odd formulation. "Enter!" exclaims the Barker. "The presentation will begin. The commencement of the beginning will start immediately." (In 1.1: "The presentation will begin! The beginning of the beginning! The commencement of the commencement will start immediately!") The opening (or near opening) of *Woyzeck* locates its datum in a pre-beginning, a commencement of the commencement from which human world history must begin. Against the inaugural force that sovereign power accrues to itself in the form of the ban, *Woyzeck* registers a counterclaim.[29] Because, as Celan contends, we are not in a position to decide between two forms of strangeness—because we are stuck with this art and its "innermost narrows"—the claim of sovereignty reveals itself as merely an attempt at rescinding a decision. "The commencement of the beginning will start immediately": we are already thoroughly exposed to the paradoxically ongoing natural historical prehistory of world history; a decision has already been made on our behalf, and we can no more decide to go back on that decision than we can pretend that it was ever ours (or anyone's) to make. What a shame, then, that sovereign power has been unable to do away with that shame—that it has been unable to rid us of our animal prehistory. And what a shame, too, that that same power is so shameless as to refuse to acknowledge the shame we all share.

In other words, Woyzeck's version of Lenz's "20th of January" marks the inescapable datum of our political thinking. It is the Barker who beckons us toward that datum; but it is his double, the Carnival Announcer, who reveals that datum to us, once we have been called inside from the outside. "Put human society to shame! . . ." he brays as he presents a horse that can answer questions, count, tell time, and, if need be, act "improperly." "That's right, put *société* to shame! You see, the beast is still nature, unspoiled nature! Take a lesson from him" (139–140). And what is that lesson, exactly? It is a lesson, vulgar but effective, in the natural history that constitutes the unthinking ground of the so-called rational animal.[30] "Yes," says the Announcer, "that's no brutish individual, that's a person! A human being, a beastly human being, but still an animal, a *bête*." Pointing, first to the "tail" hanging down between the horse's legs, then to its "inappropriate" behavior on stage, the Announcer draws out, not just our shame, but our shame at feeling ashamed—that is, the shame we feel at the shame we feel both for our animal state and for all that we put ourselves through in trying to rise above that state. One index of that multilayered shame can be heard in the huckster's language the Announcer uses to goad his audience: "Do you want to be more than dust?" That "more than" is nothing less than the "little extra life" (as Foucault terms it) promised the body by modern science and biopolitical regimes, or what the Barker succinctly calls "the progress of civilization" (139). Büchner, as it turns out, had his own answer to that question; his dying words were reportedly, "We are death, dust and ash, how could we complain?"—hardly an endorsement of the little extra life extracted (and then managed) by the discourse of the university. Perhaps, then, we should not be surprised that the Announcer's shaming language is directed, first and foremost, at "all learned societies" and their onstage representative, the horse, "a professor at our university, with whom the students learn to ride and fight duels" (139). The beast, the Announcer mockingly reminds us, has a dual presence in the discourse of the university: the embodiment both of the unthought and of those extracurricular, beastly rituals of power, the riding and the dueling, that betray its repressed truth.

The stakes of this performance are neatly captured by a comment placed at the beginning of scene 4.3 and attributed, in at least one edition of the play, to Marie: "When fools start talking sense then we're fools ourselves. It's a funny world.—No! It's a lovely world." The unsanctioned fools and lowlifes who populate the carnival in 4.3—the Old Man, the Barker, the Announcer—traffic in exactly the type of unheard-of speech that Antonio Negri identifies as an unproductive form of biopolitics.[31] Negri is right, of course: there is nothing in the foolish nonsense—in the bêtise—of the Announcer's speech that would indicate the "power and joy of the body" or "elucidate the common dimension of the productive *bíos*" required for the "construction of a new political subject." On the contrary, the Announcer speaks of nothing but the worst. It is as Büchner writes in a letter to his fiancé: we are bound to the "terrible fatalism of history," stranded after the sorrowful end of the revolution, left alone to confront the "horrifying sameness" in human nature that drives us like "an inescapable force granted to all and to no one" (185). The animal bêtise one encounters everywhere in *Woyzeck* doesn't indicate the refusal of emancipatory joy; it expresses, rather, a deep and perceptive sadness, born of our recognition that "the progress of civilization," as the Barker calls it, has yet to occur. What else can creation do, then, but continue to protest, in clamor or in silence, the unacceptable fate of being condemned, within the discourse of the university, to the muteness of its hollow ground? What else can it do but call out to one of its own, like Woyzeck, whose visions record its tremors: "Something's moving behind me, under me. (*Stamps on the ground.*) Hollow—you hear that? It's all hollow down there.... It's so strangely quiet. You feel like holding your breath.... Quiet, it's all quiet, like the world was dead" (137).

To say that *Woyzeck* resists the emergence of a new political subject constructed out of "productive *bíos*" is not to say, however, that the play presents us with no new political subject at all. It does: it gives us a subject that originates in the worst. Far from reveling in the "joy and power" of the body as conceived of by biopolitics, this new—truly new—political subject would take the form of what the Announcer, pointing to the horse, calls "a transformed person" (or, in another edition, "a transmogrified human being"). The death of God, Nietzsche teaches us, is really the death of a particular version of the human: a particular image, nature, manner of thinking. Human beings are, and ought to be, nothing but transformed persons—creatures immersed, as Woyzeck is, in natural historical becoming. Therein lies the origin, never far from shame, of *Woyzeck*'s new political subject.

That origin reveals itself, incrementally, over the course of scene 4.3. It begins with the Barker's evocation of man's natural history: "Observe the progress of civilization. Everything progresses—a horse, a monkey, a cannery-bird! The monkey is already a soldier—that's not much, it's the lowest level of the human race!" Some would distinguish the nakedness of the creature from the effect of art, which enables man to walk upright, wear a coat and trousers, carry a sword. But the Barker points to this additional insight, that it takes an enormously violent imposition of *techné* to create man, learned societies, and kings. Although emperors are only naked under their clothes, the words of the Barker remind us that only the constant maintenance of techné allows us to maintain the strained opposition between the innocent beast as God made it and the stupid soldier who believes that his uniform shields him from his own bestiality. Then comes the Announcer, who gives voice to our new origin through a garbled, motley speech that, peppered with cod French, carries with it the airs, all at once, of worldliness, rootlessness, and fraudulence. Drawing us back to the "commencement of the beginning" that the Barker had promised was about to start, the Announcer announces the institution of a compromised origin of human nature that is as nomadic and as foolish, as full of bêtise, as is the itinerant carnival and its creatures. As the Announcer himself claims, his imperative "Man, be natural" is "very unhealthy" ("Go ask the doctor," he tells us), for it carries us both forward and backward: to the "dust, sand, dirt" that makes up the *physis* of natural history; to the carnivalesque *Ur-sprung* at once reminiscent of the time before the imposition of guilt history and predictive of the time that will follow its demise.[32] One must never settle for "simple comprehension," the Announcer tells us. One must instead "think with double *raison*." "What do you do when you think with double *raison*?" asks the Announcer (139–140). The usual answer, spoken as if it were an imperative from the place of knowledge, would be "think twice as hard" or "with an increased power of reason." The correct answer, diametrically opposed to the first, is that you adopt a Woyzeckian reasoning that unfolds parallel to or alongside of—which doubles—the bestial stupor of bêtise. "Double *raison*" names the instance where too much thinking passes outside of itself and touches upon the forces of the unthought. "Double *raison*" is nothing but the thinking of origin.

To understand this new form of thinking, we turn to Deleuze. Of the philosophical and political challenges posed by bêtise, Deleuze writes that its "indeterminate or groundlessness is also the animality peculiar to thought. . . . Stupidity (not error) constitutes the greatest weakness of thought, but also the source of its highest power in that which forces it to think."[33] With its repeated staging of bêtise, *Woyzeck* adds what Deleuze calls a "new value" to classical logic, "that of the nonsensical or the absurd" beyond any traditional opposition between the true and the false. Double raison thus constitutes "the essential step of a 'critique' which should inspire in us new ways of thinking" opened up by the interregnum between sovereign power and biopolitics, the discourse of the master and of the university.[34] This new form of critique, grounded in a natural historical double raison, eschews any act of judgment, any *krísis*, that would separate the human and the animal—that would, in short, position the human as being capable of deciding to separate from the animal. It is a critique that delivers krisis, decision, over to crisis. Like Woyzeck—whose only significant lines in scene 4.3, uttered in response to Marie's rapturous exclamation, "Those lights!" are "Yeah, like a big black cat with fiery eyes. Hey, what a night!"—the Announcer thinks both too much and too little, with too many animals and too little humanity in mind. On the one hand, as the Announcer's own language tells us, the practice of double raison has the power to "assify" "all learned societies"; for if the horse only had hands, and could count, it would show itself to have more reason than humans, just as humans would be less prone to beastliness, if only they had more horse sense. On the other hand, it is that very double raison, disavowed everywhere but in the carnival, that calls into existence those same learned societies, which exist mostly to counteract double raison. But while double raison has the capacity, fundamentally natural historical, to articulate the bêtise of the learned societies it founds, its form of critique, at once bestial and "very reasonable," stops well short of congealing into another nature. What it does, rather, is sustain the disjunction that cleaves both pure reason and pure nature. Truly double, double raison forces a shift in perspective profound enough to keep reason and nature from coinciding while at the same deriving strength from the event of that shift itself, an event made apprehensible in "the transitory flash," like the fiery eyes of a big black cat, "between two orders of being."[35]

In *The Beast and the Sovereign*, Derrida observes, almost as if he were channeling the Barker and the Announcer, that "the a-human, or at least the figure of some divinanimality, would become the foreclosed, quasi-transcendental referent that grounds the symbolic order, the human order, the law, justice."[36] We locate the name for that grounding referent in the Announcer's remarkable play on words: *Viehsionomik*, which our edition of the play translates as "beastiognomy," but which might also be rendered, through a transformation appropriate to the scene, as "physionomics." Crucially, the Announcer omits the "g," making it so that Viehsionomik cannot be mistaken for the German word for physiognomy—cannot be confused, that is, with the practice of divining character through the judgment of features: the practice of creating legible bodies. On the contrary, physionomics, far from making bodies legible and knowable, instead explores the lower regions of life: their irregular laws, their erratic forms, their ways of organizing forces that work below the threshold of visibility or sense-making. Deploying language, the consummate expression of second nature, to dissolve second nature, the Announcer makes a new form of natural historical life appear before his audience.[37] Fraudulent though his performance may be, the Announcer is nonetheless effective; for he forces us to suspend our disbelief and admit the inadmissible: that the horse is a "transformed person." What is the difference, finally, between a horse that can add despite not having fingers on which to count and a drum major who, responding to the Announcer's request, "slowly and majestically" takes a watch from his pocket? Mimicking the movement of scene 4.3 as it transitions from the outside of the fairgrounds to the inside of the Announcer's tent—a kind of rival cave allegory—double raison here doubles back upon itself, going outside, into the unthought of the human, who is still "a beast, a *bête*," before then drawing that unthought-outside back within itself, where it becomes the cause of another, deeply melancholic thinking.

"On and On"

The movement from inside to outside, outside to inside continues in a pair of juxtaposed scenes, one set in an inn, the other in an "open field," that contrast two different ways of interpreting the phrase "on and on," which the historical Woyzeck was reported to have heard in his head and which Büchner makes a point of repeatedly citing in his play. The first time we hear the phrase, in the inn, it registers the accumulations of guilt history, heightened by Marie's drunkenness and lewd dancing and by an atmosphere steeped in the shamelessness of living:

> FIRST APPRENTICE: My soul, my soul it stinks like booze.—Even money eventually decays. Forget-me-not! Oh, how beautiful this world is. Brother, I could cry a barrel full of tears. I wish our noses were two bottles and we could pour them down each other's throats. . . .
>
> MARIE: (*Dancing by.*) On! and on, on and on! . . .
>
> FIRST APPRENTICE: (*Preaches on the table.*) Yet when a wanderer stands leaning against the stream of time or gives answer for the wisdom of God, asking himself: Why does man exist? Why does man exist?—But verily I say unto you: How could the farmer, the cooper, the shoemaker, the doctor exist if God hadn't created man? How could the tailor exist if God hadn't given man a feeling of shame? How could the soldier exist, if men didn't feel the necessity of killing one another? (147).

Immediately, though, Woyzeck appropriates the manic humming and spinning of Marie's machinic "on and on" and transforms it into something more like a natural historical time signature: a feverish state, bordering on psychosis, in which it becomes impossible to stop thinking, to stop projecting the interiorized outside back into the world:

> WOYZECK: On and on—on and on! (*Jumps up violently and sinks back on the bench.*) On and on, on and on. (*Beats his hands together.*) Spin around, all around. Why doesn't God blow out the sun so that everything can roll around in lust, man and woman, man and beast (147).

The Clarus report had dutifully classified the historical Woyzeck's "*Immer zu, immer zu*" as an aural hallucination. Büchner's play turns the phrase into a double citation: the citation of Marie's unwitting citation of Clarus's taxonomy, which was itself only a citation of Woyzeck's repeated expression. The seriality of Marie's "on and on" becomes the pure repetition of Woyzeck's.

Following this instance of conversion—the whirlwind of Marie's "on and on" makes Woyzeck choke, jump up, and fall back, like a demented Saul of Tarsus—Woyzeck abandons his ordinary life, renounces his vocation, and decamps to an "open field." There, in the open, Woyzeck makes the world into a cosmic echo chamber for his repetitious, duplicating thought. Now the outside world pulsates with his internal rhythm, just as he places himself in intimate proximity with the earth. He has become a kind of seismograph, registering and recording the earthquake, or a kind of barometer, tracking the changes of pressure in the atmosphere:

> WOYZECK: On and on! On and on! Shh—music. (*Stretches out on the ground.*) Ha—what, what are you saying? Louder, louder—stab, stab the bitch [*Zickwolfin*: "She-goat-wolf"] to death? Stab, stab the bitch to death. Should I? Must I? Do I hear it over there too, is the wind saying it too? Do I hear it on and on—stab her to death, to death (148).

What Clarus, consulting the definitive medical authority of the day, classified as an "idée fixe," Büchner restores to its proper standing as a politico-philosophical thought: the thinking of the outside. The "on and on" that engulfs Woyzeck's symbolic universe has nothing to do with the order of succession proclaimed, for example, in the cry, "The king is dead, long live the king!" In fact, that way of ordering time only underscores

Woyzeck's humiliation and degradation, as we see in scene 4.14, after the Drum Major has beaten Woyzeck. "One thing after another," is Woyzeck's resigned comment (149). Nor does the "on and on" have anything to do with the endless murmur of confessional speech—the articulation of desires, impure thoughts, and deep-seated faults—extracted from the subjects of power/knowledge, to say nothing of "repentant" criminals such as Woyzeck. In that respect, the "on and on" cannot be aligned with the seriality of the repetition compulsion. Rather, it inscribes the workings of a thought that, rotating and spinning, spinning and rotating, endlessly oscillating between inside and outside, drives toward the eclipse of all thinking. Clarus reports that, once Woyzeck had "conceived of a thought, and particularly of uncomfortable thoughts," he was not able "to get rid of them." That was particularly true, Clarus continues, when it came to "the incessant thinking of one single thought," which Woyzeck would do until "finally his thoughts vanished completely."[38] In his ceaselessly rotational thinking, thinking that will eventually resolve itself into the disappearance of thought, Woyzeck touches upon the unthought that thinks thought against itself. What the discourse of the university had tried to manage under the category of the idée fixe has now become, after a slight rotation, Woyzeck's own, inscrutable form of thinking: inert, inhuman, machinic, nondialogic, unproductive, anonymous, and, to those who have ears but hear not, mute.

As Höcker so aptly puts it, "In a text that deals with the problem of accountability, the voices remain that which cannot be accounted for; they have no speaker and thus escape the narrative order."[39] In Büchner's drama, such ghostly voices become impersonal, material objects, free-floating word ruins that cannot be forgotten and have turned into haunting obsessions. Büchner cites incessantly from Clarus's forensic file, like the rhythmic "immer zu, immer zu," to create word-commons without discernible source or agent: expletives, chants, and proverbs that arrive as if carried by the wind. Büchner's citational practice in *Woyzeck* is about making words and subjects unaccountable. Far from giving clear instructions, Woyzeck's voice dispossesses him of his speech and agency: "Should I, must I? Do I hear it over there too, is the wind saying it too?" (148). Clarus also dwells extensively on Woyzeck's tendency "to talk to himself," but only to make sure that the disturbing voices are firmly lodged in his overheated imagination. Clarus wastes little time in reestablishing a source for, an accountable subject of, and a narrative order to all this "noise in Woyzeck's head."[40] But while Clarus reterritorializes the voices to build his case,

Büchner makes their dispossessing power a structuring principle of the play, which proceeds by way of citable objects that cannot be accounted for. The drama is thus not primarily about recovering Woyzeck's voice out of the forensic files where it has been buried, as has often been argued.[41] It is about releasing citations and voices from their source and agent until they have lost all their juridical accountability and can enter the logic of double raison.[42]

In short, what we encounter in Woyzeck's "on and on" is the life of an infamous man (to paraphrase Foucault) thinking its way into the world.[43] Fittingly, the effects of that thinking work backward and forward. In retrospect, the discourses personified by the Captain and the Doctor sound truly mad: disjointed attempts at refashioning the universe out of the fragments left behind in the wake of Woyzeck's intervention. What Foucault observes about the early psychiatrists—that they were forced to devise the fiction of a cure "exactly patterned on the delirium itself, homogenous with the erroneous idea" harbored by each one of their patients—can also be said about the Captain and the Doctor: they inhabit discourses structured, from the very beginning, by Woyzeck.[44] Contrary to an exemplary paranoiac like Schreber, Woyzeck refuses to rebuild a livable world, one in which the foreclosed master signifier returns, in the real, as a repository of jouissance.[45] If that task falls to anyone, it is the Captain, the Doctor, and, later in the play, the Clerk, all of whom become paranoid in the sense of feeling called upon to restore the shattered world that Woyzeck had left suspended in the "on and on" of catastrophe. Believing that they continue to practice their usual, mundane vocations, they remain unaware that those vocations have been revoked in favor of a new one: fidelity to the worst, if only in the form of suturing the disastrous end.

It is not just the play's power holders who are affected by Woyzeck, however. From scene 4.11 on, the reverberations of the unthought, having been unleashed throughout the universe, return to Earth in citational form: as deranged, unhinged, nonsensical, and finally incomprehensible fragments—of folk songs, proverbs, fairy tales. Transmissibility, which under normal circumstances is used to ground a community in shared narratives and mother tongues, is here given over to the linguistic version of the worst: language as molecular and unstable; language as the mechanism that dissolves, rather than secures, collective wisdom and national identity; language as incoherent in the sense that it dislodges and disseminates those particles of the unthought that prevent a body politic either from cohering or from becoming coherent to its own members. Consider what happens to the fairy tale in scene 1.14, for example:

MARIE: Come, you little shrimps.

([*Children's games:*] *"Ring-around-a-rosy" and "King Herod.")*
Grandmother, tell a story.

GRANDMOTHER: Once upon a time there was a poor child with no
father and no mother, everything was dead, and no one was left in
the whole world. Everything was dead, and it went and searched
day and night. And since nobody was left on the earth, it wanted
to go up to the heavens, and the moon was looking at it so friendly,
and when it finally got to the moon, the moon was a piece of rotten
wood and then it went to the sun and when it got there, the sun
was a wilted sunflower and when it got to the stars, they were little
golden flies stuck up there like the shrike sticks 'em on the black-
thorn and when it wanted to go back down to the earth, the earth
was an overturned pot and was all alone and it sat down and cried
and there it sits to this day, all alone (151).

In the Grimm Brothers' ideal, the grandmother serves as the authenticating
source of a vernacular oral tradition, the matriarch of an organic counter-
empire of folk culture used both to substantiate and to constrain a republic
held together by nothing more than contracts, raison d'état, and the trappings of civilization. In *Woyzeck* she narrates a mangled, piecemeal attempt
at a fairy tale, not even pretending to shield her audience, made up mostly of
children, from cruelty. Forget the meager consolations usually provided by
the fairy tale: the poetic justice, the hopefulness, the promise that even the
most abject and undeserving fool might get lucky. What the grandmother
gives us instead is a glimpse of the worst: an orphan, stranded between
a dead Earth and a disappointing universe, sitting all alone, crying, forever. Once understood as a sign system conveying power and meaning, the
cosmos—sun, moon, stars—are given over to thwarted promise and rot,
each heavenly body having been transformed into an inhospitable monad,
windowless and incommunicative, no longer part of a sensible constellation.
In a word, the grandmother's fractured fairy tale teaches us that we are well
and truly abandoned: not in the vaguely comforting sense of being abandoned to the sovereign ban but in the generalized sense detectable, for
example, in the composition of the play, which is made up of discontinu-
ous scenes cobbled together out of fragmentary drafts, or in the parentless,
uncared-for children who roam the play's placeless settings, equipped with
little more than half-remembered snatches of nursery rhyme.

Emblematic in this regard is the figure of Karl, "an idiot." Abandoned
to the cruelty of the fairy tale, Karl is left to count off the fragments of

fairy tales to himself, to recount all the brutalities that tales like "Rumpelstiltskin" leave unexplained. Intriguingly, the only time the king returns in the play is as the final decomposition of his status in fairy tales and the mystery plays of folk tradition. Thus we encounter, not a coherent sovereign, but oblique, citational references to Herod the child murderer, ranting and raving upon the arrival of a messiah, or to the cruel and greedy king of "Rumpelstiltskin," who by the end of Karl's litany has been figuratively transformed into a blood sausage who commands a liver sausage (149). The residue of this sovereign flesh (fingers and sausages) ought not to be read, however, as an index of the increasing empowerment of the sovereign people who assume that flesh as their own. *Woyzeck* shows, rather, that the people avail themselves of the powers of this bestial, dumb flesh, now in the form of biopowers—the police, forensics, etc.—against others: the Jew, the criminal, the vagabond, the abnormal, the poor. "Idiot" though he may be, Karl appears here as the truth-teller who makes the cruelty and abandonment naturalized in the grandmother's tale encounter itself by intensifying its decomposition: "And then the giant said: I smell, I smell, I smell human flesh. Phew! That stinks already" (153). Karl's words remind us that the demise of the sovereign means the death of "man" and the image of his thought, alongside the cruelty that inheres in that unholy alliance. In this sense, the speech of the unaccountable idiot might be the play's only index of hope, for he announces the suspension, the becoming formless, of the powers that have claimed the redemptive forces of the fairy tale for their own, self-serving version of moralizing justice. No wonder, then, that in yet another version of the play, Marie turns to Karl in her despair, or that her feeble attempt at comfort is disappointed: "Karl! He's sunning himself!" (149). What else should one expect when in the midst of the worst?

Woyzeck and Marie

With flesh in mind, we turn, finally, to the tortured relationship between Woyzeck and Marie—or, perhaps we should say, to the ménage à trois among Woyzeck, Marie, and flesh. That the impingements of flesh color and even define the relationship between Woyzeck and Marie is made most obvious in the murder scene, with its earthiness and intrusive tactility, its images of Marie's "hot" lips and "whore's" breath. But the presence of flesh—flesh as the incomprehensible language particles with which we try to speak; as the impenetrable physicality of our material social relations; as the shame of denuded concepts and bodies; as that which cannot be captured, finally, by either sovereign or biopolitical arrangements of power—can be felt almost from the beginning of the play. We encounter it, for example, briefly in scene 4.2, when Marie, watching the Drum Major march past her window, declares that "he stands on his feet like a lion," and then again, in greater detail, in scene 4.6:

DRUM MAJOR: Marie!

MARIE: (*Looking at him expressively.*) Go march up and down for me.—A chest like a bull and a beard like a lion. Nobody else is like that.—No woman is prouder than me.

DRUM MAJOR: Sundays when I have my plumed helmet and my white gloves—goddamn, Marie! The prince always says: man, you're quite a guy!

MARIE: (*Mockingly.*) Aw, go on! (*Goes up to him.*) What a man!

DRUM MAJOR: What a woman! Hell, let's breed a race of drum majors, hey? (*He embraces her.*)

Setting a coarse, overbearing, almost parodic sexuality against the debasement of the heraldic tradition's sublime animal imagery, these scenes show the power that flesh has to penetrate and dissolve, from within, the structure of the social body. What had been a more or less coherent (if fanciful) sign system used to emblematize the natural power that the sovereign had taken over from the state of nature has now been transformed, after a period of revolutionary upheaval, into a set of clichés used to convey the Drum Major's sexual potency. Why, even the sovereign himself, or what's left of him, is impressed, at least according to the Drum Major: "Man, you're quite a guy," the prince always says. Still, the profanation of the sovereign's insignia has yet to translate into actual, historical change; flesh has yet to be fully appropriated by the body of the people. Potency has yet to achieve its full *potenza*.

Flesh is likewise present in another scene (scene X, in some editions) between Woyzeck and Marie, a scene where we can already witness a breakdown of the legible bodies produced by Lavater's physiognomy (later used for forensics) so thoroughgoing that even the bare matter and raw flesh of "man" fails to bestow certainty through physicality. "Every man is a bottomless pit," says Woyzeck, "you get dizzy when you look down. . . . Well, innocence, there's a mark on you. But can I know for sure? Can anyone?" (120). The encounter with the flesh of the other is ultimately a self-encounter for Woyzeck. Lacan, writing on Freud's dream of Irma's injection, provides us with a vivid account of just such a self-encounter:

There's a horrendous discovery here, that of the flesh one never sees, the foundation of things, the other side of the head, of the face . . . the flesh from which everything exudes . . . the flesh in as much as it is suffering, is formless, in as much as its form in itself is something which provokes anxiety . . . the final revelation of you are this—You are this, which is so far from you, this which is the ultimate formlessness."[46]

Following Lacan's lead, we choose to read Woyzeck's anxiety around the abysmal formlessness of flesh as a genuine political discovery. Looking down into the bottomless pit of "man," Woyzeck has a vision of community, the expropriating *munus* we all share, according to Roberto Esposito, as that which really remains once an exhausted social form of life dissolves and all that is solid melts into flesh.[47] The scene in which Woyzeck confronts Marie stages the horrific discovery that flesh is not only Woyzeck himself, the incarnation of his own question, but that flesh returns to him—to all of us—as the unavoidable and yet inscrutable question of the communal: flesh as the public Thing that we can neither assume in the form of a sovereign people nor disavow under the pretense that we are atoms without social or political bond. This might tempt us, once again, to read Woyzeck as akin to Schreber, for whom the symbolic universe has completely dissolved. But no: Woyzeck craves community and is capable of functioning, much to the satisfaction of Clarus and the Doctor, as one of its members. So he cannot be dismissed either as a psychotic or as a borderline personality who lives as if he were normal and as if he had no problem with "the reign of normality."[48] Instead, we must take Woyzeck's melancholic absorption in flesh for what it is: an absorption in the social, by way of the worst.

That is certainly the case, we would argue, in what may or may not be the climax of the play, the murder scene. For all its visceral immediacy, this scene unfolds to the beat of another, indeterminate time signature. The whole transpires, for example, in a time of suspension and arrest, introduced by Woyzeck's command to Marie to "stay here," "sit down," and abandon her daily routine. Then, all at once, as if time were collapsing in upon itself, we find ourselves immersed in linear time (Woyzeck's first question to Marie is, "Do you know how long it's been?"), liturgical time (indicated by Pentecost, with its summoning of communal spirits and foreign tongues), the prospect of eternity (Woyzeck's second question to Marie is, "And do you know how long it's going to be?"), and the natural historical time of the Apocalypse, when the moon rises red and shines like a bloody blade. Meanwhile, Woyzeck, as if filled with the Pentecostal spirit himself, seems to speak in a strange tongue—or, at least, not in a tongue that Marie can understand. "What are you talking about?" she asks. Woyzeck's response is telling: "Nothing," he says. This is an honest answer. What Woyzeck gives voice to is the "nothing" embodied by the Carnival Barker's monkey, the nothing that we all have in common: the nothing, the no-Thing, the lack even of lack—the nothing of flesh that the melancholic Woyzeck locates, or perhaps lodges, at the heart of community.

For this reason, Marie's murder should be read, not as the sudden eruption of a different time signature—the transformation of natural history into the real time of violence—but rather as its continuation: another iteration of Woyzeck's "on and on." The murder scene, as Svend Erik Larsen argues, undoubtedly demonstrates Woyzeck's attempt to assert his absolute possession and control over Marie, the other deeply melancholic character in the play.[49] It shows that Woyzeck, who in relation to Marie becomes the oppressor, is not an object of pity, as Richard Gray insists, and that the play is not simply a tragedy of social inequality.[50] True to the principle of displaced aggression and abjection, Woyzeck's disgust is not primarily directed against a single body but becomes generalized and absolute; it expresses an act of radical separation from the order that surrounds him. This is not to downplay the gravity of murder, that most sovereign of all sovereign acts. It is to propose, rather, that Woyzeck's act releases flesh from a body thoroughly patterned by power and the facile escape routes—stolen pleasures and bodily transgressions—it allows. Nor is it to make Woyzeck out to be some sort of agential hero. On the contrary, Woyzeck intends only to contain the flesh that has overwhelmed him. And yet his efforts at containment are what touch off flesh's exfoliation and fibrillation, allowing it to disperse so widely, and so suddenly, that it befalls even Woyzeck himself. Woyzeck's questions to Marie's mutilated body—"Can't you die? There! There! Ah—she's still twitching—not yet? Not yet? Still alive? (*Stabs once again.*) Are you dead?"—are thus the right ones, the questions to pose to a corpse as it enters into the afterlife of the "on and on" (152).

Still living, "twitching," quivering: in the murder scene, flesh becomes detached from a body that a master discourse, be it sovereign or biopolitical, might otherwise seek to claim for itself. What outlives the murder scene, in fact, is a fleshly combination of an agitated shame that no master would want to claim and a natural historical residue that it could never claim. The sovereign and biopolitical apparatuses each work, in part, by separating physis from nomos; their task is to create a biopolitical body, conjoined with a legal person.[51] Woyzeck's act, by contrast, separates body from person in a way that returns physis to its own, guilt-free nomos—that unleashes a flesh that cannot be mastered, a flesh that is radically masterless.

In that respect, flesh, now separated from body by Woyzeck's act of murder, shares something in common with the knife used to carry out that murder. Coming from the very margins of the outside (figured, in this case, by "the JEW") and purchased without regard for the economy of exchange ("WOYZECK How much is the knife? JEW It's good and straight. You want to cut your throat with it? Well, how about it? I'll give it to you as cheap as anybody else; your death'll be cheap, but not for nothing. How about it? You'll have an economical death. WOYZECK That can cut more than just bread. JEW Two cents. WOYZECK There! [*Goes off.*] JEW There! Like it was nothing"), the knife stands for a different oikonomia altogether, one outside of guilt history and directed, finally, toward the destruction of every oikos. The two scenes organized around the knife, 1.19 and 1.20, are easily misread as depicting a calculated effort on Woyzeck's part to conceal the murder weapon, a state of affairs that only serves to affirm his premeditation and guilt. And it is true that, at times, Woyzeck, in straining to devise a cohesive crime story that would rationalize to the world and to himself the mystery of his act, sounds a bit like Nietzsche's "Pale Criminal," "who was equal to his deed when he did it; but he could not bear its image after it was done."[52] At the same time, though, we begin to notice how Woyzeck, in fixating on the knife, becomes strangely side-tracked from his original purpose and how a kind of haunted thinking, not necessarily originating with Woyzeck himself, starts to supplant the guilt-laden thinking of a murderer suddenly astonished by the enormity of his crime. In short, what we begin to detect, in the dichotomies of Woyzeck's own thought processes, is yet another separation, set in motion by the separation of flesh from body: the separation of Woyzeck from what we will call the "Woyzeck idea."

Consider that the pure potentiality of Woyzeck's act survives even after he himself begins to behave like a common criminal. One sees this, for example, in the juxtaposition of scene 1.16, with its eerie beckoning—

FIRST PERSON: Wait!

SECOND PERSON: You hear it? Shh! Over there.

FIRST PERSON: Ooh! There! What a sound.

SECOND PERSON: That's the water, it's calling. Nobody has drowned for a long time. Let's go—it's bad to hear things like that.

FIRST PERSON: Ooh! There it is again. Like someone dying.

SECOND PERSON: It's weird. It's so fragrant—some gray fog, and the beetles humming like broken bells. Let's get out of here!

FIRST PERSON: No—it's too clear, too loud. Up this way. Come on.

—and scene 1.17, in which Woyzeck can almost be heard to address, or perhaps indict, the play's audience: "Damn it, what do you want? What's it got to do with you? Get away, or the first one who—damn it! You think I killed someone? Am I a murderer? What are you staring at? Look at yourselves! Out of my way!" (153). One sees the potentiality of the Woyzeck idea most clearly, though, in the intimation that Woyzeck's absorption in the knife— the knife that, under the force of Woyzeck's imagination, continually changes: into stone, into rust, into the secret object that, if discovered, would alter the lives of those who in the summer go swimming or diving for shells—will outlive Woyzeck while continuing the project of dissolution set in motion by his act. Expressing more than just the rationalizations of the guilty man, Woyzeck's fleeting vision of the knife rusting away under water provides a striking image for the corrosive power of natural history to dissolve guilt history, rendering transitory what had seemed eternal. An object-image smuggled from the outside into the innermost recesses of power, the knife comes to stand not only for Woyzeck's act of murder but also, in diminutive form, for all the violent instruments of a guilt history that can only comprehend Woyzeck's act as an affront to its own preroga- tive to inflict and expiate law-preserving violence. What wears away at the physical knife also wears away at the symbolic sword wielded by the pow- ers of guilt history, be they sovereign or biopolitical.

That the final scene of the play (in some versions, at least) should stage an attempt at neutralizing the lasting effects of the Woyzeck idea is almost to be expected. An inquest is called. Present are the representatives of an ascendant university discourse, an alliance of administrative rationality, popular opinion, and science—Court Clerk, Judge, Barber, Doctor—with the Clerk stepping forward as a kind of chorus tasked with assessing and aestheticizing Woyzeck's act: "[CLERK] A good murder, a real murder, a beautiful murder—as good a murder as you'd ever want to see. We haven't had one like this for a long time" (154). By this point, however, it is also to be expected that the representatives of this emerging master discourse will only betray their impotence; and that is indeed what happens. Tell- ingly, the Clerk responds to the dissolution perpetuated by the Woyzeck idea by invoking transcendental values inherited from the Middle Ages, the *bonum, verum et pulcrum*—a sign not only that the discourse of the university is still busily groping for a terminology of its own but also that it is incapable of capturing the new forms of life that it itself has pro- duced. In this case, however, those powers are already a step behind. Last we saw him, Woyzeck was wading farther and farther out into the pond, as if intending to archive himself, alongside the rusting knife, in natu- ral history. To its infinite credit, Büchner's *Woyzeck* never feeds into the frenzy that surrounds what Foucault calls "tales of murder," those hymns to disciplinary power that embellish, in great detail, the arrest, detention, interrogation, trial, conviction, incarceration, moral awakening (the silent struggle of remorse, crisis, revelation), and execution of the condemned man.[53] None of that drama of guilt, atonement, and salvation plays a role in Büchner's *Woyzeck*; no part of the documented case is romanticized or aggrandized. The character Woyzeck never rises to the status of an aestheticized, edifying exemplum that would perform for the people the tragic spectacle of an earthly justice carried out to the end or of a crime whose wounds are inevitably healed. Where Clarus, in the preface to his report, had promised the audience of Woyzeck's execution a spectacle of "penal justice" that "most people in the present generation have not yet experienced," Büchner systematically drains the character Woyzeck of all monstrosity and evil grandeur.[54] His natural historical Woyzeck does not repent or acknowledge guilt; nor does he make himself a subject. He simply wears away, without resorting to either "resistance" or obedience, at the discourses of the master and the university.

Dropping out of the play in such a manner, without trial or execution, Woyzeck leaves it to us to make sense of his act of murder and its aftermath. This is no straightforward task. We have argued that Woyzeck represents a new form of political subjectivity: a postrevolutionary melancholic subject. Typically, the melancholic remains fixated on a prior act of murder (or its close cousin, betrayal), and particularly so if that murder or betrayal exposes something rotten at the core of a given political formation. Thus Hamlet cannot get over the murder of his father, Plato the forced suicide of Socrates, or Freud (as we shall see in the next chapter) the foundational murder of Moses. Here, though, we encounter a crucial variation on that motif: a murder that, committed by a melancholic, founds the melancholic community to follow. An act of the worst, committed by the worst, in the midst of the worst, Woyzeck's murder of Marie encrypts itself as the cause of a new, postrevolutionary, universal community of the worst: a community we not only cannot get over but to which all of us now belong. Like it or not, Woyzeck's unexpiated act is our "20th of January," the irrefutable datum of every politics pursued in its wake.

CHAPTER FOUR

The Melancholic
Transformation of Dr. Freud

TO CHART THE development of Freudian psychoanalysis is to trace the arc of a strange history: the history of a quasi-political organization and its sovereign-like leader as they are undermined, year by year and in the face of fierce resistance, by the melancholic principles of their own constitution.[1] That Freud maintained an abiding interest in *Hamlet* is well known.[2] Less well known, or perhaps just underappreciated, is the degree to which Freud's thinking assumed, over time, the contours of Hamlet's counterplot against and within the state. It is as if Claudius, rather than trying to have Hamlet murdered, had instead decided to heed the latter's counsel—had decided, even, to assist in carrying out his stepson's revenge. It is as if, having entered into another scene, the would-be master was finally led, under the indifferent tutelage of the melancholic, to encounter himself. That self-encounter, unfolding, like a Platonic dialogue, in stages of compounding dissolution, would eventually culminate in what may well be Freud's most melancholic text: *Moses and Monotheism*. It begins, however, with Freud's failure to encounter himself in the one place where such an encounter might be most expected, the interpretation of his own dream.

The Dream of Irma's Injection

It was his patient Dora's "incessant repetition of the same thoughts about her father's relations with Frau K." that first called Freud's attention to the link between hysteria and melancholia:

"I can think of nothing else," [Dora] complained again and again. "I know my brother says we children have no right to criticize this behaviour of father's. He declares that we ought not to trouble ourselves about it, and ought even to be glad, perhaps, that he has found a woman he can love, since mother understands him so little. I can quite see that, and I should like to think the same as my brother, but I can't. I can't forgive him for it."

To which Freud appends the following footnote: "A supervalent thought of this kind is often the only symptom, beyond deep depression, of a pathological condition which is usually described as 'melancholia,' but which can be cleared up by psychoanalysis like a hysteria."[3]

Although we never fail to be impressed by Freud's belief in the curative powers of his own creation, that is not what interests us in this passage. What interests us is that Freud detects, in the way that Dora cannot stop thinking about how she cannot forgive her father, the workings of melancholia in one of Dora's hysterical symptoms. What interests us even more is how easily Freud becomes captivated by Dora's externalization of her melancholia, how quickly and effortlessly he becomes a conduit for her repetitious speech.[4] (The bulk of the passage consists of Freud citing Dora, supplemented by his subordinated footnote.) Most impressive of all is how skillfully Dora's performance positions Freud as yet another deluded master, convinced that he can, or should, clear up her pathological symptom. Freud himself believed that the hysteric acted out, theatrically, by way of their symptoms, a repressed trauma. Symptoms were the script, the analyst the interpreter of that script, and cathartic expulsion of trauma the goal of the theatrical production. But it would be more accurate to say that the theater in this case, the scene performed by the hysteric, is itself the trauma: that the trauma is nothing but its own representation, endlessly enacted. In such a scene, the analyst is not a master, not even an impotent one. Nor is he the spectator for whose benefit the scene is being performed. He is merely a prop within the scene, with no more insight into, agency within, or immunity from the scene than any other prop.

With that in mind, let us turn to one of the pivotal, if not foundational, scenes of psychoanalysis, the much-scrutinized dream of Irma's injection.[5] The manifest content of this dream, which Freud himself called the "specimen dream" of psychoanalysis, is easily summarized—or, perhaps we should say, staged.[6] Freud dreams that he is in a large hall receiving guests when he spots his patient "Irma," whom he takes aside and reproaches for not accepting his "solution" to her as-yet mysterious ailment. She complains of pains in her throat, her stomach, her abdomen. "It's choking me," she says. Freud, alarmed, convinced that he must be "missing some organic trouble," takes Irma to the window and, despite her "signs of recalcitrance," peers into her mouth. There, Freud is shocked to discover "a big white patch" and, in another place, "extensive whitish grey scabs on some remarkable curly structures." "All at once" Freud calls in his mentor, Dr. M., who, though he "looks quite different" than in waking life, nevertheless confirms Freud's findings. By this point, Freud's friends Otto and Leopold are also standing beside Irma, Leopold "percussing her through her bodice," pointing out a "dull area" on her left side and some "infiltrated" skin on her shoulder. Dr. M. says that it must be an infection, at which point Freud and the others are "directly aware" of the infection's origin: "Otto had given her an injection of a preparation of propyl, propyls . . . propionic acid . . . trimethylamin"—Freud can now distinctly see "the formula for this printed in heavy type." The dream then ends with Freud thinking that such injections "ought not to be made so thoughtlessly" and that "probably the syringe had not been clean."

So much for the manifest content. The core of the dream-work, like the bulk of Freud's account of the dream, consists of a detailed analysis of its latent content and implied dream-wish, and it is here that we find Freud at his most evasive and self-deceiving.[7] Proceeding as if he were performing in his own hysterical theater, Freud lays out two seductive lures in his analysis of the dream, two temptations meant to draw us away from a direct confrontation with the core of the dream, its simultaneous barrenness and rottenness. One lure is that of the lecherous Freud, the Freud who titillates us with the hint of illicit sex and intimate secrets. The other is that of the guilty Freud, the Freud who assumes the burden of his past failings and imagined transgressions, who intrigues us by promising to divulge personal indiscretions and professional jealousies.[8] Both scenarios stylize and aggrandize Freud as a heroic figure for a new age, someone willing to confront such embarrassing topics as sexuality and guilt; yet each one abides by the same logic of the veil, enticing us with the promise of more, more: more crime, more sex, more insider knowledge.[9] Like "the man who was charged by one of his neighbours with having given him back a borrowed kettle in damaged condition," Freud offers us an excess of justification and salacious biographical detail, a veritable too-muchness that only serves, as it is intended to do, to undermine Freud's analysis from within (152–153). For what we encounter once the dream has been analyzed, once its contents have been drained away, is not the opulence we were promised but its opposite: a "dull area." And we encounter, too, a Freud dulled to the workings of his own monstrous method, a Freud who hopes, perhaps, that we are too dull-witted to notice what he has injected into the world. What we encounter, in short, is a Freud still in the process of converting to the political melancholia that so absorbs him in his patients.

Except that in the case of this, the foundational dream of psychoanalysis, the "patient" involved is one that Freud does not have and will never have. She is one step removed, just out of Freud's reach: the intimate friend of Irma's of whom Freud has "a very high opinion" and who he wishes would ask him to relieve her of her hysterical symptoms but who never does, she being "of a very reserved nature" (142–143). That is of course the central point and the basis of the secret affinity Freud feels for her: she is a hysteric who does not want to be cured, a skilled performer of symptoms who does not wish to be relieved of those symptoms, particularly and precisely because they so absorb the would-be master.[10] Freud makes no attempt to hide his fantasy. "What could the reason have been for my having exchanged [Irma] in the dream for her friend?" Freud wonders.

> Perhaps it was that I should have *liked* to exchange her: either I felt more sympathetic towards her friend or had a higher opinion of her intelligence. For Irma seemed to me foolish because she had not accepted my solution. Her friend would have been wiser, that is to say she would have yielded sooner. She would then have *opened her mouth properly*, and have told me more than Irma (143).

Freud's wish is that Irma's friend would be less recalcitrant than the patient he has, more willing to open her mouth and reveal to Freud the secrets of her condition, secrets that would confirm Freud's theories. But in a sense, she does exactly that. Without saying a word (in analysis, at any rate), she leads Freud to the "unplumbable" navel of the dream by instructing him, as we shall see, in the melancholic art of staging a confrontation with flesh (143, note 2).[11]

Yet the affinity between them does not stop there. Although they come to the revelation from different angles (one might say that the friend performs for Freud what his work otherwise expresses unconsciously), both Freud and the friend understand that the cure in this case, psychoanalysis, is yet another disease—that the cure is a symptom with the power to undermine the illusory health of the social body. Paradoxical as it might sound, the friend's refusal of the cure—her persistence in the symptom— offers a model for how Freud might intensify the effects of the symptom that is the cure. As her hysterical symptom absorbs Freud, so too will Freud's cure be injected into the society that might otherwise prove recalcitrant.

Moreover, Freud and the friend share an awareness that the disease that has infiltrated the social body is a manufactured disease. It is worth noting that Dr. M. diagnoses the friend as having a diphtheritic membrane. This sounds innocuous enough, or serious enough, or legitimate enough—until one recalls that a diphtheritic membrane is a false membrane. In true hysteric fashion, the friend knows how to perform the symptoms of disease better than those who "genuinely" suffer from disease. And that symptom, simply by virtue of being performed, at once drains the social disease of its claim to naturalism or organicism while also laying the groundwork for the historical dis-solution of the social as such. For Freud's solution is, as he himself points out, and as Derrida so powerfully reiterates, a dissolution.[12] Only it is not the dissolution of the symptom through the work of interpretation. Nor is it an interiorized dissolution, the dissolution of the subject alone. It is the dissolution of a society working to immunize itself against the worst—disease, rot, decay—brought about by the power of a symptomatic cure.

Freud introduces this idea obliquely, by citing Schiller's image of Reason as a gatekeeper that must itself be carefully watched:

> "It seems a bad thing and detrimental to the creative work of the mind if Reason makes too close an examination of the ideas as they come pouring in—in the very gateway, as it were. . . . On the other hand, where there is a creative mind, Reason . . . relaxes its watch upon the gates, and the ideas rush in pell-mell" (135).

Already Freud seems to be thinking along the lines he will go on to develop, thirty years later, in *Civilization and Its Discontents*: the mental apparatus as a sort of polis or even a fortress. Yet what is it that threatens this polis if the ideas that come "pouring in," pell-mell, like an unruly mob (and is a relaxed Reason then in league with that mob?), are in fact internally generated? What is Reason guarding, exactly: the mind, or the society outside of that mind? An entire, outmoded political structure seems to be threatened by the process of free association. That Freud's analysis of the dream of Irma's injection functions, transitively, as an analysis of the society depicted in that dream is by this point well understood.[13] The image of Reason as a guard of sorts induced to relax its watch upon the gates is of a piece with that aspect, at once political and metaphorical, of the dream-work. The mind is a citadel, Reason is a guard, and analysis leads a riot of ideas through the gates. But precisely because of its political associations, the image also draws our attention to the conflicting versions of immunitarianism at work in Freud's interpretation, with the injection itself already serving as a figure for what we can and cannot, or rather should and should not, immunize ourselves against. Like the psyche, the city may try to immunize itself against threats from the outside, just as it may try to throw off the yoke of cruel repression. But against a dissolution that collapses the distinction between barrier and passage, a dissolution administered from the outside and yet generated from within, there can be no remedy.[14]

Freud's fantasy is simple enough. Using such techniques as free association, transference, and interpretation, psychoanalysis will aid the patient in constructing a benign immunitarian force capable of neutralizing the cruel and excessive auto-destructive immunitarian reaction exhibited in self-censorship and repression—a counter-immunity, as it were.[15] Later, as it evolves, psychoanalysis will place the lowering of the patient's immunitarian responses to all that threatens to disrupt the equilibrium of the psychical economy—the detrimental, the uncomfortable, the unhealthy, even the traumatic—at the very center of its political vision. But here, in the transitional stage of his career, Freud pursues the lowering of one's defenses solely in the name of personal health, which in *The Interpretation of Dreams* is understood as liberation from "the obsessional idea, or whatever it might be" (133). Here the solution is defined simply as the removal—the "unraveling," accomplished through the revelatory work of analysis—of the symptoms that plague us. The symptom stands in the way of health and therefore must be dissolved. Then, once the process of analysis has disabled the pathologically overprotective mechanisms of an "unhealthy" auto-immunitarian system of repressions and defense mechanisms, a true self (inevitably conflated with a "healthy" self) can emerge and the patient can return to the drawing room from the consulting room.

Yet what seems to elude Freud is what his patients already recognize: that the "whatever it may be" that calls up our psychical defenses may in fact be the solution of psychoanalysis. What Freud's patients fear, and what they try to immunize themselves against, is the threat posed by dissolution to the equilibrium that Freud assumes constitutes normative health, an equilibrium that will surely be restored by the dissolution of the patient's symptom. Caught up as he is in unlocking the secret of dreams, Freud never stops to consider that the melancholic core of his own method—to attentively pursue ideas that retain the character *of* ideas (rather than getting transposed into images) so that involuntary ideas might be transformed into voluntary ones—may well have unforeseen consequences (134–135). For once we learn how to will the pathological ideas that previously held us captive, we lose the comforting assurance that immunization (through the reduction of unhealthy self-censorship, say) against the cruel excesses of an immune response will automatically lead to freedom and healing. It may lead instead, as Freud's patients fear, to an ability to voluntarily pursue what had been involuntary ideas, and thus to the act of affirming whatever it is that their symptoms had kept at bay.

Freud himself contends that the relaxation of Reason's watch upon the gates is by no means difficult (136). And yet the violent resistance mounted against that relaxation by the patient's own psychical survival mechanism suggests that it is profoundly difficult, because everything is at stake. Should Reason step down, there will be no more barriers between the patient and an agitated interior world of dissolution and disgust, populated by an unruly mob. Instead of dissolving the pathological ideas that constitute an unhealthy, inauthentic, fragmented self, the dismissal of the guard can end up dissolving the supposedly true self that analysis seeks to restore, a self defined by the equilibrium of a correctly functioning mental apparatus. Analysis in this case would function as the dissolution of the very self that goes too far in its effort to counteract, or immunize itself against, the unhealthy immune response of excessive self-censorship and cruel repression. Not only does the fortress of the self come crashing down; it is brought down by the very analysis meant to shore it up. For in this case, the "proper" immunization offered by the cure, an immunization against the immune response of repression, only ends up turning against the self it seeks to restore. It is analysis, in other words, that conjures up a truth that is at once too overwhelming to bear—too symptomatic, too unrepressed—and yet truer, in its symptomatic intensity, than the balanced or authentic self that constitutes the healthy self of the psychoanalytic cure. Analysis, which styled itself the defender of a truer equilibrium against the depredations of a pathological immune reaction, has now become an attacker bent on forcing a confrontation with a truth that pays no heed to health or life or equilibrium. It has become, in short, the symptom of a curative disease.

None of that deters Freud, however. Instead, he blithely forges ahead, issuing what amounts to a categorical imperative for a new, exposed community:

> And now I must ask the reader to make my interests his own for quite
> a while, and to plunge, along with me, into the minutest details of my
> life; for a transference of this kind is peremptorily demanded by our
> interest in the hidden meaning of dreams (138).

In other words, suffer along with me. Don't be fooled by the benign appearance of the dream to follow or by the seemingly organic nature of your pathological symptoms. There is nothing organic at work here. At work here is the possibility that exposure might dissolve the pathological circularity between two mutually reinforcing metaphors: that of the healthy individual body and that of the whole social body. Be brave!

Lacan and, following him, Joan Copjec both praise this courageous version of Freud, the Freud who stays faithful to the authentic symptom revealed by analysis, the Freud who fully enjoys the symptom, expressed in his dream, that threatens his very being.[16] But while not unfounded—Freud really is the "tough customer" Lacan makes him out to be—such praise can distract us from the ambivalence in Freud's attitude, to say nothing of the backsliding.[17] For in a sense, the courage Freud displays, and that he would like his patients to display, is simply an extension of the logic of the pleasure principle, insofar as the dissolution of the self down to the core (so to speak) of the symptom offers an especially subtle way of erecting a defense against the pressures of life. It is as if the subject were sending a message to the Other: *You gave me too much life to bear, and now you will have to live without me! I hereby dissolve myself in favor of the symptom!* Such a message amounts to little more, however, than an appeal to the Other to provide the recognition that will somehow compensate for the dissolution of the self brought about by the analytical cure.

This desire for compensatory recognition finds various expressions in Freud's interpretation of his dream: his fantasy of the tablet at Bellevue commemorating his discovery, his belief that the "solution" of Trimethylamine constitutes a vatic message delivered to him as if from the gods (154). By far the most significant, however, is Freud's worry that there is an Old Testament-style punishment in store for him, one in which his daughter Mathilde must be sacrificed, in the manner of an eye for an eye, for the loss of another Mathilde, whom Freud believes he killed by treating her with an unproven medicine (and not, one infers, with his own cure). In this scenario, organized around an imaginary court scene where Freud is called to account for "a tragic event in his practice," guilt and reparation function as the ultimate form of recognition from the Other (144). Yet this is not the only guilt that Freud seeks to assuage, not the only transgression for which he wishes to be held accountable. The dream is a fulfillment of a wish, which in this case is Freud's avowed wish to be recognized for having unlocked the secret of dreams. But this particular dream also fulfills another wish: the wish to be punished, and in being punished, recognized, for having injected society with the dirty needle of psychoanalysis.[18] This is an ambivalence reflected in the dream-work itself. On the one hand, the dream expresses a profound hostility toward the medical establishment that derided Freud's theories even when its own practices, which Freud faithfully followed, brought death. Freud's great error, he comes to realize, was to allow himself to be led to believe that his patients' ailments were organic, when he suspected otherwise. On the other hand, the dream attempts to blunt that hostility by atoning for it with a succession of guilty excuses: for Freud himself, for his friends, for his hapless associates, even for the Other, who is understandably upset with Freud for having harbored such aggressive wishes in the first place.

Here then we find, in Freud's own dream, a magnificent expression of his theory that the dream is a fulfillment of a wish; for this is a dream that brings anxiety, destruction, and guilt down upon the heads of all its male characters only so that it can then turn around and gloss over their errors and transgressions. Yet glossing over is not the same as negating, and in this case the dream-work ends up working against itself by encrypting its most aggressive wishes, born of a genuinely aggressive drive, so that they elude the dissolution of interpretation. Freud is courageous; everybody says so. Yet what makes Freud courageous is not that he confronts the symptom but that he refuses to present terminality—a dissolution of the self, catharsis, negation, sacrifice, an arrested enjoyment of the merely deadly symptom—as being equivalent to the heroic attainment of analytical truth. Carefully threading the needle (a needle never to be used to suture a wound), Freud avoids having to make the false choice between playing along with the hysteric's drama, on the one hand, or moving to delimit the damage that drama might inflict, on the other. Despite how the dream piles up one terrible thing after another—diseases, ailments, rottenness, anxieties—Freud never panics. On the contrary, like the man who borrowed his neighbor's kettle, Freud *makes* the scene worse and worse by offering a succession of interpretations, explanations, qualifications, and excuses—more of them, finally, than the dream material can bear.[19] In this, however, he remains true to his own method, which entails cutting up the pieces of a dream in an act of potentially infinite, and also intensifying, dissolution: an intensification of the parts that ends up overwhelming, and draining, the whole (136).

Our interest in Freud is thus an interest in the worst. And what is the worst? It is to discover, after being forced to resort to an entirely self-generated punishment for an unconscious aggressiveness that refuses to be quelled, that there exists no Other, either whole or lacking, in whose name one must immunize himself or that must be immunized against.

There can be found no intersection between the individual body and the body politic, no boundary that must be policed in the name of life, precisely because no such life exists.[20] How could it, when the sovereign force whose ban creates the life of *bíos* is shown not to exist in the first place? Yet if Freud is able to create the worst, that is because we are already living in the midst of the worst. The symptom he creates, psychoanalysis, is simply a manifestation of the worst at the point of dissolution. Writing at the end of the nineteenth century, Freud proceeds as though he were working to dissolve the world represented by that century's social-educational novel. Gone are the vital metaphors associated with the beauty and harmony of sociability: the dances, the picnics, the table talk, the amorous escapades in the library or on the balcony. Instead we encounter a protagonist, Freud, who seems only half there, an undead interloper in the midst of a social circle comprising friends and family members with whom he experiences no social relation, no life, only disappointment: his colleagues, his patients, his wife, his calling, his ambition to heal. Though it may employ all of the elements of the social, Freud's dream steadfastly refuses to stage a scene of sociability. And while it may possess a certain haunting beauty, that beauty is lifeless.

More, then, than a world in which the social bond has disintegrated, this is a world emptied of persons who could be bonded. What we find instead are impersonals, transindividuals that act without acting, characters rendered characterless in their composite makeup, their lack of depth or dimension or relation, in their rote, mechanical response to external stimuli.[21] In ghost-like fashion, the characters on the stage of Freud's dream materialize as if they had been waiting in the wings until prompted to take their places, to enter limping or fading, to jump in or resist, to act shocked or recalcitrant (139–140). Guided by an acute sense of timing, choreography, and the employment of props, the figures populating the dream scene are outlined in stark visual detail: pale and beardless, beautifully clothed and yet sickly, with rotted flesh underneath (140). Freud's communion is not with the living; it is with these strangely undead figures, these automatons and recalcitrant hysterics, these robotic dream functionaries, all of them following the gravitational pull of a particular dream-logic.

But let us push this a bit further. If the characters in Freud's dream seem, like Freud himself, to be undead, prone to a kind of fading, that is because they are less individuals than allegories of the affects—the ambition, worry, shock, bewilderment, confusion, and dismay—that flood the scene of the dream. It is as if Freud were staging a play, only the stage was populated not by persons or even characters but by composite figures allegorizing a welter of affects. Here again, Freud could be said to follow the example set by the highly intelligent friend of Irma's, the hysteric who, in her aloofness and her mastery of the social symptom, teaches Freud how to stage a particular encounter: an encounter with flesh. Beyond the dream-work, beyond the symptom, there persists the overwhelming presence of the still-living flesh, the flesh that does not coincide with the body: the excretions and false membranes, the prostheses and instruments— dentures, syringes, drugs, formulae, poisons, injections—the bodies marked not as persons but as signifiers and citations, the composites without individuality.[22] And then the affects, free-floating and oppressive, unavoidable: shame, anxiety, guilt, desire, disgust, doubt. Freud does not hesitate to share his most intimate private distress. Against *this* overwhelming *munus*, this unavoidable burden of flesh, there can be no immunity.[23] Here is Freud's true courage; it is found in his willingness to stage this utter lack of immunity, to offer up the munus, the gift, of the worst. In place of the hysteric's eternal refrain, the *This is not it!* addressed to the Other, Freud exposes both himself and us to the *This is it!* of inescapable flesh. There is no other life than this, the life of disease and putrescence: the eternally dying life. One need no longer worry about preserving life, person, identity, individuality; one need only preserve symptom, affect, life understood as an unmaking of the curable body. If the dream of Irma's injection fulfills a wish, it is the wish, finally, to be free of life.

That is not how Freud understands it, of course. When, at the end of his analysis, Freud confidently announces that he has "now completed the interpretation of the dream," he becomes one more link in a chain of dubious authorities whose farfetched claims to mastery open them up to ridicule (151). The first link is Dr. M., whom Freud ridicules; another is the colleague whom Dr. M. ridiculed for holding a misguidedly "optimistic view" (146–147). And now we have Freud, who still believes he can assert the mastery of interpretation over the symptomatic material of his specimen dream. But the year was 1900, and Freud was still not ready to encounter himself. Nor was he yet able to admit that it is always too late to offer a solution, once the injection has been made.

Beyond the Pleasure Principle

Freud's proposal sounds so appealing that we are almost tempted: tempted to accept it, tempted to believe that it could ever be accepted, tempted to believe that Freud himself believed it to be possible, if only for a moment. "At this point," he writes (the point in question being the only inner-chapter section break in *Beyond the Pleasure Principle*), "I propose to leave the dark and dismal subject of the traumatic neurosis and pass on to examine the method of working employed by the mental apparatus in one of its earliest *normal* activities—I mean in children's play."[24] One can sympathize with Freud's desire to flee from the dismal subject of the traumatic neurosis (and its close cousin, the war neurosis) into the comforts of home and family. He was not, after all, the only one to survey the Austrian landscape in the years following the Great War and despair of oikonomia. In government there was factionalism. In the streets there was turmoil. In finance there was crushing debt, offset by inflation. Everywhere else there was unemployment.[25] Yet the problem was not only that Austria appeared to be suffering from mismanagement disguised as rationality. It was that the anarchism of the state must have seemed like an extension of the madness of the war, and the madness of the war had represented a failure of oikonomia so thoroughgoing that it had managed to implicate Freud's own economic model of mental functioning. Now daily life itself stood as an affront to the pleasure principle. But that was not the end of it. Freud, amateur classicist that he was, surely appreciated the bitter irony that the governmentality on display all around him would have had its origins in the home, the oikos: that it would have radiated outward from the very place one sought refuge from it. Wherever one turned, one could not escape from the failure of oikonomia. What was more, no one could escape from the possibility of freedom implicated by that failure. Not even Freud.

Freud opens *Beyond the Pleasure Principle* by restating the then-canonical understanding of the pleasure principle as "automatically" regulating "the course of mental events" (18:7). By the end of chapter 1, however, Freud has come to acknowledge that "the investigation of the mental response to external danger," a phenomenon exemplified by the war neurosis, "is precisely in a position to produce new material and raise fresh questions bearing upon our present problem": namely, the realization that not *all* mental events are automatically governed by the economy of the pleasure principle (18:11). Setting aside the creeping excess of Freud's own language—the longing for something to "produce new material," to bring a "fresh" product to the marketplace of ideas—which already hints at something beyond the supposedly closed economy of mental functioning, the war neurosis presents us with a crucial violation of the pleasure principle; for not only does it result in a masochistic compulsion to repeat an unpleasurable experience, but that compulsion seems to repeat its origins as an affliction imposed by humans upon other humans in the name of total, mechanized warfare. There is something vaguely mysterious about the war neurosis, as there is about all traumatic neuroses, in that it presents us with a mechanistic and automated mental process generated by the exposure of the human body to the machine. That sounds "modern," and it is. But the war neurosis itself functions by compulsively returning to a "time" (if that is the right word) before the imposition of the pleasure principle and independent of it. Considering that the affliction in question is one visited upon individual lives by anarchic state power, it can only seem as though the state were not in the business of governance or politics but of actively seeking out suffering and turmoil—as if we didn't suffer enough already from traumas generated both externally and internally. Here, then, is the basic scandal from which Freud proceeds: the state, which in certain respects ought to stand as the realization of the pleasure principle as modified by the reality principle—regulated, conditional, constant, organized around the satisfaction of needs and the deferral of immediate gratification in the interests of the whole—already indicates that there is a beyond of the pleasure principle.

And so Freud turns to an activity that he regards as explicitly economical, geared toward the management of pleasure and the achievement of equilibrium. Other theories of children's play "attempt to discover the motives which lead children to play, but they fail," according to Freud, "to bring into the foreground the *economic* motive, the consideration of the yield of pleasure involved." Fortunately, continues Freud,

> I have been able, through a chance opportunity which procented itself, to throw some light upon the first game played by a little boy of one and a half and invented by himself. It was more than a fleeting observation, for I lived under the same roof as the child and his parents for some weeks, and it was some time before I discovered the meaning of the puzzling activity which he constantly repeated (18:14).

Who would not be tempted to pull up a chair and listen as Freud, taking a few satisfied puffs on his cigar, recounted the story of his latest discovery? Alas, though, what initially promises to be a reprieve from suffering, even a return to "normal"—to home and family and the innocence of childhood—turns out to be anything but. Instead, we find ourselves confronted with yet another traumatic repetition, this one generated by Freud himself and presented to us in the dispassionate guise of an especially "scenic" case study: that of the much-scrutinized *fort-da* game.[26]

"One day," Freud tells us, he made an observation that confirmed his view that the "occasional disturbing habit" his grandson had of taking "any small object he could get hold of" and throwing it away while giving "vent to a loud, long-drawn-out 'o-o-o-o'" intended to represent "the German word '*fort*' ['gone']" was in fact a game, invented by the child himself. "The child," Freud continues, drawing us further into the innermost recesses of his family life, his home, his thought,

> had a wooden reel with a piece of string tied round it. It never occurred to him to pull it along the floor behind him, for instance, and play at its being a carriage. What he did was to hold the reel by the string and very skillfully throw it over the edge of his curtained cot, so that it disappeared into it, at the same time uttering his expressive 'o-o-o-o.' He then pulled the reel out of the cot again by the string and hailed its reappearance with a joyful "*da*" ["there"]. This, then, was the complete game—disappearance and return (18:14–15).

Freud's motives for staging this scene, ranging from the sentimental to the aggressive to the (as we shall argue here) obscurely political, are complicated, and it is not easy to untangle them. It seems likely, for example, that Freud revisits the scene of his grandson's game in an attempt to master the trauma of his daughter's death (which happened after the fact and is mentioned in a brief footnote), much as the child himself is said to play his repetitive game in order to master the "distressing experience" of his mother's unpredictable comings and goings. There seems little reason to doubt, moreover, that Freud foregrounds the "economic motive" behind children's games because he understands that the same economy structures his own research—because he understands that, on some level, his research comprises little more than an attempt to "hand on" to his reader the "disagreeable experience" of passive suffering so as to gain a "yield of pleasure from another source" (18:16). As plausible as those motives may be, however, neither should distract us from recognizing that there is another game afoot here as well. Freud may indeed resemble the game-playing child in his efforts at mastery and revenge; yet he more closely follows the child in his capacity for absorption. For, like the child, Freud continues to pursue his research-game until he has discovered, there—*da!*—in the midst of apparently innocent children's play, a compulsion to repeat that engulfs him in the life of a death drive he might otherwise have overlooked. Thus the promise of relief with which Freud first lured his reader into examining the most banal version of the repetition compulsion, the children's game, soon turns sour as we become aware of something else: a movement of endless mourning, expressed as a persistent undercurrent of rote repetition and marked by the sound, keening, almost animal-like, of a "loud, long-drawn-out 'o-o-o-o,'" from which we are offered no relief at all (18:14). Freud had meant to escape the trauma of repetition by retreating, along with the reader, into the novelty of interpretation. Instead, he finds himself slowly overwhelmed as repetition intrudes into a game that, as Freud would otherwise have it, expresses something novel in the life of the child: his "great cultural achievement" of "instinctual renunciation" (18:15); his accession to the demands of the reality principle; his immersion, "under the same roof" as his mother and grandparent, in historical time.

One way we know that Freud found something about the scene of repetition played out in the fort-da game to be particularly intriguing—and, for that reason, particularly bothersome—is that he draws on the language of pedagogical literature, the language of Rousseau and Pestalozzi, to set the mood. "The child was not at all precocious in his intellectual development," writes Freud, who then continues:

> At the age of one and a half he could say only a few comprehensible words; he could also make use of a number of sounds which expressed a meaning intelligible to those around him. He was, however, on good terms with his parents and their one servant-girl, and tributes were paid to his being a "good boy." He did not disturb his parents at night, he conscientiously obeyed orders not to touch certain things or go into certain rooms, and above all he never cried when his mother left him for a few hours (18:14).

That Freud should want to fall back upon the language of quasi-scientific observation to distance himself from the paradox at work here, the paradox of his grandson's utterly absorbing indifference to the very avatars of the master—mother, father, grandfather, doctor—that sentimentality assures us a child naturally turns to for comfort and direction, is perhaps not so surprising. All the same, we shouldn't allow Freud's distancing techniques to distance us from the strangeness of the scene itself. Freud is clearly puzzled, spooked even, by how alienated he feels from his own grandson, whom he describes in terms that make the child seem cold, mechanical, sterile, given over to solipsistic, quasi-totemic rituals. For "this good little boy," we are told,

> had an occasional disturbing habit of taking any small objects he could get hold of and throwing them away from him into a corner, under the bed, and so on, so that hunting for his toys and picking them up was often quite a business. As he did this he gave vent to a loud, long-drawn-out 'o-o-o-o,' accompanied by an expression of interest and satisfaction. . . . I eventually realized that it was a game and that the only use he made of any of his toys was to play "gone" with them (18:14–15).

One is tempted at first to interpret Freud's dispassionate inquiry as his attempt at imposing some control over the situation by bonding with a grandchild otherwise beyond his sphere of influence. Yes: this "good boy" with the "occasional disturbing habit" of becoming absorbed in a game invented by himself will validate Freud's theory that we master trauma through play. Yet Freud does not seem at all satisfied. On the contrary, one cannot help but catch, in Freud's vaguely disapproving attitude, the nagging worry that something in his grandchild's game eludes not just Freud's own mastery, or even his theory of mastery, but mastery, understood as the mastery achieved through repetition, altogether. Coolly (or so he would have us believe) observing his grandson repeatedly play a repetitious game of his own invention, Freud glimpses a realm where repetition attains an autonomy that needs no father, no mother, no grandfather, no curious researcher: a realm where the delights of play only confuse and disappoint the would-be master. That realm is not necessarily spatial, however. Mostly it expresses itself as a temporal dimension, the oddity of which is captured by the paradoxes of the child's game: at once constant and occasional, inexorable and unpredictable, rhythmically pulsating and "disturbing." What is more, that temporality intrudes upon—while also, one gets the impression from Freud's account, helping to pass—the "some weeks" of linear time in which Freud has the "chance opportunity" to carry out his observations. Simply in its peculiar time signature, then, the child's game implies the presence of another time, with a rhythm all its own, spliced through the economic time sequenced by the pleasure-reality principle. The child, whose mechanistic habits and obscure rituals make him appear more like a creature of natural history (akin to the assistants in Kafka's *The Castle*, say) than a member of Freud's immediate family, belongs to the other time of his game. And he makes Freud belong, indirectly, to that other time too.

Freud's response to this, the specter of his absence from the scene, is notable: he attempts to stage his own version of the fort-da game. Only this version of the game, in oscillating back and forth between an unsuccessful *fort!* and an equally unsuccessful *da!*—that is, between Freud's inability either to banish the child and his "disturbing game" from the ambit of Freud's concern as grandfather and researcher or else recuperate the child and his game as Freud's own possessions—doubly fails to help Freud master the trauma of his own discovery: that there is a repetition, charged with a yield of pleasure of another sort, for which his theory of the pleasure principle cannot account. Freud will end his discussion of the fort-da game by asserting that "there is no need to assume the existence of a special imitative instinct in order to provide a motive for play" (18:17).

Yet the irony is that his attempt at mastering the disturbance in his economic model of mental functioning precipitated by his grandson's game
only ends up mimicking the truth content of that game, which plays out a
drama, not of mastery, but of the master's captivation by, and subsequent
disappearance into, the natural historical realm, at once lively, rule-bound,
and artificial, of *spiel*.

At any rate, something about his grandchild's game captivates Freud,
or at least sticks with him. He could choose to stop with what he claims
the game has provided him: evidence of the continued existence and dominance of the pleasure principle. Instead, he embarks upon a wholesale
recapitulation and revision of that principle in the hopes of uncovering
evidence of what he has detected in the repetitive workings of the game,
"evidence of the operation of tendencies *beyond* the pleasure principle,
that is, of tendencies more primitive than it and independent of it" (18:17).
Chapters 3 and 4 of *Beyond the Pleasure Principle* are replete with images
of change and transformation—one might even say, along with Freud, the
speculative "work" of transformation—which make it plain that Freud has
declared a kind of fidelity not to what the fort-da game seems to accomplish but to the natural historical time it brings to light. "Unconscious
mental processes are in themselves 'timeless,'" Freud reminds us. "That
means in the first place that they are not ordered temporally, that time does
not change them in any way and that the idea of time cannot be applied
to them" (18:28). It is the unconscious that archives all of the memory-
traces that the system *Cs.*, exposed to the outside world as it is, can no
longer afford to absorb. So what would the time signature (as it were) of
that timelessness look like? How would it function, if it does not function according to the laws of an ordered temporality? Again, the constant-
occasional time scheme of the fort-da game only seems like it is meant to
master the suffering inflicted upon us by our exposure to stimuli. That is,
it only seems to be engaged with the space-time model of world history
that structures consciousness. But there is simply too much unconscious
suffering expressed in the "o-o-o-o" for this to be the case. Like the universal will to revolution evoked by Kant in "The Contest of Faculties," the
unconscious is not only timeless; it is indestructible and unforgettable,
and it wants to express itself. It does not, Freud reminds us again and
again, want to remain repressed; it wants to revolve, to come back around.
What has (not) been forgotten wants to be remembered. It *will* be remembered. But what, exactly, has been forgotten, and what is it that insists on
being remembered? There is something like a political parable at work
here: existence itself is made out by Freud to sound like the worst sort of

tyrant, despotic and cruel, delighting in humiliation. The injustices heaped upon us become unbearable. And yet, crucially, none of those injustices is ever forgotten; they survive, as memory-traces, in the unconscious. The pleasure principle may work to avoid the experience of unpleasure that recalling those injustices would surely bring; but the compulsion to repeat works to bring those injustices, that suffering, to light. Thus, at one point, Freud comes close to saying what needs to be said: that the compulsion to repeat *must* override the pleasure principle if only in the name of a just encounter with the suffering inflicted by a great wrong, a wrong barely covered over by the workings of oikonomia (18:22). Viewed from the perspective of the pleasure principle, the compulsion to repeat is noneconomical—"*more* primitive, *more* elementary, *more* instinctual"— in its excess and lack of equilibrium (18:23, emphasis added). Thus the greatest threat facing the compulsion to repeat, as Freud himself seems to recognize, is that it will be taken over by the ego and subjected to the dictates of the pleasure-reality principle, rather than retaining its autonomous existence. Freud has witnessed the struggle firsthand and been a party to it: "The phenomena of transference are obviously exploited by the resistance which the ego maintains in its pertinacious insistence upon repression; the compulsion to repeat, which the treatment tries to bring into its service is, as it were, drawn over by the ego to *its* side (clinging as the ego does to the pleasure principle)" (18:23). The greatest threat posed to the compulsion to repeat, in other words, is that it will be made to serve the interests of an oikonomia, rather than continue as the expression of, and preservation of, an unforgettable physionomos archived in the unconscious and enacted in such activities as the fort-da game. Unlike the system *Cs.*, which "ceases to have the structure proper to living matter," the deeper recesses archiving the memory-traces sloughed off by consciousness are still "living" (18:27). And what remains living there is a timeless drive to insurrection that insists on breaking through the repression imposed upon it, in the name of the pleasure principle, by "the higher strata" (18:19).

Now driven on by a game of compulsive repetition that is at once his own creation and beyond his control, Freud returns to the subject of children's play, and once again he turns children into monstrous, alien creatures possessed of a spellbinding power over any adult rash enough to be drawn into their games. Children are simply different from adults, avers Freud. Adults crave novelty: "If a joke is heard for a second time it produces almost no effect; a theatrical production never creates so great an impression the second time as the first; indeed, it is hardly possible to persuade an adult who has very much enjoyed reading a book to re-read it immediately" (18:35). But children! "Children," continues Freud,

> will never tire of asking an adult to repeat a game that he has shown them or played with them, till he is too exhausted to go on. And if a child has been told a nice story, he will insist on hearing it over and over again rather than a new one; and he will remorselessly stipulate that the repetition shall be an identical one and will correct any alterations of which the narrator may be guilty—though they may actually have been made in the hope of gaining fresh approval (18:35).

There are two things to note in this passage. The first is that it inscribes the intersection of two different conceptions of time. On the one hand, we have adult time, which is linear and organized around a succession of novel substitutions—in every way a time governed by the pleasure principle and modified by the detours, deferrals, and delayed gratifications imposed by the reality principle. On the other hand, we have children's time, which is insistent, repetitious, and categorical—in every way determined to engulf the inhabitants of adult time in the unpleasure that the seriality of the modi-fied economy of the pleasure principle, with its vague disappointments and nagging sense of emptiness, is meant to conceal. The second thing to note is how Freud then tacitly aligns psychoanalytic practice not only with children's games but also, by extension, with children's time. The passage serves, in other words, as Freud's ciphered confession that even he knows there is something monstrous about psychoanalytic practice—that there is very little daylight, finally, between the repetition staged by the analytic scene, with its one fundamental rule that the analysand free-associate, and the remorselessly repetitious games of children. Freud depicts children as little monsters playing monstrous games; and yet the primary aim of psychoanalysis is to induce the analysand to reenact, through transfer-ence and recollection, the events of childhood. Likewise, Freud wants to insist that repetition holds a pleasure all its own; and yet he finds him-self having to concede that repetition is deeply unpleasant to adults, and especially so to adults undergoing analysis, who become nothing less than infantile in their compulsions to repeat. What Freud intuits here is that analysis resembles a children's game in its strangeness and hermeticism, in the obscure dread it arouses. Just as the fort-da game played by his grandson puzzles and absorbs Freud, and just as the remorseless stipula-tions of the monstrous child exasperate the adult storyteller, so too does psychoanalysis puzzle, absorb, and exasperate, even frighten, those who become aware of its inner workings. What is transference, after all—what is the repetition structured by the analytical scene—if not an analogy to the remorseless stipulations imposed by the tyrannical child who exhausts the adult unwary enough to get drawn into the child's repetitious play: the adult forced to reenact the compulsion to repeat, to experience the suffering associated with the pleasure of another sort yielded by repetition? Freud does nothing, however, to alleviate those feelings of obscure dread. On the contrary, he intensifies them, exacerbating the same anxiety that he himself experienced upon being drawn into the "normal" activity of children's play. In a sort of infinite regression, Freud learns to exhaust his patients as he has been exhausted, in turn, by the monstrous children in his midst, children whose fresh approval he seeks even as he tries to distance himself from their activities (in both cases, like someone in analysis). The scene of reading to a child becomes, in *Beyond the Pleasure Principle*, the scene of reading into the repetition unleashed by psychoanalysis.

Unleashed by psychoanalysis even upon itself, one might say. Although it takes him five chapters to do so, Freud eventually comes around, if not to embracing the dual time-signature of psychoanalysis, then at least to exploring its more far-reaching implications. There is the economic time of the pleasure-reality principle, which aims to keep excitation at as low a level as possible so that, ideally, one moment follows the next in predictable regularity. It is a carefully managed time, predicated on the deferral of satisfaction and not the exhaustion brought about by its attainment. Its aim is a sort of telos, an infinitely receding end. That merely historical time (and here we should recall that the dominance of the pleasure-reality principle can only be established in time, that is, only sequentially, once traumatic dreams have helped to create anxiety and once "the other task of the mental apparatus, the task of the mastering or binding excitation" in the primary process has been accomplished [18:35]) is, however, spliced by another, uneconomical time. Freud makes this point quite clearly at the beginning of chapter 5. "The organism's 'instincts'—the representatives of all the forces originating in the interior of the body and transmitted to the mental apparatus," Freud writes, "have a preponderance in economic importance and often occasion economic disturbances comparable with traumatic neuroses" (18:34). The compulsion to repeat, which, Freud will breathlessly reveal, in italicized print, a few pages later, simply *is* instinct, arises from an inner realm that he had described, in the previous chapter, as being both "timeless" and "living." But there is now more to it than that. Not only is "the predicate of being 'instinctual,'" of being driven by a compulsion to repeat, lodged in the same timeless, living interior as the unconscious; it is "historically determined" (18:36, 37). Or, rather (to put words in Freud's mouth), naturally historically determined. For it is "examples from animal life"—certain fishes, migratory birds—"which seem to confirm the view that instincts are historically determined" (18:36–37). And not just animal life: "the most impressive proofs of there being an organic compulsion to repeat," Freud continues,

> lie in the phenomena of heredity and the facts of embryology. We see how the germ of a living animal is obliged in the course of its development to recapitulate (even if only in a transient and abbreviated fashion) the structures of all the forms from which it is sprung, instead of proceeding quickly by the shortest path to its final shape. This behavior is only to a very slight degree attributable to mechanical causes, and the historical explanation cannot accordingly be neglected (18:37).

It is the compulsion to repeat, then, that embeds us in natural history. And that history is deep indeed, with the power to draw every germ of every living animal into recapitulating the structures of all the forms from which it is sprung, going back millennia. Even Freud's own metaphor shows its influence; for, like a hunter in the wild, he feels that, in discovering *"that an instinct is an urge inherent in organic life to restore an earlier state of things,"* "we cannot escape a suspicion that we may have come upon the track of a universal attribute of instincts and perhaps of organic life in general which has not hitherto been clearly recognized or at least not explicitly stressed" (18:36).

Yet if the compulsion to repeat really does embed us in natural history (and Freud will go so far as to claim that, "in the last resort, what has left its mark on the development of organisms must be the history of the earth we live in and its relation to the sun" [18:38]), then it raises a question. Freud's theory is that the compulsion to repeat expresses the instinct, common to all organic life, "to restore an earlier state of things which the living entity has been obliged to abandon under the pressure of external disturbing forces" (18:36). At the same time, the compulsion to repeat is the compulsion to repeat something "distressing" or unpleasurable (18:15). That is what makes it, from the perspective of the pleasure principle at least, so perplexing. As Freud would have it, the earlier state of things that the living entity has been forced to abandon is a state of quiescence, chronologically prior to life and populated (as it were) by "inanimate things" (18:38). If there is something unpleasurable, even "daemonic," about the compulsion to repeat, it comes from the unbearable tension of straining to return to an inanimate state that the pressures of life itself, those "external disturbing forces" Freud mentions, has rendered inaccessible. The deeper into his theory Freud gets, however, the more one can begin to detect another way not only of understanding the instinctual compulsion to repeat but of evaluating the unpleasure it generates. More than repeating a moment of trauma, more even than returning compulsively to a moment of unjust coercion, the compulsion to repeat forces us to reenact, in our mental processes, what it is that has been lost but not forgotten, what remains living even in—only in—its inanimate state. There is a reason why Freud himself returns to children's games, to spiel. Like the physionomical natural history whose peculiar time signature it performs, spiel is a gestural, rule-bound activity dependent, as in the case of the fort-da game, on an inanimate object without which it could not be played. The compulsion to repeat is thus not an effort to restore a lost state but the continuous reenactment, within history, of a physionomical state.

This process can best be illustrated by comparing the different versions of the death drive that emerge in chapter 5.[27] For much of *Beyond the Pleasure Principle*, Freud seems convinced that he is advancing a version of the death drive that is, to borrow his own term, "conservative" (18:36). Its aim, says Freud, is not simply "to return to the inanimate state" whence organic life originated but to regulate tension and excitation in such a way as "to ward off possible ways of returning to inorganic existence other than those which are immanent in the organism itself" (18:38–39). We choose to call this conservative version of the death drive "sovereign" death drive for two, apparently contradictory, reasons. As the outward expression of what Freud repeatedly claims is the living organism's natural longing to "follow its own path to death" and fulfill the wish of dying "only in its own fashion," the conservative death drive cannot help but affirm the *ipseity*, the "own-ness," that constitutes the sovereign prerogative (18:39).[28] And yet it can only do so ironically, given that this same version of the death drive—this version in which, as Freud puts it in a metaphor combining both martial and immunitarian imagery, the instincts that act "as the guardians of life were originally, too, the myrmidons of death" (18:39)—has its genesis in the sovereign right to let live and make die. "The attributes of life were at some time evoked in inanimate matter by the action of a force of whose nature we can form no conception," writes Freud, simultaneously describing and occulting what sounds suspiciously like a moment of sovereign decision. "The tension which then arose in what had hitherto been an inanimate substance," Freud continues, "endeavored to cancel itself out. In this way the first instinct came into being: the instinct to return to the inanimate state" (18:38). That this mysterious action makes the supposedly "sovereign" death drive secondary to the agitation and strife of life—that it makes the ipseity of the organism that wishes to die only in its own, proper fashion dependent on the common life of germ cells—is a paradox we will return to later. Our point now is that the conservative version of the death drive can never be anything other than sovereign precisely because its ipseity emerges only in relation to the sovereign right to make die. On the one hand, the individual organism defies the sovereign's right to make die—a right executed in the "dangers" that come from the outside world and that sometimes take the form of an aggressiveness projected outward from another entity—by resisting the death that another sovereign figure might impose upon it against its will to die "only in its own fashion." On the other hand, that very resistance only ties the death of the organism to a return to a moment of sovereign decision, to a proper, economical time of death that immunizes the organism against the pressures of life, making the organism beholden to a "natural" death instituted by a sovereign force; and that only absorbs the organism deeper in an immunological form of life animated by a sovereign decision it otherwise defies, if only by trying to circumvent it. When Freud writes, in the final chapter of *Beyond the Pleasure Principle*, that "the pleasure principle seems actually to serve the death instincts," it is to this sovereign death drive that he refers (18:63).

Yet a sovereign death drive is not the only version of death drive that one might extract from the pages of *Beyond the Pleasure Principle*. The life instincts and the death drive, Freud will finally bring himself to admit in chapter 6, are "associated from the very first" (18:57). Indeed they must be, Freud concludes, because both are tied to the same moment of "chance," the moment when "the attributes of life were . . . evoked in inanimate matter by the action of a force of whose nature we can form no conception" (18:57, 38). If the death drive compels the organism to return to an original, inorganic state anterior to that moment of chance, then the "extraordinarily violent" life instincts repeat that same moment, now understood as the moment when the conjunction of cells—an activity that Freud is quick to insist runs counter to the "natural" aim toward death—caused life to quicken from out of an inert state. What allows Freud to reach this rather astonishing conclusion—in essence, the conflation of the death drive and the life instincts, the counterintuitive claim that death is natural and life unnatural—is his conjecture that "the whole path of development to natural death is not trodden by *all* the elementary entities which compose the complicated body of one of the higher organisms. Some of them, the germ cells," he continues, "probably retain the original structure of living matter and, after a certain time, with their full complement of inherited and freshly acquired instinctual dispositions, separate themselves from the organism as a whole." In fact, Freud goes on to speculate (or perhaps declare):

> [U]nder favorable conditions, they begin to develop—that is, to repeat the performance to which they owe their existence; and in the end once again one portion of their substance pursues its development to a finish, while another portion harks back once again as a fresh residual germ to the beginning of the process of development. The germ-cells, therefore, work against the death of the living substance and succeed in winning for it what we can only regard as potential immortality, though that may mean no more than a lengthening of the road to death (18:40).

A potential immortality that may be nothing more than a lengthening of the road to death: with this formulation, Freud presents us with a version of death drive significantly different from what we have described as the sovereign death drive. In this version of the death drive, we encounter a "still surviving substance" that not only does not seek to die in its own fashion—that is, according to the rules of a certain economy—but that is "oblige[d]" by "decisive external influences . . . to diverge ever more widely from its original course of life and to make ever more complicated *détours* before reaching its aim of death" (18:38–39). It is "these circuitous paths to death," Freud continues, that are "faithfully kept to by the conservative instincts" that Freud will shortly group together as the sexual instincts (18:40). Yet here Freud makes a crucial emendation. Insofar as the sexual instincts "are conservative in the same sense as the other instincts in that they bring back earlier states of living substance," they are at the same time "conservative to a higher degree in that they are particularly resistant to external influences; and they are conservative too in another sense in that they preserve life itself for a comparatively long period" (18:40). What we are left with, then, is an uncanny version of the death drive, an extended, circuitous, widely diverging, particularly resistant drive of a still surviving substance, whose vehicle is a group of sexual instincts that are themselves uneconomical according to the standards of the mental apparatus. They live in *another* way, take a *wider* and *more circuitous* path, conserve to a *higher* degree, preserve for a *longer* period than those associated with the sovereign death drive. They are, in their own way, like the monstrous child: remorseless and inexorable.

Not only, then, can this death drive of still surviving substance not die; it offers us a freedom from which we cannot escape, freedom from the destiny of worldly death. In that respect it is a profoundly unnatural, or rather natural historical, drive, a circuitous, ever-widening drive not tied to the teleological history set in motion by the intervention of a mysterious, sovereign force into inorganic existence. Yet insofar as such "immortality," as Freud calls it, is tied to the endless repetition of the moment of chance that began life, so do the germ cells subject that same moment to the repetitive wearing away brought about by natural historical turmoil. The still living substance of the germ cells ties the moment of coalescence to an uneconomical existence different from the economical life of the mental apparatus established by the sovereign, and profoundly anarchic, intervention of force that supposedly instituted life. The germ cells, in all their excessiveness, outlive the soma. But they do more than that: they record the possibility of another history—a "history of the earth we live in and its relation to the sun"; a history that "has left its mark on the development of organisms"—distinct from the restorative history traced by the sovereign death drive. "Stor[ing] up for further repetition . . . every modification which is . . . imposed upon the course of the organism's life," the germ cells serve as the archive of the inescapable life of natural history (18:38). Unlike the anarchic, inscrutable disruption of inanimate existence by a sovereign force, the germ cells patiently record and measure and conserve; they evince a synchronized order as they pulsate back and forth in a "vacillating rhythm" (18:41); they move through a natural history that has a purpose but no destiny, a history that we are in danger of forgetting once we return to the state of quiescence promised by the sovereign death drive. In the still surviving substance, we glimpse another death drive that does not aim to return to a restorative time before the moment when life was forcefully evoked, that instead moves through the history of the natural world even though, by Freud's own logic, that movement is other than "natural," its direction being not toward a death that confirms *ipseity* but through a history of continuous change, of decay and renewal. And while that movement may have its beginnings in the same singular moment of chance that initiated the sovereign death drive, the natural history it ends up inscribing is a common history of "the earth we live in," a history that obliges every germ of every living animal "to recapitulate the structures . . . of all the forms from which it is sprung," a history with its own, rotating action, its own rhythmic motion. At once repeatedly reenacting the moment of chance that first forced the conjugation of two cells and yet never aiming to go behind that moment; advancing, as Freud says of the repressed instinct, "in the direction in which growth is still possible—though with no prospect of bringing the process to a conclusion or of being able to reach the goal" (18:42); diverging, along circuitous paths, "ever more widely from its original course of life" (18:38–39): in all these ways, the death drive of the still surviving substance operates not as an affirmation of the sovereign cut that brought life into being but as a continuous cutting of that cut, a slow draining away of its vital force through a series of detours and interruptions.

For what is it that "lives" in this case? Sexuality, argues Freud, allows the still surviving substance to achieve a kind of immortality beyond the death of the soma. But if that is the case, why does Freud's own grandson seem so alien to him? Strictly speaking, the child should be a part of Freud, a soma housing the still living substance of cellular immortality that passed from Freud, through his daughter, and into his grandchild. But instead the (admittedly "good") boy seems strange, cold, curiously unfeeling and mechanical, absorbed in a repetition whose pleasure remains obscure: in most respects unrecognizable as Freud's kin. In short, he is a creature, utterly unconcerned with the transcendence promised by mastery, of a natural history whose peculiar delights elude Freud even as they captivate him. Let us return, once again, to the reel at the center of the fort-da game. Freud argues that the aim of all life is death, by which he means that all instincts seek, in the face of life, to return to an inanimate state. The reel functions as an allegory of that inanimate state, a state that, paradoxical as it might sound, continues to live. Surely it is no coincidence that the child's absorption in his game with the reel—can we go so far as to call it his *disappearance* into that game?—should coincide with the disappearance of his mirror image (18:15, note 1). Freud suggests that the child's control over, and regulation of, its relation to itself finds expression in his game with the mirror. Yet the child's disappearance into the fort-da game points to something else: namely, how the perpetuation of inanimate life can prevail over the acquisition of own-ness, ipseity, or selfhood; how the dispossession of the fort, the "gone," can fold itself into the "there" of the da—that is, into the space and time of the subject. The game has a mechanical life, a kind of rhythmic humming, that supplants the life of the soma. Pace Lacan, who holds that there is no Other of the Other, the child's repetitive game generates, in its ceaseless rotation, an Other in the place where the Other is not, an Other that, turning and turning, wears away the "there" of any Other. This is no new sovereign time, set to take the place of the Other it supplants. It is a time, rather, that hollows itself out through the serialized decay, the unceasing turning and wearing away, that Freud hears in the child's "long-drawn-out 'o-o-o-o'"—a sound that so absorbs Freud, he returns to it four times in as many pages. Thinking that he has written the secret history of consciousness, Freud has in fact

stumbled upon a game that, in its immortal "vacillating rhythm," manifests the untimely time of natural history.

Freud may seem resistant at first to that other time, that other rhythm.
Yet the current of natural history clearly affects him, given that he follows
the lead of the organism whose life he has been describing and, after having reached "a particular stage in the advance" of his argument in chapter 5,
"jerks back to a certain point" in order "to make a fresh start" in chapter 6
"and so prolong the journey" of his speculations (18:41). That journey, which
so far has taken Freud through a history of the life instincts, now prompts
him to summarize the history of scientific inquiry into cellular development
while also revisiting, along the way, the history of the libidinal theory within
the larger history of psychoanalysis. Or, to be more precise: demolishing
that history by violently reworking it. It is a remarkably melancholic move,
but not the first of its kind that Freud makes. Already in chapter 5, he had
eschewed the temptations of a destiny-driven history in order to preserve
his way, pursue *his* rhythm, wear away *his* grooves in pursuit of *his* theory of
the death drive (18:37). Now, in chapter 6, it is as though Freud melancholically tests a particular reality, the reality of the psychoanalytic movement,
and finds not only that he had overlooked what it was *not* missing—a death
drive—but also what it *was* missing: a theory to account for that death drive.
The history he retells is then shot through not only with historical time, the
time of scientific progress, but with the vacillatingly rhythmic time of natural history, a history of splitting and divergence.

All of the many faces of death drive show themselves in chapter 6.
There is, at the crudest level, the muted sadism—that is, the "displaced"
death drive—directed at Freud's erstwhile intimates Fliess and Jung, both
of whom find themselves being drawn into the metabolic activities of
Freud's recursive history (18:54). But even at the structural level, chapter 6 presents us with a linear world history spliced with a more rhythmic
and pulsating natural history, one propelled by a death drive that does not
simply return to an inorganic state but that endlessly regenerates itself by
repeating the coalescence and division of cellular life—a death drive that is
also a life drive. How telling, then, that it should be this hybrid, still-living
death drive, a death drive associated from the first with the life instincts,
that Freud ends up preserving by abruptly breaking off from his already
fragmented and truncated digest of the Platonic myth—or, to be more specific, the myth that Plato puts in the mouth of Aristophanes—with which
he concludes his history of the development of his own libido theory
(18:58). The form that Freud's retelling of that myth takes—fragmented,
paltry—is itself significant, as are its images of tearing and splitting. For

this is what Freud preserves in his reforming of the myth: a coalescence of form and subject that encrypts the force of dissolution, since the form and subject of this particular myth are both that of fragmentation. Dissolution is spliced into and preserved in the conjunction of form and subject. Then, before that version of the death drive can be lost, Freud breaks off, in the process encrypting a powerful idea: that of the powers of fragmentation and splitting being turned against themselves; that where the gods once fragmented and split earthly beings, like sorb-apples, so they too will be fragmented and split by the grinding force of natural history. In this way, Freud places his theory of the still surviving death drive on the side of a natural historical order. In the classical world, myth was used to pay tribute to the gods by praising their virtue. But the myth that Freud turns to was designed from the beginning to make the Olympian gods seem cruel and anarchic, dictatorial, more worthy of contempt and derision than of worship. Here, in fact, we encounter the sadness of a scene in which the Olympians were so insecure, so worried about not having sacrifices made to them by impious creatures, that they divided those creatures and thus brought forth a humanity beset by longing and suffering. This turning of myth against its original use, even against itself, is already present in Plato.[29] Yet Freud redoubles the effect, leaving the myth a fragmented, mechanical (or at least quite perfunctory) mess, drained of its usefulness to the gods, to say nothing of the reader. And in that way Freud uses the myth, which in its very form seems to rebel against its supposedly proper usage, to preserve and name not only the natural historical creatures overthrown by the anarchic intervention of Zeus and turned into nonbeings but also the memory of their prior rebellion. Mechanically repeating their story, but in a fragmented, truncated form, Freud wears that story away, draining it of affect until it becomes something like a cortical layer embedded in history: an inanimate layer protecting a still living core of nonbeing.

We have been arguing that *Beyond the Pleasure Principle* is spliced by, or shot through with, natural history. Such natural history is anything but anarchic, however; it moves with purpose, pulsating with a "vacillating rhythm" that bespeaks an order undetectable to the world history in which it encrypts itself. Not only is this natural history *not* wild and anarchic; it stands out against the anarchy of a state politics that actively pursues war and turmoil—that actively generates suffering—over and above the internal suffering that already besets us. In stands out, moreover, against the inexplicable intervention of a sovereign force into inorganic existence, against the selfish caprice of Zeus, against all of Freud's metaphors for the anarchic cruelty of despotic power and lawmaking violence. What matters, though, is that Freud himself does not shy away from modeling how to inject natural historical order into the midst of anomic world history. Rather than strain to recuperate his original theory of the pleasure principle, Freud instead follows his discontent with that theory until it leads him to venture beyond not only the conceptual limits of the pleasure principle but also, by extrapolation, an entire framework of classical political theory predicated on the orderly pursuit of happiness. Freud could return to Aristotle, but he does not. Instead, he goes back to Platonic myth, and further—all the way back to the pre-Socratic natural philosophers, who juggled with their four elements much as Freud and his followers juggle with the instincts—in order to construct a new theoretical foundation better able to absorb the possibilities of physionomos than his earlier economic model had been. To abandon the pleasure principle is thus to abandon, if only at the level of metaphor, the oikonomia of the home— the home of the psyche ruled by the economic model enshrined in the two principles of mental functioning; the respectable home of the Viennese bourgeoisie—in favor of the stasis, the turmoil and strife, the dualism bereft of any dialectical resolution, that dissolves the polis and that Freud sees at work even at the level of the cells torn between the life instincts and the death drive.

Civilization and Its Discontents

Freud begins *Civilization and Its Discontents* by drawing a distinction— or, to be more precise, by making a division. Freud had sent Romain Rolland a copy of *The Future of an Illusion*, and the latter had answered, according to Freud,

> that he entirely agreed with my judgement upon religion, but that he was sorry I had not properly appreciated the true source of religious sentiments. This, he says, consists in a peculiar feeling, which he himself is never without, which he finds confirmed by many others, and which he may suppose is present in millions of people. It is a feeling which he would like to call a sensation of "eternity," a feeling as of something limitless, unbounded—as it were, "oceanic."[30]

Freud is dubious. "I cannot discover this 'oceanic' feeling in myself," he tells us (21:65). He would not go so far as to "deny that it does in fact occur in other people"; but his own "experience" leaves him unconvinced of "the primary nature of such a feeling" (21:65). The "only question" that interests Freud about his friend's oceanic feeling—"it is not easy to deal scientifically with feelings," after all—"is whether it is being correctly interpreted" (21:65). And with that question in mind, Freud does something truly monstrous: he subjects Rolland's idea—an idea that, though likely present in millions of people, seems to Freud "something rather in the nature of an intellectual perception, which is not, it is true, without an accompanying feeling-tone" of the type associated "with any other act of thought of equal range" (21:65)—to psychoanalytic scrutiny.

It is like shooting feelings in a barrel. As Freud sees it, the ego, far from being expansive and open to the universe, is contractive, marked off from the outside world and "continued inward, without any sharp delimitation," into the unconscious (21:66). Not only does the ego "maintain clear and sharp lines of demarcation" toward the outside; it is little more than "the shrunken residue" of an ongoing exigency: namely, our contact with the stressful stimuli of the world around us (21:68). The ego begins, for all intents and purposes, with a cry for help, which the infant emits when the first external "object," the mother's breast, gets withdrawn (21:67). The ego disengages from the world under pressure from the pleasure principle, which seeks to avoid sensations of pain and unpleasure. Following the logic of *Beyond the Pleasure Principle*, we could therefore conclude that the ego emerges, in part, as a product of the conservative death drive. Yet the problem is that, while the ego may function as an immunitarian response to the outside, it remains fully exposed to the internal sources of pain and suffering against which it cannot defend itself. This indicates an important dichotomy. The ego's differentiation of itself from the outside world stems from the infant's "deliberate direction" of its sensory activities (21:67). This describes a process very different from the passive, apathetic immersion in the "oneness" of Rolland's oceanic feeling; it describes an act of deliberate partitioning. If anything, in fact, the oceanic feeling is itself the product of internal partitioning: little more than the ruin, the residue, of an earlier stage of ego-development existing alongside the narrower feeling of ego maturity. The oceanic feeling offers us nothing, in other words, but sensory evidence, not that the ego is boundless in space, but that it undergoes development over time. As Freud is quick to point out, however, that development cannot be "demonstrated"; it can only be "constructed" using the ruins and remnants that make up any given ego's peculiar contents (21:66). Against the outside world, the ego may emerge as the product of the conservative death drive and may thus be understood as immunitarian in its aims and origins. But within the inside into which it continues, the ego is engulfed in the natural historical turmoil or ongoing development (and here let us recall that the development of the ego cannot be empirically

demonstrated, only constructed as one might a natural historical ruin) characteristic of the still surviving death drive. The very separation of the ego
from the outside, its sharp lines of demarcation, is what exposes it to the
upheavals and turmoil—in a word, the rebelliousness—of the living interior mapped by Freud in *Beyond the Pleasure Principle*. The ego establishes
itself by making a cut against the outside world; and yet that same cut only
leaves behind a cut-up, partitioned, and self-alienated interior made up of
ruins and remnants, records of an ongoing development. If Freud cannot
discover a narcissistically expansive oceanic feeling inside himself, that is
not simply because he can boast of an especially mature ego, as he seems to
imply. It is because he remains in touch with the continuous division underway in his rebellious interior. He remains committed, as he was in *Beyond
the Pleasure Principle*, to strife.

For example: in the very first sentence of *Civilization and Its Discontents*,
Freud observes—no, Freud finds it "impossible to escape the impression,"
a sure sign that escape is only possible through the impression—"that
people commonly use false standards of measurement" (21:64). Perhaps
the falsest of those standards turns out to be the oceanic feeling itself, precisely because it does not measure; it simply expands and encompasses.
It simply engulfs. Freud, by contrast, is more attuned to measurement as
such: to lines "drawn incorrectly," to discrepancies and contradictions, to
judgments whose inaccuracy mocks itself, to variegation and diversity,
to differentiation (21:64–66). Freud, that is to say, remains more attuned
to our natural historical interior, which consists, first, of a series of partitions erected in response to the ego's demarcation of itself from the outside
world and, second, of a set of "technique[s] of living" invented to help us
cope with the suffering imposed by the life of *bíos* (21:82). There are, as
we saw in our reading of *Beyond the Pleasure Principle*, two versions of
the death drive: a conservative, sovereign death drive tied to a moment
of forceful intervention that generated life out of inanimate matter; and
a still surviving death drive that perpetuates itself through a continuously proliferating series of almost machinic divisions. The one strives to
return to a state of quiescence before the "cut" of life, the other survives
by repeatedly cutting the moment of that cut. Insofar as the ego separates
itself from "the general mass of sensations" that makes up the external
world, it remains a product of the sovereign death drive. But insofar as
it "continues inward" into a timeless, living interior to which it remains
fully exposed, the ego operates as an expression of the still surviving death
drive. Not only, then, is our relation to the world not defined by a quasi-
natural oceanic feeling born of an illusory boundlessness; it is defined by

a set of natural historical techniques of living, such as sexuality and neu-
rotic illness, whose peculiar status as processes of discontent arising out
of deprivation indicates our only chance at happiness: the perpetuation
of divisional strife, the ongoing cutting of the cut. At any rate, one will
search in vain for a "'oneness with the universe'" capable of restoring a
lost, primordial happiness.

Freud's particular analogy for the "sphere of the mind" is at once historical, architectural, and, in its own oblique fashion, political. He compares it to the history of Rome, the Eternal City (21:69–71). What interests us here is how the eternity of the place lies in its very ruination; for
this provides us with an especially powerful image of the indestructibility
of destruction. The continuous partitioning of the mind is what never
seems to be destroyed, just as "nothing which has once been formed can
perish" in the life of the mind (21:69). Nothing can be annihilated there;
everything can be brought back to life. This is a different type of repetition from the repetition compulsion. This is a repetition defined, not
by the return of the organism to an inanimate state, but by the incessant return of ruination. In the mind, Freud argues, nothing past is ever
destroyed. If there exists an exception to that rule, Freud does not know
of it. This is a very different conception of the cityscape, and thus a very
different conception of politics, from that of the polis simultaneously
founded and dissolved by the inclusive exclusion of the sovereign exception.[31] Here, the rule of return, the rule of indestructibility, has been de-
exceptionalized. Here there can be found no exception. What we find
instead is a shift in perspective—call it a potentially truer standard of
measurement—achieved through a flight of imagination. Freud can
do nothing with an oceanic feeling that leaves no room for division or
demarcation, only boundlessness. Perspective means preserving the possibility of a repetition—that is, of a starting again that might also achieve
a reversal, an inverse perspective. It means, finally, to preserve the possibility of drawing a new map of the city, a map that traces even the ruins
built atop ruin, the restorations that have become ruins themselves. What
are lineaments, after all, if not the outlines of ruins, of demarcations, of
partitions? The only remaining record is that of divisions.

In other words, the Eternal City functions as more than a metaphor
for Freud; it stands, in all its layered ruination, its ever-rising unchange-
ableness, as an expression of the still surviving death drive. "Now let us
suppose," "would be," "and so on": these temporal and speculative tags
underscore how thoroughly Rome still stands—how the Eternal City continues, how it persists and survives—within Freud's fantasy. Freud revels

in the particular idea of a still surviving, yet strangely inanimate, Rome. Nothing is lost in this odd landscape; everything that was ruined returns: palaces, statues, castles, churches. "Nothing that has come into existence will have passed away," is how Freud puts it (21:70). Even the dead—even the Caesars—have aspirations, longings that continue to speak to Freud. But they do so as imagined sites, as the images of the buildings most associated with their names. The structures of the Caesars are paraded before us, as if in triumph; but they stand upon a base of continuous strife, of ongoing ruination, of a breaking up that is also a piling up, of a destruction that preserves.

Then we reach a breaking point. Even Freud admits that there is "no point in spinning our phantasy any further, for it leads to things that are unimaginable and even absurd" (21:70). Yet this is the point: Freud's fantasy, in true death-drive fashion, spins. It rotates, it repeats, it piles up. What is more, it allows us to think the unimaginable, to come around again, all the way to a reversal of what is and an apprehension of the impossible, which in this case is nothing less than the return of everything that has been lost. Every repetition holds open the prospect of starting again. This "idle game," as Freud calls it (and the sense of arrest in that "idle" is striking), has "only one justification": to undermine mastery (21:71). To counteract the master, the sovereign who occupies the polis, one must build up another, impossible city, a city that develops according to an altogether different temporal scheme. In a word, one must make a construction.[32]

Freud, as if to emphasize the point, ends the first chapter of *Civilization and Its Discontents* by introducing the image of the father as something like a deus ex machina. "The derivation of religious needs from the infant's helplessness and the longing for the father aroused by it seems to me incontrovertible," writes Freud. "I cannot think of any need in childhood as strong as the need for a father's protection" (21:72). The suddenness of this gesture is telling, as if Freud were writing a parody of the sovereign cut. In that way, the intervention becomes its own construction, a construction that gestures toward the constructedness of authority as such. The moment of sovereign intervention gets undermined by being mirrored in the sudden imposition of a father-construction. Against the "oneness" of the universe evoked by Rolland's oceanic feeling, Freud presents us with a sovereign One that gets taken into the ego and constructed so as to drain it of its force. Force itself is thus made subject to the partitioning of the interior. "Wrapped in obscurity," sovereign force gets set off, divided, formalized in a diagram of force that remains frozen and immobilized: a master on the order of an architectural ruin (21:72).

And with the master thus neutralized, Freud can get down to his principal concern in *Civilization and Its Discontents*: the pursuit of happiness in a world of suffering. A reader new to this work could be forgiven for leaving with the impression that suffering is the natural condition of the human species. "One feels inclined to say," writes Freud, wearily, "that the intention that man should be 'happy' is not included in the plan of 'Creation'" (21:76). And yet, for all his unrelenting pessimism—or, rather, within the folds of that pessimism—Freud nonetheless manages to leave us with a peculiar image of happiness. Such happiness is not to be found, however, in the little bursts and shards of fleeting happiness derived from instinctual satisfaction and libidinal release, but in a certain dog-like (or dogged) "sniffing" described in detail by Freud in the first footnote of chapter 4:

> The incitement to cleanliness originates in an urge to get rid of the excreta, which have become disagreeable to the sense perceptions. We know that in the nursery things are different. The excreta arouse no disgust in children. They seem valuable to them as being a part of their own body which has come away from it. Here upbringing insists with special energy on hastening the course of development which lies ahead, and which should make the excreta worthless, disgusting, abhorrent and abominable. Such a reversal of values would scarcely be possible if the substances that are expelled from the body were not doomed by their strong smells to share the fate which overtook olfactory stimuli after man adopted the erect posture. . . . It would be incomprehensible, too, that man should use the name of his most faithful friend in the animal world—the dog—as a term of abuse if that creature had not incurred his contempt through two characteristics: that it is an animal whose dominant sense is that of smell and one which has no horror of excrement, and that it is not ashamed of its sexual functions (21:99–100, note 1).

Civilization as such, "the whole sum of the achievements and the regulations which distinguish our lives from those of our animal ancestors and which serve two purposes—namely to protect men against nature and to adjust their mutual relations," won't bring us happiness (21:89). Just the opposite, in fact. What brings us happiness is a certain way of rummaging among natural historical excreta, a certain immersion, at once amusingly odd and inscrutably atavistic, in the shameful incongruities of civilized life. It was when we as a species abandoned the stooped posture of the melancholic that our troubles really began.

Meanwhile, civilization looks to the heavens for a model of order that only brings us misery—and that is the greatest incongruity of all. "Order . . . like cleanliness," writes Freud, "applies solely to the works of man. But whereas cleanliness is not to be expected in nature, order, on the contrary, has been imitated from her" (21:93). We observe the "great astronomical regularities" and find there a "model for introducing order" into our lives; and yet the same nature that includes those regularities, the nature in which we dwell, is dirty. We arise from dirt, and so it is in dirt that we discover a peculiar source of happiness: the happiness of filth. But it is a happiness that civilization, which models itself on a natural order so as to achieve an unnatural cleanliness, will not let us enjoy. In fact, civilization has taught us to regard filth as a source of happiness that we can no longer abide—that we can only enjoy in the footnotes, as it were. Such is the origin of our discontent.

Given, however, that our discontent stems from our civilized intolerance for what was once a source of enjoyment—namely, our primitive immersion in filth—then it may also serve as the necessary precondition for happiness. It is strange: the lasting image one takes away from *Civilization and Its Discontents* is not that of civilization successfully mitigating the pressures of life by supplying its inhabitants with an array of what Freud calls "technique[s] in the art of living," among them intoxication, sublimation, imaginative wish fulfillment, delusion, love, and, when all else fails, neurosis. The lasting image one takes away is of the incongruities and contradictions inherent in civilization giving rise to an altogether different technique of living, one that offers us a promise of happiness in the processes of dissolution and division. Freud does not mention this other technique. He may not even have been aware of it. Nevertheless, he practices it in the way he enumerates those techniques in the art of living that the pleasure principle imposes upon us as part of what Freud calls "the programme of becoming happy" (21:83).

Deploying a method best described as "dialectical pessimism," Freud systematically undercuts every technique generated by the pleasure principle for the purpose of alleviating suffering and thus of regulating our organic existence. "An unrestricted satisfaction of every need presents itself as the most enticing method of conducting one's life, but it means putting enjoyment before caution, and soon brings its own punishment" (21:77). "Against the suffering which may come upon one from human relationships the readiest safeguard is voluntary isolation, keeping oneself aloof from other people"; but the most one could hope for here would be "the happiness of quietness." Better to become "a member of the human community" and, armed with science, go "over to the attack against nature" (21:77). "Intoxicating media"—and Freud does not think that anyone understands the mechanism of intoxication—can provide not only an "immediate yield of pleasure, but also a greatly desired degree of independence from the external world." But they are also "responsible, in certain circumstances, for the useless waste of a large quota of energy which might have been employed for the improvement of the human lot" (21:78). Since frustrated needs can cause severe suffering, "one may therefore hope to be freed from a part of one's sufferings by influencing the instinctual impulses," say, by taking up yoga. But in thus "killing off the instincts . . . the subject has, it is true, given up all other activities as well—he has sacrificed his life; and, by another path, he has once more only achieved the happiness of quietness" (21:79). One can of course gain a yield of pleasure by sublimating one's instincts, channeling them instead into "psychical and intellectual work." But while "such satisfactions" may "seem 'finer and higher,'" "their intensity is mild as compared with that derived from the sating of crude and primary instinctual impulses; it does not convulse our physical being. And the weak point of this method is that it is not applicable generally: it is accessible to only a few people" (21:79–80). What about the "satisfactions through fantasy" one gains from enjoying works of art? "People who are receptive to the influence of art cannot set too high a value on it as a source of pleasure and consolation in life. Nevertheless the mild narcosis induced in us by art can do no more than bring about a transient withdrawal from the pressure of vital needs, and it is not strong enough to make us forget real misery" (21:81). Becoming a hermit? "Whoever, in desperate defiance, sets out upon this path to happiness will as a rule obtain nothing. Reality is too strong for him. He becomes a madman" (21:81). "Loving and being loved"? "The weak side of this technique of living is easy to see. . . . It is that we are never so defenseless against suffering as when we love, never so helplessly unhappy as when we have lost our love object or its love" (21:82). Appreciating beauty? "The love of beauty seems a perfect example of an impulse inhibited in its aim" (21:83).

Freud apologizes for not having "made a complete enumeration of the methods by which men strive to gain happiness and keep suffering away," and he knows, too, "that the material might have been arranged differently" (21:81). But the lesson to be drawn from his own method is clear enough: if any happiness is to come from the techniques in the art of living, it will not be from the techniques themselves; they only lead to disappointment. It will come from the project of dismantling those very techniques. And they are techniques—nothing but techniques. Freud, we have seen, refuses to offer us recourse to any natural state of bliss, any "oceanic feeling" or its equivalent. For all the "auxiliary organs" we might put on, we humans remain, at best, only "prosthetic god[s]" (21:91–92). What we find instead is a series of natural historical formations, conventional methods for pursuing a "programme of becoming happy," countered by a natural historical activity, a dialectical practice in which Freud takes an evidently pessimistic delight. In short, Freud turns the natural history of civilization, which he sums up in an outrageously conjectural footnote tracing tool use and technology back to primitive man, urination, the renunciation of instinct, control over fire, and woman as the guardian of the domestic hearth, against itself, in the form of critical dissolution (21:90, note 1). We see this not only at the level of style—at the level of order, as Freud might have it—where *Civilization and Its Discontents* counters every evocation of happiness, every evocation of what we might call contentment with the status quo, with an evocation of some correspondingly negative affect or reaction. We see it also in Freud's account of civilization as such, which he describes, not as resting on some solid foundation, but as arising continuously out of turmoil and strife.

Freud himself does not entirely understand the widespread hostility toward civilization—he labels "astonishing" the "contention . . . that what we call our civilization is largely responsible for our misery, and that we should be much happier if we gave it up and returned to primitive conditions"—but he does have a theory about its origins (21:86). "How has it happened that so many people have come to take up this strange attitude of hostility toward civilization?" he asks. "I believe that the basis of it was a deep and long-standing dissatisfaction with the then existing state of civilization and that on that basis a condemnation of it was built up, occasioned by certain historical events," among them "the victory of Christendom over the heathen religions," the myth of the Noble Savage, the discovery ("especially familiar to us") of "the mechanisms of the neuroses, which threaten to undermine the modicum of happiness enjoyed by civilized men," and disappointment that extraordinary advances in science and technology have "not increased the amount of pleasurable satisfaction which [we] may expect from life" (21:87–88). As Freud perceives it, discontentment with civilization is both inherent and repetitive: coeval with the emergence of civilization and inseparable from its development. To be civilized is thus to be discontented. But why, Freud wonders. What would drive someone to litter the paths of the Wiener Wald (21:93)?

Here we would do well to recall Freud's own contention "that in mental life nothing which has once been formed can perish" (21:69). It is not that we can authentically recall a time of primal unity or happiness. On the contrary, whenever Freud references prehistory, it is as a time of deprivation, domination, struggle, and, in the myth of the primal father and his frustrated sons, murder (21:99–101; 115; 131). At best, it was a time, now recoverable only through wild speculation, when we could still revel in "olfactory stimuli" and extinguish fires by urinating on them. No, it is that we cannot forget the sense of injustice that has "formed" in us over the steep price civilization extracts from its members, the price of instinctual renunciation. In chapter 3, Freud had singled out "justice" as "the first requisite of civilization," but even then he had admitted, albeit ambivalently, that "what makes itself felt in a human community as a desire for freedom may be their revolt against some existing injustice and so may prove favourable to a further development of civilization; it may remain compatible with civilization" (21:95–96). Now, in chapter 4, Freud can only conclude that "the rift between [genital love and civilization] seems unavoidable," for reasons vaguely connected to the dictates of political economy (21:103). In restricting sexual life to expand the cultural unit, explains Freud,

> civilization is obeying the laws of economic necessity, since a large amount of the psychical energy which it uses for its own purposes has to be withdrawn from sexuality. In this respect civilization behaves towards sexuality as a people or a stratum of its population does which has subjected another one to its exploitation. Fear of a revolt by the suppressed elements drives it to stricter precautionary measures (21:104).

But such suppression cannot be justified, contends Freud. Puberty rites are one thing. But the proliferation of "taboos, laws and customs" that began with "perhaps the most drastic mutilation which man's erotic life has in all time experienced," namely "the prohibition against an incestuous choice of object," is quite another (21:104). For

> the requirement, demonstrated in these prohibitions, that there shall be a single kind of sexual life for everyone, disregards the dissimilarities, whether innate or acquired, in the sexual constitution of human beings; it cuts off a fair number of them from sexual enjoyment, and so becomes the source of serious injustice (21:104).

One can only take so much, Freud protests. "If more is demanded of a man, a revolt will be produced in him or a neurosis, or he will be made unhappy" (21:143). Like the individual superego, the "cultural superego" is a tyrant that "does not trouble itself enough about the facts of the mental constitution of human beings. It issues a command and does not ask whether it is possible for people to obey it" (21:143). And yet "in mental life nothing which has once been formed can perish," not even our primal memory of injustice. *Sic semper tyrannis.*

One need not resort to open rebellion, however. One might also express their hostility toward civilization by abiding by one of its "ideal demands." "It runs," Freud tells us—and his tone of disbelief is unmistakable—"'Thou shalt love thy neighbour as thyself'" (21:109). Adopting "a naïve attitude" toward that demand, "as though . . . hearing it for the first time," Freud finds himself "unable then to suppress a feeling of surprise and bewilderment. Why should we do it?" he asks. "What good will it do us? But, above all, how shall we achieve it? How can it be possible?" (21:109). Superficially, Freud's skepticism concerning the injunction to neighbor-love presents us with the image, built up over the course of *Civilization and Its Discontents*, of inescapable suffering and natural aggression. "Men are not gentle creatures who want to be loved, and who at the most can defend themselves if they are attacked," insists Freud:

> [T]hey are, on the contrary, creatures among whose instinctual endowments is to be reckoned a powerful share of aggressiveness. As a result, their neighbour is for them not only a potential helper or sexual object, but also someone who tempts them to satisfy their aggressiveness on him, to exploit his capacity to work without compensation, to use him sexually without his consent, to seize his possessions, to humiliate him, to cause him pain, to torture and to kill him. *Homo homini lupus* (21:111).

Worse still is the bitter irony of the situation. Civilization ought to relieve us of suffering; and yet the injunction to love even one's aggressive neighbor indicates how thoroughly the demands imposed by civilization upon its individual members only compound their suffering. Freud writes:

> The commandment "Love thy neighbour as thyself" is the strongest defence against human aggressiveness and an excellent example of the unpsychological proceedings of the cultural super-ego. The commandment is impossible to fulfil; such an enormous inflation of love can only lower its value, not get rid of the difficulty. Civilization pays no attention to all this; it merely admonishes us that the harder it is to obey the precept the more meritorious it is to do so (21:143).

Here, then, is the great and unbearable irony at the heart of civilized life. "What a potent obstacle to civilization aggressiveness must be," exclaims Freud, "if the defence against it can cause as much unhappiness as aggressiveness itself!" (21:143). But look again: Freud would not take exception to the imperative were it more economical (21:110). The problem for him is that it remains wildly uneconomical—an "expenditure of energy" so intense that it fractures the law of civilization it is supposed to advance (21:112). Ideally, the commandment is meant to counter that "primary mutual hostility of human beings" in consequence of which "civilized society is perpetually threatened with disintegration" (21:112). And yet the commandment, strictly speaking, counters nothing. On the contrary, it enjoins us to do something without restraint, beyond prohibition: love thy aggressive neighbor as thyself. Freud cannot quite get over how the neighbor, who ought to bind us to community, makes community impossible. How are we to love a neighbor who externalizes their death drive as sadism (21:121–122)? But that, as Lacan observes in *The Ethics of Psychoanalysis*, is exactly what Freud misses about this own theory.[33] Pushed to love our own aggressiveness toward the neighbor in the neighbor's aggressiveness toward us, we discover, in our shared death drive, a new communal bond. And not just any bond, but the bond of dissolution. Aggressiveness, Freud argues, threatens civilized society with disintegration; hence the restrictions, inhibitions, and prohibitions imposed on our instinctual life (70). But why should a civilization that imposes such widespread suffering on its own members be spared disintegration? Why not follow the commandment to love thy neighbor as thyself all the way, to the letter, as Lacan might put it: until the point that, forced to acknowledge the neighbor's aggressiveness as one's own, love disintegrates even the disintegrating force of aggressiveness? Freud is so focused on the splitting introduced by the neighbor, the "stranger" we are enjoined to love by an imperative that is equally "strange," that he fails to recognize how that stranger provides us, in that very splitting, with a chance at happiness (21:109).

For the road to happiness runs, as it turns out, through the death drive. Reviewing the "painfully" slow development of the drive theory, Freud writes that "in the course of time" his belief in "the existence of an instinct of death or destruction . . . gained such a hold upon" him that he could no longer think in any other way (21:119). In this he confesses more than he realizes. Not only did the assumption of the existence of an instinct of death or destruction gain a hold up on him; the death drive gained such hold upon him that he began to carry out its work of division and destruction. Of course, the death drive in question here is not the conservative death drive, not the return to an inanimate state posited by Freud in *Beyond the Pleasure Principle*. It is the repetition of splitting and divergence, the endless starting again. Freud describes the instinct for death or destruction as being itself "indestructible," and that about sums up the matter (21:114). The only thing that remains indestructible, finally, is destruction. We should not conclude from this, however, that destruction is simply the "natural" antithesis to civilization. "The inclination to aggression" may be, according to Freud, "an original, self-subsisting instinctual disposition in man" (21:122). But he thrice describes it, natural historically, as being "alloyed" with eros, with eroticism, or with libido—in a word, with life (21:119–121). The story of civilization Freud says he wants to tell is a simple one. It is the story of "the struggle between Eros and Death, between the instinct of life and the instinct of destruction, as it works itself out in the human species" (21:122). And yet in telling that reassuring story of oppositional struggle, Freud not only dissolves the parts of *Civilization and Its Discontents* that lead up to it; he also fails to reckon, once again, with the commandment to love thy neighbor as thyself. That commandment, Freud tells us, is "strange" in the same way that the neighbor is "strange." Logically, then, to follow that strange commandment and love thy neighbor as thyself is also to love the commandment as thyself. And the commandment is just that: a commandment, an imperative, a positive injunction that prohibits nothing. In short, it is on the order of a drive. To follow the commandment is thus—again, logically—not only to love the commandment as thyself but a drive as thyself. And yet it is no less difficult to love that drive than it is to love thy neighbor. In fact, it is far more difficult. The neighbor is merely aggressive; the drive we suffer in trying to fulfill the injunction to neighbor love is doubly aggressive, in that it cruelly demands that one love the aggressive neighbor as oneself. In that respect, it truly is a drive to death or destruction, not only because it exhibits the same degree of sadism as when the neighbor externalizes their own death drive, and not only because it effectively dissolves any illusion of a unified, autonomous self, but because "nothing else runs so strongly counter to the original nature of man." The death drive expressed in the commandment to neighbor-love destroys our original nature, precisely by turning that nature into its opposite. At the same time, however, the death drive cannot be a part of "unnatural" civilization, since by forcing you to love thy aggressive neighbor as thyself, it violates the primary purpose of civilization, which according to Freud is "to protect men against nature and to adjust their mutual relations" (21:89). If anything, the commandment, by enjoining us to do something without restraint, demolishes the entire logic of prohibitory law. The death drive, then, is neither natural nor civilized; it is natural historical, with the power to dissolve both the "original nature" that threatens civilization with disintegration and the civilization that brings misery and suffering in the name of protecting life. And by gaining such a hold upon Freud that he could no longer think in any other way, it enlists him in its project of dissolution.

As is so often the case with Freud's texts, this process of dissolution finds a formal expression, this time in Freud's multiple citations. Freud's own memories of happiness are invariably citational, tied to an act of reading. When Freud wants to make a point, he tends to deploy a quotation: of poets, of anecdotes, of his own past work. These quotations are, on the one hand, Freud's amusements, providing him with an opportunity to proudly and self-consciously display his erudition. In that respect, they are on the same order as his "stupid" enjoyment of antiques, which allows him to construct, in his own work environment, the alienated space of displaced things. On the other hand, Freud's citations have a way of draining the main text of its tragic shadings, of undermining Freud's grandeur just enough to undermine, in turn, the image of the sovereign and of the suffering that supposedly gives rise to the conservative death drive. Divisions, divergences, contradictions, discrepancies: these are the labors of the nonsovereign death drive, the labors that Freud performs with his citational style. Happiness, then, is citational and recursive—in a word, repetitive. The processes of civilization that supposedly bring fleeting moments of happiness, the sublimation and intellectualization, are merely citational. Not vital processes, but citations. And if it is true that every citation is a kind of crypt, the memorialization of one text encrypted in another, then Freud's form of escape is to retreat into the crypt of a citation, to lay himself out in a parable. His peculiar, and peculiarly melancholic, way of taking a break from the demands of civilization is to rummage about in its ruins.

We should pay attention to this form of escape if for no other reason than it provides us with a way of counteracting the guilt history that tempts Freud in the last two chapters of *Civilization and Its Discontents*. Disappointingly, Freud introduces a new topography of the psyche, complete with superegoic watchtower: an internal landscape very different from the ruins of the Eternal City (21:136). But in a manner similar to the way in which the heightening of guilt as a sensation implies its eventual ruination—its heightening and heightening, its piling up until it collapses under its own, uneconomical weight, under the ruination it can no longer support—recursiveness provides a map of the passageways and catacombs leading us out of that new topography. Freud's citations function as a form of revolution, a repetition that promises a reversal of how things are, a continuous starting over. They hint at another history different from the guilt history that dooms us to suffering. And they operate through a death drive, characterized by unremitting division and dispersal, not tied to suffering. Freud himself is not the master of that death drive. Rather, his citations have a life of their own, an uncanny life, without vitality, that engulfs Freud, drawing him back and down, into a paradoxically foundationless foundation—and that leads him, in time, to write *Moses and Monotheism*.

Moses and Monotheism

The German title that Freud gave his last major work, *The Man Moses and Monotheistic Religion*, is both misleading and instructive. On the one hand, as Freud repeatedly states, the Egyptian Moses was nothing but a man: terrestrial, telluric, sublunary. Later, after he had been murdered by his chosen people, some of Moses's attributes as a leader would get transposed onto the volcano god Yahweh. But historically Moses was a man, a man who preserved "the monotheistic idea" introduced by the Pharaoh Akhenaten—an idea encompassing a "highly spiritualized notion of god, the idea of a single deity embracing the whole world, who was not less all-loving than all-powerful, who was averse to all ceremonial and magic and set before men as their aim a life in truth and justice"—long enough to impose it upon the Jewish people.[34] On the other hand, Moses became something more than a man once he had been killed *into* a people and an institution as their constitutive idea. Moses the Egyptian had to be destroyed as a man so that the idea of destruction—an idea repeated in Akhenaten's destruction of the old Egyptian religion, in the Egyptian priests' destruction of the memory of Akhenaten, in the "catastrophe" visited upon Moses by his chosen people, and in the eventual supersession of the Mosaic religion over the "priestly revisions" of subsequent generations—could become the universal ground on which constitutive force as such might assert itself. Through destruction, Moses the man, whose death preserves what Freud had once called the loss of an ideal kind, is transformed into an immanent, melancholic idea.

Freud writes that he found it impossible to set aside his project on Moses because "it tormented [him] like an unlaid ghost" (23:103). Not to be deterred, he eventually "found a way out by making two pieces of it independent and publishing them" in *Imago* while holding back on "the remainder, which included what was really open to objection and dangerous—the application [of these findings] to the genesis of monotheism and the view of religion in general" (23:103). Freud assumed that he would have to hold back on this third part "for ever"; but in the event, forever did not last very long. In March 1938, Freud was forced to leave Vienna for London, a move that freed him from, among other things, his anxiety "lest [his] publication might conjure up a prohibition of psychoanalysis in a place where it was still tolerated" (23:103). It is in the writing of Freud's text, then—writing as both form and process—that we comprehend the idea of Moses. On the one hand, that idea asserts itself as the unlaid ghost of a destroyed destruction, discernable not only in the initial destruction of the iconoclastic Aten religion and the murder of the man Moses, immediately disavowed, but in the shape of Freud's fragmented, repetitious, piecemeal text. On the other hand, and only by virtue of that ruined status, the idea of Moses manifests as a ghost with the power to bring destruction to destruction. That Freud's struggle with this unlaid ghost has superegoic overtones is hinted at by his anxiety around prohibition—an anxiety that he soon surmounts, that indeed he transforms into an anxiety to be turned back upon the would-be agents of prohibition. Yet in another, more crucial way, that struggle is against, even about, the superego. The superego may destroy everything but proper places, positions, and prerogatives (including its own). Yet this unlaid, tormenting ghost, now unleashed upon an unsuspecting public, not only destroys the agency of destruction, figured in the man Moses who continued Akhenaten's work of overthrowing the ancient religion in favor of the "monotheistic idea"; it also destroys the economy of guilt and reparation in which one might function as a high priest carrying out the work of destruction, the work of murdering the man Moses, in the misguided hope of propitiating an angry god.[35]

Which is to say: monotheism should not be misconstrued as the destruction only of paganism and animism. It also acts as the ruination of monotheistic terror. Monotheism, as Lacan argues in his seminar on the ethics of psychoanalysis, introduces lack into the structure of history.[36] To be tormented, as Freud is, by an unlaid ghost—and not just any unlaid ghost, but the ghost of a maimed work on Moses, a figure of origins—is to go one step further, to an apprehension of the lack of lack. Whereas the superego, like monotheism, binds through the cut of a law from which there is no turning back, the unlaid ghost that torments Freud—call it the ghost of a Mosaic work that must be repeatedly written, a history whose origin cannot be wiped out—cuts us off from the foundational act of cutting and leaves us stranded in a barren no-place, a desert condition. Witness Freud's own condition or the attenuated condition of *Moses and Monotheism*, with its audacious speculations compromised through drab repetition. Like Moses the foundational figure of a worldwide community, Freud now finds himself, at the end of his career, exiled and terminally ill, alienated from the people he called together under a new dispensation, a lawgiver with no new law to give, an old man repeating himself.

It is like *Totem and Taboo*, if the myth at the heart of that work, the myth of the primal horde, were inverted and drained of all its powers of enchantment.[37] In the myth of the primal horde, the primal father retains exclusive access to sovereign enjoyment. Or at least he does until he is murdered and devoured by his sons. Subsequent to that, no participant in the social contract underwritten by that death can accede to the now fore-closed exceptional position once held by the father. In this way the dead father becomes even more powerful than the living one had been. Freud knows all this (it is his myth, after all). One foot in the grave, he knows that after his "sons" (and "daughters") have feasted on his, the founding father's, flesh, he will be subjected to all of the same betrayals that awaited the primal father after he had been incorporated. Rather than assume the role of the admonitory superegoic father doling out revenge to the genera-tions of renegades to come, Freud instead delineates the restrictions of a superegoic regime founded on an economy of prohibition, transgression, crime, guilt, punishment, and expiation. Where before he had grafted himself onto an orthodox image of Moses as the superego of the Israel-ites, now Freud works to transform the exceptional position of the primal father—a position occupied, in this particular narrative, by the founders Moses and Freud—into a widely dispersed, unlocatable, ghostly univer-sal. Like a composite of the Egyptian Moses and the people who rose up against him, Freud destroys the edifice of psychoanalysis that he himself established but that he knows full well will be allowed, like the puristic monotheistic idea of Moses, to fall into disrepair, both through the attacks of his enemies and, worse, the compromises of his followers. And those compromises would indeed come. In Exodus, we have the story of the Golden Calf. In the history of psychoanalysis, we have the development of ego psychology, depth psychology, the collective unconscious, and Nazi psychoanalysis, among other compromise formations that retreat from the rigors of Freud's psychoanalytic idea.

But Freud is hardly an innocent victim of the betrayals of his follow-ers. On the contrary, it is Freud himself who makes betrayal a *topos* of psychoanalysis. In the years around 1900, he betrays Breuer and Fliess. In 1919, he leaves his most orthodox followers bereft and adrift when he reorients psychoanalysis around the death drive. Now, in 1938, Freud, the serial betrayer, coolly dismantles the pillars of his doctrine and replaces them with an outlandish political-historical-theological construction. Gone is the family romance, gone the internal topography governed by the superego, gone the central tenet of the ambivalence of love and hate. All that is held most dear, not only by Freud's admirers but by his detractors, Freud himself actively demolishes in these pages. What we find instead is an impersonal, strangely nonrelational, eerily unpopulated, atemporal history—or rather a-history—of a people and their interloping imposter of a founder. But in this, Freud is only following Moses once again. For betrayal is inscribed from the very beginning into the fabric of Moses's twin existences: Moses the traitor and Moses the victim of betrayal.

And so, like a new Moses bearing a new tablet, Freud delivers to his readers a prescription for wholesale destruction—of the image and narrative of Moses, of the Jewish people, of historiography, and, ultimately, of the very place from which destruction is meted out. That place can go by many names: the superego, the primal father, sovereign jouissance, the conservative version of the death drive, monotheistic terror. Here it might be called the Moses-complex. In any case, the point is that Freud, like a self-negating primal father, effectively disallows the possibility of having mastery over destruction by denying, to his followers and everyone, the prerogative of enjoying destruction. Henceforth only Freud can enjoy destruction, precisely because he destroys destructiveness. It is as if Freud were at once enacting and dismissing the residual fantasy of omnipotence that had captivated him ever since he confessed to Fliess his wish to see a "marble tablet" placed on the wall at Bellevue. Heretofore, that fantasy had taken the form of a specter on the order of Marx's specter: the psychoanalyst as deeply troubling revolutionary subject determined to overthrow the morality of the bourgeois subject. Now it takes the much more discomfiting—and, if the reception of *Moses and Monotheism* is any guide, shame-inducing—form of a ragged, desiccated, destitute, unfashionable, unproductive, rotten, and unwelcome ghost.

This raises several questions. Can Freud, in his attempt to abjure the specter in favor of the ghost, reassert his control over the destiny of psychoanalysis by declaring a new foundational moment for his discipline? Can psychoanalysis, once refounded as a ghostly discourse, maintain the status that it first took over from the hysteric, that of the grand inquisitor of masters and fathers? Or has it imperceptibly left the territory demarcated by castration and entered into a wilderness populated by nonsovereign creatures? Moreover, has the focus on the ghostly work of Moses undermined the analyst's discourse, reliant as it is on the affective alchemy of transference and counter-transference?

Our initial answer to all of these questions is that Freud, in *Moses and Monotheism*, presents us with a magnificently precise articulation of the discourse of the melancholic, a discourse that will eventually, through the workings of a particular dialectic, engulf even Freud's own attempts at monopolizing sovereign violence. Formalized as an impossible inversion of Lacan's discourse of the hysteric—a structurally inconceivable, fifth quarter-turn, as it were—the discourse of the melancholic is, like *Moses and Monotheism* itself, a construction: a formal intervention into an already fabricated history; a matheme in the place where an origin cannot be.[38] Insofar as it can be put into practice, insofar as a subject can come to occupy it, the discourse of the melancholic originates in "a tradition sunk in oblivion" (let's call it the Mosaic tradition of destruction and catastrophe) that nevertheless "continued to operate (from the background, as it were), which gradually acquired more and more power over people's minds and which in the end succeeded in changing the god Yahweh into the Mosaic god and in reawakening into life the religion of Moses that had been introduced and then abandoned long centuries before" (23:70). In Freud's hands, the Moses-complex, our term for the peculiar dialectic whereby the idea of the Egyptian Moses comes to negate the Midianite Moses whose name had negated his, becomes a cipher for history as it gets written by the repetition of destruction, even if the interval between those repetitions lasts "long centuries" or, as happened when the "Reformation . . . brought to light once more the frontier between the Germany which had at one time been Roman and the Germany which had remained independent," "over a thousand years" (23:38). But then, avers Freud, "history is fond of reinstatements like this, where a later fusion is undone and an earlier separation re-emerges" (23:38).[39]

So how is it that *Moses*, of all people, should emerge as the figure of serial destruction? How is it that the Moses-complex, to phrase the question a different way, should emerge as another name for the dialectic of natural history? We begin by noting, once again, that the man Moses—or perhaps we ought to say, the actions of the man Moses—repeat the actions of the Pharaoh Akhenaten, whose religion Moses takes over and, as it were, intensifies. This is where things get complicated. Akhenaten had destroyed the old religion of the Egyptians and replaced it with the first true monotheism, as Freud calls it. That larger destruction had entailed the particular demolition of all that tied the Egyptian religion to the natural world and to a particular geographical place. Monotheism in that sense parallels the imperialism of the Eighteenth Dynasty; it spread until it was no longer tied, and could no longer return, to a specific locale, a native terrain. But then, after Akhenaten's death, the priests of the old folk religion embarked on a campaign to obliterate the memory of Akhenaten and his monotheistic idea. In short, they set out to destroy destruction, and they mostly succeeded.

Except for the fact that the Egyptian Moses kept the idea of the Aten religion alive long enough to impose it upon his "chosen people," who, so far as Freud can tell, had never asked to receive it. Truly, the Egyptian Moses performs as a destructive character; he is even harsher and more restrictive than his predecessor. Now there is not even a reference to the sun god of old. Moses is also—and this trait fundamentally distinguishes him as a repetition of Akhenaten—melancholic, in that he preserves and intensifies the memory of a loss of an ideal kind. He visits the destruction of the destroyed idea upon the Jewish people, who then, in a repetition of their own, rise up against the Egyptian Moses, the interloper in their midst. Now we have even more destruction: the destruction of the revival of the destroyed religion of destruction. This is the "catastrophe" that befalls Moses; and yet it is precisely that catastrophe which ensures his survival as an idea. The Jewish religion that emerges in the wake of catastrophe will try to supplant the Egyptian man Moses with the Midianite Moses. But in a strange dialectical process, a sort of deferred action, the idea of the murdered Moses—or, rather, the man Moses as an idea—will come to overwhelm the second Moses. And what is that "Moses idea"? More than just an idea of destruction, it is an immanent idea of destruction. Gone are the central tenets of the old Egyptian religion: the assurance of a life after death and the reassurances of explanatory myth. Gone is any connection to the natural environment of a particular locale. What we get instead is an alienation from the world that denies a transcendence of that world. On the one hand, the Mosaic religion dispenses with any mention of a life after death. On the other hand, the idea of Moses preserves the concept of truth and justice (as Freud puts it) while also preserving the memory of revolt against the harshness of the tyrant, embodied in the figure of the Egyptian Moses himself. There is a critical dialectic at work here: Moses establishes the possibility of liberation from the guilt history he otherwise imposes, and that his murder makes possible after the fact.

The motif that makes this clear, oddly enough, is that of circumcision. Like the Egyptian Moses, who, according to Freud, brings the practice with him from Egypt, circumcision is imposed upon the Jewish people from outside (23:26). Rather than inventing the practice as part of their covenant, in other words, the Jewish people adopt and repeat a practice that has no organic connection to their cultural or religious practices. Yet herein lies its significance. Circumcision, divorced from its origins— having no origins, really—no longer signifies the cut of the law. On the contrary, it now indicates a repetition and a dispersal at the point of the cut: a potentially infinite cutting of the cut, so to speak (23:30). In this way, Freud succeeds in making circumcision, the putative cut of the law, into a figure for nonsovereignty. More than that, he somehow succeeds in separating circumcision from the guilt history it had been made, retroactively, to serve. There is no autochthonous connection between the Jewish people and the practice of circumcision. It represents, finally, a break from the natural that is also a break, in its repetition and division, from a guilt history of indebtedness to the father.

Later on in *Moses and Monotheism*, Freud will detail the ways in which both Judaism and Christianity (especially Christianity) work to re-naturalize, and indeed re-mythologize, the de-naturalizing monotheism brought by the Egyptian Moses. Freud is at his most Mosaic, we might say, when he acts to counter those attempts at returning monotheism to nature (and away from idea) by offering a construction, in the psycho-analytic sense of the term, in place of the absent history of the Mosaic moment. There is nothing "natural" about a construction; but neither is a construction "historical," strictly speaking. A construction, like the staging of a theatrical scene, is an imposition of itself. A construction is intended, moreover, not only to take the place of symptoms but also to diminish the affects that have rushed in to fill the void left behind by a forgotten fragment of the past. Its purpose, simply put, is to establish something deadened and scenic, even inert, in the place of a paradoxically lively lost history. But there is something else here as well. In "Constructions in Analysis," written during the same period as *Moses and Monotheism*, Freud draws a surprising comparison between constructions and delu-sions. Both are said to reject reality in favor of bringing back a (usually painful) "historical truth," a truth that had been repressed in the name of the sort of economic equilibrium we examined in our study of *Beyond the Pleasure Principle*.[40] In that respect, a construction is deeply melancholic. Moses, then, could be said to make a sort of construction on behalf of his chosen people, a construction that brings back the repressed memory of the lost religion of Akhenaten. And it goes without saying that Freud then makes a construction having to do with that construction, that interven-tion into history. But Freud's construction in this case goes slightly awry. It is designed to account for the rise of a guilt history tied to the super-ego, to explain the weighty presence of the law. The very makeup of a construction—fabricated and unmoored from the history it supposedly recovers or recounts—is what evacuates the man Moses. There is no lon-ger anything natural about his actions or his position; and the same can be said of Freud, or of any master. In trying to be like Moses by denaturalizing the position of master, Freud makes the very gesture impossible as anything other than the repetition it already is. And to repeat a repetition, to multiply it, is simply to evacuate, through a process of continual wearing away, the thing being repeated.

Repetition, serial destruction, cutting: What do these actions accomplish? They are all nonsovereign gestures, all ways of diminishing the force of the sovereign cut. They might also be used to describe the peculiar form taken by Freud's text, in which every section, every idea, seems to get repeated and in which every repetition makes for a reduction and a diminishment. Writing itself seems to turn against Freud's project, destroying it and all its Mosaic proclamations, much as the Jewish people turn against the Egyptian Moses and his uncompromising monotheistic idea. Like Moses, the outsider who brought the Aten religion to a chosen people who had not asked to receive it, Freud unleashes upon an unsuspecting world the harsh, unyielding "truth" of psychoanalysis. Both men move, then, to assume the masterful position of the superego. But can that position ever be assumed? Or can it only be usurped? In neither case is the usurper in question, Moses or Freud, related to his followers (with the notable exception of Anna Freud). The connection between them cannot then be described as genealogical or, for lack of a better word, organic. Moses, Freud: these are not primal fathers. These are outsiders, interlopers, and their relationship to their followers, not being direct, cannot be said to give rise to a guilt history rooted in the inexhaustible obligations imposed by filial duty; it can only be said to institute a construction. If Freud fears that he will be betrayed by his followers, as Moses was betrayed by his, that is because Freud's own construction of the history of Moses preserves the idea, the memory, of revolt against the position of the superego. The superego itself can be destroyed, cut up, and then preserved as the idea of its destruction rather than as the legacy of its capacity to act as a berating agency.

Freud considered *Moses and Monotheism* to be a companion work to his *Totem and Taboo*, and in a way he was correct; both works feature a superegoic primal father figure. But whereas the father of the primal horde retains a kind of life after death, a vitality exemplified by the communal eating of the totem meal, the man Moses is stripped of his flesh and drained of his vitality, worn away until he is nothing but an idea, a potentiality. And what is that Mosaic idea, exactly? It is, in the first place, a melancholic idea, an idea that comes to dominate the thinking of a people whose act of murder constituted it as an idea in the first place—an idea and not a man. The priests try to supplant the man Moses with the

Midianite Moses and the volcano god Yahweh. But the undead idea of Moses—the "supervalent idea" of truth and justice—ends up taking the place of both. Strangely, though, that idea cannot be called disembodied, since it was realized when the Jewish people revolted against Moses and the unyielding demands of his harsh religion. If the murder of the primal father institutes a guilt history in which none of his sons can rise to take the father's vacated place—if they can only procreate and extend that history through time—then the killing of Moses, never to be commemorated and yet never forgotten either, sets in motion a history of repetition that can only be constructed, that is nothing but constructed: a history in which the idea of the man Moses returns to destroy the very point of command from which that idea issued.

What are we left with, then? Freud returns to the terrain of *Totem and Taboo* only to find that terrain changed into something unrecognizable. The very position of exceptionality is cut up, subjected to repetition, reduced to the idea of its own destruction, its power of decision transformed into a construction. Nothing lives in such a terrain. At the end of his life and his career, Freud writes a text that, abandoning us to the desert condition of the master, points the way out of captivity.

CHAPTER FIVE

Melancholia under Capitalism

MARX, SCHUMPETER, ADORNO

BEFORE BEGINNING THIS chapter in earnest, we must first take a moment to secure the object. In the wake of Derrida's forceful intervention into the tradition of psychoanalysis, we have come to understand Freud's version of melancholia as profoundly ethical, an immersive, if also paradoxical, fidelity to the indestructible and unforgettable lost object.[1] Yet that way of conceptualizing melancholia becomes increasingly difficult to maintain once capitalism intrudes upon the world-historical scene. Not only does the status of the object change radically under capitalism; with the emergence of so-called second nature, the status of reality itself changes, along with the activity, reality-testing, that Freud identified as central to both mourning and melancholia.[2] When all that is solid melts into air, what then becomes of melancholia?

For Freud, reality-testing names the process whereby consciousness confirms that a presentation in the psyche corresponds to an object perceivable in external "reality." The "healthy" mourner tests reality, finds that it no longer includes the object still present to the psyche, then sets about the laborious task of withdrawing his libido from that object and transferring it to another—the task, that is, of reconciling himself to reality. The melancholic, by contrast, persists in holding on to the presented object, despite the fact that such a presentation no longer accords with a reality bereft of the object to which the melancholic stubbornly clings. Like the mourner, the melancholic tests reality. But where the mourner's explorations prompt him to heed the call of reality, the melancholic, having tested external reality and finding it impoverished, refuses that call in favor of a psychical topography in which fidelity to the object might still be possible.

The shortcomings of this dichotomy were evident even to Freud himself, who came to understand that we are all melancholics after a fashion, our psyches a repository of abandoned object-cathexes and the unresolved conflicts that attend them.[3] Yet those shortcomings do not necessarily concern us here. What concerns us, rather, is that reality-testing, arguably the mechanism that defines melancholia (if only by allowing us to distinguish it from mourning), becomes impossible under a historical regime of commodification.[4] Post-Freudian melancholia rests on the idea that we retain, if only unconsciously, a privileged lost object: an object neither fungible nor exchangeable. Arguably, though, all objects are lost objects under commodification, because all objects get displaced by their status as commodities.[5] How, then, is one to maintain even unconscious fidelity to the lost object—the essence of melancholia—if one cannot separate that object from out of the welter of lost objects generated by commodification? In short, what reality-testing is possible or necessary—what reality is there to test—under commodification?

We might reframe this as a question of fetishism, in both the Freudian and Marxian senses of the term. As Freud understands it, the fetish functions as a means of "fending off" a confrontation with lack.[6] Such an operation cannot be said to apply to the melancholic, however, since the melancholic's interest lies not in disavowing lack but in staging, as it were, the lack of lack. The melancholic has no need, then, of the fetish as psychoanalysis defines it. The commodity fetish, on the other hand, confronts the melancholic with a genuine dilemma. Clearly, the melancholic is not one to be taken in by the commodity's mystification of the antagonistic split between classes—the way, that is, that the commodity fetish masks the lack of the social relation by putting real social relations, relations of labor and value, out of sight.[7] If anything, the melancholic remains fixated on that split insofar as it indicates an eruption of the real and thus an impasse at the heart of community. Instead, the problem that commodity fetishism presents to the political melancholic is, as we have already suggested, that commodification transforms every object into a lost object, an object that can no longer be perceived as such because it has been supplanted by the commodity in its place. So we ask again: How is one to melancholically test—and, having tested, repudiate—a reality that is nothing more than the virtual reality of commodification?

The obvious answer to this question would be that the political melancholic simply refuses that virtual reality—refuses, that is, to heed the call of a reality structured by commodification. If that simple explanation fails to suffice, however, it is because of the complex nature of melancholia itself. Melancholia, as Agamben argues in a passage from *Stanzas* that we looked at in both our prologue and our chapter on *Hamlet*, is "not so much the regressive reaction to the loss of the love object as the imaginative capacity to make an unattainable object appear as if lost." This characterization of melancholia—the imaginative substitution of loss for unattainability—holds some far-reaching implications. One could argue, for example, that such a characterization accurately describes psychical life under commodification; for even if one could see through the commodity fetish to the real social relations it obscures, the nature of that fetish still dictates that unmediated access to the object remains fundamentally impossible. The commodity always gets in the way, the screen is always there. Carried to its logical extreme, this would suggest that melancholia as Agamben describes it—melancholia as a pact with unreality—is operationally complicit with commodity fetishism. But it would suggest, too, that a melancholia dependent on reality-testing and directed toward the faithful preservation of a privileged lost object is now impossible. The commodity fetish, to express the matter paradoxically, has rendered melancholia inaccessible. Little wonder, then, that left-wing melancholics are so profoundly melancholic.[8] Not only have they suffered the loss of the loved object; they have suffered the loss of the melancholia that would allow them to maintain fidelity to that object.

Even in spite of that double loss, however, hope remains, and it does so precisely because of what Agamben describes as "the strategy of melancholia." That strategy, he writes, "opens a space for the existence of the unreal and marks out a scene in which the ego may enter into relation with it and attempt an appropriation such as no other possession could rival and no loss possibly threaten."[9] For the time being—the time, that is, of capitalism and its attendant regime of commodification—the political melancholic must secret away, not the object, which has been rendered utterly inaccessible, put out of reach by layer upon layer of mediation, but rather melancholia itself, which the political melancholic appropriates so that no other possession might rival it and no loss possibly threaten it. On the contrary, melancholia, in the manner of the melancholic object, can now be infinitely destroyed and so prove its indestructibility. Nor will it ever be forgotten, because its encryption has placed it beyond the reach of destructive memory. Melancholia, and the hope for a better world it makes possible, remains in safekeeping.

But what of the melancholic himself? No longer the living archive of the lost object, the melancholic has instead become the custodian of a melancholia that can no longer be practiced, only preserved. That leaves him little choice, then, but to embrace a new role, defined by a different tactic. The tactic we have in mind here, while ultimately derived from what Walter Benjamin would describe as an absorption in the realm of "petrified unrest," finds its fullest expression in the work of Benjamin's interlocutor Theodor W. Adorno.[10] In "Reflections on Class Theory," for example, Adorno observes, as part of a larger effort aimed at critiquing capitalism's ongoing efforts to naturalize prehistorical hierarchies, that

> to recognize the catastrophic violence in the latest form of injustice, that is to say, the latent injustice contained in fair exchange, means simply to identify it with the prehistory that it destroyed. If all the oppression than man ever inflicted on man culminates in the modern age in the cold inhumanity of free wage labor, then the past is revealed in conditions and things . . . as the trace of former suffering. The archaic silence of pyramids and ruins becomes conscious of itself in materialist thought: it is the echo of factory noise in the landscape of the immutable.[11]

That the disposition here adopted is one of "melancholy" is made clear by Adorno in a lecture delivered on January 12, 1965. Explaining why, in his view, the "interweaving of nature and history must in general be the model for every interpretive procedure in philosophy," Adorno goes on to declare that "the relationship of nature and history provides us with the primal image of interpretive behavior, something that has been handed down through intellectual history in the form of allegory." He then continues:

> Beneath this gaze, the profound gaze of allegory, which is perhaps the model for the philosophical gaze as such—because the attitude of melancholic contemplation may well be the attitude on which philosophical inquiry has been founded—nature stands revealed. Nature, I say, reveals itself beneath this gaze as history, just as in all allegory the death's head owes its central importance to the fact that as a natural object its own expression reveals its historical nature. Conversely . . . beneath this gaze history stands revealed as nature in so far as it turns out to be permanent transience.

Such a melancholy attitude, because it "perceives transience in everything historical," is not just recollective of the past, according to Adorno; it is also "critical," given over to the dialectical negation of both nature and history. Thus "we can say," picking up on Adorno's argument,

> that the transition from philosophy to criticism represents something like a secularization of melancholy. This is a melancholy that has

become active, not a melancholy that makes do, that remains stuck fast in an unhappy consciousness, not at home with itself, but a conscious-ness that exteriorizes itself as a critique of existing phenomena. Such a melancholy is probably the pre-eminent critical, philosophical stance. In other words, if you read the phenomena of history as the cyphers of their own transience or their own natural deterioration, they will also always be defined by their own negativity.[12]

What emerges here is an image of the melancholic akin to Benjamin's famous, and famously contemplative, angel of history, whose face, we know, is turned toward the past, where a pile of debris ("wreckage upon wreck-age," writes Benjamin) "grows skyward" even as the storm called progress "irresistibly propels him into the future to which his back is turned."[13] But where the angel remains fixated on, even struck by, the "one single catastro-phe" that we call history, the melancholic's gaze is, as Adorno insists, criti-cal, capable of "read[ing] the phenomena of history as the cyphers of their own transience." The vehicle for a consciousness able to exteriorize itself in the transformative act of critique, the melancholic gaze contemplates a storm whose apparent naturalness can still be historicized.

If this version of melancholia—critical, contemplative, philosophical—sounds nothing like the caricature of "left-wing melancholia" promulgated by Benjamin and, following him, Wendy Brown, that is because both crit-ics are content to accept the orthodox Freudian understanding of melan-cholia and then apply it transitively. The symptoms of the unfortunate affliction, Left melancholia, they then take it upon themselves to diag-nose do indeed sound worrisome. "A refusal to come to terms with the particular character of the present, that is, a failure to understand his-tory in terms other than 'empty time' or 'progress'"; "a certain narcissism with regard to one's past political attachments and identity that exceeds any contemporary investment in political mobilization, alliance, or trans-formation"; "a mournful, conservative, backward-looking attachment to a feeling, analysis, or relationship that has been rendered thing-like and frozen in the heart of the putative Leftist"; a commitment "more to cer-tain long-held sentiments and objects than to the possibilities of political transformation in the present": If we checked any of those boxes on a diagnostic questionnaire, we would seek professional help.[14] But the con-dition described by Benjamin and Brown (or Brown paraphrasing Ben-jamin) is not political melancholia. Like the garden-variety melancholia from which it derives, Left melancholia involves the disappointed ego's narcissistic identification with a lost object (in this case, "a movement" and "a historical moment"; "a theoretical and empirical coherence"; "a way of life and a course of pursuits") that it can neither relinquish nor forgive. The Left melancholic, to put the matter in the quasi-clinical terms adopted by Brown, refuses to cathect their libidinal energies in any object other than the disappointed leftism of the last century. Yet nothing could be further from the tactics of the political melancholic, who, as we argued in our prologue, cathects not to the object as such but rather to the persistent conflictual love associated with the object. The immobilized leftist melancholic can do nothing but turn their ambivalence inward, directing their ire at the heretical betrayals, the identity politics and insufficiently empirical poststructuralism, of the movement they loved. Political melancholia, by contrast, is characterized by its tendency to turn round into mania, at which point the political melancholic directs their passions outward, into a world that needs not just changing, but rethinking. What Benjamin and Brown perceive as the leftist melancholic's inability to move forward becomes, in the political melancholic, a manifestation of stasis.

That Benjamin failed to recognize as much is disappointing. But Brown then compounds the problem through an incomplete reading of Benjamin's own theory of melancholia. "Benjamin," she writes,

> is particularly attuned to the melancholic's investment in "things." In *The Origin of German Tragic Drama*, he argues that "melancholy betrays the world for the sake of knowledge," here suggesting that the loyalty of the melancholic converts its truth ("every loyal vow or memory") about its beloved into a thing, indeed, imbues knowledge itself with a thinglike quality. Benjamin provides another version of this formulation: "in its tenacious self-absorption [melancholy] embraces dead objects in its contemplation." More simply, melancholia is "loyal to the world of things," a formulation that suggests a certain logic of fetishism—with all the conservatism and withdrawal from human relations that fetishistic desire implies—contained within the melancholic logic. . . . We come to love our Left passions and reasons, our Left analyses and convictions, more than we love the existing world that we presumably seek to alter with these terms or the future that would be aligned with them.[15]

It is this melancholic investment in things, Brown argues, that the leftist must resist; otherwise, the movement becomes inert, history ceases its forward progress, and the future is lost. That may well be true. But what the Left melancholic is admonished to resist, the political melancholic rushes to affirm. That is because, unlike the Left melancholic, whose attachment to the past no doubt impedes the transition from one historical formation to another, the political melancholic remains loyal to the world of things in order to lay claim to the transformative power of natural history. The political melancholic, as Adorno observes, is both philosophical and critical; their externalized critical consciousness apprehends itself in the objective world of things. Brown's injunction to the Left melancholic to *get over it* and *move on* assumes there must be lack in the present (the lack of the object) for there to be a future. The political melancholic knows that only by allowing ourselves to be arrested by the lack of lack, realized in the contemplative embrace of insistent things, will we ever be forced to think something truly new.

One characterization we agree with, however, is that the political melancholic has no time for mobilization or alliance, activities they are content to leave to those committed to effecting the transition from one historical formation to another. The tactics and talents of the political melancholic lie elsewhere, in the authentically critical processes of thought, action, and judgment. That may sound like a lonely pursuit; and yet the political melancholic under capitalism is no more (or less) alone than was Plato or Hamlet or Woyzeck or Freud. On the contrary, even as he is blown, like the angel of history, backward into the future, the pile of debris before him growing ever skyward, the melancholic's contemplative gaze cannot help but take in, and indeed fuse with, the activities of the other melancholic figures under capitalism. One of those, to whom we will turn in a moment, is the haunted agent of what Marx terms "living labor." The other is the capitalist himself; and it is toward that strange fusion, that peculiar coming together of melancholic and capitalist, where we will initially direct our own critical gaze in this chapter.

The Melancholic Capitalist of Marx's Capital

There are good reasons to regard the capitalist as melancholic in the more conventional sense. Here is a figure, after all, who refuses to give up a nothing that, strictly speaking, he has never in fact possessed, despite having appropriated it: surplus value.[16] Of more immediate interest to us, however, is what Benjamin perceived in his fragmentary sketch from 1921, "Capitalism as Religion."[17] The problem with capitalism, Benjamin argues, is not that it disenchants the world—Max Weber's thesis—but rather that it reenchants the world with new practices and rituals, new beliefs and deities. Like the psychiatrist in relation to his paranoiac, the capitalist becomes so enthralled by the delirium induced by the reenchanted world of capitalism, with its spectral invisible hands, that he ends up taking on the contours of that delirium in his own practices.[18] In short, the capitalist becomes haunted.[19] The capitalist can become so haunted—so completely immersed in the liturgy of capitalism, so captivated by its misty world of ghosts, invisible forces, and such afflictions of the spirit as guilt and debt—that he loses sight of capitalism's authentically melancholic dimension. That dimension has nothing to do with spirits or specters. It has to do, rather, with the unfolding of a physionomos defined, like capitalism, by accumulation. This slightly alters the aim of the political melancholic. Now that aim must be to disenchant the world, the world under capitalism, once and for all. The aim of the political melancholic, in other words, must be to intensify the concern of the capitalist—to accumulate and accumulate—until his burden becomes unbearable. An understanding of the emancipatory potential held by accumulation: that is what the political melancholic has to offer the *homo oeconomicus*.

This turns out to be a task for which the melancholic is especially well suited, for the simple reason that the melancholic intervenes at the exact point where capitalism and guilt history intersect: the point of accumulation. That capitalism works through accumulation—that capital as such simply is what is accumulated (as opposed to hoarded or dispersed through wages)—is of course one of the core arguments advanced in *Capital*.[20] There is a "law" that governs capitalism, according to Marx, and that law is the law of accumulation. It is the law of accumulation, in fact, that ensures capitalism's reproduction of itself (771). Through the generation—or, rather, the extraction—of surplus value from labor, capital begets capital. But to describe accumulation as a law, *the* law, of capitalism: What does that mean? Capitalism, at least in the way that Marx describes it, is inherently *nomic*, a process of division, calculation, apportionment, dispensation. But it is also, and more pointedly, a process of continuous building up, of incessantly producing and accumulating surplus. From the perspective of capital, that surplus is the surplus value extracted from labor. From our perspective, however, it also includes the surplus of bodies that make up the standing reserve army of labor and the uneconomical forces of resistance and conflict produced when capitalism produces "an active and cooperative working class."[21] In short, the production of surplus value necessitates the production of antagonism. The "living labor" alienated in the production of commodities is never passive in the way that abstract labor is; by virtue of its capacity to force transformation, living labor "functions as both the condition and limit to the development of the capitalist mode of production."[22] Living labor is more than productive. In its objectification of the conflictual energy that leads to change, it is akin to that "melancholy consciousness" that, according to Adorno, "exteriorizes itself as a critique of existing phenomena." One way of thinking about capitalism as melancholic would thus be to acknowledge that the surplus accumulated by capitalism is not simply surplus value but, more specifically, the "unrest" (*Unruhe*) of the maker, extinguished in the product through the activity of labor (287). Truly, according to that way of reckoning, capitalism is haunted by the objectification of innumerable, and highly critical, ghosts.

But if capitalism is a sort of nomos, a quasi-legal order rooted in the endless division and accumulation of the life-activity expressed in labor, then it is at the same time only a nomos—that is to say, a nomos with no direct connection, ultimately, to *physis*. That is not how capitalism understands itself, of course. And heaven knows that it is not how capitalists understand capitalism. In their not disinterested view, capitalism is a physis in the sense that it would realize its essential properties if only it were left to follow its own, supposedly natural course of development. The Lutherans saw matters more clearly. Their worry, as Weber notes, was that, without capitalism, they would fall back into their sinful natural state.[23] Witness to the historical beginnings of capitalism, the Lutherans could recognize it for what it was and what it yet remains: an entirely world-historical phenomenon. To recognize that capitalism is world historical or merely nomic is not to argue, however, that it is therefore divorced from the patient workings of natural historical physionomos—that it could not be profaned; that it could not be returned to the capitalist as profaned. Herein lies the truly radical dimension of Marx's thought in *Capital*, and the one that a politics of melancholia calls to our attention.[24] Woven through the accumulative workings of capitalism, like a natural historical law equivalent to the law of accumulation, is a physionomos that also operates through accumulation—so much so, in fact, that it cannot help but accumulate the capitalist himself, who emerges as little more than an unwitting agent of physionomos.[25]

Marx makes this plain enough in the opening pages of part 3 of *Capital*, on the production of absolute surplus-value, where his own actions as a critic mirror and invert those of the capitalist. It is notable that the capitalist should be the only human figure that Marx allows into the final paragraphs of this section, a section that begins, equally notably, with a natural historical analogy comparing the worst architect with the best of bees (284).[26] Standing at the present end of "an immense span of time," the latest in a long line of descent that includes the stone-wielding savage,

the managerial Cincinnatus, and the cruel slave driver, the anxious capitalist now finds himself the inheritor of a property that includes, among
its many amenities, a vast cellar filled with barrels (292). Those barrels,
countless in number, environ more than wine alone, however. They also
foster Marx's own, implicit metaphor for physionomos: fermentation. On
the one hand a process available for use by any given capitalist, who "by
the purchase of labour-power . . . incorporates labour, as a living agent of
fermentation, into the lifeless constituents of the product," fermentation is
also, and more fundamentally, an ongoing cycle of controlled rot or natural historical decay that is both a manifestation of petrified unrest and a
politicized apprehension of metabolic germination (292). In fermentation,
as in melancholia, that which is apparently most dead most actively works
through the living (292). Working his way down to the most basic molecular level, Marx comes to understand how seemingly nonliving agents such
as yeast and bacteria, operating through the process of dissolution that
transpires when things, nature, and human labor come into contact with
one another, produce the convivial luxuries that we associate with life
under a regime of commodification. Marx thus concludes his brief natural
history of the labor process with a thought-image that mimics capitalist
practice by first accumulating, then metabolizing, the technological devel-
opments of his own present day. The power of micro-organic, bacterial life
discovered through the work of Pasteur, Swann, and others—life activity
operating below the threshold of everyday perception, "life without air"—
germinates, like some sort of high-yielding, fast-growing fermentative
agent, in Marx's own critical analysis. One might go so far as to say that
such micro-organisms act as the unacknowledged, metaphoric driving
force within Marx's materialist dialectics. For it is in that dialectics, as
it is in the secret workings of fermentation unlocked by the advances in
microbiology taking place in the 1850s, that forms of life once regarded as
idle and inoperative turn out to be supremely fecund, and that elements
of nature once dismissed as "unorganized ferments" turn out to be highly
organized, perhaps even politically potent. Once accumulated by Marx,
metabolized by him, drawn up into his materialist dialectics, microbio-
logical forms-of-life, with their distributed networks and quorum-sensing,
not only evade being owned or possessed (however much they might be
subjected to the seal of copyright and patent law); their silently persistent physionomos goes on bubbling away within the products and commodities that the capitalist claims as his own. And indeed those things
are the capitalist's own, but not entirely in the way that he believes or that
Marx implies. Rather, those commodities "belong to him" in a way that the

capitalist finds it impossible to own up to. For try as he might, he cannot get rid of the surplus life he has incorporated (in good melancholic fashion) simply by transmuting its excessive, incessant activity into surplus value. The laws of capitalist fermentation dictate that such life belongs to the capitalist as much as he belongs to it.

With that in mind, let us revisit the comparison with which Marx begins chapter 7 of *Capital*: that of the worst architect, "who builds the cell in his mind before he constructs it in wax," and "the best of bees" (284). Taken in isolation, this analogy seems to affirm humankind's radical difference from nature—seems to affirm, that is, the putative gulf that separates the "worst architect" from the "best of bees." Subject the image to the critical metabolism practiced by Marx himself, though, and it dissolves within a larger narrative charting humankind's convergence with nature at the very moment, and in the very place, that we seek to assert our mastery over it. It is not only, as Marx's own reliance on natural imagery suggests, that nature furnishes the material substratum through which ideas (such as the idea that we are somehow separate from the nature we continue to transform) are constructed. In the sweeping drama that unfolds over the first pages of chapter 7, humans do more, but also less, than transform their own nature by transforming nature. Traversing the bounds of nature, they realize themselves in nature so thoroughly that they have no choice but to subordinate their will to that which they have transformed. The more impersonal the laborer becomes, the more they come to realize their life not as something alienated in the production of commodities but as something metabolized with and through the same nature that produced their own actions and organs.[27] Humankind's metabolism of nature leads, in time, to the metabolism of the idea of humankind. We ourselves confront the materials of nature as yet another force of nature.

But Marx is interested in more than just the reciprocal metabolism that takes place between humans and nature. What truly interests him is how the metabolic interactions between human laborers and the world (which is really just another way of saying the dialectical relationship between them) generates a return: the return of a "complex of things," things marked by their transformative powers, their transient existence, and their suspended torment, within the mechanisms of production (285–286). Inherently melancholic, labor acts as a form of communion between the past and present, the living and the dead.[28] To enter into the workings of natural history is not only to realize one's own life in the impersonalization of labor. It is to unearth (as it were) those relics of past means of labor wherein one discerns the lineaments of lost forms of social organization.

There is something more than lyrical about the process of decay or the appearance of a ruin. Commodity fetishism being what it is, we only ever really become aware of the past labor objectified in a commodity—only ever really become aware of the petrified unrest encrypted in a product of labor—when that commodity breaks down far enough to reveal its inherent dysfunctionality, its uneconomical, inoperative core. In a crowded universe of things, perished forms of life reappear. Redemption depends upon the disenchantment and profanation of the erstwhile commodity.

And what are we, the living, meant to do with this extinguished life-activity, this petrified unrest? "Past labor," as Marx calls it, having once produced what are now idle objects, returns to conjure the revitalizing sparks inherent in our own living labor. This is how melancholia and labor come together to form a new universal. Not only are the transient things around us and to hand the "results of labor"; they also make up "its essential conditions," the spaces and materials and instruments through which and upon which labor expends itself. Living labor's first task, then, is to lay hold of the moribund corpus constituted by dead labor and decaying things. Meanwhile, the process of decay, insofar as it is a metabolic process possessed of its own inexorable force—a process that encompasses things and materials, tools and machines, life forms and forms of life—calls living labor to it and, in so doing, calls living labor to itself. Generated by the same labor process into which it is then entered (and which consumes it either immediately or slowly, over time), the product also allows that process to carry out its redemptive work by realizing its revitalizing force. The true value of things lies, then, not in their use-value, and certainly not in their surplus-value, but in their return as relics of past labor. For it is then that they redeem living labor by calling it to further their consumption—further, that is, their disappearance into natural history—and, in that gesture, ensure their own redemption.

Marx, then, understands labor as a melancholic universal; and in that understanding we discover a critical paradigm that actualizes the labor implicit in the German word *Stoffwechsel*. Meaning "change of stuff" or "change of materials," but ordinarily translated as "metabolism," Stoffwechsel names the ongoing natural historical process actively pursued by the melancholic theoretician, who grasps that every production of theory injects a differential into the operations of political economy (290). Thought itself furthers the ends of metabolism. Going well beyond the simple historicization of political economy, Marx, the practitioner of a critical, melancholic metabolism, ties the end of things to new beginnings, like a montage artist whose found objects consist of different states, temporalities, and collectives. But Marx does not stop there. Instead, he reinserts those conjoined states, recomposed things, and newly forged collectives into the very apparatus of capitalist consumption that previously dissolved their original, innate ties.[29] Such a move then allows Marx to arrive at an altogether different consummation: a consuming that creates, by devouring the "living means" used in the process of (critical) labor, a novel product "distinct from the consumer," at once outside of her control and operative in the economy at large (290). Marx, in other words, so thoroughly metabolizes the objects he scrutinizes that he ends up composing an entirely new body, prosthetic and monstrous, made up entirely of relics, a category that now includes not only tools and bones but economies that have fallen so far out of recorded history, dropped so far from view, that they are rendered imperceptible even to the natural sciences (286).

Could we go so far as to call those relics reliquaries or even crypts, material objects containing, in the form of the petrified unrest of past labor, the spirits whose return preoccupies melancholic thought? In his own writing, Marx rather dramatically reuses an array of obstinately persistent objects, up to and including machines that, having been taken out of circulation, fall into disrepair and lose their use-value, in order to demonstrate how close objects must come to being extinguished before their true value, the power to call living labor into redemptive action, can be realized. Past labor can only ever return—return to haunt us, to redeem us—once it loses its mediating purpose, along with all of the other objects and forms of life-activity that once sustained it; for only in their ruination can the products of past labor realize themselves as relics liberated from the drudgery of a specific usefulness or the life-context that animated them and lent them sense.

Mindful, then, that his own critical activity is itself a form of labor, and thus part of a new universal, Marx's melancholic critic returns incessantly to objects that return, consuming them further in the process of his living labor activity. In so doing, the Marxian critic not only describes, but in describing effects, a new way of understanding accumulation: not as the amassing of surplus-value, but as the process whereby the objects of labor and the means and materials of production proliferate until "the distinction between principal subject and accessory vanishes," along with the "original composition" of all substances and products (288). The capitalist, by drawing a distinction between the finished product, which interests him only insofar as it is a commodity, and the raw materials, means of production, and labor activities that went into its making, turns all means, things, and processes into substances. The critic, by contrast, liquefies those same substances, transforming them into accidents by reintroducing them into natural historical—that is, metabolic and laborious—circulation. What Marx conjures here is a radically different version of the relationship between nature and history than that found in the classical natural order of the Physiocrats, with its hierarchies and distributions, its overall properness (176, 284, 644). But while Marx's conception might be uneconomical, it is not without an order of its own. Rather, it describes a physionomos in which semi-manufactured things—things produced by the metabolic interaction between labor and nature—"may have to go through a whole series of different processes," "changing [their] shape constantly" depending upon "the position [they] occupy" within the labor process, until they achieve their complete extinction, at which point they fulfill their role in the destructive power of nature by calling out living labor (289). What Marx invents, then, is a completely new, ever expanding, potentially infinite universe of means and things, subtended by a physionomical logic in which every product of labor—in other words, nearly everything—gets unsettled by the unrest extinguished in it. And in that way he shows himself to be a universalizing thinker keenly attuned to a natural historical level of existence wherein minute things—bacteria, stones, bones, dye, rust—comingle with the grandest accomplishments of humankind—canals and such—both past and present.

Viewing history from that perspective, Marx cannot help but regard the capitalist as a latecomer to a millennia-old drama, a latecomer who, having traversed a thingly technical history, is incapable ot separating himself from the metabolism he serves and by which he, like all things, will finally be consumed. Marx, we know, had an abiding interest in crisis, which he understood not as a parlous situation demanding management and resolution (let alone exploitation) but as one of the motive forces within capitalism.[30] Did he also understand it as inherently redemptive? Etymologically, *crisis* stems, in part, from the symptomatic analysis of a diseased body or—why not?—body politic.[31] Marx, nonimmunitarian thinker that he is, is not concerned with bodies. Unlike the capitalist, whose livelihood depends upon the effective administration and distribution of bodies—bodies to consume and to be consumed in the process of labor, bodies to be used up or cast aside, inexhaustible bodies, elite bodies to be disciplined and perfected—Marx's melancholic critic fixates on those things that a privileging of the body encourages us to treat as pathogenic or parasitical: the technical prostheses that expand our corporeal boundaries, the fascination of exfoliating cadavers, the energy of decaying things and forms of life. The capitalist identifies the symptoms of crisis only insofar as he might profit thereby; his response to the symptom is always to turn it toward the resuscitation of an economy perpetually on the verge of collapse. What everyone else suffers, the capitalist enjoys. The melancholic critic, meanwhile, retains a very different understanding of *symptom*. Ultimately derived from the Greek word (σύμπτωμα) for "chance," "accident," "mischance," "disease," it comes from the stem of *sympiptein*, "to befall," which in turn is formed from syn- "together" + piptein "to fall."[32] A symptom, then, is what befalls us. It is the worst that could happen, the source of crisis in both its medical and sociopolitical dimensions. Above all, the symptom is evental. It befalls all of us and excludes no one, not even the capitalist. As much, then, as the capitalist might want to separate himself from the universal of labor by laying claim to the symptom as surplus to be enjoyed (if only as what corroborates his sense of himself as a careful manager of crisis), the melancholic knows otherwise. Her tactic, which she pursues in utter indifference to the needs of the economy, is to make the extinguished unrest that "belongs" to the capitalist instead "befall" the capitalist, and to such a commonizing extent that the capitalist becomes yet another agent of physionomos, subject, as are all things, to the twin *nomoi* of fermentation and accumulation.

The Melancholic Accumulation of Guilt: The Case of Joseph Schumpeter

The capitalist accumulates something else besides the symptomatic unrest of extinguished labor, however. He also, as Benjamin points out in "Capitalism as Religion," accumulates guilt and debt, a historical process that begins with so-called primitive accumulation.[33] It was then, at that particular historical juncture, that the capitalist could have opted not to pass on indebtedness to later generations or withhold from them the possibility of justice that the melancholic encrypts in the form of the lost object. Instead, the early capitalists, those pioneering exploiters of living labor, actively perpetuated the primitive accumulation that would go on to be perfected and accelerated in the historical development of capitalism. From that point on, capitalists began to accumulate guilt at an exponential rate; and should we not wish to accrue that guilt ourselves by passing on such injustice to subsequent generations, then it falls to us to relieve previous generations of their guilt by disrupting the cycle of capitalist accumulation—in other words, by breaking capitalism's fundamental "law."

To understand how that might happen, we turn to an unlikely source: Joseph Schumpeter's *Capitalism, Socialism and Democracy*. "Can capitalism survive? No, I do not believe that it can."[34] The opening sentence of Schumpeter's section on capitalism reads as if it were written to strike fear into the hearts of capitalists everywhere. And it only gets worse as the book wears on. "Crumbling Walls," "Growing Hostility," "Decomposition": with each succeeding chapter, particularly as the section draws to a close, Schumpeter presents us with the image of a capitalism prone to the same transience and decay that besets every historical formation. The most famous (or perhaps notorious) of those chapters, dedicated to "The Process of Creative Destruction," brings out that image in the starkest relief. "Capitalism," Schumpeter writes, "is by nature a form or method of economic change and not only never is but never can be stationary" (82). Like life in the animal kingdom, the life of the capitalist enterprise is one of relentless competition, a never-ending struggle for survival. Surprisingly, perhaps, Schumpeter's account of creative destruction echoes some of Marx's language in *Capital*. At one point, for example, Marx writes that

> the attraction of capitals no longer means the simple concentration of the means of production and the command over labour, which is identical with accumulation. It is concentration of capitals already formed, destruction of their individual independence, expropriation of capitalist by capitalist, transformation of many small into few large capitals. . . .
>
> Here competition rages in direct proportion to the number, and in inverse proportion to the magnitude, of the rival capitals. It always ends in the ruin of many small capitalists, whose capitals partly pass into the hands of their conquerors, and partly vanish completely (777).

Like Marx, Schumpeter regards capitalism as a natural process, comprehensible in terms of evolution, genetic mutation, and climatic phenomena (82–84). But Marx leaves us with the clear impression that the capitalist, as yet another thing to be metabolized, another life to be used up, should worry about being devoured. Schumpeter, by contrast, leaves us with the sure knowledge that the capitalist should be worried, while obscuring what it is, exactly, he should be worried about. This ambiguity is due, we think, to Schumpeter's reliance on figurative language.[35] Were "the perennial gale of creative destruction" an actual gale, the capitalist would have reason to fear being wiped out by a natural force, his entrepreneurial ambitions scattered to the winds (84). The same would be true if industrial "mutation" involved actual genetic material or if capitalism really were "organic" (83). Then the capitalist would have legitimate cause to worry about being subjected to the implacable workings of evolution. Yet none of those ways of describing capitalism is anything other than metaphorical.

Capitalism is not natural; Schumpeter's own language belies the claim. It is, rather, a series of diagrammatic arrangements, evolutionary only in the sense that each new arrangement of forces evolves, historically, out of the one before it.

This is not to suggest that capitalism has no "real" effects. It is to underscore how Schumpeter's efforts to present capitalism as natural—a presentation that can only take place at the level of metaphor—are meant to promote the assumption of capitalism's given-ness and inevitability. More than that, it is to emphasize that the very language needed to promulgate such an idea calls attention to its own lack of naturalness, even its construct-edness, and, in doing so, alerts us to what truly should worry the capitalist. It is not the creative-destructive forces of a natural capitalism; it is the natu-ral historical state of a historical formation, capitalism, the only given of which is its tendency to transience and decay. This is not to be understood, however, as the transience and decay that Schumpeter claims is inherent, like some sort of natural groundlessness, in capitalism. We refer instead to the natural historical transience and decay—the process by which, on the one hand, any given historical formation is subject to evolution while, on the other, even those apparently "natural" forces that threaten to engulf us become historicizable, subject to human intervention—to which even "the perennial gale of creative-destruction" is subject.

Whether wittingly or not, then, Schumpeter points to a way out of guilt history simply by presenting, as a matter of course, the diagram-matic structure of the world-historical formations through which guilt reproduces itself. And the effect of that presentation is only intensified by Schumpeter's theory regarding the dire fate of capitalism as he envi-sions it. That fate does not involve the out-and-out destruction of the whole capitalist enterprise; it involves, instead, the steady rationalization of capitalist practices—a process that will continue, Schumpeter argues, until capitalism is no longer its "natural" self, precisely because it will have been drained of all its vital "destructive" powers.[36] In other words, Schum-peter anticipates the inevitable, and total, disenchantment of capitalism: a capitalism denied its terrifyingly mythical dimension, its conflation of the natural and the spectral, the aleatory and the fated. This is a capital-ism in which the capitalist need no longer worry, since there is no lon-ger anything to worry about. The perennial gale of creative destruction will have been quelled. Paradoxically, however, this denaturalizing disen-chantment of capitalism, insofar as it denies the capitalist the pleasure of remaining captivated by the mysterious forces of the spirit world, simul-taneously releases him to become absorbed in natural history. No less than

Marx, with his constellated complex of "stone implements and weapons," "domesticated animals," "relics of bygone instruments of labour processes," "extinct economic formations of society," "the bones and muscles of production," "pipes, tubes, baskets, jars etc.," Schumpeter inserts a deadened diagram into the midst of capitalism's historical formation.

Adorno's Creature

This puts Schumpeter in some surprising company; for the other figure who early on grasped the power of profanation to force a diagrammatic rearrangement of capitalism's historical formation was Adorno. This time, however, that grasp was knowing and strategic. In 1934, Adorno wrote to Benjamin to express his profound admiration for the "intentions behind" the latter's essay on Kafka.[37] Adorno's enthusiasm is palpable. "Do not take it for immodesty if I begin by confessing that our agreement in philosophical fundamentals has never impressed itself upon my mind more perfectly than it does here," he gushes (66). But he is also intent on correcting what he sees as an oversight on Benjamin's part. "The most important difficulty seems to me to be that of Odradek," insists Adorno, referring to the creature from Kafka's short story "Cares of a Family Man." "For it is merely archaic to have him spring forth from the 'immemorial world and guilt,' rather than re-reading him precisely as that prolegomenon which you so penetratingly identified in the problem of scripture." Adorno then poses a series of forceful questions concerning Odradek, followed by an equally forceful assertion:

> If his origin lies with the father of the house, does he not then precisely represent the anxious *concern* and danger for the latter, does he not anticipate precisely the overcoming of the creaturely state of guilt, and is not this concern—truly a case of Heidegger put right side up— the secret key, indeed the most indubitable promise of *hope*, precisely through the overcoming of the house itself? Certainly, as the other face of the world of things, Odradek is a sign of distortion—but precisely as such he is also a motif of transcendence, namely of the ultimate limit and of the reconciliation of the organic and the inorganic, or of the overcoming of death: Odradek "lives on" (68–69).

That Adorno, from out of "distortion," the "commodity that has survived to no purpose" (as Adorno describes Odradek in another letter to Benjamin), and the crisis of the patriarchal form of life, could somehow extract "the promise of *hope*" is of no small consequence for a politics of melancholia.[38]

One does not, after all, typically associate melancholia with hopefulness. So what is it that gives Adorno, whom no one would mistake for a cock-eyed optimist, hope?

Consider the dialectical character of the German word *Sorge*, meaning "care" or "concern." The concern that the house-father has for Odradek presents us with a case of "Heidegger turned right side up," according to Adorno. We interpret this to mean that Odradek makes it possible to transform a patriarchal economy predicated, depending on how one wants to look at it, either on dutiful guilt and worry or on ennobling care, into an economy disorganized—and thus potentially redeemed—by an un-economical concern with a worn-out commodity that has survived to no purpose. In other words, Odradek holds out the promise of hope because he provides the house-father with a chance at genuine melancholia: a melancholic immersion in physionomical natural history.[39] What can be said to befall a subject (the house-father, in this case) whose affective attachment to the outside world is mediated by an elusive, mobile object unmoored from any specific place or time? What happens to a subject's worldview when it comes into contact with an object as unpredictable and unlocat-able as Odradek? One thing is certain: what Heidegger calls the Age of the World Picture, defined by man's ability to make the representation of an object dependent upon how he places himself in the scene—man's ability, that is, to position himself in relation "to beings as the objective"—has surely come to an end.[40] The Age of the World Picture means that we humans find ourselves at home in a time and place wherein a stable subject-object opposition licenses man to subjectivize himself in relation to an outside world of objects while at the same time subjecting those objects to the fixed position and measure of man. No such relationality is possible, however, in a world populated by whimsical, ill-disciplined, obstinate, and vaguely impish things, like Odradek, that withdraw from us only to return in their own peculiar manner, their own strange, syncopated time.

Yet if the childlike comings and goings of Odradek threaten the fix-ity of the Age of the World Picture, they also present a problem—a whole new source of worry, one might say—for Heidegger's own, essentially tragic notion that care (Sorge) defines *Dasein's* being-in-the-world. That such an understanding of care, stemming as it does from so weighty and ponderous a vision of Dasein's fallenness and being-toward-death, necessarily plays into the house-father's exalted sense of himself as a grand figure attuned to the tragic necessity of duty—a figure who thoroughly suffers, and thus thor-oughly enjoys, the privilege that comes with being a Dasein of care dwelling in a home sustained by care—should not surprise us. Is it not an indulgently doomed and fatalistic vision of life? Does it not confront us with just the right, tragic admixture of pride and humility? What a vigorous struggle life is, what a vital contest! And how ennobling, the sense of fulfillment one feels upon giving oneself over at last to the satisfactions and secondary gains that flow from embracing the burden of care! And yet, for all of the fear and anxiety that underwrite Dasein's unsheltered being in the world— the speechless exposure to "the nothingness of *Zuhandenheit* [handiness]," the icy terror of being called into Dasein's everyday existence—the house-father can still rest easy (§40, 187).⁴¹ After all, such troubles concern him as they do everyone else: a sheer ontological facticity both sustains and unlocks Dasein's fundamental situatedness (*Befindlichkeit*) in the "world-as-such" (§40, 187). Dasein's groundlessness, anxiety-provoking though it may be, simply provides existence with a new ground.

Not only, then, does the house-father have no reason to worry about his anxious care; he can take comfort in knowing that his home sits comfortably atop two solid pilings, one made from a stable concept of time, the other from a powerfully seductive version of the political. The fundamental ontological structure of the world's as-suchness (the "historicity of Dasein" as such), being deeply rooted in Dasein's being toward death, functions like an innate, impassive nature whose "own time" and "authentic historicity" (§74, 385) establish the "ontological genesis of history as science" (§75, 392). However dishearteningly fatalistic it may seem to accept that our collective "world-historical" destiny io gɪafled onto Dasein's being-toward death, It is not altogether disconcerting. For the fact remains that such a fatalistic destiny, unfolding as it does with a predictable rhythm toward a definitive end, constitutes an ordered arrangement, one might even say an oikonomia, of time. And the situation is much the same with politics. Repeating the central gesture of the philosophy of the tragic that he had inherited from Schelling and Hegel, Heidegger posits that we must first choose to assume Dasein's fate before we can comprehend and then seize its inherent freedom. Yet Heidegger goes one step further by transforming what had been an individual act of choosing and assuming into something more insidious: a people's resolute decision to assume its collective destiny. The moment it embraces both "the *higher power*" of its "finite freedom" and "the *powerlessness*" of being abandoned to its fate, Dasein's Sorge, its careful being-toward-death, suddenly finds itself transformed into a shared political destiny: "Fateful Dasein essentially exists as being-in-the-world in being-with others, its occurrence is an occurrence-with and is determined as destiny. With this term, we designate the occurrence of the community, of a people" (§74, 384).

But let us have a care of our own. The problem we face here is not simply that the house-father cares, and cares deeply—that he has always cared, always lain awake at night worrying about his responsibilities. The problem is that we are expected, as political beings in the world, to care about the father and his cares: to enlist ourselves in the father's epic, existential struggle, as if we remained indebted to the father for his care, as if his fateful destiny were ours as well. It is no secret that the father of the family stands at the gateway to modern economic and political thought. Marx certainly knew as much, as did Freud, Lacan, and Foucault, to name but the most prominent examples. The Roman paterfamilias, with his right over the life and death of his children and his right to enjoy the usufruct of the products generated by their labor, establishes the archetype for the modern sovereign, capitalist, manager, and master. The family may be sovereign in origin and grounded in the *patria potestas* of Roman law, yet it still constitutes the cell of modernity's disciplinary archipelago. In the family structure, as Foucault reads it, the flat, isotopic politics of contiguity associated with discipline joins the hierarchical, asymmetrical politics of verticality associated with the sovereign. All, then, that the care and welfare provided by the *parens patriae* can be said to do is add a biopolitical dimension to the "double role," at once sovereign and disciplinary, already performed by the family man. Thus Foucault, quoting Montesquieu: "In Rome, after fathers were no longer permitted to put their children to death, the magistrates inflicted punishment that the father would have prescribed." Yet if juridical and disciplinary power radiates outward from the family unit to government and the state, then this holds several implications, the most obvious being that the Roman magistrates step forth as the crucial relay between the paterfamilias and the house-father: the first figures to occupy the threshold between sovereign, disciplinary, and biopolitical regimes. As a matter of practical administration, the doctrine of the parens patriae establishes, once and for all, the obligation of the state to care for the legally incompetent and the infirm. Where once the father of the family had concerned himself primarily with the production of obedient and efficient offspring, now he finds himself responsible, in his new governmental guise, for all those who, like Odradek, have "no fixed abode": "the uneducatable, the undisciplineable, the unstable and unwanted human waste" produced by and yet anathema to biopolitics. As a theoretical matter, on the other hand—a matter of history—the fact that the father acts as the linchpin for all three diagrams of governmental power (the juridical, the disciplinarian, and the biopolitical) means that he embodies the origin, at once foundational and dispersed, but always uncannily returning, of our primordial investment in the political and social spheres. Or, to put this another way, it is only through the father that we come to find ourselves invested in those spheres in the first place. By amassing legal and moral obligations, establishing a network of permanent relations and loyalties, and consolidating, among his sons and heirs, a regime of contractual and personal indebtedness to himself, the paterfamilias of Rome set in motion—one might even go so far as to say invented—a guilt history tying us, through bonds of obligation, both to the past and to a future genealogy. The more the father cares, the greater our debt to him grows.

The house-father, then, is ennobled by care, inflated by anxiety, uplifted by indebtedness. But what if the father secretly hoped to be relieved of the duties imposed upon him by the administration of care? What if the father wanted out of the house? One of the more intriguing details of Kafka's story is that the house-father finds it "almost painful" that Odradek will outlive him, that he will be survived by the commodity that survives to no purpose. Why *almost* painful? The answer is simple: the house-father takes a secret delight—extracts the secret enjoyment, we might say—from the knowledge that the economy of guilt and indebtedness at whose head he sits will be brought down by its own waste product. If the father is anxious, it is not because he has embraced the fateful destiny of his being-toward-death. It is because he worries that Odradek might not "live on" in such a way as to relieve the house-father's children from the burden of care—that is, to offer them an uneconomical concern in place of an economy of care.

That the house-father might hope to be relieved of his duty—his calling, his fate—and that such relief might come through his utter absorption in and concern with the mysterious comings and goings, the revolutions, of the creature Odradek—that his redemption might rest upon Sorge's encounter with itself—was an idea that Benjamin had already hinted at in "Capitalism as Religion." "Capitalism as Religion" proceeds from the premise that "capitalism is a purely cultic religion, perhaps the most extreme that has ever existed." "Capitalism," contends Benjamin,

> is the celebration of a cult *sans rêve et sans merci*. There are no "week-days." There is no day that is not a feast day, in the terrible sense that all its sacred pomp is unfolded before us; each day commands the utter fealty of each worshiper. And third, the cult makes guilt pervasive. Capitalism is probably the first instance of a cult that creates guilt, not atonement (288).

Here, Benjamin is expanding upon—one might say intensifying—Max Weber's thesis in *The Protestant Work Ethic and the Spirit of Capitalism*, a work that had shown Benjamin how "the adaptation of the divine to the secular was not accomplished by means of a theocratic organization such as state or church, but by means of a decentralized economic ethic tangible only in its effects."[42] But whereas Weber, according to Benjamin, had understood capitalism to be "a formation conditioned by religion," Benjamin goes one step further to discern a religion in capitalism—and not just any religion, but a religion of "pure cult, without dogma" (289)— that Weber himself had vividly described but that he stopped short of naming as such.

The character of that religion, as any reader of Weber's study knows, is bleak indeed. Salvation comes through grace alone. Every individual member of the cult lives in isolation. One's calling, from which one cannot escape, provides the only means of serving God. Work is incessant. One exists for God and his laws; God does not exist for us. Humans are inherently guilty and, for that reason, utterly indebted to God for His grace. All of this is easily taken over by capitalism, to whose inscrutable and incontrovertible laws we remain entirely beholden. Every day is a feast day on which we take part, involuntarily, in the rituals devoted to celebrating the "miracle" of the commodity. There are no days reserved solely for rest or play; and every day results in the accumulation either of profit or of debt. Under capitalism, we are forced to be monks—or, worse, mendicant friars—all of the time. What is more, capitalism is a cult devoted to the worship of a "spirit," as Weber calls it: an "idea of duty in one's calling" that "prowls about in our lives like the ghost of dead religious beliefs."[43] In that respect, as Benjamin points out, capitalism is not simply a cult; it remains, for all its rational ordering, atavistic and "heathen."

Here then we behold the providential oikonomia ruled over by the house-father in Kafka's story: an economy of guilt and indebtedness, of endless labor—an economy in which Dasein's icy call becomes indistinguishable from one's worldly calling. As Adorno points out, however, Odradek is a product of that same economy; his "origin is with the father." But if that is the case, then what sort of product is he? Marxism holds that the "modern family" is little more than the "embryo" of "slavery" and "serfdom," revealing "in miniature all the antagonisms which later developed on a wide scale within society and the state."[44] With that in mind, let us draw a small equation. If the father of the family stands at the origin of the modern economy, and Odradek's origin is with the father, then one can see how Odradek as a product, a particular sort of commodity surviving to no purpose—surviving without necessarily circulating—stands to short circuit the very economy of which he is a scandalous progeny.

Marx provides us with a model for thinking a dynamic of this sort in his analysis of the way that value circulates, as M-C-M, within the closed system of capitalism. To illustrate his point, Marx draws a blasphemous, if highly effective, analogy. Entering "into a private relationship with itself, as it were," value

> differentiates itself as original value from itself as surplus value, just as God the Father differentiates himself from himself as God the Son, although both are of the same age and form, in fact one single person; for only by the surplus-value of £10 does the £100 originally advanced become capital (256).

As with the incestuous relation of self-knowledge carried out between God the Father and God the Son, value's ability to add to itself ex nihilo operates within a closed system that, strictly speaking, only generates its own reproduction; it never produces anything new. The analogy to the mystery of the Trinity is therefore essential, as it evokes capitalism's ability to draw us so thoroughly into its inner workings that those workings appear not simply occulted but natural and inevitable. Incapable of producing anything genuinely new, in the sense that it can only generate commodities and capital—that is, itself—capitalism lulls us into believing not only that we cannot get outside of it but that there is no outside of it, that there is no day that is not a feast day. Everything, all difference, gets drawn into the self-contained, self-identical, and self-replicating "family" dynamic of the cycle M-C-M.

And of course there is some truth to this. "The simple circulation of commodities," Marx reminds us,

> is a means to a final goal which lies outside circulation, namely the appropriation of use-values, the satisfaction of needs. As against this, the circulation of money as capital is an end in itself, for the valorization of value takes place only within this constantly renewed movement. The movement of capital is therefore limitless (253).

Nevertheless, should the circulation of value be suspended—if, for example, money, rather than being employed as capital, and thus used to generate surplus value, is "withdrawn from circulation" and "petrified into a hoard" where it could "remain . . . until the Last Judgment without a single farthing accruing to it" (252)—then we find ourselves straying into a strange zone in which nothing is being produced and yet nothing dies: a zone of petrified unrest in which, to paraphrase Adorno, we meet Odradek, "the commodity that has survived to no purpose" other than (or so it seems) to bemuse the house-father. Value, as Marx repeatedly emphasizes, is purely social: a product of a particular, and historicizable, mode of production. Yet there is something natural about value as well—or at least so Marx's metaphors (of value as a crystal, for example) might lead us to believe. Or perhaps the better way of putting this would be to say that value is on the order of a natural metaphor: that it is both natural and historical to the same degree that a natural metaphor (or a metaphor drawn from nature) is. This is where we meet Odradek, then: in the objective realm of natural history that announces its presence, within a capitalist economy, in the figure of a commodity that survives to no purpose, like a hoard of money that will remain in that inert state until doomsday.

Not that that isn't already the case with the cycle M-C-M, which presents itself as something like a self-generating, self-enclosed lifecycle, despite the fact that it can never produce anything new, because it can never produce anything outside of itself. Marx, however, reveals M-C-M for what it is: something essentially deadened and de-animated; a tombstone. Yet a tombstone is still a stone, still a natural property that remains such even as it allegorizes death; and, in that respect, it returns us to the same paradoxical register occupied by Odradek. The mistake that the classical political economists made was to believe that value was a natural property of the commodity. They therefore construed value as something natural even as they understood that same value to be social by virtue of its constant circulation. They erred by putting out of sight—or rather, by naturalizing—the social reality of value. Odradek disrupts that fantasy (if we can call it that) precisely by being so close to it. Even in its schematic presentation as M-C-M, the capitalist cycle of value is not natural. Nor is it given or inevitable, like the seasons. It is historical and contingent, the form assumed by one particular mode of production. At the same time, M-C-M remains profoundly embedded in the natural world, even as it thrives on the systematic reproduction of its own mystified, airy abstraction. Thus the strangeness of Odradek, whose status is that of waste and debris, the stuff left over when commodification has run its course and all that was solid has melted into air. Consider the labor that goes into the making of a commodity. What happens to that "congealed" labor once the commodity has been used up, once it ceases to circulate? It "lives on" in Odradek, albeit to no apparent purpose. In that respect, Odradek confronts the house-father with all that the commodity fetish puts out of sight: the decay and destruction, the waste, the turmoil and antagonism, the death drive at work within the social. Something survives to no purpose in Odradek; yet as spectral as that sounds, it would be misleading to call Odradek "spirit," as that would put him in the same category as the putative "spirit" of capitalism. Odradek is something more complex: the object that persists in the commodity and that can only be detected once the commodity begins to decay. Adorno locates Odradek in "the zone in which it is impossible to die," which is also, says Adorno, "[t]he no man's land between man and thing." We need not emphasize that this sounds an awful lot like Lacan's "space between two deaths," which happens to be the space of the Thing; but the comparison is an apt one all the same. Like the Thing, Odradek has been taken out of circulation but nonetheless always returns to the same place. Moreover, his presence disrupts a simple economy of lack, because Odradek is not lacking. Rather, he insists on coming and going in the place where lack ought to be. To put this another way: Odradek's surplus enjoyment—the inscrutable laugh, the enigmatic timetable—impinges itself upon the house-father to such an extent that it cannot be appropriated. The surplus value usually generated by capitalistic circulation (M-C-M again) is made impossible by the overwhelming presence of Odradek's surplus enjoyment, which cannot be appropriated any more than the perishing at work in natural history can be appropriated.

Let us phrase this another way: Odradek calls the house-father away from his calling. The house-father tries to practice managerial care whenever he happens to meet Odradek coming and going in his usual, mobile fashion (like a parody of capitalistic circulation): in the hallway, on the stairs. But Odradek is having none of it; and that enigmatic resistance, which may simply be indifference, or perhaps infinite patience, draws the house-father further out, or deeper down, into concern: the opposite of mastery. One might call this Odradek's gift to the father, the reason why the latter (to refresh our memory) finds it *almost* painful that Odradek will outlive him. The celebration of the commodity—the total commitment to the cult of capitalism—is the most dangerous form of absorption, as Benjamin well understood; it simply engulfs us in a self-reproducing guilt history. Concern, on the other hand, expresses another type of anxiety, one that alerts us to the proximity of the true object of melancholia. This is what Odradek does for the house-father: he answers the questions with which we began this chapter. What hope is left us if there can be no melancholic reality-testing of the world as it is supposedly is? And yet what reality-testing, what affirmation of the object, can there be if we can never set foot outside of the *oeconomia*, the cult that makes total claims upon us? Odradek holds out hope for the father because, as waste and leftover, he reveals to the father that the object survives to no purpose, at once outside of, and yet also a product of, the circulation of value.

Yet to the extent that Odradek "lives on," holding out "the promise of immortality in commodities," as Adorno puts it, he does so in such a way as to call into question the category of "life" itself. Odradek does not simply live on; he lives on in the sense that he is not entirely bound to the home economy of which he is both the offspring and the refugee, the product and the prodigal. Odradek lives on, but his life falls outside the jurisdiction not only of sovereign power, which seems unable to make him die, but also of biopower, which seems incapable of making him live according to its particular agenda or abide by its particular timetable. He lives on, in a zone where it is impossible to die, in his own peculiar, enigmatic fashion. He lives on, but the life he leads is a life unsanctioned even by the powers that brought it into the world: a form of life outside any recognizable form-of-life.

This is a strange form of life indeed: a postcommodified life, an assemblage (or, to use Adorno's language, a "reconciliation") of the organic and the inorganic, the natural and the historical (in the sense of being fabricated). Odradek, to use *our* language, is the physionomical byproduct of the capitalist economy. This is not simply because Odradek is pieced together out of the natural, essential materials whence the commodity comes and into which it inevitably returns: that natural historical realm whose presence we detect in Odradek's inscrutable laugh, which the father likens to the rustling of fallen leaves. It is not simply because Odradek embodies the ruination and decay associated with physis. It is because Odradek appears to us not as physis only, an emissary from the world of things, but as the nomos that cannot be separated from physis. Nomos may signify order, but it derives from the root word for *division* and *apportionment*. In truly nomical fashion, the unpredictable comings and goings of Odradek slowly, rhythmically apportion the objective presence of revolution. Mobile and elusive though he may be—like the mystified circulation of value—Odradek alerts us, with every return, to the survival of authentic justice, or to something at large within the capitalist mode of production. But more than that, Odradek confronts us with a nomos that divides, that piles up, that accumulates—a vast body of waste and debris and accumulated unrest, relics of exhausted labor—in one place, inside the home. It is this process that Benjamin seems to have in mind when he alludes, in "Capitalism as Religion," to "intensification": the accumulation of commodities that is at the same time the cumulative buildup, the intensification, of guilt and worry at a particular historical site. It would be a mistake, however, to see accumulation in this case as simple assemblage.

Building up is subtly different from putting together. This is the accumulation, and subsequent intensification, of nomical division. The guilt and
worry that ensue in this case are not then the guilt and worry described so
vividly by Weber. They are, rather, the concern that intensifies in the face
of accumulated unrest, the concern that builds up to such a fever pitch
that even the house-father, even God himself (according to Benjamin),
gets called away from his calling. Capitalism in this respect remains deeply
melancholic, even if the commodity fetish makes the precapitalist version
of melancholia, which relies on reality-testing in the interest of envision-
ing a better, different, and truly new world, impossible, at least for now.

CHAPTER SIX

Arendt's Melancholic Revolution

IT MAY SEEM odd to end a book devoted to excavating a politics of melancholia with a chapter on Hannah Arendt. Arendt was too well acquainted
with the ancient "Greek doctrine of the passions" to be hopeful, and no one
would accuse her of being sanguine.[1] But no one would compare her to
Hamlet, either. It is not even clear, despite her admiration for Walter Benjamin, whose works she edited, that she realized how thoroughly she exemplified "the attitude of melancholic contemplation . . . on which," according
to Adorno, "philosophical inquiry has been founded." Mostly she seems
bemused, in an objective, philosophical manner, by the melancholic tendencies she detects in others. Why do people settle for the "desert psychology"
of today?[2] Why did the revolutionaries of the eighteenth century look to the
failures of the past for their models for the future? Why do we fight for freedom only to succumb to the rule of necessity? Why, in our founding gestures,
do we so often conflate natality with the grave? But just as Plato's politics can
be melancholic despite his disavowal of the melancholic temperament, so too
can Arendt provide us with a model of melancholia despite the fact that she
herself was not "melancholic" in any conventional, clinical, or clichéd sense.
It is Arendt, for example, who not only recovers but also embodies Kant's
idea of the melancholic witness to the revolution: the figure who, though not
an active participant in the revolution itself, holds on to the searing memory
of the revolution and its disappointed aftermath and so ensures that the
unfinished work of revolution will return to haunt future generations. In
a similar vein, it is through Arendt's writings, *On Revolution* in particular,
that we come to appreciate how quickly a discourse on the worst can find
itself transformed into a conduit for the worst. Against her better judgment,

and certainly against her temperament, Arendt becomes engulfed by the revolutionary energies of her own cautionary citations, her own melancholy communion with the writings of Melville, Virgil, Tocqueville, and Jefferson. What matters, though, is that she does not resist becoming engulfed; and in that she becomes an exemplar of the melancholic institution of literature she otherwise questions. Finally, it is Arendt whose profound dissatisfaction with what she calls the "desert condition" of the modern world leads to a revolutionary return to beginnings and origins—truly an immersion in natural historical turmoil—that any reader of Benjamin's work on the Trauerspiel would recognize as typical of the melancholic disposition.[3] Not only then is it fitting to end a book on political melancholia with a chapter on Hannah Arendt. It is only fitting that her example should inspire us to expand our understanding of political melancholia itself.

Revolution and the Worst

In "Lives of Infamous Men," his introduction to "an anthology of existences" recovered from archives of internment compiled between 1660 and 1760, Foucault's discourse takes an extreme turn toward the worst: toward "lowly lives reduced to ashes in the few sentences that struck them down."[4] What fascinates Foucault about these fragmentary records is that, in them, ill-fated, gray, ordinary existences, lives bereft of any brilliance or form and destined to disappear without ever having been narrated, were able to leave behind faint but persistent traces. They were only able to do so, however, because of their "encounter with power," a "collision" without which "it's very unlikely that any word would be there to recall their fleeting trajectory" (161). But something else about these terse accounts of obscure personages also fascinates Foucault. It is "that at the turn of the seventeenth and eighteenth centuries relations of discourse, power, everyday life, and truth were knotted together in a new way, one in which literature was also entangled" (172). Guided by "a kind of injunction to ferret out the most nocturnal and most quotidian elements of existence," literature from the seventeenth century onward ("literature in the modern sense of the word") would arrogate to itself "the duty of saying what is most resistant to being said—the worst, the most secret, the most insufferable, the unforgettable, the shameless" (172–174). Thus "the power on lives, and the discourse that comes of it," a discourse of which literature is an integral component, ends up conferring upon those lives a sort of immortality in their very infamy: "an energy," like that of particles, "all the greater for their being small and difficult to discern" (174, 161).

The remarkable affinities between Foucault's thought and that of Hannah Arendt—remarkable because, so far as we can tell, Foucault never seriously engaged with Arendt's work—have lately been noted, and here we see one particularly striking example.[5] For like Foucault, Arendt homes in on the idea, at once fleeting and persistent, of the worst—so much so, in fact, that the idea might be said to constitute the origin of her political thought. From her early articles onward, Arendt remains completely faithful to the inconspicuous energy that dwells in lives weirded by the worst, lives at odds with the world, or bereft of world, or withdrawn from it altogether. Being thus attuned, however, is also what allows Arendt to discern the basic paradox of such lives. On the one hand, the energy of those lives, "all the greater for their being small and difficult to discern," exerts tremendous pressure on the tradition of political thought. It may even exceed the pious reach of our memory and conscience. On the other hand, that energy can never establish a tradition of the oppressed and defeated or serve as the groundwork for an alternative history; for such a history would never substantially differ from the history of the dominant classes and would soon find itself guided by the dictates of necessity. Arendt's melancholic absorption in the melancholic strata of infamous lives gives rise, over time, to a melancholic vision of history.

It is a vision she extends to politics and to her philosophical touchstones. Arendt views even the most established figures, despite their fame and glory, through the prism of the worst, retroactively bestowing upon their otherwise celebrated lives the air of a rebellious infamy: Socrates, the condemned philosopher, the stingray who exacerbates the *stasis* already present in the Greek agora; Kant, the melancholic *"Alles-Zermalmer"* ("all-pulverizer"); Lessing, whose "destructive, revolutionary temper" was profoundly at odds with his time; Rosa Luxemburg and Walter Benjamin, the permanent exiles who drop out of contemporary life altogether. It is as if each one of those figures partook, in some fashion, albeit at times remotely and paradoxically, in the general destiny of the modern pariah, in the loss of world characteristic of the persecuted and the refugee.[6] Not for nothing does Oedipus, the man of infamy par excellence, the old wandering beggar with his terrifying words *"mê phunai"* ("better not to be born"), repeatedly appear in Arendt's work, most prominently in the concluding lines of *On Revolution*.[7] For Foucault, the duty of saying the worst is a self-styled imperative of literature. For Arendt, it is the very engine of her political thought.

For Arendt, in fact, the thinking of politics and the thinking of the worst are coeval and indistinguishable. Arendt, as we saw in our reading of Plato, emphasizes time and again that the philosopher's concern with politics emerges only belatedly, as a response to the "trial and death of Socrates, the condemnation of the philosopher by the polis." As early as 1954, Arendt insists on the fateful origin of political philosophy as being, in essence, the traumatized reaction to murder. Political philosophy, Arendt suggests, is the half-thought answer to "the question, which had haunted Plato . . . : How can philosophy protect and liberate itself from the realm of human affairs? What are the best conditions ('the best form of government') for philosophical activity?"[8] The skeptical, if not outright hostile, attitude of the philosopher toward politics—toward the whole sphere of public affairs—is born from the primal scene of executing the preeminent philosopher of his time. The deadly blow that spurs political thought into being fascinates philosophy while at the same time remaining, like melancholia's lost object, constitutively inaccessible to it as a problem for thought. The "political" in political philosophy, which is not a noun, is in this respect not an adjective, either. It is a scar and the cipher of a scar. If it is true, as Arendt contends, that contingent political action, expressed as arbitrary violence, constitutes the originary trauma or "dark precursor" for the history of political philosophy, then her account remains consistent with Freud's claims about the ontogenesis of the superego in melancholia. If, in other words, Socrates is to political philosophy what Moses is to monotheism (that is to say, the great figure whose mourned absence precipitates the inheritance of its superego), then Athenian imperial power will have been political philosophy's Egypt—and the empire of philosophy itself built upon a melancholic foundation and heritage.

For Arendt, this remains a serious problem: at once the burden from which philosophy must free itself and the reason why Arendt seeks to free herself from the burden of philosophy. She thus protests vehemently when, during an interview conducted in 1964, Günter Gaus tries to induct her into "the circle of philosophers": "I have to protest. I do not belong to the circle of philosophers. . . . My profession is political theory . . ." Most philosophers have looked down on politics and political theory. "The philosopher cannot be objective or neutral with regard to politics. Not since Plato." There is a "vital tension between philosophy and politics . . . between man as a thinking being and man as an acting being," but the philosopher's enmity "is extremely important for the whole problem." "I want no part in this enmity, that's it exactly!" declares Arendt. "I want to look at politics, so to speak, with eyes unclouded by philosophy."[9]

Arendt comes by her concerns honestly. Philosophers since Plato have repeatedly and systematically denigrated the object of politics: its way of seizing power, its thoughtless, busybody activism, its fundamental faith in the justice of the stronger. Because of this deep-seated hostility, political philosophy has made a series of fateful decisions. First came Plato's division of knowing and doing, followed in due course by the separation of speaking and acting, the substitution of rulership for action, and the isolation of contemplation and thought from political praxis. The effect of these separations and divisions has been particularly striking, Arendt emphasizes, "in the series of revolutions, characteristic of the modern age, all of which—with the exception of the American Revolution (and the Hungarian Revolution)—show the same combination of the old Roman enthusiasm for the foundation of a new body politic with the glorification of violence as the only means for 'making' it."[10] What, Arendt wants to know, is a revolution unguided by philosophy?

The exception to this philosophical tradition, according to Arendt, is Kant, since for him the contestation between politics and philosophy "is not a personal question. It lies in the nature of the subject itself."[11] Not only can philosophy, as Kant redefines it, not eschew the conflict usually associated with politics; it has no choice but to engage with that conflict philosophically, and toward philosophical ends. True to his vision, this is exactly the route Kant follows in his analysis of the "sympathy," even the "enthusiasm," exhibited by the spectators of the French Revolution: a route that leads him through tension, conflict, a contest of faculties, and, finally, the need to affirm a fundamental reversal of all ideas, albeit without enmity, without war. In Kant's view, it is not the revolutionary actions themselves that are transformative; rather, it is the sympathetic "attitude" ("*Haltung*") of the spectator that gives those actions a lasting form. What enduringly changes the course of history is the spectator's undying fidelity to the revolutionary truth-content, now encrypted as sign of history, practice of thinking, and commemorative act. Although, as Kant clarifies, the onlooker is far from being a neutral observer, she differs from the revolution's actors in that she is not completely consumed by the revolutionary events and their disillusioning aftershocks. Her vision can thus attain a revolutionary form because it remains attuned to the fallouts of the revolution, to its failures and betrayals, to future wreckage and past suffering. Precisely because she perceives that worry, pain, and sorrow always outweigh the gratifications and pleasures of revolutionary action, the spectator's will to revolution persists beyond the failures of the moment. The revolution never outlives its own time and place; the revolutionary attitude shapes all times and all aspects of life.

That such an attitude turns out to be deeply melancholic is a matter worth pausing over. Notably, the sympathy of Kant's spectator, "which borders on enthusiasm," no matter if the revolutionary drama itself "succeeds or fails, or if it accumulates misery and atrocity," makes no attempt to disguise itself or retreat from the world. Rather, it "reveals itself *in public* while the drama of great political changes is taking place."[12] Hence, the revolution takes on both a phenomenal and a noumenal dimension: the one exhilarated and ephemeral, the other enthusiastic-anxious and untimely—but also, for that reason, indestructible. Alongside the revolutionary action, there appears an anxious audience that, far from weighing risks and benefits, instead manifests its sympathetic attitude for everyone to see, regardless of present dangers. Elevating the members of that audience to the same level as the actors they observe, Kant deadens the frenzy of revolutionary exploits and histories, their clamor and their struggles, in order to immortalize their revolutionary form, the cause and the will that drive them, through the figure of the melancholic witness. The pivotal historical role played by revolutionary actors turns out to be, then, that they propel the melancholic witness backward toward another, more taciturn and irresistible type of history, one that asserts itself as the true force of change. Although Kant does not envision a transformation that arises magically, "as if from the bowels of the earth," it is one that is similarly irresistible and natural historical.[13] At some moment, the revolutionary actors will have reached a point of no return; the unrest will have created facts—thoughts, signs, and attitudes—that are irrevocable. The revolution is the lost object that cannot be killed, precisely because, as Kant himself emphasizes, it "can never be forgotten."[14]

For Arendt, then, Kant remains the quintessential melancholic philosopher, the one who brings the old perplexities inherent in political praxis to the fore, because he is able to maintain a split vision. On the one hand, he understands that deeds start unforeseeable processes, that single acts constitute the realm of politics; on the other, he recognizes that those deeds alone are incapable of bringing about their own permanence, let alone lasting institutions. Kant reminds us, according to Arendt, that human actions and words, "unless they are remembered, are the most futile and perishable things on earth," "almost never fulfill [their] original intention," and can never "be recognized by [their] author[s] as [their] own."[15] Like Horatio to Hamlet, the melancholic witness ensures the afterlife of deeds and words that would otherwise have perished—deeds and words whose very survival attests to the permanence of perishing. Arrested by the unrest unleashed by the revolutionary actor, the melancholic witness stands as living proof that "whoever begins to act must know that he has started something whose end he can never foretell, if only because his own deed has already changed everything," including the conditions for its own preservation and perpetuation.[16]

Arendt, siding unequivocally with Kant's spectator of the French Revolution, positions herself in the role of that melancholic witness: the one who differs from the actors she observes, not being completely consumed by the revolutionary events and their disillusioning aftershocks; the one whose vision can attain a revolutionary form because it remains attuned to the fallouts of the revolution, to its failures and betrayals, to future wreckage and past suffering; the one who comes closest to establishing something like a lasting melancholic institution. For Arendt, however, thinking the worst entails more than encrypting the as-yet unrealized potential of the revolution by recalling the heartbreaking failure or betrayal of the revolution. It entails, too, remaining attuned to the revolutionary energies—the unrest, the discontent—of all those whom the revolution passed over: the forgotten, the undocumented, the unfortunate. It entails, finally, thinking in such a melancholic manner—a manner given over to the slow-moving, taciturn history momentarily drowned out by revolutionary clamor—that thinking itself becomes revolutionary, consuming but not consumed. Thinking the worst, to round it off to a formula, is the worst.

Consider the following scene from *On Revolution*. In a critical moment after American independence was declared, James Madison tarried with this problem, that the cause of revolution remains linked with the revolutionary fervor of desperate men who lived through the worst: men who "sunk below the level of men"; men "who, in the tempestuous scenes of civil violence, will inadvertently remain an unhappy species of the population" (214). In *On Revolution*, Arendt writes about Madison's observation:

> These words of Madison are true enough, except that we must add, if we are to apply them to the affairs of European revolutions, that this mixture of the unhappy and the worst received their chance to rise again "into the human character" from the despair of the best, who, after the disasters of the French Revolution, must have known that all the odds were against them, and who still could not abandon the cause of revolution—partly because they were driven by compassion and a deeply and constantly frustrated sense of justice (214).

The disappointed aftermath of revolution is all that ensures the continued existence of revolution, as Arendt clearly perceives. Yet continued existence is never far, in Arendt's thinking of the worst, from disappearance and even oblivion. Why is her inquiry always on the verge of bottoming out, as when she asks, with Leibniz and Kant, "'Why is it necessary that men should exist at all?'" and "'Why should there be anything and not rather nothing?'" Arendt agrees with Leibniz that this is the first question philosophy must ask itself: that it must confront the moment when, as Kant says, enjoyment, life, and happiness sink "below zero" and are marked by an essential "melancholy haphazardness."[17] Thus, in her 1943 essay "We Refugees," Arendt makes the argument that political philosophy ought to be built on the figures of the stateless and the persecuted no-count, figures with a fleeting trajectory who are forever falling out of history, but who therefore confront us with the trembling contours of an entirely new political consciousness. Arendt's new paradigm would make this precarious condition universal, its obscurity and sullenness legible. The Platonic tradition, traumatized by the murder of Socrates, had insisted that political philosophy ought to be unencumbered. Arendt insists that political philosophy ought to be engulfed.

For the German-Jewish refugee, this is deeply personal. She knows all too well that the "humanity in the form of fraternity" which "invariably appears historically among persecuted peoples . . . is the great privilege of pariah peoples" but that "the privilege is dearly bought"; for "it is often accompanied by so radical a loss of the world . . . that in extreme cases, in which pariahdom has persisted for centuries, we can speak of real worldlessness."[18] Such worldlessness is both a perverse blessing—"I do not mean to imply that this warmth of persecuted peoples is not a great thing," Arendt writes. "In its full development it can breed a kindliness and sheer goodness of which human beings are otherwise scarcely capable" (13)—and a political curse. "[I]n 'dark times,'" observes Arendt, "the warmth which is the pariahs' substitute for light exerts a great fascination upon all those who are so ashamed of the world as it is that they would like to take refuge in invisibility" rather than enter the public realm and assume their responsibility for a world common to all people (16). "In such a state of worldlessness," Arendt continues, "it is easy to conclude that the element common to all men is not the world, but 'human nature.'" Yet herein lies the danger. For

> this "human nature" and the feelings of fraternity that accompany it manifest themselves only in darkness, and hence cannot be identified with the world. What is more, in conditions of visibility they dissolve into nothingness like phantoms. The humanity of the insulted and injured has never yet survived the hour of liberation by so much as a minute (16).

Centuries after the dark times that gave rise to them, the nation states founded on principles of ephemeral fraternity are showing signs of strain. But it is not only geopolitical states that are on the verge of dissolving. Humanity, citizenship, man, rights, a sovereign people: all the hailed achievements of the great revolutions of the eighteenth century, born of "that enthusiastic excess in which individuals feel ties of brotherhood to all men," but ultimately "only psychological substitutes, localized in the realm of invisibility, for the loss of the common, visible world," have begun to reveal their limitations in the face of inescapable visibility (16). Compassion, the privilege of those privileged enough to take refuge from the world in a "warmth" not rightfully belonging to them, is no substitute for politics (16).

A political theory that derives much of its energy from the worst, by contrast, attunes itself to the forgotten, to the lives rendered undead and placeless, reduced to political means: lives existing only within the precarious domicile of the archive. As Arendt writes in the *Origins of Totalitarianism*, this systematic undeadening in contemporary politics reaches its apotheosis in the "insane mass manufacture of corpses preceded by the historical and political preparation of living corpses."[19] This, the totalitarian version of the worst, appropriates the insight of Luther's lonely man, who "thinks everything *to* the worst": to the point where no one, not even God, can be trusted.[20] By contrast, Arendt thinks the political *from* and *within* the worst, within suffering and the threat of annihilation. Her aim, as she writes in the epilogue to *The Promise of Politics*, is to never adapt to the desert conditions of our times, to not carry sand into the few oases that are left to us: the capacities to act, think, and judge.[21] The very fact that we suffer from this loss of world, from the waning of public life and plurality in the desert, proves that we are not yet one with it. Though we may live in the desert at present, we do not originate from it, and thus we cannot make our peace with it.

And yet the desert, already set in motion as the "sandstorms" that "menace even those oases in the desert without which none of us could endure," spreads, as Arendt says with Nietzsche. The totalitarian version of the worst is not the property of totalitarian practices alone. Rather, as Arendt shows in *On Revolution*, it continues to exert its sway over political life in our Western democracies. The deeply disillusioning "death of immortality," of which both Arendt and Adorno speak, ranks among its most enduring marks, as does our entrapment in an outmoded political terminology.[22] Moreover, since Arendt regards arbitrary memory, the inability to think, and traceless oblivion as being all of a piece, even the most famed life and established history can never be secure from the dangers of infamy and loss of world that return to us from the tradition of the forgotten. The melancholic thinking of the worst must, for that reason, never allow that tradition itself to be forgotten. But neither can it accept it as our fate.

The Melancholic Institution of Literature
(Homer, Virgil, Melville, Jefferson)

For Arendt, the question of the proper attitude to assume in dark times—a question "especially familiar to the generation and group to which I belong," she writes—was far from abstract.[23] Her provisional answer, as we know from her address on Lessing, was to attune her vision—her writing, her thought—to the worst, and to do so in the poetic-cum-political manner that Foucault would formalize, some years later, in his essay on the lives of infamous men. Arendt understood, better than most, that the encroachment of the worst renders human beings without world. At the same time, however, being attuned to the worst, insofar as it leaves us with no choice but to excavate the purity of a beginning—insofar as it nudges us to imagine a *novus ordo seclorum*, a new ordering of worldly time— makes our thinking, like our actions, political, courageous, and just. This duality of the worst confronted Arendt with a dilemma. Seeking a way of engaging with the world that would allow for a beginning without, at the same time, abandoning the realm of the forgotten, Arendt regularly turns to poets both ancient and modern: to Homer and the tragedians, to Auden and René Char. Her writings are possessed by citations. Yet herein lies her dilemma; for it is at those moments when she cites other writers that Arendt's own writing betrays all of the inconsistencies that plague the faculties of thinking, judging, and acting—all of the inconsistencies, that is, which allow us to be political beings in the world, engaged in the creation of a novus ordo seclorum, yet at the price of becoming more and more unreconciled to its present state.

Many of Arendt's writings "grapple with the perplexities of beginning," as she puts it in *On Revolution*, where that grappling continues for several chapters before ending in a draw (199). How can one give birth to something truly new, particularly when one finds oneself referring back to other beginnings to guide one's thinking and actions in the present? How is one to channel the revolutionary spirit when one is haunted by the losses of the past? This ongoing struggle with the perplexities of beginning finds an interesting, if inadvertent, resolution in *On Revolution*. Arendt's citations of poetry and other literature in that work make for encounters with things, as Saint Augustine would say: things that do not refer away from themselves, but instead act as intermediaries in a secret meeting between past generations, founders, and initiators, on one side, and us, on the other. Citations, however, turn out to be untrustworthy courtiers. For while they are meant to act as go-betweens in that secret encounter between past and present, what actually transpires is something far more astonishing: Arendt's citations rise up against her. Rather than working smoothly, according to their preordained script, the poetic examples that Arendt marshals in support of what she calls her "strange and sad story" of spontaneous revolutions betrayed by revolutionists develop a revolutionary life of their own—a birth that Arendt never intended.

What happens is that Arendt's writing ends up facilitating an infinite proliferation of the very perplexities she is trying to explain. Intending to take up a "strange and sad story that remains to be told and remembered," Arendt sets *On Revolution* to a melancholy key (247). And yet the text reads as though Arendt had implanted, unconsciously and involuntarily, mute counter-stories designed to draw out all of the discrepancies present both in her own account and in the revolutionary narratives that empower it. A revolution takes place within Arendt's revolutionary recounting; her tales about thwarted revolutions "do not modestly lie at the feet of [her melancholy] doctrine . . . but unexpectedly raise a mighty paw against it," to paraphrase what Benjamin writes of Kafka's parables.[24] "Something else" appears, as Arendt herself likes to say, and that something else disturbs the rule of necessity which always seems to lead, once the dust has settled, to the failure of the revolutionary beginning. At those moments, Arendt's melancholy perspective on history ceases to be possessed and winds up dispossessed instead. Conjured to resolve the difficulties she creates in the process of telling her strange and sad story, Arendt's poetic examples now stalk that story's progress and invert its meaning. Subtly, almost inconspicuously, the inversions and reversals of poetic citations betray the political betrayal of the revolution carried out under the pressures of necessity. Stasis breaks out in the pages of *On Revolution*.

The roots of that conflict, which we might characterize as a revolt against the demise of revolution, can be traced back to Arendt's enduring fascination with the historical and political legacy of the prehistorical and prepolitical Trojan War—a legacy personified, in all its complexity, by the volatile figure of Achilles. In *The Promise of Politics*, to cite but one example, Arendt writes that the "tale of how Rome's political existence originated in Troy and the war that engulfed it . . . is surely among the most remarkable and amazing events in Western history" (174). Remarkable and amazing: what never ceases to astonish Arendt is, as she puts it in *On Revolution*, "the profoundly Roman notion" that even the "first act" of founding Rome "had been already a re-establishment, as it were, a regeneration and restoration. In the language of Virgil the foundation of Rome was the re-establishment of Troy, Rome actually was a second Troy" (200). The political lesson Arendt seeks to draw from this Virgilian scheme is both subtle and, for that very reason, conflicted. Strictly speaking, what impresses Arendt is that the Romans were able to fulfill, in reality, what in Homer had remained a merely poetic achievement: full justice for the cause of the defeated. Embellishing upon the memory of Trojan defeat preserved in Homer's poetry, the Romans figured the founding of the Eternal City as the reversal of the annihilation of Troy. Yet this could only mean that the foundation of Rome, and thus the foundation of a political order rooted in the bond of law (*lex*), was not, strictly speaking, a beginning; it was a revolution back to the same war that the Greeks regarded as the prepolitical origin of the polis, the polis being nothing more than the space that made permanent the theater of action realized in the camps of the Achaeans. The Romans may have fulfilled the Homeric project of annihilating the annihilation of Troy; but what they could not do was annihilate the destruction wrought by the Trojan War itself, without which Rome would not exist. And so it would appear, according to Arendt, that there really had been a war that matches Heraclitus's definition of it as the father of all things (or at least of the *polis* and the *civitas*).

But if the Trojan War really is the father of all things in the Western political tradition, then that leaves us with the unresolved issue of Achilles and his melancholic wrath. In his own treatment of Arendt's political thought, Roberto Esposito makes the following observation. While "it is true," he writes, "that violence per se is not politics . . . it is still what 'founds,' 'protects,' and 'expands' it, that is, what accompanies it along the entirety of its historical 'arch.' "[25] As Arendt sees it, the political is necessarily the preservation, or transmutation, of its conceptual and experiential opposite, the prepolitical. *Polemos*, the agonistic struggle exemplified by the rivalry between Achilles and Hector, inheres in the polis as its ever-present origin. In that respect, politics as Arendt understands it is inescapably melancholic. "Not historically, of course, but speaking metaphorically and theoretically," she writes in *The Human Condition*, "it is as though the men who returned from the Trojan War had wished to make permanent the space of action which had arisen from their deeds and suffering, to prevent its perishing with their dispersal and return to their isolated homesteads" (198). Approached metaphorically and theoretically—Arendt was not above making constructions of her own—the founding of the polis (as distinct from the oikos) is an act of memorialization, intended to outlast the perishing of conflict.[26] Not content to return to their lives as despots, as rulers of the oikos who must themselves submit to the rule of necessity, the surviving victors of the Trojan War refused to let go of the space of action they had created over ten years of struggle and combat outside the gates of Ilium. However, as Arendt herself repeatedly emphasizes, the model of the great actor remained Achilles, just as the consummate example of struggle was that between Achilles and Hector. The space that the founders of the polis sought to recreate at home is a space dominated, haunted even, by the undying memory of Achilles and his deeds.

But in memorializing Achilles, what was it that the survivors of the Trojan War actually preserved? Arendt argues that the Greeks, in re-founding the polemical space of action inside the walls of the polis, also re-founded the space of freedom, which for the Greeks could only be realized in the struggle among equals, wherein each combatant could be fully realized. Here again, the figure of Achilles provided the standard. Yet it is difficult to say that Achilles is, or was, free. Rather, he seems absorbed in losses—of Briseis, Patroclus, his honor (*tīmē*) most of all—for which there can be no compensation. Alongside lingering polemos, then, the polis encounters at its origin a sorrow that cannot forget and that slips imperceptibly into anger. Achilles's combat with Hector, the model for all rivalry, including that found in political struggle, does more than simply reveal who Achilles really is; it unleashes what Arendt herself elsewhere calls Achilles's implacable wrath, his *mênis*.[27] In the *Iliad*, Achilles's grief over his lost honor undergoes a lethal transformation, and not only for himself. His mênis indicates something beyond a simple reaction to loss; it marks the precise moment when grief becomes affirmative and absolute, when it assumes its active principle and morphs into an absolute anger "that can never ever be erased from the mind."[28] With the introduction of Achilles's mênis, observes Nicole Loraux, "mourning and wrath are naturally associated with each other insofar as they both participate in nonoblivion [*alaston*]." Achilles's wrath expresses the pathos of an irreparable loss whose obsessive and relentless presence never abates. This "nonoblivion is a ghost," adds Loraux; it is "the worst enemy of politics: anger as mourning makes the ills it cultivates 'grow' assiduously, and it is a bond that tightens itself until it resists all untying." This tireless mourning-wrath in Achilles attains cosmic dimensions and sets itself up not only as a rival to Zeus's divine fury but also "as a powerful rival of the political."[29] It cannot be reduced merely to the passivity of what is unforgettable, for Achilles's devotion to his grief enacts an affirmative, active stance. In his implacable mourning-wrath, Achilles displays fidelity to an inscrutable thing, what Loraux calls the "*unforgetful*: the very thing, in Greek poetics, that does not forget and that inhabits the mourner so that it says 'I' in the mourner's voice."[30]

If it is indeed the case, then, that "the full Homeric effect of the poet's description of the Trojan War can be found in the way in which the polis incorporates the concept of struggle into its organizational form, not only as a legitimate pursuit, but also, in a certain sense as the highest form of human activity," then it is also the case that the polis incorporates, alongside the prepolitical polemos, the prehistorical, or rather natural historical, "unforgetful" mourning-wrath of Achilles.[31] One might go so far as to argue, in fact, that the founders of the polis acted in a doubly melancholic fashion, retaining what they had lost—the space of action that vanished once they struck camp—as a pretext not just for holding on to conflict, as we saw in the case of Hamlet, but also for ensuring that the sublime wrath modeled by Achilles would not perish even with the founding of the polis.

The legacy of that wrath then returns, with a vengeance, to trouble Arendt's handling of the American Revolution. As she writes in *On Revolution*:

> When the Americans decided to vary Virgil's line from *magnus ordo seclorum* to *novus ordo seclorum*, they had admitted that it was no longer a matter of founding "Rome anew" but of founding a "new Rome," that the thread of continuity which bound Occidental politics back to the foundation of the eternal city and which tied this foundation once more back to the prehistorical memories of Greece and Troy was broken and could not be renewed (204).

Yet that founding gesture, that introduction of something new—something unheard of in either time or space—is itself so violent that it must sit in tension with what Arendt elsewhere writes concerning the founding of Rome:

> To be sure, this enterprise also was accompanied by violence, the violence of war between Aeneas and the native Italians, but this war, in Virgil's interpretation, was necessary in order to undo the war against Troy; since the resurgence of Troy on Italian soil . . . was destined to save "the remnant left by the Grecians and Achilles' wrath" and thus to resurrect the *gens Hectorea* . . . the Trojan War must be repeated once more (198, 201).

One can found a new Rome rather than Rome anew. Nevertheless, the violence necessary for such fabrication cannot help but repeat the wrathful deeds of Achilles, if only because the memory of those deeds, preserved in the very makeup of the polis, is what gave the American revolutionaries the courage to act in the first place. But then, having done the deed—having founded a new Rome and broken the link of tradition that tied that foundation back to prehistory—the Americans then immediately set about putting an end to what they had begun. In short, the principle inherent in the beginning of the new nation put an end to revolution. The Achaeans had annihilated Troy; Homer's impartial poetics had then annihilated that annihilation; Virgilian Rome then continued Homer's poetic innovation by reversing the course of Trojan annihilation in the founding of the Eternal City; and now the American Revolution had somehow annihilated that whole tradition and, in so doing, annihilated the very possibility of revolution. Yet such a sequence runs up against what Arendt observes in *The Promise of Politics*, where she argues that, precisely because the Greeks "turned struggle into an integrating component of the polis and the political sphere," they left "any concern as to what might happen with the defeated and vanquished . . . to the poets and historians," whose works also "became part of the polis and its politics" (171–172). The poetic texts that inspired the American revolutionaries and gave them the courage to act, modeling themselves after Achilles (and also Aeneas), have not perished in the meantime, any more than polemos or mênis vanished upon the creation of the polis. What the founders of the new Rome could not do away with was the foundation, the origin, of Rome—which is to say, the beginning of Rome in the annihilation of Troy precipitated by the wrath of Achilles. In putting an end to revolution, the Founding Fathers unknowingly repeated what the founders of the first polis had done upon returning home from war: they preserved stasis.

Such perplexities, recurring throughout *On Revolution*, have come no closer to being resolved by the time we reach the book's final pages, where Arendt stages an encounter between the contemporary and the ancient, between the modern French poet René Char, who joined the Resistance during World War II, and the Sophocles of *Oedipus at Colonus*. Char's notes and fragments, written down shortly before the liberation, describe the happiness found in the immediate encounter with oneself and with all creatures, the knowledge that every revolutionary action must invent itself anew. Char describes that feeling, which he anticipates will be lost once he and his fellow partisans have been liberated "from the 'burden' of public business" as well as from German occupation, as his "treasure" (272). It is a treasure whose worth Arendt knows well but whose "actual content" resists articulation (271). She writes in her *Denktagebuch*: "Notre héritage n'est precede d'aucun testament" (Our inheritance was left to us by no testament): perhaps the strangest of the strangely abrupt aphorisms in which Char compressed what four years in the Resistance had come to mean to a whole generation of European writers and men of letters.[32] There is no testament for revolutionary action. Thinking, acting, and writing cannot be guided by any received experience. The experiment of freedom that dwells in the spirit of the revolution must create itself—ex nihilo—from out of itself, so that an unheard-of time, a new temporality is, as it were, blasted into the course of time. Only then can that experiment weave its own thread into the world or assume its place in the future as a task to be mulled over.

Notably, though, Arendt concludes that Char's "reflections," while significant, "are perhaps too 'modern,' too self-centered, to hit in pure precision the center of that 'inheritance which was left to us by no testament'" (273). By way, then, of sealing the significance of Char's testimony, Arendt immediately follows it up by juxtaposing two moments from Sophocles's *Oedipus at Colonus*. The first is "the famous and frightening" lines of the choral verse: "Not to be born prevails over all meaning uttered in words; by far the second-best for life, once it has appeared, is to go as swiftly as possible whence it came." The second, which provides the book's concluding line, features the words of Theseus, the legendary founder of Athens: "It was the polis, the space of men's free deeds and living words, which could endow life with splendor" (273). What are we to make of this bewildering welter of citations, the second of which seems to cancel out the horror of the first? The line "Not to be born prevails over all meaning uttered in words" marks the birth of the Athenian polis from the spirit of Oedipus's death wish, as Arendt herself intimates. In that case, the polis, far from promising any escape from or sublimation of Oedipus's words, grounds itself instead in the strange afterlife of the infamous man, a true biography of the worst: a life whose end and flash-like existence declares fidelity to the perplexity of an irrevocable beginning. Theseus's words, conjured by Arendt to underscore her point that the "rare treasure of the political . . . promises to brighten up the *triste epaisseur*, the *Erdenschwere*, and the strange mourning of all creatures," would appear, from their positioning as the literal last words of *On Revolution*, to retroactively qualify those of Oedipus. But in this case, the qualification works in both directions at once. The rare treasure of the political, and that which really brightens up our common melancholia, is its beginnings in the worst.

Shuttling back and forth between happiness and mourning, joy and *Schwermut*, Arendt's citations reflect the ambivalent process by which melancholy undergoes its transformation into political melancholia. Oedipus's unreconciled and impossible struggle to become unborn describes the struggle to find a placeless home, that is, to inhabit a new home, a symbolic order, without mother tongue or fatherland, founded on an unrecognizable burial site, a grave with no marker. Like Thomas Jefferson, whose own melancholic attitude we will turn to in a moment, Arendt thinks through an institution without testament or perhaps even inheritance, a paradoxical form of constitution that contains within itself, within its constitutive powers, a "destituent power"—a deformative death drive in the midst of political foundations—that preserves the self-critical spirit of the revolution.[33]

That Arendt can only think through such an institution by turning repeatedly to poetry and other forms of literature points to what may be *On Revolution*'s greatest perplexity, its true blind spot. Waxing melancholy as she considers how mass political movements preclude "those few from all walks of life who have a taste for public freedom and cannot be 'happy' without it" from experiencing "the joys of public happiness and the responsibilities of public business" precisely because those joys and responsibilities have been imposed upon all of us, Arendt laments that "this, and probably much more, was lost when the spirit of revolution—a new spirit and the spirit of beginning something new—failed to find its appropriate institution" (271). In an almost textbook melancholic fashion, she continues, *"There is nothing that could compensate for this failure or prevent it from becoming final, except memory and recollection"* (272, italics ours). But can we truly speak of a failure to conceive of an "appropriate institution" for the "spirit of revolution—the spirit of beginning"—when we consider the institution of poetry to which Arendt turns throughout *On Revolution*, and particularly so in her conclusion? Arendt turns to the poets because "from the poets we expect the truth," as she writes in her *Denktagebuch*. But this truth is not so much about memory and recollection, about "the storehouse of memory watched over by the poets, the ones who find and make the words we live by" (another of Char's aphorisms). The truth Arendt discloses at the conclusion of her book concerns the necessity of forcing a confrontation of the revolutionary spirit with tradition in order to create a kind of memory of the future: the production of works of art that function, as Benjamin puts it, like shots taken on film for which an adequate means of development has not yet been discovered. Even if Arendt is correct that the realization of the beginning is repeatedly missed once necessity intrudes upon the scene, "something else" appears, something akin to what Arendt describes as the "involuntary self-discourse" testified to by René Char's reflections on his time in the Resistance. Something else about the labor of the poet is revealed, something altogether different that releases him from his duty as watchman over the treasure house of words and memory. Perhaps poets point, by traversing the worst and the insufferable, toward a political revolution that joins forces with a poetic revolution, that is, toward a revolution of the very concept of the political revolution. This thought of the political, in its double sense, would perhaps be able to escape from the "same chain of wrongdoing" broken, as Arendt argues elsewhere in *On Revolution*, by Melville's Billy Budd or even from the repetition compulsion of creating ever more intricate forms of mastery and sovereignty. Arendt's involuntary self-discourse can become the means of derailing historical necessities, provided one can construct "silent depositories" of the indestructible—political monads, so to speak— from them. This indestructible can be infinitely destroyed because it has, like Oedipus, taken on the labor of destruction and assumed the deadly impact of thought and poetic speech that is now directed at our political tradition.

This would be a revolutionary labor indeed, for not only would it liberate things from the drudgery of usefulness and politics from the goal of historical progress; it would free the subject to appear in the repetitions of a beginning, again and for the very first time. What is more, it would be a citational labor, carried out within the revolutionary institution of literature, where words live. "Language alone remains," is how Arendt puts it in her essay on Benjamin:

> finally naming through quoting became for Benjamin the only possible and appropriate way of dealing with the past without the aid of tradition. Any period to which its own past has become as questionable as it has to us must eventually come up against the phenomenon of revolution rooted in our language, for in it the past is contained ineradicably, thwarting all attempts to get rid of it once and for all. The Greek polis will continue to exist at the bottom of the sea like an *Urphänomen*, surviving in new crystallized forms and shapes that remain immune to the elements—for as long as we use the word "politics."[34]

Earlier we looked at how some of Arendt's citations rebel against their intended use. Yet that is only one of the ways in which the melancholic institution of literature carries out its work. We recognize another when we note that Arendt's citations rarely endorse or memorialize the traditions from which she extracts them. On the contrary, they disrupt those traditions to reveal a *principium*: a beginning or a law; the promise of a forgotten past. In that respect, Arendt's work follows Heidegger's idea of historical destruction (*Destruktion*), that "inconsiderateness in the face of tradition is reverence for the past." Some pasts are lost irretrievably, as are some beginnings; and yet it is on such forgotten ground that the great revolutions of the eighteenth century were founded and their historical legibility ensured. True, the spectacles of those revolutions proved to be fleeting and were quickly replaced by dissimulating traditions and institutions incapable of preserving the revolutionary spirit. But Arendt's work is not concerned with traditions derived from the past (which they only obscure). Arendt's work is concerned with the transmissibility of beginnings lost in the past. Its purpose is to convey the experience of revolution through an apprehension of the worst.

As usual, this involves a great deal of ambivalence and internal conflict. According to Arendt, the "briefest and most grandiose definition of revolution" is the one found in Robespierre's famous sentence, "Death is the beginning of immortality." Such a sentiment cannot help but collide, however, with her verdict, reached elsewhere, about the "death of immortality." As Arendt writes in her account of the death of immortality in *The Human Condition*, the shock of this discovery has been so overwhelming that any attempt to build an immortal city on earth is now regarded "as vanity and vainglory."[35] This is a quintessentially melancholy attitude, and its origins, which we can trace back to the (legendary) loss of Troy and the (historical) fall of the Roman Empire, are ancient. Why even try? But it cannot possibly be reconciled with Robespierre's declaration, which seems to equate revolutionary action with the death of the death of immortality.

Given this tension between melancholy and the promise of revolution, between the death of immortality and death as the beginning of immortality, it was inevitable that Arendt should turn her curious gaze upon the American revolutionaries, who looked obsessively to ancient precedents for their mode of beginning, the foundation of Rome in particular, and who regularly cited Virgil's *Aeneid* as one of their central sources. As Arendt shows in *On Revolution*, Virgil's myth of the foundation of the *Imperium Romanum* in the *Aeneid*, and indeed the whole notion of a birth of Rome, run completely counter to the idea of a new beginning capable of overcoming the transience and fatal flaws of empire. Virgil's story of liberation, the aimless wanderings of Aeneas after he escaped the burning Troy, the melancholy trope of Rome as a second Troy, founded to undo the sacking of Troy (as in Aristotle's *Ethics*), the reversal of Homer and salvaging of the remnants of Achilles's wrath: none of these can bridge the irreducible hiatus between the authoritative return of a past and a new, revolutionary beginning.[36] Revolution understood in this fashion could never manifest the birth of a new order—of natality—and of genuine freedom; it could only ever be a rebirth.

A revolution worthy of its name thus has to create this hiatus between past and future, produce new times of transition. It falls into holes of oblivion and gaps of historical time, risking the worst—traceless oblivion and loss of world—so as to think the best: political freedom. Revolutionary time in this sense prompts what Arendt calls a "thinking without banister" (*Denken ohne Geländer*), with "nothing whatsoever to hold on to": no God, no heritage, no tradition, no *auctoritas*, no precedent, except for the idea of natality itself. The revolutionary moment, emerging as if out of nothing, inaugurates an entirely new map and calendar. Its currents are irresistible, overwhelming; anyone caught up in them radically drops out of the customary temporal and spatial orders. No longer are revolution, birth, the miracle of action, and forgiveness altogether different from the traceless oblivion of existence that Arendt shows to be the hallmark of the worst. The radical freedom of revolution begins to converge, strangely and perplexingly, with the sandstorm of the desert. The dissolution of tradition and the archives causes shame and anxiety to flare up, catching the protagonists of the revolution in a "hiatus between end and beginning, between a no-longer and a not-yet" (197).

Among the Founders, however, only Jefferson was melancholic enough to have a clear premonition that the revolutionary spirit could not generate lasting institutions. "He refused to be consoled," Arendt tells us, for his greatest fear was indeed that the future democracy would inadvertently lack the concrete institutions capable of remaining faithful to their own revolutionary beginning. Along with his idea that every generation has the right to repeat the revolution, Jefferson's clairvoyance that the ecstatic days of revolution are sure to be followed by a hangover suddenly resembles Marx's diagnosis of the drunken spectacle of the bourgeois revolutions in "The Eighteenth Brumaire of Louis Bonaparte," that the form of the new is only used to better perpetuate the status quo. As Arendt shows, this unavoidable disillusion occurs whenever the worst that literature brings to the fore encounters the greatest aspirations in the political sphere. Virgil, too, was in Philadelphia.

Arendt also insists, however, that even as it threatens to hamper the revolutionary spirit, such a deep-seated sense of melancholy about fallen empires, lost pasts, and future betrayals needs to be understood as the motor force of revolution, and thus, we would add, as the first step in the transformation of melancholy into political melancholia. Throughout *On Revolution*, Arendt endeavors to combine two incompatible ideas: the irresistibility of natural historical occurrences with the novelty of a beginning, incessant repetition with the singular event. This is an impossible task, as

Jefferson well knew. And yet if those incompatible ideas can be thought together—if the pathos of novelty, the unprecedented, can be conjoined with a continuous citation and repetition of the past—one will have produced a new logic, an unheard-of revolutionary form. Such an aggregate, revolution-repetition, would no longer be a figure; it would be the real of politics and might not even resemble what we call, in a still familiar way, a revolution. But it would therefore be, by virtue of this very novelty, itself an event: the first and only possible event—an im-possible. What Arendt incessantly thinks through, then, are events that combine the persistence of repetition with the novelty of beginnings; she gravitates toward this one single scene, this scene where anonymous collectives, forgotten spirits, lost sites, and obliterated pasts are sutured to the singularity of an action or appearance, poetry and history to politics. An aggregate state where revolutionary repetition meets a singular beginning: that is Arendt's idea of the revolution. Melancholic and impossible, such a revolution would link the irresistible force that inheres in the prerevolutionary idea of revolution, Copernicus's 1543 *De revolutionibus orbium coelestium*—the revolution in the natural history of the planetary order—with the idea that has characterized the term *revolution* since the eighteenth century: "to begin the world over again" (225).

Poverty, Natural History, and Revolution

Published two years after Franz Fanon's *The Wretched of the Earth*, Arendt's *On Revolution* presents a rival and very perplexing account of the question of poverty, which erupts, volcano-like, as a mass phenomenon in the eighteenth century. In a decisive passage concerning the emergence of the social question in the French Revolution, Arendt turns to the poets, in particular Dostoyevsky and Melville, to uncover the revolutionary and contradictory truths about poverty. According to Arendt, the vehemence of mass poverty is a prepolitical, even a profoundly antipolitical, force; and yet it is what politicizes both philosophy and poetry. Though it may not be possible to directly politicize poverty or create lasting institutions from its energy of despair, the poor nonetheless dwell in the midst of politics, just as the wretched of the earth today are at once excluded from and fully included in the shadow economies of the world. For both Arendt and Fanon, the despair and destitution of poverty linger at the intersection between nature and history, and at the conflicted site where politics, poetry, and philosophy meet.

In this way, the defamed spirits of poverty unleash novel forms of poetry and aesthetics even as they continue to embody the most unpoetic fact of suffering. According to Arendt, the exigencies of poverty are like an elementary force of this earth that is not of this earth; contact with it requires passing through a kind of death and through passions, like Arendt's melancholia and Fanon's anger, that have yet to find an institutional, political expression. The exigency of poverty thus cannot be used to establish an alternative tradition or a different type of politics, for the simple reason that it marks the crisis of tradition and the end of transmitted political wisdom. But that does mean that it does not remain profoundly political. Tellingly, as soon as Arendt's "*penialogy*" (not to be confused with Foucault's analysis of *penology*) gravitates toward Fanon, toward Benjamin, and toward poetry, it begins to lend credence to the Socratic myth about *penia* (poverty); for here, too, that miserable, "grievous thing" (Alcaeus), afflicted with shame, is revealed to be an affirmative form of distress and destitution capable of wearing down our preoccupation with socioeconomic needs and biological or historical necessities. As Arendt shows, the contradictory nature of poverty comes to embody, in tragic fashion, the discordant afterlife, hobbled by necessity and yet insistently poetic, of the two great political revolutions of the eighteenth century.

In *On Revolution*, Arendt remarks that if freedom and poverty are incompatible, then the compelling needs of mass poverty, interpreted in political terms, must eventually prompt an uprising, not only for the sake of wealth, but also for the sake of freedom (52). Marx learned from the French Revolution that poverty can be a political force of the first order, even an irresistible natural historical torrent. This interpretation of poverty reveals its underside from the outset: poverty is a crucial driver of history. Once linked to the iron laws of historical necessity, poverty as such converges with the struggle for liberation from poverty to comprise the secret undercurrent of historical progress. Marx's early analysis of the transformation of the social question into a political power—that poverty itself is a *political*, not a natural, phenomenon: the result of domination—joins his later "scientific" contention about the objective laws of the dialectics between freedom and necessity in history, with this result: the transformation of need into historical necessity ultimately conjoins corporeal necessities, our immediate needs and urges, with the question of history.

What Marx describes here, according to Arendt, is nothing less than the primal sin of our times. "This," she tells us, "is the most pernicious doctrine of the modern age, namely that life is the highest good, and that the life process of society is the very center of human endeavor . . . to liberate the life process of society from the fetters of scarcity so that it could swell into a stream of abundance. Not freedom but abundance became now the aim of revolution" (54). From now on, according to Arendt, we live in a realm of "spiritual poverty" where formerly poor people seek their redemption solely in private wealth and fantasies of abundance (the closest Arendt comes to a critique of capitalism and liberal democracies), where questions of politics turn into those of society and public freedom, and where the capacity for a new beginning—the novus ordo seclorum— gets reduced to the desire for bureaucratic-administrative care.

It was at this juncture, Arendt claims, that the failure of the revolution was sealed. She writes: "It was necessity, the urgent needs of the people and the preoccupation with poverty that unleashed the terror and sent the Revolution to its doom" (50). And she is not alone in her opinion. Adorno tells us, in the final sentence of *Minima Moralia*, that philosophy must continue its melancholic, custodial labor "because the moment of its realization had been missed," while Robespierre's prophecy, issued in his last speech, haunts all revolutionary movements: "We shall perish because, in the history of mankind, we missed the moment to found freedom." So it is all the more remarkable that in Arendt's reading of poverty, the popular attack and outrage of the destitute and the *malheureux* (unfortunates) is also revealed to be the nucleus and secret moving force of our concept of history, even our historiography. Arendt writes that the multitude of the poor and downtrodden, whom "every century before had hidden in darkness and shame," now enters the historical scene "for the first time in broad daylight" to claim the same carefree political participation as those who already dwelled in its free space and light (38). Poverty, although a prepolitical state, is initially, before it devolves into a question of societal caretaking and wealth-governmentality, a politicizing and indispensable historical power. Poverty is the substratum, the *Bodensatz*, of history—its obscure undercurrent, the other side of history. Moreover, it is the condition sine qua non of revolution and thus also of today's entire political terminology.

As Arendt contends, the uprising of the people for freedom is from the beginning mixed with the riot of the mobs of the great cities, both of which are made irresistible by the sheer force of their numbers. "Suddenly," with the appearance of the poor on the political scene, "an entirely new imagery begins to cluster around the old metaphor [of the revolution] and an entirely new vocabulary is introduced into political language" (39). The despair of poverty and the vehemence of the poor, Arendt admits, had, unbeknownst to the political actors of the time, revolutionized their concepts, their language, their idea of freedom, and their purpose. No longer simply wishing to found Rome anew, they were now on their way to creating a new Rome—and to seizing the chance for a political natality that suddenly opened Desmoulins's *torrent revolutionnaire*. In its rushing waves, the actors of the revolution were borne away.

It is poverty and the poor, then, that hint at the natural history—the mighty current of the revolution, "the volcanic lava stream which spares nothing, and which nobody can arrest"—coursing through our idea of world history. The presence of natural history signals that the revolutionary spectacle has fallen under the sign of Saturn, that despite being amidst an abundance of freedom, "the actors themselves . . . clearly no longer believed they were free agents" (40). Its actors described the revolutionary process not as the work of men but as a convergence of natural historical forces: at once the renewal of an earlier state *and* an unheard-of novelty. They coined the metaphors of the ravishing stream, the devastating storm, and the swelling current to signify that novelty and freedom do not stand opposed to repetition and necessity (40). As Arendt argues, "The raging storm of revolutionary events had changed [the revolutionaries] and their innermost convictions in a matter of a few years" (40). Unwittingly, completely against their will, and due to the lava stream of outrage from the poor, the revolutionaries were forced to embrace a kind of freedom they neither wanted nor expected. The appearance of poverty, its inexorable force, confronted the actors of the French and American revolutions with the necessity of freedom; they embraced therein the freedom of a necessity that arises from the torrents of revolutionary upheaval.

What Arendt evokes here is not the speculative-tragic dialectics of freedom and necessity, in which assuming necessity preemptively allows for the tragic act, thereby providing a yield of freedom. This is a natural historical dynamic of destruction, transience, downfall, and the powers of creaturely despair. As with revolution, poverty is not a question of having to choose between need, history, and necessity on one side, and politics, novelty, and freedom on the other, as Arendt at times argues. On the contrary, as Benjamin writes in "Experience and Poverty," the pressures of war and the exigencies of economic crisis—poverty—necessitate a new beginning and the emergence of a destructive character.[37] With sobriety and coldness, this character erases the traces of traditional wisdom and the falsity of experience in order to embrace the inhuman barbarism that constitutes the new attitude, at once critical and affirmative, of poverty.

In many respects, Arendt's memorialization of the great revolutions of the eighteenth century is not as far removed from Benjamin's demand as is commonly argued. The "metaphors of stream and torrent and current" display all the more glaringly that the revolutionary actors, "however drunk they might have become with the wine of freedom," encountered something akin to a superhuman-inhuman power at precisely the moment that they insisted most vehemently on the dignity of man and the inviolability of human rights (40). And it is the unfortunate ones, the ones who, in the process, are transformed into the *enragés*, the people with blind rage—this rage being the only means by which misfortune can become active—that possess that inhuman power of true suffering (*Leiden*), that extraordinary, "diamond-hard" capacity to suffer (*Leidensfähigkeit*) which cannot be resisted. It is as though the passion (*Leidenschaft*) of the enraged ones, their revolutionary acts, infinitely greater and more enduring than the compassion of Rousseau and Robespierre, conspired with the elements of the earth in order to lead them to their own destruction (101–102). Ever the melancholic witness, Arendt incessantly tracks that inhuman (revolutionary) kernel at the heart of mankind, where it manifests in highly conflicted forms: as poverty, as the intrusion of the absolute, or as natural historical vehemence—in short, all that Saint-Just combines in his phrase "*les malheureux sont la puissance de la terre*," the unfortunate are the power of the earth, that Arendt uses to bookend her chapter on "The Social Question" (49).

Arendt does not envision a continuous process of history as a kind of baseline against which a torrential revolutionary upsurge occasionally reasserts itself in order to posit an alternative axis of superhuman unrest. Rather, Arendt explores revolutionary time entirely in terms of what the ancients called stasis: civil strife, where "crimes of tyranny," the despair of poverty, and the "progress of liberty" continuously provoke one another, "so that movement and counter-movement neither balanced nor checked nor arrested each other, but in a mysterious way seemed to add up to self-opposed streams of progressing force, despite their internal unrest flowing in the same direction with an ever-increasing rapidity." The surprising discovery, Arendt continues, is that the historical movement of revolutionary time can never lead to the restoration of a known state or beginning, but on the contrary extends regularly into an unknown future. Once the question of poverty took hold of the revolutionary cause, it was no longer the proud architects who were in charge, the men who built their new houses upon accumulated wisdom, but "men swept willy-nilly by revolutionary stormwinds into an uncertain future" (46–47).

Prologue

1. Arendt, *The Promise of Politics*, 95.
2. On this point, see Arendt, *The Promise of Politics*, 6–7.
3. Gilroy, *Postcolonial Melancholia*; Cheng, *The Melancholy of Race*; Butler, *The Psychic Life of Power*; Eng and Kazanjian, eds., *Loss*.
4. For a lucid account of Derrida's translation of melancholia into the ethical "work of mourning," see Brault and Naas, "To Reckon with the Dead."
5. Winters, *Hope Draped in Black*, 21–24.
6. Winters, *Hope Draped in Black*, 17.
7. Winters, *Hope Draped in Black*, 17, 16.
8. Flatley, *Affective Mapping*; Comay, *Mourning Sickness*; Lear, *Radical Hope*.
9. See Flatley, "How a Revolutionary Counter-Mood Is Made."
10. Proceeding from Walter Benjamin's thinking of primal origin (*Ursprung*) in *The Origin of German Tragic Drama*, Esposito writes that "*Ursprung* refers . . . to a movement of continuous self-generation that, in its distance from the simplicity of *Beginn* [beginning], is very close to [Hannah] Arendt's *Anfang* [beginning/origin]. While [*Beginn*] exhausts itself—such as in the Creation of the world—*Anfang-Ursprung* never ceases to give itself origin. It is the very source of commencement. It is what precedes—as commencement's presupposition—but also what follows; or even better, it is what always leaps beyond itself. . . . This means that *Ursprung* [origin], unlike Genesis, both belongs to and does not belong to the sphere of history, or, more precisely, it belongs to it from the point of view of its 'not': from what is not *yet* and what is *no longer* history." Esposito, *The Origin of the Political*, 21. Politics, which, as we argue in our final chapter, springs from its prepolitical, prehistorical others, *polemos* and *mênis*, is the origin of the political.
11. On this aspect of melancholia, see Agamben, *Stanzas*, 20.
12. Benjamin, *The Origin of German Tragic Drama*, 139. Subsequent references will appear in the text.
13. Kierkegaard, *Either/Or* and *Stages on Life's Way*, cited by Adorno, *Kierkegaard*, 60.
14. Adorno, *Kierkegaard*, 88.
15. Kierkegaard, *Stages on Life's Way*, cited by Adorno, *Kierkegaard*, 61.
16. Kierkegaard, *Either/Or*, cited by Adorno, *Kierkegaard*, 61.
17. Adorno, *Kierkegaard*, 175–181.
18. Caygill, "Non-Messianic Political Theology in Benjamin's 'On the Concept of History,'" 222.
19. In contrast to Deleuze, who pits repetition against the logic of representation, Kierkegaard and Benjamin use the power of presentation (critical, theatrical, novelistic) to tease out different modes of repetition and to demonstrate why repetition keeps insisting. Vice versa, repetition becomes the pivotal force through which new

modes of presentation and new genres, like Kierkegaard's *Posse* (farce) or Benjamin's *Trauerspiel*, emerge.

20. On the "afformative," see Hamacher, "Afformative, Strike," 1138–1140. As opposed to the performative speech act, "which posits conventions and legal conditions," the afformative event "deposes" "all acts of positing and the dialectic" of lawmaking violence ("the cycle of laws and their decay") that they perpetuate.

21. Hamacher, "Afformative, Strike," 1148.

22. The quotations from Aristotle, Cassian, and Pinel are found in Radden, ed., *The Nature of Melancholy*, 57, 71, 205.

23. Freud, "Mourning and Melancholia," in *The Standard Edition*, 14:244. Subsequent references to this edition will appear in the text.

24. Freud, *The Ego and the Id*, in *The Standard Edition*, 14:246. Subsequent references to this edition will appear in the text.

25. See Fisher, *The Vehement Passions*.

26. Agamben, *Stanzas*, 20.

27. Foucault, *The Courage of Truth*, 113–114.

28. Sebald, *Die Beschreibung des Unglücks*, 12.

29. Sebald, *Die Beschreibung des Unglücks*, 12.

30. Loraux, *Mothers in Mourning*, 101.

31. Loraux, *Mothers in Mourning*, 99.

32. Badiou, *The Meaning of Sarkozy*, 72–73.

33. Loraux, *Mothers in Mourning*, 99.

34. Žižek, *In Defense of Lost Causes*, 35.

35. Loraux, *Mothers in Mourning*, 96.

36. Derrida, *Politics of Friendship*, 244; and "Ulysses Gramophone," 298, 304.

37. Eng and Kazanjian, "Introduction: Mourning Remains," in *Loss*, 2. Subsequent references will appear in the text.

38. Lacan, *The Ethics of Psychoanalysis*, 186.

39. Buck-Morss, *The Origin of Negative Dialectics*, 70.

40. Adorno, *Negative Dialectics*, 354.

41. Adorno, *Negative Dialectics*, 354, 357.

42. Adorno, *History and Freedom*, 135.

43. Adorno, *History and Freedom*, 133.

44. Adorno, *History and Freedom*, 133–134. Žižek reaches a similar conclusion in *How to Read Lacan*, where he writes that "melancholy (disappointment with all positive, empirical objects, none of which can satisfy our desire) is the beginning of philosophy" (68).

45. Adorno, *History and Freedom*, 134.

46. Agamben, *Homo Sacer*, 31–32.

47. Plato, *Complete Works*, 1224–1291.

48. *Physionomos*, a construction of *physis* and *nomos*, should not be taken as a natural law; it is more like an order that is universally valid, a nomos, and at the same time true or essential, like physis. The physionomos is an order before law and yet apart from nature. Never resolving itself into a spuriously "natural" order, a force of law that supposedly originates in nature, physionomos is rather an immemorial order: unforgettable and indestructible as well as elusive, since it cannot be appropriated

by sovereign power or harnessed by governmentality. An essential order but not an "original" natural order outside of history, physionomos is ultimately a name for that which is at once sought and realized in the melancholic idea of natural history.

49. Klibansky, Panofsky, and Saxl, *Saturn and Melancholy*, 284.

50. On the ancient meaning of stasis, see Loraux, *The Divided City*, 10, 64.

51. Melchinger, *Das Theater der Tragödie*, 27, 33, 55.

52. Gurd, *Aeschylus' Oresteia*, 238.

53. Agamben, *Stasis*, 22.

54. Lacan, *Encore: On Feminine Sexuality*, 16.

55. Esposito, *Terms of the Political*, 29.

56. Freud, *Project for a Scientific Psychology*, in *The Standard Edition*, 1:331.

57. On Lacan's appropriation of the Freudian Thing, see Reinhard, "Toward a Political Theology of the Neighbor," 32.

58. Adorno, "The Idea of Natural-History," 123.

59. Esposito, *Terms of the Political*, 29.

60. Esposito, *Terms of the Political*, 32.

61. Esposito, *Terms of the Political*, 32.

62. Agamben, *Homo Sacer*, 6.

Chapter 1: The Eros of Stasis

1. Campbell, *Greek Lyric*, 321.

2. Strauss, *On Plato's Symposium*, 121.

3. Strauss, *City and Man*, 111.

4. Freud, "Mourning and Melancholia," in *The Standard Edition*, 14:247–250.

5. Campbell, *Greek Lyric*, 395.

6. Plutarch, *Hellenistic Lives*, 19. Foucault provides an excellent analysis of this anecdote in *The Courage of Truth*, 273–287.

7. Diogenes Laertius, *Lives of the Eminent Philosophers*, 18–42.

8. Herodotus, *The Histories*, 1.31.

9. Plutarch, *Consolation of Apollonius*, cited by Hubbard, "The Capture of Silenus," 55.

10. Nietzsche, *The Birth of Tragedy*, 42.

11. Foucault, *The Courage of Truth*, 283, 286.

12. Foucault, "A Preface to Transgression," 36.

13. Roochnik, *Of Art and Wisdom*, 239, 241.

14. Lacan's formula in *Transference* that "love is to give what one hasn't got" combines Socrates's statement to Agathon that "love needs beauty, then, and does not have it" (200b) with Diotima's claim that love is "judging things correctly without being able to give a reason" (202a). Giving what "one does not have" means giving "a discourse, a valid explication, without having it." See Lacan, *Transference*, 148. For Lacan's claim that the erotic philosopher "loves with his lack," see Lacan, *Anxiety*, 108.

15. Lacan, *Transference*, 185–186.

16. See Desjardins, "Why Dialogues?" 119.

17. See Brogan, "Socrates' Tragic Speech," 33.

18. Wohl, "The *Eros* of Alcibiades"; Larivée, "*Eros Tyrannos*"; Lisi, "Philosophische und Tyrannische Liebe."

19. Gerhardt, "Person als Institution," 255.

20. Galli, *Political Spaces and Global War*, 137–191.

21. Loraux, *The Divided City*, 122; 229–244.

22. Euben, *The Tragedy of Political Theory*, 273.

23. Saxonhouse, "Democracy, Equality, and *Eidê*," 279.

24. Badiou, "The Democratic Emblem," 13.

25. Euben, *Tragedy of Political Theory*, 188–189.

26. McKim, "Shame and Truth in Plato's *Gorgias*," 47.

27. On this point, see Havelock, "*Dikaiosune*: An Essay in Greek Intellectual History," 49–70.

28. Esposito, *Nove pensieri sulla politica*, 17–18.

29. Wallach, *The Platonic Political Art*, 291.

30. Clay, "Reading the *Republic*," 26.

31. Henri van Effenterre, cited by Loraux, *The Divided City*, 93.

32. Loraux, *The Divided City*, 84.

33. See Wallach, *The Platonic Political Art*, 290–91; and Saxonhouse, "Democracy, Equality, and *Eidê*," 274, 277.

34. Saxonhouse, "Democracy, Equality, and *Eidê*," 274.

35. Loraux, *The Divided City*, 93–122.

36. The prayer in the *Iliad* (16:112–13) says: "Tell me now, Muses, who have dwellings on Olympus, how fire was first flung on the ships of the Achaeans."

37. Wallach, *The Platonic Political Art*, 323.

38. Deleuze and Guattari, *What is Philosophy?*, 70.

39. See Parry, *Logos and Ergon in Thucydides*.

40. Saxonhouse, "Democracy, Equality, and *Eidê*," 279.

41. Saxonhouse, "Democracy, Equality, and *Eidê*," 282.

42. Campbell, *Greek Lyric*, 321.

43. Loraux, *The Divided City*,105.

44. Parry, "The Unhappy Tyrant," 403.

45. Kahn, *The Art and Thought of Heraclitus*, 276.

46. Baas, *Le Désir Pur*, 18.

47. Nightingale, *Genres in Dialogue*, 133.

48. Orwin, "On the *Cleitophon*," 69.

49. Arendt, *The Promise of Politics*, 19.

50. We have used some parts of Metcalf's translation from "The Philosophical Rhetoric of Socrates' Mission," 144.

51. Metcalf, "Socrates and Achilles," 74; and Metcalf, "The Philosophical Rhetoric of Socrates' Mission," 145.

52. Arendt, *The Promise of Politics*, 25.

53. See Foucault, *The Government of Self and Others*, 273–287; 314.

54. Gonzalez, "Caring and Conversing about Virtue Every Day," 129.

55. Talero, "Just Speaking, Just Listening," 25.

56. Lacan, *The Other Side of Psychoanalysis*, 22.

57. Foucault, "Truth and Juridical Forms," 31.

58. Foucault, "Truth and Juridical Forms," 32.

59. Kirkland and Johnstone, *Ontology of Socratic Questioning*, 49.

60. Euben, *Corrupting Youth*, 32.

61. Sophocles, *Antigone*, lines 332–333.

62. As Jung told Lacan, when Freud "arrived in New York harbor and caught their first glimpse of the famous statue illuminating the universe, [he said] 'They don't realize we're bringing them the plague.' . . . To catch their author in the trap, *Nemesis* had only to take him at his word. We would be justified in fearing that *Nemesis* had added a first-class return ticket." Lacan, *Écrits*, 336.

63. Metcalf, "Socrates and Achilles," 80.

64. Patricia Fagan contends that Socrates's *Apology* shares many features with epic poetry like Hesiod's *Theogony*: the inspiration by the muses, the bard who does all the talking and the "power to sing the things that are, the things that were, and the things that will be." See her "Plato's Oedipus," 96–97. But Plato also transforms the conventions of epic poetry by making Socrates the bard *and* hero of his myths.

65. Loraux, "Therefore, Socrates Is Immortal," 165.

66. Lacan, *Transference*, 77.

Chapter 2: Hamlet, the Melancholic Prince

1. We rely on the excerpts found in Conway, *The Writings of Albrecht Dürer*, 262–273.

2. We draw here on our introduction to *Sovereignty in Ruins*, 12–15.

3. See Foucault, "The Confession of the Flesh," 194–228.

4. On the lack of lack, see Lacan, *Anxiety*, 42, 54.

5. Our thinking here is indebted to Lacan, *The Ethics of Psychoanalysis*, in particular chapters 4, 5, and 6.

6. See Derrida, "Forward: *Fors*," xiv.

7. Agamben, *Stanzas*, 20.

8. On natural history, see page 20, above.

9. Shakespeare, *The Tragedy of Hamlet, Prince of Denmark*, act 1, scene 1. Subsequent references will appear in the text.

10. On the claim that "*Hamlet* enacts the advent of—calls forth—a modern subject, or what has been described as the liberal, proto-Kantian subject," see Pye, *The Vanishing*, 109. A helpful overview of the topic can also be found in Fitzmaurice, "The Corruption of *Hamlet*," 139. For his own part, Pye reminds us that the argument made on behalf of Hamlet's emergent modern subjectivity "overlooks precisely what is most vexed about such an emergence," namely the operations of oedipal identification, misrecognition, and interpellation that reveal themselves in the play's many instances of hesitation, indecision, and delay (117–122). Meanwhile, Fitzmaurice makes the persuasive case that Hamlet's subjectivity, such as it is, is "political" (and thus, from the point of view of Renaissance philosophy, moral) rather than interiorized.

11. "plot, n.," def. 1b. OED Online. June 2020. Oxford University Press. https://www-oed-com.dartmouth.idm.oclc.org/view/Entry/145915?rskey=nzHqrN&result=1&isAdvanced=false. Accessed August 31, 2020.

12. Benjamin, *The Origin of German Tragic Drama*, 44.

13. Were we to be persuaded otherwise, it would perhaps be by Franco Moretti's theory that "the historical 'task' effectively accomplished by [tragic form] was precisely the destruction of the fundamental paradigm of the dominant culture. Tragedy disentitled the absolute monarch to all ethical and rational legitimation. Having deconsecrated the king, tragedy made it possible to decapitate him." In the specific case of what he calls "Shakespearean 'poetry,'" Moretti writes: "It is made possible by, and is identical with, the stupefied perception that cultural paradigms, abruptly defaulting, are no longer capable of guiding the world. A chasm has opened up between signified and referent that, while it provides the imagination with an unexpected semantic freedom, empties reality and history of that meaning which had seemed consubstantial with them." See Moretti, *Signs Taken for Wonders*, 42, 71. As his madcap antics suggest, however, Hamlet finds this situation less tragic than politico-poietic: an occasion for making. And indeed the situation is not tragic, insofar as it fails to generate the lack in which a new polis will emerge. What it produces instead is an "emptiness" filled by Hamlet and his dying voice. We might also be inclined to accept Hugh Grady's argument that *Hamlet* is a tragedy about a Montaignian subject forced to maneuver within a political environment that remains Machiavellian. Yet we would hold to our conviction that the courtier-as-event turns Machiavellianism against that same political environment, precisely because it is not political in any meaningful sense of the term. See Grady, *Shakespeare, Machiavelli, and Montaigne*, 243–265.

14. See Reinhard Lupton, "Tragedy and Psychoanalysis: Freud and Lacan," 96–97.

15. Our thinking here is indebted to Benjamin's *The Origin of German Tragic Drama*, the "Epistemo-Critical Prologue" and "Trauerspiel and Tragedy" in particular.

16. See Lacan, "Desire and the Interpretation of Desire in *Hamlet*," 39–41.

17. In their extended gloss on Benjamin's reading of *Hamlet*, Simon Critchley and Jamieson Webster note that "[f]or Benjamin, Hamlet betrays not the ancient world of heroic action and fate but the world of knowledge—embracing only dead objects, a world absent of radiance, deprived of soul. Mourning is characterized by a chronic deepening of intention and a surfeit of intention over action. This yields an intense contemplation" of the world of things, an "inertia," that, as Critchley and Webster further note, "is also depicted by Benjamin as a turning to stone." They then raise an intriguing question: "Is not Hamlet himself, for Benjamin, this mute rock erupting in the play in the form of mourning?" They rightly answer, yes; but they then betray Hamlet by reaching the following conclusion: "That Hamlet cannot face this force of fate, that he always flees it, means he is condemned to mirror it—silence, ruin, excess, stone." This is to condemn Hamlet to mere inertia: an intention that never translates into action. Our argument is that Hamlet captures the rest of the court in his intense contemplation, draws them in to his inertia. In short, he turns Elsinore into the stone that he has already become. This is the intention (or object) of the melancholic, translated (or objectified) into action. See Critchley and Webster, *Stay Illusion!*, 64–69.

18. On the distancing function of comedy and its connection to ideological complacency, see Zupančič, *The Odd One In*, 4–5.

19. Lacan, *The Ethics of Psychoanalysis*, 248, 295. On the ghost's pathetic failure to enforce his will, see Charnes, *Hamlet's Heirs*, 62–66.

20. On this point, see Freud, *The Interpretation of Dreams*, 298–299, and Lacan, "Desire and the Interpretation of Desire in *Hamlet*," 41–45.

21. Our reading here diverges somewhat from that of Charnes, who, following Slavoj Žižek, identifies Hamlet as literature's first noir detective. "The *noir* detective," she writes, "learns to his disgust that the local crimes he uncovers originate in the very law that authorizes his actions: that the Name of the Father covers over a metastatic corruption that reproduces its crimes precisely at the same moment that it also reproduces its authority." Charnes, *Hamlet's Heirs*, 42. Hamlet, we argue, is not trying to get to the bottom of things in the manner of a detective. He listens to the ghost too carefully to concern himself with crime or corruption. Rather, he is practicing how to make the most of the worst.

22. Lacan, "Desire and the Interpretation of Desire in *Hamlet*," 49–52.

23. For a suggestive, if different, interpretation of Hamlet's so-called "tables" speech, see Cavell, *Disowning Knowledge*, 184. But what Cavell reads as a moment of deferred obedience, we see as a moment of consummate fidelity to the ghost behind the ghost. Hamlet fulfills the ghost's injunction precisely by destroying it. He is a very dutiful son.

24. For a crisp account of "the competing models of memory in *Hamlet*"—the medieval ars memoria vs. the emerging art of "remembering oneself" as a form of discipline—and their political implications, see Blake, "The Art of Memory Meets the Art of Government in *Hamlet*." As we understand it, Hamlet's forgetfulness manages simultaneously to ruin the position of sovereign occupied by his father and reorient the incipient governmentality practiced by Claudius—no mean feat.

25. Lacan, "Desire and the Interpretation of Desire in *Hamlet*," 43–44.

26. By Freud, for example, who argues that "Hamlet is able to do anything—except take vengeance on the man who did away with his father and took that father's place with his mother, the man who shows him the repressed wishes of his own childhood realized." *The Interpretation of Dreams*, 299.

27. For a different take, see Stephen Greenblatt, who argues that "the Ghost's return is a reminder, an injunction to sharpen what has become dull"—that is, Hamlet's remembrance. *Hamlet in Purgatory*, 224.

28. Lacan, "Desire and the Interpretation of Desire in *Hamlet*," 45–49.

29. Our thinking on flesh in *Hamlet* is informed by three sources: Reinhard Lupton and Reinhard, *After Oedipus*, 60–88; Esposito, *Bíos*, 157–169; and Santner, *The Royal Remains*, 5–12 and passim.

30. On this point, see Jennifer Ann Bates, who argues that Gertrude's "crime, in Hamlet's eyes, is that she has forgotten Hamlet senior. She has instead re-collected a king who is not the one she loved and with whom she bore young Hamlet. The depth of transgression here is precisely that she continues in the flow of things without taking the time to mourn. Time is out of joint even as it appears to move forward." However, we disagree with Bates's conclusion (hardly exclusive to her) that, inspired by his disgust at his mother's forgetfulness, "Hamlet must set time's joint in two ways: he must solve the existential corruption of the court and of the 'original scene' [of trauma]." On the contrary, Hamlet is on his way to learning to share Gertrude's melancholic indifference, precisely so that he can affirm a time out of joint. See Bates, "Hamlet and Kierkegaard on Outwitting Recollection," 44–45.

31. Esposito, *Bíos*, 159.

32. Esposito, *Bíos*, 159–160, 169.

33. See Badiou, *Ethics*, 129–130.

34. Esposito, *Bíos*, 157–159. But see as well Santner, *The Royal Remains*, 12–22.

35. We mean "event" here in the restricted, specific sense given the term by Alain Badiou: "The event is both *situated*—it is the event of this or that situation—and *supplementary*, thus absolutely detached from, or unrelated to, all the rules of the situation.... We might say that since a situation is composed by the knowledges circulating within it, the event names the void inasmuch as it names the not-known of the situation." See Badiou, *Ethics*, 68–69. The courtier is the necessary, if scheming and secretive, supplement—both the addition to and substitute for—the sovereign. They are also the harbinger of governmentality within the situation structured by sovereignty. Elsinore would cease to function without them. Elsinore will cease to exist because of them.

36. Benjamin, "The Storyteller," 108.

37. For an exhaustive catalog of the proverbs in *Hamlet*, see Champion, "'A Springe to Catch Woodcocks,'" especially 28–30.

38. Schmitt, *Hamlet or Hecuba*, 44. For a dazzlingly adroit, critical distillation of Schmitt's thesis, see Santner, *The Royal Remains*, 142–159. For an evenhanded, and much welcome, demolition of Schmitt's reactionary privileging of a fateful "real" history over aesthetic play, see Kahn, *The Future of Illusion*, 38–53.

39. Rust and Reinhard Lupton, "Introduction: Schmitt and Shakespeare," xxv–xxvi.

40. Fitzmaurice argues that "Shakespeare's contemporaries would have seen Hamlet not as a modern subject but as a man who withdraws from the corruption of political life." "The Corruption of *Hamlet*," 140. But this is only half right, we think. The internal evidence of the play suggests that they would have seen him as Claudius and Polonius do: as a man who intensifies the corruption, the rottenness, of what passes for political life in Elsinore, turning the forces of natural historical decay to his advantage. Hamlet's political melancholia is his (dis)solution to the problem that Fitzmaurice claims Shakespeare explores in this play: "namely, why was it that the republican tradition was in ruins and beyond repair, and why is it that we get tyrants as rulers in the first place?" (155).

41. Here we find ourselves in sympathy with Cavell, who observes that "the condition of this work [of mourning—detaching oneself from—the object] is that you *want* to live. Hamlet is making claim to, or laying hold of, a power of perception that curses him, as Cassandra's cursed her, one that makes him unable to stop at seems, a fate to know nothing but what people are, nothing but the truth of them." See Cavell, *Disowning Knowledge*, 186.

42. On the allegorical nature of this and several other scenes in *Hamlet*, see Grady, "*Hamlet* as Mourning-Play." Grady does a thoroughgoing job of confirming Benjamin's mostly intuitive reading of *Hamlet* the play as the paradigmatic *Trauerspiel*, and of demonstrating how Hamlet the character works by way of allegorizing—fragmenting, sundering, and ruining—what otherwise threatens to achieve a spurious coherence. For a succinct account of Benjamin's theory of allegory, see Comay, "Paradoxes of Lament," 264–265.

43. Lacan, *The Ethics of Psychoanalysis*, 307.

44. Benjamin, *The Origin of German Tragic Drama*, 177–182.

45. On mortification as a method of the allegorician, see Benjamin, *The Origin of German Tragic Drama*, 182.

46. On this point, see Comay, "Paradoxes of Lament," 270. Our reading of the end of *Hamlet* aligns with Comay's in several respects. But where Comay argues that in electing Fortinbras with his dying voice, Hamlet "occupies the empty seat of power, if only long enough to vacate it," we argue that Hamlet continues to occupy that seat in absentia (so to speak) so that no one else can claim it. His dying voice deprives everyone else of the consolation of vacancy.

47. Lacan, *Encore: On Feminine Sexuality*, 16.

48. For more on the inadequacy of what she calls Horatio's "new historicist" narration of Hamlet's story, see Charnes, *Hamlet's Heirs*, 99–103.

Chapter 3: Woyzeck Is the Worst

1. As chronicled by Michel Foucault in *Discipline and Punish* and elsewhere.

2. Foucault, "*'Omnes et Singulatim*,'" 311.

3. Deleuze, *Foucault*, 70–93.

4. Robert Hullot-Kentor, the editor and translator of Adorno's "The Idea of Natural-History," cites the classical description by Francis Adams of the Hippocratic face as "the physiognomy of a person suffering from 'the worst': a sharp nose, hollow eyes, collapsed temples, the ears cold, contracted, and their lobes turned out: the skin about the forehead being rough, distended, and parched; the color of the whole face being green, black, livid, or lead colored." Adorno, "The Idea of Natural-History," 120, n. 10.

5. Benjamin, *The Origin of German Tragic Drama*, 166. But see also Adorno, who cites Benjamin in his essay "The Idea of Natural History," 120.

6. Georg Büchner, Letter to Wilhelmine Jaegle, March 10, 1834, in *The Major Works*, 184.

7. Georg Büchner, *Lenz*, in *The Major Works*, 100.

8. On the "surplus of immanence" generated by the fragmentation and attenuation of the sovereign, see Santner, *The Royal Remains*, xxi, 28–32.

9. Büchner, *Woyzeck*, in *The Major Works*, 144. Subsequent references to this edition will appear in the text, either by scene or page number.

10. Celan, *The Meridian*, 9.

11. In all that follows, we are indebted to David G. Richards's *Georg Büchner's Woyzeck: A History of Its Criticism*, in particular the chapters "International Criticism: 1966–1979" and "Recent Criticism: 1980–1999."

12. Lacan, *Encore: On Feminine Sexuality*, 16–17.

13. We nod here to Walter Benjamin's "Theses on the Philosophy of History," 253–264.

14. Marx, "The Eighteenth Brumaire of Louis Bonaparte," 595–598.

15. On the breakdown of the sovereign and its aftermath, see Santner, *The Royal Remains*, in particular the preface and the chapter "Sovereignty and the Vital Sphere."

16. Foucault, *Psychiatric Power*, 19–35.

17. On this (contentious) point, see John Reddick, "*Natur* and *Kunst*," in Büchner, *The Major Works*, 359.

18. An idea outlined by Adorno in "The Idea of Natural History," 117–121.

19. See the so-called second Clarus report in Büchner, *Sämtliche Werke und Briefe*, 522.

20. Campe, "Johann Franz Woyzeck: Der Fall im Drama," 215.

21. Pethes, "'Viehdummes Individuum,' 'unsterbliche Experimente,'" 76.

22. Höcker, *The Case of Literature*, 122.

23. Wilbrand, *Handbuch der Naturgeschichte des Thierreichs*, 21. Winkler demonstrates how the rhetoric of the doctor about classifying forms of life and inanimate matter, about the spiritual freedom of mankind, man as crown of creation, draws heavily from Wilbrand's handbook on natural history. Winkler, *Georg Büchners "Woyzeck,"* 120.

24. Kant, *Introduction to Logic*, 458.

25. Büchner, *Werke und Briefe*, 146, 580.

26. Celan, *The Meridian*, 2.

27. Celan, *The Meridian*, 10.

28. Celan, *The Meridian*, 8.

29. Agamben, *Homo Sacer*, 28–29; 82–83.

30. Here we share the view of Reddick, who writes that "'Kunst,' that entire man-made contrivance that is culture, society, civilization, is perhaps merely an overlay that might disguise our essential creatureliness and nothingness, but can never change or overcome it. . . . The whole episode" involving the performing horse "turns out to have a moral," he continues, "which is duly delivered—and carries us with shocking suddenness from piss and shit to ultimate questions of ontology." "*Natur* and *Kunst*," in Büchner, *The Major Works*, 364–365.

31. Negri, "The Political Subject and Absolute Immanence," 235–236.

32. On the concept of guilt history, see Hamacher, "Guilt History." We will return to Benjamin's sketch in chapter 5. For the time being, the hallmarks of guilt history can be summed up by paraphrasing Hamacher: Whatever is prior has had something taken from it by what follows; or whatever is prior has withheld something from that which follows. Every "having" is thus declared as a having from something else that previously had it. Every state of the world is guilty to the extent that it releases another deficient state of the world and bears guilt for it. Every state of the world is therefore an incomplete one, a morally or legally lacking condition.

33. Deleuze, *Difference and Repetition*, 275.

34. Deleuze, *Difference and Repetition*, 153.

35. On that "flash," see Alenka Zupančič's discussion of Lacan's four discourses in Zupančič, *The Shortest Shadow*, 115.

36. Derrida, *The Beast & the Sovereign*, 127.

37. We mean second nature in the way that Georg Lukács defines it: "[O]n the one hand, men are constantly smashing, replacing and leaving behind them the 'natural,' irrational and actually existing bonds, while, on the other hand, they erect around themselves in the reality they have created and 'made,' a kind of second nature which evolves with exactly the same inexorable necessity as was the case earlier on with irrational forces of nature." Lukács, *History and Class Consciousness*, 128

38. Büchner, *Sämtliche Werke und Briefe*, 518.

39. Höcker, *The Case of Literature*, 129.

40. Büchner, *Sämtliche Werke und Briefe*, 522.

41. Meier, *Georg Büchner: Woyzeck*, 21.

42. Campe, "Three Modes of Citation," 14, and Höcker, *The Case of Literature*, 129.

43. Foucault, "Lives of Infamous Men," 157–175.

44. Foucault, *Psychiatric Power*, 34.

45. See Lacan, *The Psychoses*, 133.

46. Lacan, *The Ego in Freud's Theory*, 154–55.

47. See, for example, Esposito, *Terms of the Political*, 14–15.

48. Agamben, *The Time That Remains*, 36.

49. Larsen, "The Symbol of the Knife in Büchner's *Woyzeck*," 269.

50. Gray, "The Dialectic of Enlightenment in Büchner's *Woyzeck*," 93–94.

51. For a succinct genealogy of that "task," see the introduction to Esposito, *Third Person*, esp. 1–13.

52. Nietzsche, *Thus Spoke Zarathustra*, 38.

53. Foucault, "Tales of Murder," 207.

54. Büchner, *Sämtliche Werke und Briefe*, Vorwort, 488.

Chapter 4: The Melancholic Transformation of Dr. Freud

1. That Freudianism contains a political philosophy or, more prosaically, a theory of social relations and a critique of power and authority, is well attested. See, for example, Brunner, "*Oedipus Politicus*," 80–93, and Eli Zaretsky, whose *Political Freud* makes a persuasive case "that psychoanalysis [has] had a critical and political side from the first" (3). We in no way dispute that psychoanalysis can provide us with a means of analyzing, say, the irrational underpinnings of political structures. However, our interests lie less in rehabilitating Freudianism as a tool for political activism than in diagramming it as a kind of polis, complete with aristocracy, apostates, passions, rivals, exiles, enemies, walls, and a charismatic ruler who can't stop himself from repeatedly taking on the role of Socrates, much to the dismay of his followers. Psychoanalysis is to politics as the side stage in *Hamlet* is to Elsinore: both its spectral counterpart and the scene of its unplotting. In this we follow the example of Derrida, who bequeathed us an understanding of psychoanalysis as operating much like the psychosocial structures it studies: a body governing and administering cruelty while being endlessly undermined by its own "archive fever," Derrida's term for "the perverse work that the death drive performs—the work that allows for the forgetting of the memory that the archive wishes to preserve *in the first place* but also the possibility that the memory that it wants to preserve might be irretrievably lost in the process of archivization, without remainder." On this point, see Khan, "Aneconomy, Indirection, Undecidability," 140. Following the supplementary logic of the prosthesis, the death drive in its guise as archive fever erases the own-ness of the master by undermining the work of the archon, the keeper of records, laws, and case files, on which mastery depends. Then, working silently and without leaving a trace of its own, death drive erases itself. See Derrida, "Psychoanalysis Searches the States of Its Soul," 238–280, and *Archive Fever*. Our understanding here has been aided by Ryder, "Politics after the Death of the Father."

2. See, in particular, Freud, *The Interpretation of Dreams*, 298–299. Subsequent references to this edition will appear in the text.

3. Freud, *Fragment of an Analysis of a Case of Hysteria*, in *The Standard Edition*, 7:54.

4. For a fascinating account of how Dora expertly manipulated Freud into acting as the vehicle for "broadcasting to the world her desperate message" concerning adult injustice, see Paul, "Purloining Freud," 182.

5. Already in the mid-1950s, Lacan could wryly remark, before embarking upon his own, influential interpretation of the dream, that "amongst those people whose function it is to teach analysis and to train analysts, I'm not the only one to have had the idea of taking up the dream of Irma's injection again." *The Ego in Freud's Theory*, 147. Likewise, in the 1990s, Derrida coyly concedes that "I will not say anything new about this 'Dream of Irma's Injection.' The sense of this text, if not of this dream . . . will have surely been exhausted for some time now by the enormous analytic literature that, throughout the world, has submitted it to investment and investigation from every angle." Derrida, *Resistances of Psychoanalysis*, 5. All the same, we admire Eric Santner's deft treatment of "the inaugural dream of psychoanalysis" in his *The Royal Remains*, 64–69. Like us, Santner interprets the dream as staging an encounter with flesh.

6. See the chapter "The Method of Interpreting Dreams: An Analysis of a Specimen Dream," in Freud, *The Interpretation of Dreams*, 128–154.

7. For a useful account of the dream-work, see Žižek, *The Sublime Object of Ideology*, 12–13.

8. For an account of Freud's "guilty experience with a woman patient named Mathilde"—that is, Freud's second lure—see Felman, "Competing Pregnancies: The Dream from Which Psychoanalysis Proceeds," 188.

9. Ken Frieden, for one, seems quite enticed by Freud's lures. *Freud's Dream of Interpretation*, particularly Frieden's discussion of "repressed sexual dynamics" and "competitive wishes" in the chapter "Freud: Interpreter and Seducer."

10. Here we part company with those who "emphasize Freud's latent identification" with Irma, rather than his more obvious, if no less furtive, identification with the nameless friend, who really gets under Freud's skin. See, for example, Sprengnether, "Mouth to Mouth," 259.

11. We mean "flesh" in the sense given it by Roberto Esposito: an "existence without life" that cannot be integrated into a body politic organized around the normativization and "negative protection" of life. "Flesh is intrinsic to the same body from which it seems to escape (and which therefore expels it). Existence without life is flesh that does not coincide with the body; it is that part or zone of the body, the body's membrane, that isn't one with the body, that exceeds its boundaries or is subtracted from the body's enclosing." See Esposito, *Bíos*, 159. Although we share an interest in flesh with Eric Santner, alongside whom we began reading Esposito's work, we suspect that our understanding of the term diverges from his around the question of the genesis of flesh, and also of its destiny. If we understand him correctly, Santner collapses flesh with trauma and thus ends up tying flesh to the shifting fortunes of the sovereign exception and the "life" it ex-cites into being. By contrast, we understand flesh as an existence without life and thus as unbeholden to the logic of the sovereign exception. Flesh rots the body politic by offering an escape from life.

12. "[A]s regards these [psycho-pathological] structures (which are looked on as pathological symptoms) unravelling them coincides with removing them," runs

Strachey's English translation, where (a footnote informs us) "unravelling" translates *Auflösung* ["dissolution"] and "removing" translates *Lösung* ["solution"]. Freud, *The Interpretation of Dreams*, 132 note 2. For influential discussions of the dissolution/solution nexus, see Lacan, *The Ego in Freud's Theory*, 150 and passim; and Derrida, *Resistances of Psychoanalysis*, 3–10.

13. On the inherent, mundane political and sociocritical nature of *The Interpretation of Dreams*, see the chapter "Politics and Patricide in Freud's *Interpretation of Dreams*," in Schorske, *Fin-de-Siecle Vienna*, 181–207. For a sketch of the frankly claustrophobic social scene represented in the dream of Irma's injection, see the chapter "The Dream of Psychoanalysis," in Appignanesi and Forrester, *Freud's Women*, 117–145.

14. Our thinking on immunity, autoimmunity, and immunization is rooted in the work of Roberto Esposito. For a succinct account, see his "Community, Immunity, Biopolitics," 2–3. But see as well Esposito, *Communitas*, 12–14. We have benefitted enormously from Timothy Campbell's introduction to Esposito's *Bíos*, vii–xlii.

15. Though brief, Samuel Weber's comments on Derrida's late-career turn to "autoimmunity" and its bearing on Derrida's earlier engagements with Freudian notions of apparatus, system, and economy are characteristically lucid. See Weber, "Sidestepping," 10.

16. See Lacan, *The Ego in Freud's Theory*, 146–171, and Copjec, *Read My Desire*, 119–123.

17. Lacan, *The Ego in Freud's Theory*, 155.

18. Here we part company with Lacan, who argues that Freud's "desire," fulfilled in the dream, is "to be relieved of his responsibility for the failure of Irma's treatment" and, more dramatically, *"to be forgiven for having dared to begin to cure these patients, who until now no one wanted to understand and whose cure was forbidden."* Lacan, *The Ego in Freud's Theory*, 151, 170 (italics in the original).

19. On this point, see Lacan, *The Ego in Freud's Theory*, 151

20. We mean "life" in the precise sense developed by Agamben: life abandoned to and by the ban of the law. "[1] he inclusion of bare life in the political realm constitutes the original—if concealed—nucleus of sovereign power. *It can even be said that the production of a biopolitical body is the original activity of sovereign power.* In this sense, biopolitics is at least as old as the sovereign exception." Agamben, *Homo Sacer*, 6 (italics in the original). But see as well 28–29, 82–83, and 104–111.

21. On the impersonal, which is not to be confused with "that process of depersonalization and reification that inheres in the very *dispositif* of the person," see Esposito, *Terms of the Political*, 117–122. For a more extensive treatment, see Esposito, *Third Person*, 104–151.

22. Esposito, *Bíos*, 159.

23. Esposito, *Communitas*, 12.

24. Freud, *Beyond the Pleasure Principle*, in *The Standard Edition*, 18:14. Subsequent references to this edition will appear in the text.

25. See Gay, *Freud: A Life for Our Time*, 446–447.

26. For what is surely the most influential reading of the fort-da game, see Derrida, "Freud's Legacy," part 2 of "To Speculate– on 'Freud.'" For an engaging analysis of Derrida's career-long fascination with *Beyond the Pleasure Principle*, see Rottenberg, "Intimate Relations." For a thoughtful reading of the fort-da game as an instance

of Aristotelian "courage-in-the-making," see Lear, *Happiness, Death, and the Remainder of Life*, 89–98. Meanwhile, for a gloss on Lear's reading that is also an interpretation of the fort-da game in its own right, see Santner, *The Royal Remains*, 69–73. Where we diverge from both Lear and Santner is around the question of trauma and its mastery. Both critics persist in reading the game from Freud's perspective—that is, as an instance of the child mastering the psychic trauma of his mother's absence—whereas we understand it as Freud's flailing attempt to master the trauma of his grandchild's absorption in the game and thus as an important step in his own melancholic transformation.

27. Much has been written about the death drive. For a canonical treatment, see Laplanche, *Life and Death in Psychoanalysis*, in particular chapters 5 and 6. For vigorous defenses and rigorous deployments of drive theory, see Rowland Smith, *Death-Drive*, and Fong, *Death and Mastery*. For a critical assessment, see Dufresne, *Tales from the Freudian Crypt*. For a nuanced revision of the concept, see Lear, *Happiness, Death, and the Remainder of Life*. We have benefitted enormously from Azeen Khan's lucid exposition in "Aneconomy, Indirection, Undecidability."

28. On sovereign ipseity, see Derrida, *The Beast and the Sovereign*, 66–67.

29. See Plato, *The Symposium*, in *Complete Works*, 472–477. We have benefitted enormously from Samuel Weber's discussion of the same episode in *The Legend of Freud*, 188–206.

30. Freud, *Civilization and Its Discontents*, in *The Standard Edition*, 21:64. Subsequent references to this edition will appear in the text.

31. Agamben, *Homo Sacer*, 105–106.

32. On the peculiar temporality of psychoanalytic constructions, see Reinhard, "The Freudian Things": "Construction is logically rather than chronologically preliminary to interpretation: a moment of disarticulating intervention, an invasive reorganization of the interpretive work of analysis with a narrative which is almost by definition farfetched, egregiously extreme, a blatant imposition—both merely and profoundly 'constructed'" (68).

33. Lacan, *Ethics of Psychoanalysis*, 186.

34. Freud, *Moses and Monotheism*, in *The Standard Edition*, 23:63, 50. Subsequent references to this edition will appear in the text.

35. Here we part company with Jonathan Lear, who takes Freud at his word that psychoanalysis "offered a thoroughly disillusioned—and thus completely secularized—way to acknowledge guilt." See Lear, *Happiness, Death, and the Remainder of Life*, 151. That may be the case with psychoanalysis, but it is not the case with *Moses and Monotheism*, which works to dissolve guilt history in the name of natural history. What *Moses and Monotheism* provides us is not a way to acknowledge guilt but a vehicle for affirming the worst.

36. Lacan, *The Ethics of Psychoanalysis*, 172–173.

37. Freud, *Totem and Taboo*, in *The Standard Edition*, 13:141–143.

38. For the four discourses (of the master, university, hysteric, and analyst), see Lacan, *Encore: On Feminine Sexuality*, 16.

39. Here again we part company with Lear, who regards the whole notion of an immemorial primal crime or "phylogenetic inheritance" as a fantasy contributing to the establishment of what Lear calls a "metaphysics of aggression." "The primal crime

itself—the killing of the primal father—is unanalyzable," Lear argues, "because Freud treats it as an actual event rather than a fantasy." But that is to discount the role played in psychoanalysis by constructions, the purpose of which is to force a confrontation with the real and thus to make an event happen. In short, it is to mistake a construction like *Moses and Monotheism* for an actual history and thus to misconstrue Freud's text. See Lear, *Happiness, Death, and the Remainder of Life*, 141–155. Derrida makes a similar observation concerning Josef Hayim Yerushalmi's *Freud's Moses*, that it confuses "historical" and "material" truth.

40. Freud, "Constructions in Analysis," in *The Standard Edition*, 23:267.

Chapter 5: Melancholia under Capitalism

1. See, for example, Derrida, "Mnemosyne" and "Forward: *Fors*." As Brault and Naas put it in "To Reckon with the Dead": "Derrida invokes throughout [his] essays of mourning the possibility of an interiorization of what can never be interiorized, of what is always before and beyond us as the source of our responsibility. This is the 'unbearable paradox of fidelity,'" whereby fidelity to the dead equates to an act of (ethical) infidelity toward one's own interior (11).

2. On second nature, see Lukács, *History and Class Consciousness*:

> The commodity can only be understood in its undistorted essence when it becomes the universal category of society as a whole. Only in this context does the reification produced by commodity relations assume decisive importance both for the objective evolution of society and for the stance adopted by men towards it. Only then does the commodity become crucial for the subjugation of men's consciousness to the forms in which this reification finds expression and for their attempts to comprehend the process or to rebel against its disastrous effects and liberate themselves from servitude to the "second nature" so created (86).

But see as well 90–92.

3. Freud, *The Ego and the Id*, in *The Standard Edition*, 19:28, 152.

4. As Jason Read so carefully explains: "For Marx . . . an opposition between truth and falsity misses the central question—the question of the particular appearance, or form, itself. It is by answering this question that we can approach an understanding of the simultaneous 'factual' and unconscious nature of abstract labor. In the section on commodity fetishism Marx refuses any psychological or intentional understanding of this illusion. It is not, like Immanuel Kant's famous antinomies, an illusion hardwired into human consciousness, nor has anyone been deceived by a ruling class—operating the smoke and mirrors from offstage. 'It constitutes, rather, the way in which reality (a certain form or social structure) cannot but appear.'" Read, *The Micro-Politics of Capital*, 69. The final sentence quotes Étienne Balibar.

5. This much was evident to Adorno, who, because he "accepts that the commodity form is a 'structuring principle' of modern society," also "regards attempts to invoke an immediate access to use-value as an ideological cover for the way in which all human activity is mediated by commodity exchange." Jarvis, *Adorno*, 55. But the situation is even more extreme today, now that capitalist production "has either directly appropriated the production of culture, beliefs, and desires, or it has indirectly linked them to the production and circulation of commodities. . . . In short, capitalist production

has taken on a dimension that could be described as 'micro-political,' inserting itself into the texture of day-to-day social existence and, ultimately, subjectivity itself." Read, *The Micro-Politics of Capital*, 2.

6. Freud, "Fetishism," in *The Standard Edition*, 21:154.

7. See Žižek, *The Sublime Object of Ideology*, 16–26.

8. For critical appraisals of left-wing melancholia, see Benjamin, "Left-Wing Melancholia," and, building upon Benjamin's criticism, Brown, "Resisting Left Melancholia."

9. Agamben, *Stanzas*, 20.

10. Benjamin, "Central Park," 169.

11. Adorno, *Can One Live after Auschwitz?*, 94.

12. Adorno, *History and Freedom*, 133–134.

13. Benjamin, "Theses on the Philosophy of History," 257.

14. Brown, "Resisting Left Melancholia," 20–22.

15. Brown, "Resisting Left Melancholia," 21.

16. Marx, *Capital*, 643–654. Subsequent references will appear in the text.

17. Benjamin, "Capitalism as Religion." Subsequent references will appear in the text. Our understanding of Benjamin's enigmatic sketch relies heavily on two commentaries: Hamacher, "Guilt History"; and the chapter "Closing the Net: 'Capitalism as Religion' (Benjamin)," in Weber, *Benjamin's -abilities*, 250–280. Also of interest is Mauro Ponzi's commentary in *Nietzsche's Nihilism in Walter Benjamin*.

18. Foucault, *Psychiatric Power*, 34.

19. On the haunted nature of capitalism, see Vogl, *The Specter of Capital*.

20. For an authoritative exposition of "the general law of capitalist accumulation," see Harvey, *The Limits to Capital*, 156–166.

21. Read, *Micro-Politics of Capital*, 76.

22. Read, *Micro-Politics of Capital*, 14.

23. Weber, *The Protestant Ethic and the Spirit of Capitalism*, 65.

24. In this respect, a politics of melancholia pays heed to the "immanent causality" that Althusser extracted from *Capital*. See Read, *Micro-Politics of Capital*, 8–10.

25. Although we arrived at our interpretation of Marx the old-fashioned way, by explicating the relevant sections of *Capital*, we feel vindicated in our "critical strategy of reading" by our subsequent study of Read's *Micro-Politics of Capital* (14). We thank Christian Haines for bringing Read's excellent work to our attention.

26. For a lucid, if residually humanistic, exposition of this section of *Capital*, see Harvey, *A Companion to Marx's* Capital, 109–134.

27. As Read observes, criticisms of Marx that "focus on [his] early presentation of production as isolated and asocial . . . fail to grasp the extent to which abstract labor acts not only in the market of commodities and labor but also in the production process itself as a norm that is forcefully imposed on the diverse bodies of different labors. In Marx's terms they are attentive to 'how capital *produces*, but not how capital is *produced*.' What is overlooked is the manner in which the capitalist mode of production must be made and remade, not just at the level of economic relations but also at the intimate level of power relations affecting the body, habits, and subjectivity of the worker. Furthermore, by deriving abstract labor solely from the commodity form, they present it as a deed already accomplished with the emergence of commodity

production, thus overlooking the antagonistic relations internal to the social production of abstract labor." Read, *Micro-Politics of Capital*, 75–76.

28. It is here that a politics of melancholia intersects with the so-called autonomist hypothesis of Antonio Negri, Mario Tronti, Paolo Virno, and others, which holds
that "the transformation of capital, its extension into new spaces and technologies,
is the effect and displacement of prior conflicts. The modern high-tech productive
processes conceal and maintain the traces of past struggles." As Read elaborates: "In
the pages Marx devotes to 'primitive accumulation' (the violence necessary to destroy
precapitalist social relations), the struggle over the length of the working day, and the
conflict over machinery. . . . there is an analysis of the manner in which the subjectivity of the working class, the demands and desires of what Marx sometimes calls 'living
labor,' functions as both the condition and limit to the development of the capitalist mode of production. . . . [T]he autonomist hypothesis challenges the very idea of
capitalism functioning like an economy, a self-sufficient series of market relations that
function as 'natural laws' of society, by exposing the antagonistic and overdetermined
historicity of the formation and development of capitalism." Read, *Micro-Politics of
Capital*, 14–15. The melancholic dimension of this dynamic comes from the petrified
unrest of past labor, which necessarily coincides with the prior conflicts that survive,
in displaced form, in the high-tech productive processes that make up the capitalist
mode of production today. The living labor that, according to the autonomist hypothesis, generates the conflicts that transform capitalism, is called to itself by the petrified
unrest of its own past activities. The motor force of the capitalist mode of production
is the melancholic, and thus conflictual, disposition of living labor.

29. One might characterize this as Marx's revolution of the violence of primitive
accumulation.

30. See, for example, Marx, "Crisis Theory." But see as well his postface to the
second edition of *Capital*, in Marx, *Capital*, 103.

31. See Koselleck, "Crisis," 360 361.

32. From the OED: "In early use, in medieval Latin form *synthoma*, *sinthoma*,
corrupt forms of late Latin *symptōma*, < Greek σύμπτωμα chance, accident, mischance,
disease, < συμπίπτειν to fall together, fall upon, happen to (compare πτῶμα fall, misfortune), < σύν sym- *prefix* + πίπτειν to fall." "symptom, n." OED Online. June 2020.
Oxford University Press. Accessed September 08, 2020.

33. Benjamin, "Capitalism as Religion," 288. On the myth of "so-called primitive
accumulation," see Marx, *Capital*, 873–874.

34. Schumpeter, *Capitalism, Socialism and Democracy*, 61. Subsequent references
will appear in the text.

35. In this Schumpeter follows a long-standing tradition of economics, which over
its history has sought to justify its scientific aspirations by borrowing the language
of physics, mechanics, medicine, and biology. See Resche, "Towards a Better Understanding of Metaphorical Networks in the Language of Economics," 87. But see as
well Mouton, "Metaphor and Economic Thought: A Historical Perspective."

36. Schumpeter, *Capitalism, Socialism and Democracy*. See, in particular, the
chapters "Crumbling Walls" and "Growing Hostility."

37. Adorno and Benjamin, *The Complete Correspondence*, 69.

38. See Adorno, "Letters to Walter Benjamin," 114.

39. Adorno's and Benjamin's inaugural exchange on the enigmatic Odradek has been taken up by critics such as Jane Bennett, for whom Odradek "brings to the fore the becoming of things," and Eric Santner, who follows Werner Hamacher to arrive at an understanding of Odradek as manifesting the homelessness of flesh in the aftermath of the historical demise and dispersal of the sovereign exception. See Bennett, *Vibrant Matter*, 8; and Santner, *The Royal Remains*, 83–86. But see as well Santner, *The Weight of All Flesh*, 62–65, for a glancing critique of Bennett and for a pithy description of Odradek as "a figure of *Un-economic* man par excellence, a paradoxical 'busy-body' serving no apparent use and yet not ever quite going to waste." For our part, we parse Adorno to arrive at an interpretation of Odradek as, simultaneously, the return of *Unruhe* in the worn-out commodity, a natural historical relic, and an object that eludes the domination of the concept.

40. Heidegger, *Off the Beaten Track*, 69.

41. Heidegger, *Being and Time*. Subsequent references will appear in the text.

42. Caygill, "Non-Messianic Political Theology," 220.

43. Weber, *The Protestant Ethic and the Spirit of Capitalism*, 96.

44. Engels, "The Origin of the Family, Private Property, and the State," 737.

Chapter 6: Arendt's Melancholic Revolution

1. Arendt, *Men in Dark Times*, 6.

2. Arendt, *The Promise of Politics*, 201.

3. Arendt, *The Promise of Politics*, 201.

4. Foucault, "Lives of Infamous Men," 157, 158. Subsequent references will appear in the text.

5. See the editors' introduction to Campbell and Sitze, *Biopolitics: A Reader*, 23, 38–39 note 67.

6. Arendt, *Men in Dark Times*, 13.

7. Arendt, *On Revolution*, 273. Subsequent references will appear in the text.

8. Arendt, *Essays in Understanding*, 428–29.

9. Arendt, *Essays in Understanding*, 1–2.

10. Arendt, *The Human Condition*, 228. Subsequent references will appear in the text.

11. Arendt, *Essays in Understanding*, 2.

12. Arendt, *Men in Dark Times*, 13. Subsequent references will appear in the text.

13. Kant, "The Contest of Faculties," 182.

14. Kant, "The Contest of Faculties," 184.

15. Arendt, *Between Past and Future*, 84.

16. Arendt, *Between Past and Future*, 85.

17. Arendt, *Lectures on Kant's Political Philosophy*, 24.

18. Arendt, *Men in Dark Times*, 13.

19. Arendt, *The Origins of Totalitarianism*, 447.

20. Arendt, *The Origins of Totalitarianism*, 477.

21. Arendt, *The Promise of Politics*, 201–204.

22. See Claude Lefort's critique of Adorno and Arendt in "The Death of Immortality?" in Lefort, *Democracy and Political Theory*, 256–81.

23. Arendt, *Men in Dark Times*, 17.

24. Benjamin, "Some Reflections on Kafka," 144.

25. Esposito, *The Origin of the Political*, 25.

26. The locus classicus for Arendt's ambivalent stance toward the Homeric origin of politics, Rome, and the revolution is Canovan, *Hannah Arendt*, 136–137, 142–145.

27. Arendt, *The Promise of Politics*, 166, 173.

28. Nagy, "Foreword" to Loraux, *Mothers in Mourning*, xii.

29. Loraux, *Mothers in Mourning*, 100 and passim, 98.

30. Loraux, *Mothers in Mourning*, 96.

31. Arendt, *The Promise of Politics*, 166.

32. Arendt, *Between Past and Future*, 3.

33. Laudani, *Disobedience in Western Political Thought*, 4–5.

34. Arendt, *Men in Dark Times*, 204–206.

35. Arendt, *The Human Condition*, 21.

36. Aristotle, *Nicomachean Ethics*, 1139b7-11.

37. Benjamin, "Experience and Poverty," 731–736.

BIBLIOGRAPHY

Adorno, Theodor W. *Can One Live after Auschwitz? A Philosophical Reader.* Edited by Rolf Tiedemann. Translated by Rodney Livingstone et al. Stanford, CA: Stanford University Press, 2003.

———. *History and Freedom.* Translated by Rodney Livingstone. Cambridge: Polity Press, 2006.

———. "The Idea of Natural-History." Edited and translated by Robert Hullot-Kentor. *Telos* 60 (Summer 1984): 97–124.

———. *Kierkegaard: Construction of the Aesthetic.* Translated by Robert Hullot-Kentor. Minneapolis: University of Minnesota Press, 1989.

———. "Letters to Walter Benjamin." In Ernst Bloch et al., *Aesthetics and Politics.* London: New Left Books, 1977.

———. *Negative Dialectics.* Translated by E. B. Ashton. New York: Continuum, 1973.

Adorno, Theodor, and Walter Benjamin. *The Complete Correspondence, 1928–1940.* Edited by Henri Lonitz. Translated by Nicholas Walker. Cambridge: Harvard University Press, 2001.

Agamben, Giorgio. *Homo Sacer: Sovereign Power and Bare Life.* Translated by Daniel Heller-Roazen. Stanford, CA: Stanford University Press, 1998.

———. *Stanzas: Word and Phantasm in Western Culture.* Translated by Ronald L. Martinez. Minneapolis: University of Minnesota Press, 1993.

———. *Stasis: Civil War as a Political Paradigm.* Translated by Nicholas Heron. Stanford, CA: Stanford University Press, 2015.

———. *The Time That Remains.* Translated by Patricia Dailey. Stanford, CA: Stanford University Press, 2005.

Appignanesi, Lisa, and John Forrester. *Freud's Women.* New York: BasicBooks, 1992.

Arendt, Hannah. *Between Past and Future: Eight Exercises in Political Thought.* New York: Penguin Books, 2006.

———. *Essays in Understanding, 1938–1954: Formation. Exile and Totalitarianism.* Edited by Jerome Kohn. New York: Schocken Books, 1994.

———. *The Human Condition.* 2nd ed. Chicago: University of Chicago Press, 1998.

———. *Lectures on Kant's Political Philosophy.* Edited by Ronald Beiner. Chicago: University of Chicago Press, 1992.

———. *The Life of the Mind.* San Diego: Harcourt Brace, 1978.

———. *Men in Dark Times.* San Diego: Harcourt Brace, 1968.

———. *On Revolution.* New York: Penguin Books, 2006.

———. *The Origins of Totalitarianism.* San Diego: Harcourt, 1994.

———. *The Promise of Politics.* Edited by Jerome Kohn. New York: Schocken Books, 2005.

Aristotle. *Nicomachean Ethics.* Translated by Terrence Irwin. Indianapolis: Hackett Publishing, 1999.

Baas, Bernard. *Le Désir Pur: Parcours Philosophiques dans le Parages de J. Lacan.* Leuven: Peeters Publishers, 1992.

Badiou, Alain. "The Democratic Emblem." In *Democracy in What State?* Translated by William McQuaig. New York: Columbia University Press, 2012.

———. *Ethics: An Essay on the Understanding of Evil.* Translated by Peter Hallward. London: Verso, 2001.

———. *The Meaning of Sarkozy.* Translated by David Fernbach. London: Verso, 2008.

Bates, Jennifer Ann. "Hamlet and Kierkegaard on Outwitting Recollection." In *Shakespeare and Continental Philosophy*, edited by Jennifer Ann Bates and Richard Wilson. Edinburgh: Edinburgh University Press, 2014.

Benjamin, Walter. "Capitalism as Religion." In *Selected Writings*, vol. 1, *1912–1926*, edited by Marcus Bullock and Michael W. Jennings. Cambridge: Belknap Press, 1996.

———. "Central Park." In *Selected Writings*, vol. 4, *1938–1940*, edited by Marcus Bullock and Michael W. Jennings. Cambridge: Belknap Press, 2006.

———. "Experience and Poverty." In *Selected Writings*, vol. 2, *1927–1934*, edited by Marcus Bullock and Michael W. Jennings. Cambridge: Belknap Press, 1999.

———. *Illuminations: Essays and Reflections.* Translated by Harry Zohn. New York: Schocken Books, 1968.

———. "Left-Wing Melancholia." In *Selected Writings*, vol. 2, *1927–1934*, edited by Marcus Bullock and Michael W. Jennings. Cambridge: Belknap Press, 1999.

———. *The Origin of German Tragic Drama.* Translated by John Osborne London: Verso, 1985.

———. "Some Reflections on Kafka." In *Illuminations*.

———. "The Storyteller." In *Illuminations*.

———. "Theses on the Philosophy of History." In *Illuminations*.

Bennett, Jane. *Vibrant Matter: A Political Ecology of Things.* Durham: Duke University Press, 2010.

Blake, Katherine. "The Art of Memory Meets the Art of Government in *Hamlet*." *Early Modern Literary Studies* 20, no. 1 (2018): 1–22.

Brault, Pascale-Anne, and Michael Naas. "To Reckon with the Dead: Jacques Derrida's Politics of Mourning." In Jacques Derrida, *The Work of Mourning*, edited by Pascale-Anne Brault and Michael Naas. Chicago: University of Chicago Press, 2001.

Brogan, Walter. "Socrates' Tragic Speech: Divine Madness and the Place of Rhetoric in Philosophy." In *Retracing the Platonic Text*, edited by John Russon and John Sallis. Evanston: Northwestern University Press, 1999.

Brown, Wendy. "Resisting Left Melancholia." *boundary 2* 26, no. 3 (1999): 19–27.

Brunner, José. "*Oedipus Politicus*: Freud's Paradigm of Social Relations." In *Freud: Conflict and Culture*, edited by Michael S. Roth. New York: Alfred A. Knopf, 1998.

Büchner, Georg. *The Major Works.* Edited by Matthew Wilson Smith. Translated by Henry J. Schmidt. New York: W. W. Norton, 2012.

———. *Sämtliche Werke und Briefe. Historisch-Kritische Ausgabe*, vol. 1. Edited by Werner R. von Lehmann. Hamburg: Christian Wegner, 1967.

———. *Werke und Briefe. Gesamtausgabe.* Edited by Fritz Bergemann. Wiesbaden: Insel, 1958.

Buck-Morss, Susan. *The Origin of Negative Dialectic: Theodor W. Adorno, Walter Benjamin, and the Frankfurt Institute.* New York: The Free Press, 1977.

Butler, Judith. *The Psychic Life of Power: Theories of Subjection.* Stanford, CA: Stanford University Press, 1997.

Campbell, David A., ed. and trans. *Greek Lyric: Sappho and Alcaeus*. Cambridge: Harvard University Press, 1982.

Campbell, Timothy, and Adam Sitze. Introduction to *Biopolitics: A Reader*, edited by Timothy Campbell and Adam Sitze. Durham, NC: Duke University Press, 2013.

Campe, Rüdiger. "Johann Franz Woyzeck: Der Fall im Drama." In *Unzurechnungsfähigkeiten. Diskursivierungen unfreier Bewußtseinszustände seit dem 18. Jahrhundert*, edited by Michael Niehaus and Hans-Walter Schmidt-Hannissa, 206–236. Frankfurt am Main: Suhrkamp, 1998.

———. "Three Modes of Citation: Historical, Casuistic, and Literary Writing in Büchner." *Germanic Review: Literature, Culture, Theory* 88, no. 1 (2014): 44–59.

Canovan, Margaret. *Hannah Arendt: A Reinterpretation of Her Political Thought*. Cambridge: Cambridge University Press, 1992.

Cavell, Stanley. *Disowning Knowledge: In Seven Plays of Shakespeare*. Updated Edition. Cambridge: Cambridge University Press, 2003.

Caygill, Howard. "Non-Messianic Political Theology in Benjamin's 'On the Concept of History.'" In *Walter Benjamin and History*, edited by Andrew Benjamin. New York: Continuum, 2005.

Celan, Paul. *The Meridian: Final Version–Drafts–Materials*. Edited by Bernhard Böschenstein and Heino Schmull. Translated by Pierre Joris. Stanford, CA: Stanford University Press, 2011.

Champion, Larry S. "'A Springe to Catch Woodcocks': Proverbs, Characterization, and Political Ideology in *Hamlet*." *Hamlet Studies* 15, no. 1–2 (Summer/Winter 1993): 24–39.

Charnes, Linda. *Hamlet's Heirs: Shakespeare and the Politics of a New Millennium*. New York: Routledge, 2006.

Cheng, Ann Anlin. *The Melancholy of Race: Psychoanalysis, Assimilation, and Hidden Grief*. New York: Oxford University Press, 2001.

Clarus, Johann Christian August "The Legal Accountability of the Murderer Johann Christian Woyzeck, Demonstrated with Documentary Evidence According to the Principles of the Science of Public Health." In Büchner, *The Major Works*.

Clay, Diskin. "Reading the *Republic*." In Griswold, *Platonic Writings/Platonic Readings*.

Comay, Rebecca. *Mourning Sickness: Hegel and the French Revolution*. Stanford, CA: Stanford University Press, 2010.

———. "Paradoxes of Lament: Benjamin and Hamlet." In *Lament in Jewish Thought*, edited by Ilit Ferber and Paula Schwebel. Berlin: De Gruyter, 2014.

Conway, William Martin, ed. and trans. *The Writings of Albrecht Dürer*. New York: Philosophical Library, 1958.

Copjec, Joan. *Read My Desire: Lacan against the Historicists*. Cambridge: MIT Press, 1995.

Critchley, Simon, and Jamieson Webster. *Stay Illusion! The Hamlet Doctrine*. New York: Vintage Books, 2014.

Deleuze, Gilles. *Difference and Repetition*. Translated by Paul Patton. New York: Columbia University Press, 1994.

———. *Foucault*. Translated by Sean Hand. Minneapolis: University of Minnesota Press, 1988.

Deleuze, Gilles, and Félix Guattari. *What Is Philosophy?* Translated by Hugh Tomlinson and Graham Burchell. New York: Columbia University Press, 1994.

Desjardins, Rosemary. "Why Dialogues? Plato's Serious Play." In Charles L. Griswold, *Platonic Writings/Platonic Readings*. University Park: Pennsylvania State University Press, 1988.

Derrida, Jacques. *Archive Fever: A Freudian Impression*. Translated by Eric Prenowitz. Chicago: University of Chicago Press, 1998.

———. *The Beast and the Sovereign*, vol. 1. Edited by Michael Lisse, Marie-Louise Mallet, and Ginette Michaud. Translated by Geoffrey Bennington. Chicago: University of Chicago Press, 2009.

———. "Forward: *Fors*: The Anglish Words of Nicolas Abraham and Maria Torok." Translated by Barbara Johnson. In Nicolas Abraham and Maria Torok, *The Wolf Man's Magic Word: A Cryptonymy*. Translated by Nicholas Rand. Minneapolis: University of Minnesota Press, 1986.

———. "Mnemosyne." In *Memoires for Paul de Man*. Translated by Cecile Lindsay. New York: Columbia University Press, 1989.

———. *The Politics of Friendship*. Translated by George Collins. London: Verso, 1997.

———. "Psychoanalysis Searches the States of Its Soul." In *Without Alibi*, edited and translated by Peggy Kamuf. Stanford, CA: Stanford University Press, 2002.

———. *Resistances of Psychoanalysis*. Translated by Peggy Kamuf, Pascale-Anne Brault, and Michael Naas. Stanford, CA: Stanford University Press, 1998.

———. "To Speculate—on 'Freud.'" In *The Post-Card: From Socrates to Freud and Beyond*. Translated by Alan Bass. Chicago: University of Chicago Press, 1987.

———. "Ulysses Gramophone." In *Acts of Literature*, edited by Derek Attridge. New York and London: Routledge, 1992.

Diogenes Laertius. *Lives of the Eminent Philosophers*.

Dufresne, Todd. *Tales from the Freudian Crypt: The Death Drive in Text and Context*. Stanford, CA: Stanford University Press, 2000.

Edmondson, George, and Klaus Mladek, eds. *Sovereignty in Ruins: A Politics of Crisis*. Durham, NC: Duke University Press, 2017.

Eng, David L., and David Kazanjian, eds. *Loss: The Politics of Mourning*. Berkeley and Los Angeles: University of California Press, 2003.

Engels, Friedrich. "The Origin of the Family, Private Property, and the State." In Tucker, *The Marx-Engels Reader*.

Esposito, Roberto. *Bíos: Biopolitics and Philosophy*. Translated by Timothy Campbell. Minneapolis: University of Minnesota Press, 2008.

———. *Communitas: The Origin and Destiny of Community*. Translated by Timothy Campbell. Stanford, CA: Stanford University Press, 2010.

———. "Community, Immunity, Biopolitics." Translated by Michela Russo. *e-misférica* 10, no. 1 (2013): 1–10.

———. *Nove pensieri sulla politica*. Bologna: Il Mulino, 1993.

———. *The Origin of the Political: Hannah Arendt or Simone Weil?* Translated by Vincenzo Binetti and Gareth Williams. New York: Fordham University Press, 2017.

———. *Terms of the Political: Community, Immunity, Biopolitics*. Translated by Rhiannon Noel Welch. New York: Fordham University Press, 2013.

———. *Third Person*. Translated by Zakiya Hanafi. Malden: Polity Press, 2012.

Euben, J. Peter. *Corrupting Youth: Political Education, Democratic Culture, and Political Theory*. Princeton, NJ: Princeton University Press, 1997.

———. *The Tragedy of Political Theory: The Road Not Taken*. Princeton, NJ: Princeton University Press, 1990.

Fagan, Patricia. "Plato's Oedipus: Myth and Philosophy in the *Apology*." In Fagan and Russon, *Reexamining Socrates*.

Fagan, Patricia, and John Russon, eds. *Reexamining Socrates in the "Apology*." Evanston, IL: Northwestern University Press, 2009.

Felman, Shoshana. "Competing Pregnancies: The Dream from Which Psychoanalysis Proceeds." In *The Claims of Literature: A Shoshana Felman Reader*, edited by Emily Sun, Eyal Peretz, and Ulrich Baer. New York: Fordham University Press, 2007.

Fisher, Philip. *The Vehement Passions*. Princeton, NJ: Princeton University Press, 2002.

Fitzmaurice, Andrew. "The Corruption of *Hamlet*." In *Shakespeare and Early Modern Political Thought*, edited by David Armitage, Conal Condren, and Andrew Fitzmaurice. Cambridge: Cambridge University Press, 2009.

Flatley, Jonathan. *Affective Mapping: Melancholia and the Politics of Modernism*. Cambridge: Harvard University Press, 2008.

———. "How a Revolutionary Counter-Mood Is Made." *New Literary History* 43, no. 3 (2012): 503–525.

Fong, Benjamin Y. *Death and Mastery: Psychoanalytic Drive Theory and the Subject of Late Capitalism*. New York: Columbia University Press, 2016.

Foucault, Michel. "The Confession of the Flesh." In *Power/Knowledge: Selected Interviews and Other Writings 1972–1977*, edited by Colin Gordon. New York: Pantheon Books, 1980.

———. *The Courage of Truth: The Government of the Self and Others II: Lectures at the Collège de France, 1983–1984*. Edited by Frédéric Gros. Translated by Graham Burchell. New York: Palgrave Macmillan, 2011.

———. *Discipline and Punish: The Birth of the Prison*. Translated by Alan Sheridan. New York: Vintage, 1977.

——— *Essential Works of Foucault, 1954–1984: Power*. Edited by James D. Faubion. Translated by Robert Hurley et al. New York: The New Press, 1994.

———. *The Government of Self and Others: Lectures at the Collège de France, 1982–1983*. Edited by Michel Senellart. Translated by Graham Burchell. New York: Palgrave Macmillan, 2010.

———. "Lives of Infamous Men." In *Power*, edited by James D. Faubion.

———. "'*Omnes et Singulatim*': Toward a Critique of Political Reason." In *Power*, edited by James D. Faubion.

———. "A Preface to Transgression." In *Language, Counter-memory, Practice: Selected Essays and Interviews*, edited and translated by Donald F. Bouchard. Ithaca, NY: Cornell University Press, 1977.

———. *Psychiatric Power: Lectures at the Collège de France, 1973–1974*. Edited by Jacques Legrange. Translated by Graham Burchell. New York: Picador, 2006.

———. "Society Must Be Defended." In *Essential Works of Foucault, 1954–1984: Ethics: Subjectivity and Truth*, edited by Paul Rabinow. Translated by Robert Hurley et al. New York: The New Press, 1994.

———. "Tales of Murder." In *I, Pierre Rivière, having slaughtered my mother, my sister, and my brother . . . A Case of Parricide in the 19th Century*, edited by Michel Foucault. Translated by Frank Jellinek. Lincoln: University of Nebraska Press, 1982.

Foucault, Michel. "Truth and Juridical Forms." In *Power*, edited by James D. Faubion.

Freud, Sigmund. *The Interpretation of Dreams*. Edited and translated by James Strachey. New York: Avon Books, 1965.

———. *The Standard Edition of the Complete Psychological Works of Sigmund Freud*. Edited and translated by James Strachey. 24 vols. London: Vintage Books, 2001.

Frieden, Ken. *Freud's Dream of Interpretation*. Albany: State University of New York Press, 1990.

Galli, Carlo. *Political Spaces and Global War*. Edited by Adam Sitze. Translated by Elisabeth Fay. Minneapolis: University of Minnesota Press, 2010.

Gay, Peter. *Freud: A Life for Our Time*. New York: Anchor Books, 1989.

Gerhardt, Volker. "Person als Institution." In *Die Weltgeschichte—das Weltgericht?: Stuttgarter Hegel-Kongress 1999*, edited by Rüdiger Bubner and Walter Mesch. Stuttgart: Klett-Cotta, 2001.

Gilroy, Paul. *Postcolonial Melancholia*. New York: Columbia University Press, 2005.

Gonzalez, Francisco J. "Caring and Conversing about Virtue Every Day: Human Piety and Goodness in Plato's *Apology*." In Fagan and Russon, *Reexamining Socrates in the "Apology."*

Grady, Hugh. "*Hamlet* as Mourning-Play: A Benjaminesque Interpretation." *Shakespeare Studies* 36 (2008): 135–165.

———. *Shakespeare, Machiavelli, and Montaigne: Power and Subjectivity from Richard II to Hamlet*. Oxford: Oxford University Press, 2002.

Gray, Richard. "The Dialectic of Enlightenment in Büchner's *Woyzeck*." *The German Quarterly* 61 (1988): 78–96.

Greenblatt, Stephen. *Hamlet in Purgatory*. Princeton, NJ: Princeton University Press, 2013.

Griswold, Charles L., ed. *Platonic Writings/Platonic Readings*. University Park: Pennsylvania State University Press, 1988.

Gurd, Sean. *Aeschylus' "Oresteia": Silence, Criticism, Tragedy*. PhD diss., University of Toronto, 2001.

Hamacher, Werner. "Afformative, Strike." Translated by Dana Hollander. *Cordoza Law Review* 13 (1991–1992): 1133–1157.

———. "Guilt History: Benjamin's Sketch 'Capitalism as Religion.'" Translated by Kirk Wetters. *diacritics* 32, no. 3–4 (2002): 81–106.

Harvey, David. *A Companion to Marx's "Capital."* London: Verso, 2010.

———. *The Limits to Capital*. London: Verso, 2006.

Havelock, E. A. "*Dikaiosune*: An Essay in Greek Intellectual History." *Phoenix* 23, no. 1 (1969): 49–70.

Heidegger, Martin. *Being and Time*. Translated by John Macquarrie and Edward Robinson. New York: Harper and Row, 1962.

———. *Off the Beaten Track*. Edited and translated by Julian Young and Kenneth Haynes. Cambridge: Cambridge University Press, 2002.

Herera-Soler, Honesto, and Michael White, eds. *Metaphor and Mills: Figurative Language in Business and Economics*. Berlin: De Gruyter Mouton, 2012.

Herodotus. *The Histories*. Edited by Robert B. Strassler. Translated by Andrea L. Purvis. New York: Anchor Books, 2009.

Höcker, Arne. *The Case of Literature: Forensic Narratives from Goethe to Kafka*. Ithaca, NY: Cornell University Press, 2020.

Hubbard, Margaret. "The Capture of Silenus." *The Cambridge Classical Journal* 21 (1975): 53–62.

Jarvis, Simon. *Adorno: A Critical Introduction*. New York: Routledge, 1998.

Kahn, Charles H. *The Art and Thought of Heraclitus: A New Arrangement and Translation of the Fragments with Literary and Philosophical Commentary*. Cambridge: Cambridge University Press, 1979.

Kahn, Victoria. *The Future of Illusion: Political Theology and Early Modern Texts*. Chicago: University of Chicago Press, 2013.

Kant, Immanuel. "The Contest of Faculties." In *Political Writings*, edited by Hans Reiss. Translated by H. B. Nisbet. Cambridge: Cambridge University Press, 1991.

———. *Kant's Introduction to Logic*. Translated by T. K. Abbott. London: Longmans, Green, 1885.

Khan, Azeen. "Aneconomy, Indirection, Undecidability: Derrida's 'Principled' Critique of the Death Drive." *differences* 31, no. 1 (2020): 135–162.

Klibansky, Raymond, Erwin Panofsky, and Franz Saxl. *Saturn and Melancholy: Studies in the History of Natural Philosophy, Religion and Art*. London: Thomas Nelson and Sons, 1964.

Kirkland, Sean, and Bruce Johnstone. *The Ontology of Socratic Questioning in Plato's Early Dialogues*. Albany: SUNY Press, 2012.

Koselleck, Reinhart. "Crisis." Translated by Michaela W. Richter. *Journal of the History of Ideas* 67, no. 2 (2006): 357–400.

Lacan, Jacques. *Anxiety, 1962–1963*. Book 10 of *The Seminar of Jacques Lacan*. Edited by Jacques-Alain Miller. Translated by A. R. Price. Malden: Polity Press, 2016.

———. "Desire and the Interpretation of Desire in *Hamlet*." In *Literature and Psychoanalysis*, edited by Shoshana Felman. Baltimore, MD: Johns Hopkins University Press, 1982.

———. *Écrits*. Translated by Bruce Fink. New York: W. W. Norton, 2006.

———. *The Ego in Freud's Theory and in the Technique of Psychoanalysis, 1954–1955*. Book 2 of *The Seminar of Jacques Lacan*. Translated by Sylvia Tomaselli. New York: W. W. Norton, 1991.

———. *Encore, 1972–1973: On Feminine Sexuality, the Limits of Love and Knowledge*. Book 20 of *The Seminar of Jacques Lacan*. Translated by Bruce Fink. New York: Norton, 1998.

———. *The Ethics of Psychoanalysis, 1959–1960*. Book 7 of *The Seminar of Jacques Lacan*. Translated by Dennis Porter. New York: Norton, 1992.

———. *The Other Side of Psychoanalysis, 1969–1970*. Book 17 of *The Seminar of Jacques Lacan*. Translated by Russell Grigg. New York: W. W. Norton, 2007.

———. *The Psychoses, 1955–1956*. Book 3 of *The Seminar of Jacques Lacan*. Translated by Russell Grigg. New York: W. W. Norton, 1993.

———. *Transference, 1960–1961*. Book 8 of *The Seminar of Jacques Lacan*. Edited by Jacques-Alain Miller. Translated by Bruce Fink. Malden: Polity Press, 2015.

Laplanche, Jean. *Life and Death in Psychoanalysis*. Translated by Jeffrey Mehlman. Baltimore, MD: Johns Hopkins University Press, 1976.

Larivée, Annie. "*Eros Tyrannos*: Alcibiades as the Model of the Tyrant in Book X of the *Republic*." *International Journal of the Platonic Tradition* 6 (2012): 1–26.

Larsen, Svend Erik, "The Symbol of the Knife in Büchner's *Woyzeck*," *Orbis Litterarum*, 40 (1985): 258–281.

Laudani, Raffaele. *Disobedience in Western Political Thought: A Genealogy*. Cambridge: Cambridge University Press, 2013.

Lear, Jonathan. *Happiness, Death, and the Remainder of Life*. Cambridge: Harvard University Press, 2000.

——. *Radical Hope: Ethics in the Face of Cultural Devastation*. Cambridge: Harvard University Press, 2008.

Lefort, Claude. *Democracy and Political Theory*. Cambridge: Polity Press, 1988.

Lehmann, Johannes F. "Erfinden, was der Fall ist: Fallgeschichte und Rahmen bei Schiller, Büchner und Musil." *Zeitschrift für Germanistik N. F.* 19 (2009): 361–380.

Lisi, Francisco L. "Philosophische und Tyrannische Liebe." In *Plato's "Symposium": Proceedings of the Fifth Symposium*, Platonicum Pragense. Edited by Aleš Havlíček and Martin Cajthami. Prague: Oikoymenh, 2007: 176–188.

Loraux, Nicole. *The Divided City: On Memory and Forgetting in Ancient Athens*. Translated by Corinne Pache. New York: Zone Books, 2006.

——. *Mothers in Mourning*. Translated by Corinne Pache. Foreword by Gregory Nagy. Ithaca, NY: Cornell University Press, 1998.

——. "Therefore, Socrates Is Immortal." In *The Experiences of Tiresias: The Feminine and the Greek Man*. Translated by Paula Wissing. Princeton, NJ: Princeton University Press, 1995.

Lukács, Georg. *History and Class Consciousness: Studies in Marxist Dialectics*. Translated by Rodney Livingstone. Cambridge: MIT Press, 1971.

Lupton, Julia Reinhard. "Tragedy and Psychoanalysis: Freud and Lacan." In *A Companion to Tragedy*, edited by Rebecca Bushnell. Malden: Blackwell, 2005.

Lupton, Julia Reinhard, and Kenneth Reinhard. *After Oedipus: Shakespeare in Psychoanalysis*. Ithaca, NY: Cornell University Press, 1993.

Marx, Karl. *Capital*, vol. 1. Translated by Ben Fowkes. New York: Penguin Books, 1990.

——. "Crisis Theory." In Tucker, *The Marx-Engels Reader*.

——. "The Eighteenth Brumaire of Louis Bonaparte." In Tucker, *The Marx-Engels Reader*.

McKim, Richard. "Shame and Truth in Plato's *Gorgias*." In Griswold, *Platonic Writings/Platonic Readings*.

Meier, Albert. *Georg Büchner: Woyzeck*. Munich: Wilhelm Fink, 1980.

Melchinger, Siegfried. *Das Theater der Tragödie: Aischylos. Sophokles. Euripides auf d. Bühne ihrer Zeit*. Munich: C H Beck, 1974.

Metcalf, Robert. "The Philosophical Rhetoric of Socrates' Mission." *Philosophy & Rhetoric* 37, no. 2 (2004): 143–166.

——. "Socrates and Achilles." In Fagan and Russon, *Reexamining Socrates*.

Moretti, Franco. *Signs Taken for Wonders: Essays in the Sociology of Literary Forms*. New York: Verso, 1988.

Mouton, Nicolaas T. O. "Metaphor and Economic Thought: A Historical Perspective." In Herera-Soler and White, *Metaphor and Mills*.

Negri, Antonio. "The Political Subject and Absolute Immanence." In *Theology and the Political: The New Debate*, edited by Creston Davis, John Milbank, and Slavoj Žižek. Durham, NC: Duke University Press, 2005.

Nietzsche, Friedrich. *The Birth of Tragedy* and *The Case of Wagner*. Translated by Walter Kaufmann. New York: Vintage, 1967.

———. *Thus Spoke Zarathustra.* Translated by Walter Kaufmann. New York: Penguin Books, 1978.

Nightingale, Andrea Wilson. *Genres in Dialogue: Plato and the Construct of Philosophy.* Cambridge: Cambridge University Press, 2000.

Orwin, Clifford. "On the *Cleitophon.*" In *The Roots of Political Philosophy: Ten Forgotten Socratic Dialogues*, edited by Thomas L. Pangle. Ithaca, NY: Cornell University Press, 1987.

Parry, Adam. *Logos and Ergon in Thucydides.* New York: Argos Press, 1981.

Parry, Richard D. "The Unhappy Tyrant and the Craft of Inner Rule." In *The Cambridge Companion to Plato's "Republic,"* edited by G.R.F. Ferrari. Cambridge: Cambridge University Press, 2007.

Paul, Robert A. "Purloining Freud: Dora's Letter to Posterity." *American Imago* 63, no. 2 (2006): 159–182.

Pethes, Nicolas. "'Viehdummes Individuum,' 'unsterbliche Experimente': Elements for a Cultural History of Human Experimentation in Georg Büchner's Dramatic Case Study *Woyzeck.*" *Monatshefte* 98, no. 1 (2006): 68–82.

Plato. *Complete Works.* Edited by John M. Cooper. Indianapolis: Hackett Publishing, 1997.

Plutarch. *Hellenistic Lives: Including Alexander the Great.* Translated by Robin Waterfield. Oxford: Oxford University Press, 2016.

Ponzi, Mauro. *Nietzsche's Nihilism in Walter Benjamin.* New York: Palgrave, 2017.

Pye, Christopher. *The Vanishing: Shakespeare, the Subject, and Early Modern Culture.* Durham, NC: Duke University Press, 2000.

Radden, Jennifer, ed. *The Nature of Melancholy: From Aristotle to Kristeva.* New York: Oxford University Press, 2000.

Read, Jason. *The Micro-Politics of Capital: Marx and the Prehistory of the Present.* New York: SUNY Press, 2003.

Reinhard, Kenneth. "The Freudian Things: Construction and the Archeological Metaphor." In *Excavations and Their Objects: Freud's Collection of Antiquity*, edited by Stephen Barker. New York: SUNY Press, 1996.

———. "Toward a Political Theology of the Neighbor." In *The Neighbor: Three Inquiries in Political Theology*, edited by Slavoj Žižek, Eric L. Santner, and Kenneth Reinhard. Chicago: University of Chicago Press, 2005.

Resche, Catherine. "Towards a Better Understanding of Metaphorical Networks in the Language of Economics: The Importance of Theory-Constitutive Metaphors." In Herera-Soler and White, *Metaphor and Mills.*

Richards, David G. *Georg Buchner's "Woyzeck": A History of Its Criticism.* Rochester, NY: Camden House, 2001.

Roochnik, David. *Of Art and Wisdom: Plato's Understanding of Techne.* University Park: Pennsylvania State University Press, 1996.

Rottenberg, Elizabeth. "Intimate Relations: Psychoanalysis Deconstruction / La psychanalyse la deconstruction." *Derrida Today* 11, no. 2 (2018): 178–195.

Rowland Smith, Robert. *Death-Drive: Freudian Hauntings in Literature and Art.* Edinburgh: Edinburgh University Press, 2010.

Rust, Jennifer R., and Julia Reinhard Lupton. "Introduction: Schmitt and Shakespeare." In Schmitt, *Hamlet or Hecuba.*

Ryder, Andrew. "Politics after the Death of the Father: Democracy in Freud and Derrida." *Mosaic: An Interdisciplinary Critical Journal* 44, no. 3 (2011): 115–131.

Santner, Eric L. *The Royal Remains: The People's Two Bodies and the Endgames of Sovereignty*. Chicago: University of Chicago Press, 2011.

———. *The Weight of All Flesh: On the Subject-Matter of Political Economy*. Oxford: Oxford University Press, 2016.

Saxonhouse, Arlene. "Democracy, Equality, and *Eidê*." *American Political Science Review* 92, no. 2 (June 1998): 273–283.

Schmitt, Carl. *Hamlet or Hecuba: The Intrusion of the Time into the Play*. Translated by David Pan and Jennifer R. Rust. Candor, NY: Telos Press Publishing, 2009.

Schorske, Carl E. *Fin-de-Siecle Vienna: Politics and Culture*. New York: Alfred A. Knopf, 1980.

Schumpeter, Joseph A. *Capitalism, Socialism and Democracy*. 3rd ed. New York: Harper Collins, 2008.

Sebald, Winfried Georg. *Die Beschreibung des Unglücks*. Frankfurt/Main: Fischer, 2003.

Shakespeare, William. *The Tragedy of Hamlet, Prince of Denmark*. Edited by Sylvan Barnett. New York: Signet Classics, 1998.

Sophocles. *Antigone*. In *Sophocles*, vol. 2, 1–128. Edited and translated by Hugh Llyod-Jones. Cambridge: Harvard University Press, 1998.

Sprengnether, Madelon. "Mouth to Mouth: Freud, Irma, and the Dream of Psychoanalysis." *American Imago* 60, no. 3 (2003): 259–284.

Strauss, Leo. *City and Man*. Chicago: University of Chicago Press, 1978.

———. *On Plato's "Symposium."* Chicago: University of Chicago Press, 2003.

Talero, Maria L. "Just Speaking. Just Listening: Performance and Contradiction in Plato's *Apology*." In Fagan and Russon, *Reexamining Socrates*.

Tucker, Robert C., ed. *The Marx-Engels Reader*. 2nd ed. New York: W. W. Norton, 1978.

Vogl, Joseph. *The Specter of Capital*. Translated by Joachim Redner and Robert Savage. Stanford, CA: Stanford University Press, 2015.

Wallach, John R. *The Platonic Political Art: A Study of Critical Reason and Democracy*. University Park: Pennsylvania State University Press, 2001.

Weber, Max. *The Protestant Ethic and the Spirit of Capitalism*. Edited by Richard Swedberg. New York: W. W. Norton, 2009.

Weber, Samuel. *Benjamin's -abilities*. Cambridge: Harvard University Press, 2008.

———. *The Legend of Freud*. Stanford, CA: Stanford University Press, 2000.

———. "Sidestepping: 'Freud after Derrida.'" *Mosaic: An Interdisciplinary Critical Journal* 44, no. 3 (2011): 1–14.

Wilbrand, Johann Bernhard. *Handbuch der Naturgeschichte des Thierreichs*. Gießen: Heyer, 1829.

Winkler, Hans. *Georg Büchners "Woyzeck."* Greifswald: Ratsbuchhandlung L. Bamberg, 1925.

Winters, Joseph R. *Hope Draped in Black: Race, Melancholy, and the Agony of Progress*. Durham, NC: Duke University Press, 2016.

Wohl, Victoria. "The *Eros* of Alcibiades." *Classical Antiquity* 18, no. 2 (1999): 124–170.

Yerushalmi, Josef Hayim. *Freud's Moses: Judaism Terminable and Interminable*. New Haven, CT: Yale University Press, 1991.

Zaretsky, Eli. *Political Freud: A History*. New York: Columbia University Press, 2015

Žižek, Slavoj. *How to Read Lacan*. New York: W. W. Norton, 2007.

——. *In Defense of Lost Causes*. London: Verso, 2008.

——. *The Sublime Object of Ideology*. London: Verso, 1989.

Zupančič, Alenka. *The Odd One In: On Comedy*. Cambridge: MIT Press, 2008.

——. *The Shortest Shadow: Nietzsche's Philosophy of the Two*. Cambridge: MIT Press, 2003.

A NOTE ON THE TYPE

THIS BOOK has been composed in Miller, a Scotch Roman typeface designed by Matthew Carter and first released by Font Bureau in 1997. It resembles Monticello, the typeface developed for The Papers of Thomas Jefferson in the 1940s by C. H. Griffith and P. J. Conkwright and reinterpreted in digital form by Carter in 2003.

Pleasant Jefferson ("P. J.") Conkwright (1905–1986) was Typographer at Princeton University Press from 1939 to 1970. He was an acclaimed book designer and AIGA Medalist.

The ornament used throughout this book was designed by Pierre Simon Fournier (1712–1768) and was a favorite of Conkwright's, used in his design of the *Princeton University Library Chronicle*.

Printed in the USA
CPSIA information can be obtained
at www.ICGtesting.com
CBHW030600160324
5426CB00010B/550